DAVID BISHOP
Grinnell College

INTRODUCTION TO
CRYPTOGRAPHY
WITH JAVA™ APPLETS

JONES AND BARTLETT PUBLISHERS
Sudbury, Massachusetts
BOSTON   TORONTO   LONDON   SINGAPORE

World Headquarters

Jones and Bartlett Publishers
40 Tall Pine Drive
Sudbury, MA 01776
978-443-5000
info@jbpub.com
www.jbpub.com

Jones and Bartlett Publishers Canada
2406 Nikanna Road
Mississauga, ON L5C 2W6
CANADA

Jones and Bartlett Publishers
International
Barb House, Barb Mews
London W6 7PA
UK

Library of Congress Cataloging-in-Publication Data

Bishop, David 1963-
   Introduction to cryptography with Java applets / David Bishop.
     p. cm.
   Includes index.
   ISBN 0-7637-2207-3
1. Computer security. 2. Cryptography. 3. Java (Computer program language) I. Title.

QA76.9.A25 B565 2003
005.8—dc21

                                   2002034167

Editor-in-Chief, College: J. Michael Stranz
Production Manager: Amy Rose
Editorial Assistant: Theresa DiDonato
Associate Production Editor: Karen C. Ferreira
Senior Marketing Manager: Nathan J. Schultz
Production Assistant: Jenny L. McIsaac
V.P., Manufacturing and Inventory Control: Therese Bräuer
Cover Design: Night and Day Design
Interior Design: Anne Flanagan
Illustrations: Dartmouth Publishing
Composition: Northeast Compositors
Printing and Binding: Malloy Incorporated
Cover Printing: Malloy Incorporated

Printed in the United States of America
06 05 04 03 02   10 9 8 7 6 5 4 3 2 1

4 G & Gjr

Form is exactly emptiness, emptiness exactly form;
so it is with sensation, perception, mental reaction, and consciousness.
All things are essentially empty, not born, not destroyed;
not stained, not pure; without loss, without gain.
Therefore in emptiness there is no form,
no sensation, perception, mental reaction, or consciousness;
no eye, ear, nose, tongue, body, mind,
no color, sound, smell, taste, touch, object of thought;
no seeing and so on to no thinking;
no ignorance, and no end to ignorance;
no old age and death, no end to old age and death,
no anguish, cause of anguish, cessation, path;
no wisdom and no attainment.
Since there is nothing to attain, the Bodhisattva lives thus:
with no hindrance of mind; no hindrance, and hence, no fear;
far beyond deluded thought,
RIGHT HERE IS NIRVANA.

—From The Great Prajna–Paramita Heart Sutra

I saw myself seeing Nirvana,
but I was there, blocking my view;
"I see only me," I said to myself,
to which I replied, "Me too."

—David Bishop

Preface

Cryptography is the art of secret writing. It involves transforming information into apparently unintelligible garbage so that unwanted eyes will be unable to comprehend it. This transformation, however, must be done so that it is reversible, so that individuals intended to view the information may do so. This is the traditional use of cryptography.

I agree with the philosophy that it is wiser to publish your encryption methods than to try to keep them secret. Thus, this book and others like it exist. Only government agencies endeavor to keep their encryption methods hidden. It is generally thought that publishing your ciphers exposes them to an army of brilliant people who will take great joy in pointing out any weaknesses they have. This gives the developer a chance to correct these weaknesses. On the other hand, trying to protect your methods from someone who really wants to know what they are probably won't work. A few bribes here and there will take care of that, and once they know your algorithms, they will pay very intelligent people to find weaknesses to exploit. The difference, of course, is that you won't know that this has happened, nor that the precious information you are sending with this cryptosystem is being monitored.

A great deal of modern cryptography depends upon the clever manipulation of huge integers. Thus, both number theory and abstract algebra play a large role in contemporary methods of hiding information. In many respects, Java is a pioneer in computer languages, with system security one of its primary missions. Java provides a BigInteger class, and through the use of this class, one may write cryptographic routines unbreakable by even the fastest supercomputers in the world. This will not change in the near future, nor probably even the distant future. The solution to modern cryptanalysis is not more powerful hardware, but more powerful mathematics, for modern cryptosystems depend on the intractability of certain mathematical problems.

Java already has security classes defined for it; they are in a package consisting of various abstract classes and interfaces, like Cipher, Message, and so on. This book does not cover these; rather, the emphasis is in learning the mathematical theory of cryptography, and writing algorithms "from the ground up" to implement the theory. For an excellent exposition of Java security providers and the Java security classes, one should consult Knudsen's book, *Java Cryptography* by O'Reilly.

This book is intended for undergraduate students taking a first course in cryptography. I wrote it with both the mathematical theory and the practice of writing cryptographic algorithms in mind. The chapters present the number theory required, and, in most cases, cryptosystems are presented as soon as the material required to understand them has been completed. No prior knowledge of number theory is necessary, though you should know how to use matrices, and should be familiar with the concept of mathematical induction, and other methods of proof. There are many math exercises for you, and I believe this is necessary to deepen one's understanding of cryptography. A working knowledge of Java is assumed. You should have little trouble programming cryptographic algorithms in Java once the mathematics is understood. We begin the cryptographic programming "from the ground up." For example, we will first develop our own large integer class in order to gain a deeper appreciation of the challenges involved in such construction.

With Java, one may construct secret key cryptographic systems or public key schemes. The concept of secret key cryptography is the traditional view, where both the encryption key and the decryption key must be kept secret, or the messages will be compromised. Secret key cryptography is often said to involve only one key (often it does), because either the encryption key or decryption key is easily obtainable from the other. With public key cryptography, each user generates his or her own public key, which he makes known to anyone, and a private key, which he keeps to himself. Anyone knowing some individual's public key can encrypt and send messages to that person, but only the intended recipient can decrypt it with the private decryption key. It is interesting to note that knowing the public encryption key is of almost no help at all in finding the decryption key.

There are many other aspects of cryptography that Java may also be used to implement; for example:

Signing Messages. A problem with public key cryptosystems is knowing whether or not someone who has sent a message actually is the person they claim to be. The concept of signing is a technique the sender uses so that the message is known to have come from her. This is simply one of various methods used to authenticate people.

Key Agreement. Since public key encryption and decryption tends to execute more slowly than secret key systems, public key systems are often used just to establish secret keys, which are then used in message exchange using a quicker method of encryption and decryption.

Database Enciphering. We can use cryptography to encipher entire databases in such a way that individuals can recover certain files or records without giving them access to the entire database.

Shadows. This is a method of enciphering highly sensitive information that can be reconstructed only with the combination of a certain minimum number of keys or shadows (as they are more commonly known) assigned to various individuals.

Hashes or Message Digests. A message digest is a special marker sent referencing a message. It is used to verify that the message is authentic. Messages, like people, are authenticated using various techniques.

Generating Random Numbers. Since computers are designed to operate in a completely deterministic fashion, they actually have a very difficult time producing true random numbers. Many of the same mathematical transformations that are used to disguise data are also used to produce "pseudorandom" sequences of numbers.

As you can see, the world of cryptography has many faces. I hope everyone who reads this will come to enjoy the beauty in all of them.

About The Applets

Since the Internet has swept across the face of the Earth, penetrating homes, businesses, and classrooms, people have been trying to figure out how to use it in a way that best suits them. The modern Internet streams digital video, audio, photos, and text through high-speed connections. Since the receiving device is usually a computer, even more sophisticated messages can be sent; for example, programs can be downloaded and run live within a Web page. One can even run programs on a server thousands of miles away, and have the output sent to the receiver. Via the connection of multiple computers storing myriad types of data, one can view live maps, weather information, government forms, and so on. One can interact with these other machines by the simple click of a mouse.

The impact of the Internet is highly visible in schools. Never have individuals had such easy access to materials for learning, and the tools available now go far beyond text, diagrams, and footnotes. This book, in particular, uses an easily accessible method to demonstrate its concepts: Java applets. Applets are programs that run within a Web page, and with a few restrictions, behave like regular windowed applications with buttons, text fields, check boxes, and so on.

What makes applets different is that these programs are referenced from an HTML document, and are downloaded and run automatically through the Internet connection. The user simply goes to a Web page, and the program pops up and starts running. Contrast this to users downloading programs the old-fashioned way:

- Download the source code.
- Obtain a compiler for the language the program is written in (this step is often difficult and expensive).
- Compile the program(s).
- If the programs compile (often not the case), you can now finally run them.

Anyone with the time, patience, and experience for all this will have a wonderful time plodding through all these steps. The rest of us want results now, and with this text, we have it. To access the applets in the book, go to the book's Web site:

http://computerscience.jbpub.com/cryptography

Here you will see links to all of the following course resources:

- The applets
- Sample data files
- Program files
- Instructor's manual

The applet names begin with "Test," and the HTML document associated with each applet will have a name something like "TestSomethingApplet.html". By clicking on such a document, you invoke, download, and run some applet. For example, by selecting TestDiscreteLogApplet.html, an html document is brought up, which immediately references an applet on the server. In this case, the applet TestDiscreteLogApplet.class is requested, downloaded, and run within the browser window on your computer.

You always invoke the applet by selecting its associated HTML document.

Program Files

If you wish to view the Java source code for the applets or any of the other classes in the text, select the Program Files link. We have included on the next page an example of the source code for an applet that demonstrates a block affine cipher in "TestBlockAffine-CipherApplet.java".

```
Opened: C:\Documents and Settings\David\Local Settings\Temporary Internet Files\C...
import java.math.*;
import java.applet.*;
import java.awt.*;
import java.awt.event.*;
public class TestBlockAffineCipherApplet extends Applet implements ActionListener {

    BigInteger shift=null;
    BigInteger multiplier=null;
    int blockSize=0;
    byte[] msgArray=null;
    byte[] encmsgArray=null;

    Label Label1=new Label("Plaintext");
    TextField msg=new TextField(40);
    Label Label2=new Label("Ciphertext");
    TextField encmsg=new TextField(40);
    Label shiftLabel=new Label("Shift value:");
    TextField entryShiftValue=new TextField(40);
    Label blockLabel=new Label("Block size (in bytes):");
    TextField entryBlockValue=new TextField(40);
    Label multLabel=new Label("Multiplier (must be relatively prime to modulus):");
    TextField entryMultValue=new TextField(40);
    Button encipherButton=new Button("Encipher");
    Button decipherButton=new Button("Decipher");
    TextField outmsg=new TextField("");

    public void init() {
        setLayout(new GridLayout(13,1));
        add(Label1);
        add(msg);
        add(Label2);
        add(encmsg);
        encmsg.setEditable(false);
        add(blockLabel);
        add(entryBlockValue);
        add(shiftLabel);
        add(entryShiftValue);
        add(multLabel);
        add(entryMultValue);
        add(encipherButton);
        encipherButton.addActionListener(this);
        add(decipherButton);
        decipherButton.addActionListener(this);
```

Sample Data Files

Because cryptography often involves manipulating very large numbers, there are examples in the text that incorporate them. These examples are also stored on the book's Web site. Click on the Sample Data Files link to view them. By copying these files and pasting the large numbers into a math computation engine, you can verify the results claimed in the book.

Instructor's Manual and Resources

Instructors of a course using this text have access to a manual that provides solutions to the more difficult exercises in the text. There are also programs written just for instructors that can be used to generate additional exercises. Permission must be obtained to use this portion of the site. Please contact your publisher's representative at 1-800-832-0034 for your username and password.

A Word of Thanks

I would like to extend my sincere thanks to Charles J. Colbourn of Arizona State University and K. T. Arasu of Wright State University, who reviewed this book in its early stages. Their insightful comments and suggestions were of great value, and I appreciate the time and energy they put in to their reviews.

To You, THE READER

I hope you have as much fun reading this book as I had writing it, and I SINCERELY hope you use the many applets provided for you online. If you are a student, this goes double for you, and if you are a teacher, quadruple. Without the applets, this book is just another crypto book, but with them, **IT'S AN ADVENTURE!**

HAVE FUN!

Contents

CHAPTER 1

A History of Cryptography

This chapter provides an overview of some of the classical methods of cryptography and some idea of how they evolved. None of the methods described here is used today, because they are considered either insecure or impractical. We begin with some definitions:

Definition   A cipher, or cryptosystem, is a pair of invertible functions:

- f_k (known as the enciphering function), which maps from a set S to a set T, based on a quantity k called an enciphering key.
- $g_{k'}$ (known as the deciphering function), the inverse of f_k. k' is known as the deciphering key.

The function f_k maps an element x in S to an element $f_k(x)$ in T so that determining the inverse mapping is extremely difficult without knowledge of k'. An element of S is called plaintext, whereas an element of T is called ciphertext.

Some ciphers are better at satisfying this definition than others. The terms encipher and encrypt are synonymous, as are the terms decipher and decrypt.

Definition   If, for some cipher $k = k'$, or if k' is easily computable given k, such a cipher is called a secret key cipher. However, if k' is extremely difficult to obtain even with knowledge of k, such a cipher is called a public key cipher. In this case k is called a public key, whereas k' is called a private key.

> ***Definition***   Cryptology consists of two disciplines: cryptography and cryptanalysis.
> - Cryptography refers to the study of concealing information with the use of mathematical transformations. One who studies and/or practices cryptography is called a cryptographer.
> - Cryptanalysis refers to the practice of revealing information hidden by cryptography using analytical and mathematical techniques, without the consent of the cryptographer. One who practices cryptanalysis is called a cryptanalyst.

Note   A cryptanalyst uses mathematical means to break ciphers. One can also break a cipher by spying on the users of a system, stealing the decryption key, bribing the cryptographer, injecting him with truth serum, pointing a light (or a gun) in his face, bashing him over the head with a rock, as well as various other tactics. This refers to a rather different discipline known as intelligence.

1.1   CODES

We must first make an important distinction between ciphers, which are the main topic of this book, and codes. Ciphers usually transform units of a fixed length, by means of some mathematical function that describes how to encipher any particular item. Ciphers can work virtually independently of the language being used in the message. Codes, on the other hand, map words to words and thus depend on the language being used. Encoding is not described by some mathematical transformation; rather, a large reference, called a codebook, specifies how each word is to be mapped.

An encoding codebook might be ordered alphabetically by the plaintext words, as shown in Table 1.1.

TABLE 1.1   A Sample Encoding Codebook

Word	Codeword
...	...
At	Lion
Attack	Run
...	...
Dawn	Computer
...	...
Enemy	Explode

TABLE 1.2   A Sample Decoding Codebook

Codeword	Word
...	...
Computer	Dawn
...	...
Explode	Enemy
...	...
Lion	At
...	...
Run	Attack
...	...

A decoding codebook would provide the reverse mappings, organized alphabetically by codeword, as shown in Table 1.2.

In practice, both the encoding and decoding codebooks would probably be incorporated into one book.

So, using the previous codebook, the message

ATTACK ENEMY AT DAWN

would be encoded as

RUN EXPLODE LION COMPUTER.

Though there is some evidence that codes may be more secure than most ciphers, they are not used widely today because of the high overhead involved in distributing, maintaining, and protecting the codebooks.

1.2   MONOALPHABETIC SUBSTITUTION CIPHERS

The oldest cryptosystems were based on monoalphabetic substitution ciphers. These ciphers mapped individual plaintext letters to individual ciphertext letters. They are considered insecure because they are all vulnerable to a type of analysis called frequency analysis, which breaks these ciphers.

The oldest cipher known is called the Caesar cipher. The enciphering and deciphering transformations map an individual letter to another letter in the same alphabet. Specifically, a plaintext letter is shifted down 3 letters, with letters near the end of the alphabet wrapping around again to the front, as shown in Table 1.3.

Thus, using this cipher,

FIRE MISSILE

TABLE 1.3

Plaintext letter	A	B	C	D	......	W	X	Y	Z
Ciphertext letter	D	E	F	G	......	Z	A	B	C

would be enciphered as

ILUH PLVVLOH.

In practice, however, one usually groups these letters into blocks, say 5 letters each. A cryptanalyst can easily guess certain mappings if the ciphertext words are the same size as the plaintext words. Thus, we would probably send the previous message as

ILUHP   LVVLO H.

To decipher, one simply shifts each ciphertext letter 3 letters up the alphabet, again taking wrap-around into account.

Every cipher has at least one key, which may need to be kept secret. In the case of the Caesar cipher, the key is the shift value, say $k = 3$. This key must certainly be protected from unauthorized users, as knowing it allows decryption. In general, we can choose any shift value we wish for a Caesar cipher.

1.3 FREQUENCY ANALYSIS ON CAESAR CIPHERS

Of course, the Caesar cipher is easily breakable, using what is called frequency analysis. We can proceed in the following way:

1. Suppose the message is English text. (The message may not be English text, but the principle remains the same.)
2. Note that the most common letter appearing in English text is "E."
3. Examine as much ciphertext as possible. The character appearing most often is probably the character "E" enciphered.
4. The distance between "E" and the enciphered character is the shift value.

Of course this guess may be wrong, but it is a pretty fair guess with this simple cipher. Frequency analysis exploits the fact that languages are biased in that some letters appear much more frequently in text than others, and that some ciphers preserve this bias. Frequency analysis is only useful for simple ciphers, however, such as this one.

EXAMPLE.   Take a look at the following ciphertext, which was produced using a Caesar cipher:

WFIDZ JVORT KCPVD GKZEV JJVDG KZEVJ JVORT KCPWF IDJFZ KZJNZ KYJVE
JRKZF EGVIT VGKZF EDVEK RCIVR TKZFE REUTF EJTZF LJEVJ JRCCK YZEXJ

```
RIVVJ JVEKZ RCCPV DGKPE FKSFI EEFKU VJKIF PVUEF KJKRZ EVUEF KGLIV
NZKYF LKCFJ JNZKY FLKXR ZEKYV IVWFI VZEVD GKZEV JJKYV IVZJE FWFID
EFJVE JRKZF EGVIT VGKZF EDVEK RCIVR TKZFE FITFE JTZFL JEVJJ EFVPV
VRIEF JVKFE XLVSF UPDZE UEFTF CFIJF LEUJD VCCKR JKVKF LTYFS AVTKF
WKYFL XYKEF JVVZE XREUJ FFEKF EFKYZ EBZEX EFZXE FIRET VREUE FVEUK
FZXEF IRETV EFFCU RXVRE UUVRK YEFVE UKFFC URXVR EUUVR KYEFR EXLZJ
YTRLJ VFWRE XLZJY TVJJR KZFEG RKYEF NZJUF DREUE FRKKR ZEDVE KJZET
VKYVI VZJEF KYZEX KFRKK RZEKY VSFUY ZJRKK MRCZM VJKYL JNZKY EFYZE
UIRET VFWDZ EUEFY ZEUIR ETVRE UYVET VEFWV RIWRI SVPFE UUVCL UVUKY
FLXYK IZXYK YVIVZ JEZIM RER
```

If we count the occurrences of each letter in the text, we come up with the following counts:

```
A: 1  B: 1  C: 16 D: 14 E: 82 F: 69 G: 10 H: 0  I: 27 J: 47 K: 61 L: 15
M: 3  N: 5  O: 2  P: 8  Q: 0  R: 45 S: 5  T: 21 U: 28 V: 69 W: 9  X: 15
Y: 28 Z: 47
```

The letter E appears most frequently, but this would be the identity map, not a smart choice. Otherwise, the most frequently occurring letters are F and V, which each appear 69 times. Thus, the shift value is likely to be

distance(E, F) = 1, or distance(E, V) = 17.

If we try the shift value of 1, we see that we get only garbage. If we shift each letter of the ciphertext to the left by 17, though, we get the beautiful expression:

```
FORMI SEXAC TLYEM PTINE SSEMP TINES SEXAC TLYFO RMSOI TISWI THSEN
SATIO NPERC EPTIO NMENT ALREA CTION ANDCO NSCIO USNES SALLT HINGS
AREES SENTI ALLYE MPTYN OTBOR NNOTD ESTRO YEDNO TSTAI NEDNO TPURE
WITHO UTLOS SWITH OUTGA INTHE REFOR EINEM PTINE SSTHE REISN OFORM
NOSEN SATIO NPERC EPTIO NMENT ALREA CTION ORCON SCIOU SNESS NOEYE
EARNO SETON GUEBO DYMIN DNOCO LORSO UNDSM ELLTA STETO UCHOB JECTO
FTHOU GHTNO SEEIN GANDS OONTO NOTHI NKING NOIGN ORANC EANDN OENDT
OIGNO RANCE NOOLD AGEAN DDEAT HNOEN DTOOL DAGEA NDDEA THNOA NGUIS
HCAUS EOFAN GUISH CESSA TIONP ATHNO WISDO MANDN OATTA INMEN TSINC
ETHER EISNO THING TOATT AINTH EBODH ISATT VALIV ESTHU SWITH NOHIN
DRANC EOFMI NDNOH INDRA NCEAN DHENC ENOFE ARFAR BEYON DDELU DEDTH
OUGHT RIGHT HEREI SNIRV ANA
```

It is not necessary that a monoalphabetic mapping be based on a shift. We can map the plaintext alphabet letters to a permutation of the alphabet, as shown in Table 1.4.

This particular mapping is based on a keyphrase "THE HILLS ARE ALIVE." Note that the first few letters in the ciphertext column are the initial occurrences of each letter in the phrase. This was often done in practice, as it made the permutation easy to reconstruct. However, a permutation certainly need not be based on such a keyphrase.

TABLE 1.4

Plaintext Letter	Ciphertext Letter
A	T
B	H
C	E
D	I
E	L
F	S
G	A
H	R
I	V
J	B
K	C
L	D
M	F
N	G
O	J
P	K
Q	M
R	N
S	O
T	P
U	Q
V	U
W	W
X	X
Y	Y
Z	Z

1.4   FREQUENCY ANALYSIS ON MONOALPHABETIC SUBSTITUTION CIPHERS

Frequency analysis can be used for any permutation of single letters of an alphabet, not just a shift as in the Caesar cipher. The relative frequencies of all letters in English text (and many other languages) are well known. These frequencies can be used to break any cipher that maps individual letters. The approximate frequency distribution of letters in typical English text is shown in Figure 1.1.

If analysts have enough ciphertext, they can use this distribution to make fairly good guesses about how individual letters are mapped in a monoalphabetic substitution cipher. For example, the most common letter in the ciphertext probably corresponds with the plaintext letter "E," the second most common letter in the ciphertext probably corresponds with "T," and so on. Once the analyst starts filling in these more common letters, they can begin to make some good guesses for the other letters, and they eventually fill out enough letters so that they uncover the secret mapping.

EXAMPLE.   Consider the following ciphertext, which was produced by a mapping of the alphabet A . . . Z to a permutation of the alphabet.

```
HUFMD  JCXNE  ONUFZ  UFJCX  NUYMM  TDHLF  XTGYT  HUFEY  KFNEF  MXFCD
GTXTQ  JFFTZ  YNHSJ  FNUFM  FYCNE  FLFNX  CFPSX  FHGYH  FJNUF  JFNHD
JFNEO  NDSMU  FQSXC  FNEFX  TZYHU  NDBJX  QUHFD  SNTFN  NBDJU  XNTYE
FNNYK  FFAFT  HUDSQ  UXGYM  KHUJD  SQUHU  FAYMM  FODBH  UFNUY  CDGDB
CFYHU  XGXMM  BFYJT  DFAXM  BDJOD  SYJFG  XHUEF  ODSJJ  DCYTC  ODSJN
HYBBH  UFORD  EBDJH  EFODS  ZJFZY  JFYHY  LMFLF  BDJFE  FXTHU  FZJFN
FTRFD  BEOFT  FEXFN  ODSYT  DXTHE  OUFYC  GXHUD  XMEOR  SZDAF  JBMDG
NNSJF  MOQDD  CTFNN  YTCMD  AFGXM  MBDMM  DGEFY  MMHUF  CYOND  BEOMX
BFYTC  XGXMM  CGFMM  XTHUF  UDSNF  DBHUF  MDJCB  DJFAF  J
```

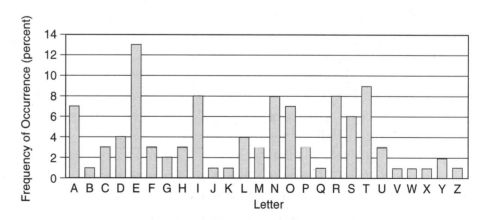

FIGURE 1.1   **Relative Frequencies of English Letters (percent)**

We must count the frequency of each letter in the ciphertext, and then compare these frequencies with the relative frequency table. Here are the counts for each letter:

```
A: 6       B: 17      C: 17      D: 39      E: 17      F: 67
G: 13      H: 25      I: 0       J: 26      K: 3       L: 4
M: 29      N: 30      O: 15      P: 1       Q: 6       R: 3
S: 15      T: 21      U: 28      V: 0       W: 0       X: 26
Y: 26      Z: 7
```

F is by far the most common letter, and its plaintext partner is probably E. The next most common letters are D, N, M, U, J, X, and Y, which are likely the mappings of A, I, N, O, R, S, and T. The least frequent ciphertext letters are I, V, and W, which are likely the mappings of Q, X, and Z. These guesses may of course be wrong, but once you start trying different combinations words will start to appear in the plaintext. As you progress, you can start to make educated guesses about the mappings; this process starts out slowly, but quickly speeds up. Table 1.5 shows the mapping for this cipher.

Using this mapping, we see that the plaintext is:

```
THELO RDISM YSHEP HERDI SHALL NOTBE INWAN THEMA KESME LIEDO
WNING REENP ASTUR ESHEL EADSM EBESI DEQUI ETWAT ERSHE RESTO
RESMY SOULH EGUID ESMEI NPATH SOFRI GHTEO USNES SFORH ISNAM
ESSAK EEVEN THOUG HIWAL KTHRO UGHTH EVALL EYOFT HESHA DOWOF
DEATH IWILL FEARN OEVIL FORYO UAREW ITHME YOURR ODAND YOURS
TAFFT HEYCO MFORT MEYOU PREPA REATA BLEBE FOREM EINTH EPRES
ENCEO FMYEN EMIES YOUAN OINTM YHEAD WITHO ILMYC UPOVE RFLOW
SSURE LYGOO DNESS ANDLO VEWIL LFOLL OWMEA LLTHE DAYSO FMYLI
FEAND IWILL DWELL INTHE HOUSE OFTHE LORDF OREVE R
```

1.5   POLYALPHABETIC SUBSTITUTION CIPHERS

As one can readily see, monoalphabetic substitution ciphers are notoriously easy to break. In the case of the Caesar cipher, the shift value can be uncovered rather easily. One way classical cryptographers dealt with this was to use different shift values for letters depending on their position in the text. For example, one may do something like the following:

- Let $a_1, a_2, \ldots, a_n$ be the letters in a plaintext message. Consider the letter a_p:
- If p is divisible by 4, shift a_p 7 letters down the alphabet.
- If p is of the form $4k + 1$ for some k, shift a_p 5 letters down the alphabet.
- If p is of the form $4k + 2$ for some k, shift a_p 13 letters down the alphabet.
- If p is of the form $4k + 3$ for some k, shift a_p 2 letters down the alphabet.

Using this scheme, we can encipher the message

DEFCON FOUR

as shown in Table 1.6.

TABLE 1.5

Plaintext Letter	Ciphertext Letter
A	Y
B	L
C	R
D	C
E	F
F	B
G	Q
H	U
I	X
J	I
K	K
L	M
M	E
N	T
O	D
P	Z
Q	P
R	J
S	N
T	H
U	S
V	A
W	G
X	V
Y	O
Z	W

TABLE 1.6

Plaintext	D	E	F	C	O	N	F	O	U	R
Shift value	5	13	2	7	5	13	2	7	5	13
Ciphertext	I	R	H	J	T	A	H	V	Z	E

A	B	C	D	E	F	G	H	I	J	K	L	M	N	O	P	Q	R	S	T	U	V	W	X	Y	Z
0	1	2	3	4	5	6	7	8	9	10	11	12	13	14	15	16	17	18	19	20	21	22	23	24	25

TABLE 1.7

The message to send is

IRHJT   AHVZE.

Note that the way we group the letters has nothing to do with how many shift values are being used; in fact, we don't want to give the analyst any clues by grouping the letters in blocks the same size as the number of shift values!

It was difficult for classical cryptographers to remember shift values when using a large number of them. They certainly didn't want to write them down, because the shift values were the secret key. So instead they used letters to represent the shifts in the form of a keyword, or a long keyphrase. Each letter in the alphabet was associated with its position, as shown in Table 1.7.

From now on, when our alphabet consists of only capital English characters we will call this the "ordinary" alphabet. These keywords and keyphrases were easily remembered. For example, the keyphrase

BLAST OFF

represents the shift values

1   12   0   18   19   14   5   5.

These are the 8 shift values that would be used on a message, repeating the sequence every eighth letter.

1.6 THE VIGENERE CIPHER AND CODE WHEELS

One convenient tool used for the previous type of cipher (called a simple shift Vigenere cipher) was a code wheel. The outer ring of the wheel represented plaintext letters, and the inner wheel represented ciphertext letters. Using a letter from a keyword or keyphrase, say "S," one would rotate the inner wheel and position the keyword letter under the letter "A." To encipher, one would go to the plaintext letter in the outer wheel, say "G," and find its corresponding ciphertext letter, in this case "Y." This is the position of the wheel illustrated in

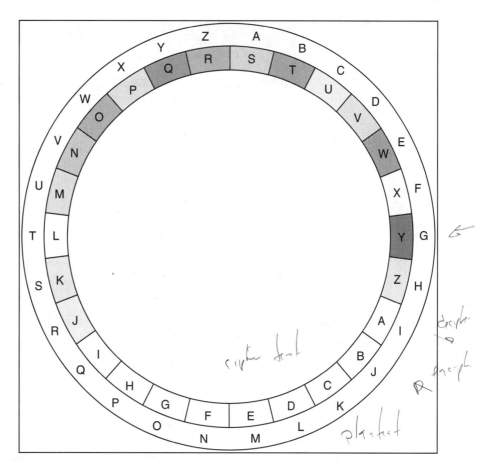

FIGURE 1.2   A Sample Code Wheel

Figure 1.2. To decipher, one would position the keyword letter under "A," but would go from the inner ciphertext wheel to the outer plaintext wheel.

1.7   BREAKING SIMPLE VIGENERE CIPHERS

If enough ciphertext is received, and if the analyst makes a good guess for the key length, say *n*, frequency analysis also breaks these types of polyalphabetic substitution ciphers. An analyst can separate the ciphertext into *n* categories, and then do a separate frequency analysis on each category. In this way, one could derive all of the *n* shift values. The problem with using a keyword in this way is that it would eventually repeat, and this fact could be exploited.

TABLE 1.8

Key Length = 5				
Category 1	Category 2	Category 3	Category 4	Category 5
XIPGL	ZIASN	QSWGO	TTRPX	YNTOF

Suppose we have the ciphertext message

XZQTY   IISTN   PAWRT   GSGPO   LNOXF.

If the analyst assumes (correctly) that the keyword is of length 5, she would separate the ciphertext into 5 categories, as described in Table 1.8.

She then does a separate frequency analysis for each category; in this way she can derive the shift values for all letters in categories 1, 2, 3, 4, and 5. (Of course, this example does not provide nearly enough ciphertext to do this, but the method works as described.) How does one determine the key length? Random guessing may work, but perhaps only after a lot of work. The method described here is often useful.

1.8 THE KAISISKI METHOD OF DETERMINING KEY LENGTH

The Kaisiski method is a way of determining key length. This method takes advantage of the fact that languages contain not only frequent individual characters, but also frequently occurring letter pairs and letter triples. We can use this to spot recurring triples in the ciphertext. This will happen when a common triple falls on, and is enciphered by, the same portion of the keyword. By noting the distance between these recurring blocks of text in the ciphertext, we can make a good guess for the key length.

EXAMPLE. Suppose the triple FSI appears in the ciphertext 12 times, and the distance between the first character (F) of each is as shown in Table 1.9.

Note that all but 2 of the distances in the table are multiples of 7. (The sixth appearance of FSI came about probably by coincidence, and probably does not represent the same plaintext triple). A good guess for the key length being used here is 7.

EXAMPLE. Consider the following ciphertext, which was formed using a Vigenere cipher on uppercase English letters:

LJVBQ STNEZ LQMED LJVMA MPKAU FAVAT LJVDA YYVNF JQLNP LJVHK
VTRNF LJVCM LKETA LJVHU YJVSF KRFTT WEFUX VHZNP

If we use the Kaisiski method, we see that the triple LJV keeps reappearing. The distances between each occurrence of LJV are shown in Table 1.10.

This tells us that it is very likely that the key length is 5. We now separate the ciphertext into 5 categories, and do a frequency analysis on each category, as shown in Table 1.11.

In each category, the most common letter probably corresponds with the plaintext letter E, T, I, N, or R. It would be easier to determine the shift values if we had more text to work

TABLE 1.9

i	Distance between $(i-1)$th and ith occurrence
2	56
3	14
4	35
5	63
6	9
7	5
8	28
9	35
10	33
11	21
12	35

TABLE 1.10

Occurrence	Distance
2	15
3	15
4	15
5	10
6	10

with, since E is more likely to appear than any other letter in plaintext. However, we have even more information: The most common triple in English is THE, and in this example it probably corresponds with the triple LJV. Even with this short amount of text, we can try a few possibilities. The one that works is shown in Table 1.12.

Thus, we derive the keyword

SCRAM

Category	Letters				Most Common Letter
1	LSLLM	FLYJL	VLLLY	KWV	L
2	JTQJP	AJYQJ	TJKJJ	REH	J
3	VNMVK	VVVLV	RVEVV	FFZ	V
4	BEEMA	ADNNH	NCTHS	TUN	N
5	QZDAU	TAFPK	FMAUF	TXP	A

TABLE 1.11

Category	Plaintext Letter	Maps to Ciphertext Letter	Shift value
1	T	L	18 = S
2	H	J	2 = C
3	E	V	17 = R
4	N	N	0 = A
5	O	A	12 = M

TABLE 1.12

and based on this, we can recover the plaintext.

```
THEBE ARWEN TOVER THEMO UNTAI NYEAH THEDO GWENT ROUND THEHY
DRANT THECA TINTO THEHI GHEST SPOTH ECOUL DFIND
```

1.9 THE FULL VIGENERE CIPHER

The full Vigenere cipher is similar to the simple shift Vigenere in that it uses a keyword or keyphrase. However, in the full Vigenere cipher, rather than using a series of shift values k_1, $k_2, \ldots, k_n$, each letter in the keyword refers to a general permutation $e_1, e_2, \ldots, e_n$ of the alphabet. Enciphering in this way is aided by the use of a table such as Table 1.13.

TABLE 1.13

	A	B	C	D	E	F	G	H	I	J	K	L	M	N	O	P	Q	R	S	T	U	V	W	X	Y	Z
A	F	W	Y	G	B	D	Z	I	X	V	H	A	L	K	J	U	E	T	C	N	R	P	S	M	O	Q
B	G	A	Y	O	M	X	C	W	H	Z	N	B	S	T	E	V	P	D	K	Q	U	L	F	R	I	J
C	L	Y	B	O	N	I	Z	C	K	M	J	X	H	G	A	E	T	Q	F	V	D	W	P	R	S	U
D	F	D	I	V	Z	H	E	G	U	Y	B	T	K	P	W	C	S	N	Q	J	M	O	A	L	X	R
E	Q	T	G	S	A	R	Z	P	B	H	X	F	J	O	Y	K	U	D	W	I	M	V	C	N	L	E
F	M	X	C	P	O	N	F	W	E	V	I	Q	B	D	G	H	L	Z	U	K	R	Y	J	T	A	S
G	F	E	P	Z	D	Y	O	I	C	W	B	Q	X	J	S	N	H	A	R	T	G	L	K	V	M	U
H	O	B	Z	M	N	Y	A	L	U	R	D	C	K	P	H	Q	F	X	J	E	S	T	G	I	W	V
I	N	F	Y	D	Z	H	O	E	A	G	P	W	C	V	M	I	J	T	R	B	Q	L	K	S	U	X
J	S	A	U	M	E	K	O	N	J	F	C	P	T	H	Y	V	L	G	Q	Z	D	X	I	R	B	W
K	E	W	N	D	L	X	U	K	O	F	V	M	T	C	S	R	I	P	Z	G	Q	J	Y	H	A	B
L	M	B	L	T	A	S	N	X	J	W	D	U	V	O	C	K	Q	P	I	F	Z	G	R	E	Y	H
M	J	I	O	C	W	H	U	M	B	V	G	N	Y	F	P	K	L	Y	D	X	E	R	Q	S	Z	A
N	E	S	C	Y	G	Z	R	U	D	P	O	F	A	H	T	V	K	Q	I	M	B	X	J	L	W	N
O	B	Z	K	J	W	P	U	Y	L	A	X	H	V	R	M	I	F	Q	G	O	S	N	C	T	E	D
P	Z	Y	O	U	M	W	N	B	V	D	G	P	K	T	A	R	H	C	X	J	I	E	L	Q	S	F
Q	I	V	E	H	Q	J	F	D	K	U	Z	G	R	A	T	P	C	S	Y	M	W	O	L	B	X	N
R	C	B	U	Y	T	G	N	P	E	S	D	Q	Z	O	A	M	F	L	W	K	I	R	X	J	H	V
S	V	E	R	D	S	Q	W	O	G	F	C	P	Y	J	U	N	H	L	X	I	K	Z	T	B	A	M
T	W	B	R	A	P	O	D	F	T	C	M	X	Y	G	U	E	Q	N	I	Z	V	L	S	H	K	J
U	R	B	O	M	A	N	T	C	D	V	L	Q	J	Z	E	S	K	U	I	W	Y	P	H	F	X	G
V	C	Z	B	N	G	L	O	Y	F	X	K	M	W	H	R	D	P	J	S	A	I	Q	U	E	V	T
W	A	S	P	Y	Q	R	G	F	D	E	Z	H	O	T	V	I	B	X	N	U	J	L	K	W	C	M
X	P	Q	O	Z	M	X	Y	W	S	L	N	U	K	V	T	I	J	D	G	B	R	E	A	F	C	H
Y	M	Y	X	O	A	N	V	C	L	U	W	B	I	T	G	K	Q	J	P	Z	H	R	S	E	D	F
Z	Q	P	W	O	Y	Z	N	X	H	M	S	J	L	I	U	A	G	C	T	E	F	V	D	K	B	R

Each row is a permutation of the ordinary alphabet; the leftmost letter of each row is referenced by the keyword. The first row in the table represents the plaintext letter. To encipher the plaintext letter T using the key letter D, for example, we find the letter in the cell referenced by row D, column T. This yields the ciphertext letter J.

EXAMPLE.   Encipher the message

HARKONNEN RULZ

using the keyphrase

SPICE.

By locating each ciphertext letter in the manner described previously, we get

OZTJY   JTZGD   KPX.

Decryption should be simple to figure out. What makes the full Vigenere cipher slightly superior to the simple shift Vigenere is that the full relative frequency distribution of the language may be necessary to break the former, whereas only the most common letter is needed to break the latter.

1.10   THE AUTO-KEY VIGENERE CIPHER

Vigenere ciphers are our earliest examples of stream ciphers. Stream ciphers are those that encipher letters based on their position in the plaintext. Ideally, the key being used should never repeat, as this aids the cryptanalyst. Some stream ciphers make the plaintext and/or the ciphertext part of the encryption process; such is the case with the auto-key Vigenere.

This type of cipher begins with a priming key of length n, say $k_0, k_1, \ldots, k_{n-1}$. Encryption for the first n characters is done the same way (using the key) as for the simple shift Vigenere, but after that, to encipher the ith character of the plaintext, we add to it (with wrap-around) the $(i - n)$th letter of the plaintext. This is easily seen with an example.

EXAMPLE.   For this example, it is convenient to see the letter–number associations of the ordinary alphabet. (See Table 1.14.)

Suppose we wish to encipher the message

LIGHT SPEED CHEWIE NOW

A	B	C	D	E	F	G	H	I	J	K	L	M	N	O	P	Q	R	S	T	U	V	W	X	Y	Z
0	1	2	3	4	5	6	7	8	9	10	11	12	13	14	15	16	17	18	19	20	21	22	23	24	25

TABLE 1.14   Letter–Number Associations of the Ordinary Alphabet

TABLE 1.15

Plaintext	L I G H T S P E E D C H E W I E N O W
Key	A R G H L I G H T S P E E D C H E W I
Ciphertext	L Z M O E A V L X V R L I Z K L R K E

using the keyword

ARGH

and an auto-key Vigenere. First, we write the plaintext, and underneath it we write the priming key, followed by as much of the plaintext as necessary to fill out the line. Underneath this, we do a simple shift to generate the ciphertext shown in Table 1.15.

How does one recover the plaintext when the plaintext is part of the key? It should be easy to see that only knowledge of the priming key is necessary. Once we use the key to decrypt the first n characters of the ciphertext, we derive the first n characters of the plaintext, and hence can use it to decrypt more ciphertext.

One must be particularly careful with ciphers like these that no errors are made in the encryption phase, for a single miscalculated character affects an entire series of characters following it. Care must also be taken to ensure that no errors occur during transmission.

1.11   THE RUNNING KEY VIGENERE CIPHER

Another alternative to the auto-key Vigenere is called a running key Vigenere. It makes use of a very long key in the form of meaningful text, as in a book, of which both the sender and intended receiver have a copy.

EXAMPLE.   Suppose we are working with the ordinary alphabet. Again, we show the ordinary letter/number associations, in Table 1.16, for quick reference.

To encrypt the message

TORA TORA TORA

we use a passage from a book, such as a particular edition of the Bible, as the key:

AND GOD SAID LET THERE BE LIGHT.

The encryption proceeds as a simple shift, as shown in Table 1.17.

To decrypt, one simply needs to know which passage from which book to use, and the plaintext is easily regained.

A	B	C	D	E	F	G	H	I	J	K	L	M	N	O	P	Q	R	S	T	U	V	W	X	Y	Z
0	1	2	3	4	5	6	7	8	9	10	11	12	13	14	15	16	17	18	19	20	21	22	23	24	25

TABLE 1.16   Letter–Number Associations of the Ordinary Alphabet

TABLE 1.17	Plaintext	T	O	R	A	T	O	R	A	T	O	R	A
	Key	A	N	D	G	O	D	S	A	I	D	L	E
	Ciphertext	T	B	U	G	H	R	J	A	B	R	D	E

1.12 BREAKING AUTO-KEY AND RUNNING KEY VIGENERE CIPHERS

Though the auto-key Vigenere and the running key Vigenere evade the problem of the repeating key, they are still vulnerable to frequency analysis. This is because plaintext is being used for the key. Even though this plaintext never repeats, it still provides information. This is because high frequency letters in the key will often encipher high frequency letters in the message. This information is often enough to recover messages.

1.13 THE ONE-TIME PAD

One solution to thwarting frequency analysis on polyalphabetic substitution ciphers was to use a truly random key that would never repeat. Such a key was called a one-time pad. These were notebooks consisting of sheets with tables of random numbers on them. The random numbers were used as shift values. Each sheet in the pad was different from every other, and each sheet was used only once. Encrypting using a one-time pad would look something like Table 1.18.

Using this particular sheet from a one-time pad, the ciphertext message

NHTAB   FJTAUCDHZL

is produced from the plaintext message

ENGAGE WARP DRIVE.

If the message does not fill out the sheet, the rest of the sheet is ignored. After the sheet is used, it is destroyed. The recipient of the message would also have an identical one-time pad. The messages are numbered, so the recipient would know which sheet to use. They would use the same shift values to shift back to the plaintext.

The one-time pad is the ultimate cipher, if used properly. In terms of ciphertext analysis, it is totally secure. In fact, it is the most secure cipher possible. There is no way an ana-

Plaintext letter	E	N	G	A	G	E	W	A	R	P	D	R	I	V	E					
Shift value	9	20	13	0	21	1	13	19	9	5	25	12	25	4	7	25	0	8	8	7	24
Ciphertext letter	N	H	T	A	B	F	J	T	A	U	C	D	H	Z	L					
Plaintext letter																				
Shift value	2	6	18	16	10	23	5	11	12	13	6	22	22	17	3	8	0	0	19	4	15
Ciphertext letter																				

TABLE 1.18

lyst can guess the key if it is a potentially infinite sequence of random numbers. It is mathematically provable that *any* plaintext message could map to some particular ciphertext message if random numbers are used; thus, the ciphertext provides absolutely no information to the analyst at all.

Of course, the reason one-time pads are not used today is because they are simply impractical. The distribution and protection of the pads is a logistical nightmare. For example, if all the sheets in a pad were used up, it would have to be replaced with a new pad consisting of entirely different random numbers. However, one-time pads have been used; in particular, certain embassies have used them for highly sensitive communications with their governments.

1.14 TRANSPOSITION CIPHERS

Transposition ciphers were simply a permutation of the letters in a plaintext message; that is, they reordered the letters of the message. This reordering was specified for blocks of a predetermined size, and the reordering would occur within each block. Say we choose a block size of 5, and for a particular block we specify the following:

The 1st letter becomes the 4th letter,

the 2nd letter becomes the 3rd letter,

the 3rd letter becomes the 1st letter,   (*)

the 4th letter becomes the 5th letter, and

the 5th letter becomes the 2nd letter.

A short way of denoting this permutation is to use the notation

$$(1\ 4\ 5\ 2\ 3),$$

which becomes meaningful if you just rearrange the statements in (*).

The 1st letter becomes the 4th letter,

the 4th letter becomes the 5th letter,

the 5th letter becomes the 2nd letter,

the 2nd letter becomes the 3rd letter, and

the 3rd letter becomes the 1st letter.

Suppose we have the plaintext message

THE SKY FALLING PLEASE ADVISE

which we split into blocks of length 5:

THESK YFALL INGPL EASEA DVISE

If we use the permutation defined by (*), we get the following scrambled blocks, which comprise the ciphertext.

EKHTS ALFYL GLNIP SAAEE IEVDS

By themselves, transposition ciphers are considered very weak ciphers. Anyone who has played anagrams or has done unscrambling puzzles in the newspaper can testify to this. However, when transposition is used in combination with substitution, one can produce very powerful ciphers. Many modern ciphers are based on this idea.

1.15   POLYGRAM SUBSTITUTION CIPHERS

Mapping single letters to single letters is far too vulnerable to be useful. Thus, cryptographers eventually came up with the idea of mapping entire blocks of plaintext letters to blocks of ciphertext letters. The ciphertext blocks didn't necessarily have the same length as the plaintext blocks. For example, suppose we wish to map 8 letter blocks to 8 letter blocks. In general, we could specify the mapping shown in Table 1.19.

There are clearly a lot of 8-letter plaintext blocks in the range AAAAAAAA through ZZZZZZZZ (26^8, exactly). If one wanted to do frequency analysis on such a scheme, he would require a table of $26^8 = 208,827,064,576$ blocks, and would have to know the relative percentages for which each 8-letter block appears in typical English text (if that is the language being used). Then, he would need an enormous amount of ciphertext so that he could determine the relative frequency of the 8-letter ciphertext blocks, and equate ciphertext blocks to plaintext blocks. This is clearly infeasible, both in terms of the time and storage requirements. Thus, doing frequency analysis on blocks of letters is much harder than doing frequency analysis on individual letters. However, if the cryptosystem does not use a sufficiently large block size, frequency analysis is still possible. An example follows.

1.16   THE PLAYFAIR CIPHER

The Playfair cipher was a cryptosystem that mapped digraphs (2-letter pairs) to digraphs. The letters were arranged in a 5×5 square. There are 26 letters in the ordinary alphabet, so the letters I and J were equated. This is the simplest 5×5 Playfair square:

A	B	C	D	E
F	G	H	I/J	K
L	M	N	O	P
Q	R	S	T	U
V	W	X	Y	Z

TABLE 1.19

AAAAAAAA	maps to	ZXCIJCDV
AAAAAAAB	maps to	APQODFIM
. . .	. . .	. . .
ZZZZZZZZ	maps to	SSTFQQWR

The letters in the square, however, were usually permuted, often based on a keyword or keyphrase. The Playfair Square that follows is derived from the keyphrase "The quick brown fox jumped over the lazy dogs."

T	H	E	Q	U
I/J	C	K	B	R
O	W	N	F	X
M	P	D	V	L
A	Z	Y	G	S

It is easy enough to see how this is done. You fill in the square with letters from the keyphrase, avoiding duplicates. If the keyphrase does not contain all 26 letters, you fill out the rest of the table with the unused letters, in order. A Playfair square based on the keyphrase "Since by man came death" follows.

S	I/J	N	C	E
B	Y	M	A	D
T	H	F	G	K
L	O	P	Q	R
U	V	W	X	Z

Here is how to encrypt with the square: The plaintext pair of letters p, q is mapped to the ciphertext letters c, d as follows:

1. If p and q are in both different columns and different rows, they define the corners of a square. The other 2 corners are c and d; c is the letter in the same column as p.

2. If p and q are in the same row, c is the letter to the right of p, and d is the letter to the right of q (wrapping around if necessary).

3. If p and q are in the same column, c is the letter below p, and d is the letter below q (with wrap-around).

4. If p = q, the letter "X" is inserted into the plaintext between the doubled letters. The evaluation continues with the new pair p, and q = "X." If there is only one letter trailing at the end (instead of a full pair), add a final letter "X."

EXAMPLE.   We use the following square

L	O	V	E	I/J
S	A	M	N	Y
P	D	R	T	H
G	B	C	F	K
Q	U	W	X	Z

to encrypt the message

AMBASSADOR SHOT.

First, group the letters in pairs

AM BA SS AD OR SH OT.

Now look for any doubled letter pairs and insert an X between them. Regroup the plaintext.

AM BA SX SA DO RS HO TX

If there are not enough letters to make the final pair, add another X at the end, as done here. If one follows the rules outlined previously, one should obtain the following ciphertext:

MN UD QN AM BA MP ID FE

The rules for decryption should be easy to figure out; the same Playfair square is used. (Of course—the square is the key.) The ciphertext pair of letters c, and d, are mapped to the plaintext letters p and q in the following way.

1. If c and d are in both different columns and different rows, they define the corners of a square. The other 2 corners are p and q; p is the letter in the same column as c.
2. If c and d are in the same row, p is the letter to the left of c, and q is the letter to the left of d (wrapping around if necessary).
3. If c and d are in the same column, p is the letter above c, and q is the letter above d (with wrap-around).

Because of the way enciphering was done, doubled letter ciphertext pairs will not occur. The recipient must remove from the recovered plaintext any letter X's which do not make sense. They must also determine, since I and J are equated, whether a recovered plaintext I/J is an I or a J.

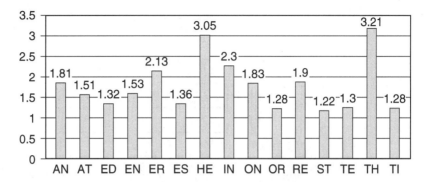

FIGURE 1.3   Percentage of Common Digraphs in English Text

1.17   BREAKING SIMPLE POLYGRAM CIPHERS

The Playfair cipher, for all its complicated rules, is not secure. Digraphs are not large enough blocks to rule out the use of frequency analysis. Tables that record the relative frequency of digraphs in typical English text exist (as well as for many other languages). For example, the most common digraph in English text is "TH," followed by "HE." Using such tables, one can break a Playfair cipher given enough ciphertext. A complete table is often not even necessary; a partial table will often be enough, such as the chart shown in Figure 1.3.

Relative frequency tables for English exist even for trigraphs (3-letter blocks); the most common is "THE," followed by "AND" and "THA." Such tables exist for even larger blocks. Modern polygram ciphers use a block size of at least 8 characters.

1.18   THE JEFFERSON CYLINDER

None other than the American statesman Thomas Jefferson invented the Jefferson cylinder. It was an ingenious device that provided very secure ciphers, and it was used for many years. The cylinder consisted of 36 wheels. Each wheel had printed on it a complete (scrambled) alphabet. A simplified drawing of a typical Jefferson cylinder is shown in Figure 1.4.

To encipher, one needed to rotate the wheels so that the plaintext appeared along one of the rows in the cylinder. To select the ciphertext, one would simply select any of the other 25 rows. Rotating the wheels so that the ciphertext would appear in one of the rows did deciphering. Then they would search the other 25 rows of the cylinder for meaningful text.

What made the Jefferson cylinder so powerful was the huge size of its rows, or blocks; frequency analysis on such blocks, each consisting of 36 characters, was literally impossible at the time.

The Jefferson cylinder eventually fell into disuse because of its impracticality. (This is why most of the excellent classical ciphers were rejected; they were too hard to implement.) Every authorized user of the cryptosystem would need his or her own cylinder. If a single

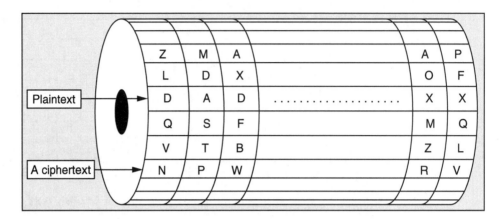

FIGURE 1.4   Simplified Drawing of a Typical Jefferson Cylinder

cylinder fell into the wrong hands, the cipher would become useless; in that case, one solution would be to reorder the wheels on the cylinder, ensuring that no unauthorized persons receive this vital information.

1.19   HOMOPHONIC SUBSTITUTION CIPHERS

Another approach taken to thwart frequency analysis was the use of homophones. This was a system of enciphering wherein letters that occurred more frequently in the language were given multiple choices of ciphertext symbols. The more frequent a plaintext letter was, the more choices it would have.

For quick reference, the relative frequencies of letters in typical English text are shown again, in Figure 1.5.

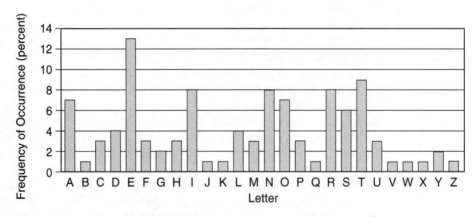

FIGURE 1.5   Relative Frequencies of English Letters (percent)

The following table is a sample of a homophonic substitution scheme. This scheme is based on the distribution of letters in typical English text. So, for example, because the letter E appears about 13 percent of the time in such text, there are 13 choices of ciphertext replacements for E in the table. This is called a table of homophones. (See Table 1.20.)

Using this table, the message "RETREAT" could be enciphered as

DQ AW CC AQ CO BS DB.

It could also be enciphered in other ways depending on our choices for those letters having multiple selections. It is important to make a selection as randomly as possible. This randomization "evens out" the relative frequency distribution of the ciphertext digraphs, so equating "humps" in the ciphertext to "humps" in the plaintext becomes difficult, if not impossible.

Note that the ciphertext is larger than the plaintext. This is necessary if individual letters have multiple choices without introducing new alphabetic symbols. Encryption is a

Plaintext letter	Choices for ciphertext unit											
A	BU	CP	AV	AH	BT	BS	CQ					
B	AT											
C	DL	BK	AU									
D	BV	DY	DM	AI								
E	DK	CO	AW	BL	AA	CR	BM	CS	AF	AG	BO	BN	BE
F	BW	CM	CN									
G	DN	BJ										
H	AS	CL	CK									
I	DJ	BI	AX	CJ	AB	BP	CU	CT				
J	BX											
K	DI											
L	AR	BH	CI	AJ								
M	DH	BG	AY									
N	BY	DG	DF	CH	AC	BR	DU	DT				
O	DZ	BF	DX	AK	CG	BQ	DR					
P	BZ	DE	AZ									
Q	DD											
R	AQ	DC	DQ	AL	CE	CF	CV	DS				
S	AP	AN	AO	CD	DW	DV						
T	CB	DB	DP	CC	AD	CY	CW	CX	AE			
U	CA	AM	BA									
V	BB											
W	CZ											
X	BD											
Y	DO	DA										
Z	BC											

TABLE 1.20   A Sample Table of Homophones

one–to–many mapping, but note that decryption is not, for none of the letter pairs in the previous table appear more than once. (You may wish to verify this.) Thus, decryption always produces the correct message.

Those decrypting would probably have the inverse mappings organized according to the ciphertext symbols, to aid in decryption. A listing of the inverse mappings of our sample homophone is shown in Table 1.21.

Homophonic ciphers were very effective, and were used extensively in the past. Because of their heavy dependence on the language being used, and because modern powerful block ciphers are primarily independent of language, homophones are not commonly used today.

1.20   COMBINATION SUBSTITUTION/TRANSPOSITION CIPHERS

When substitution and transposition are used simultaneously, and especially when the respective block sizes are different, the result can be a very powerful cipher.

EXAMPLE.   The following is a cipher that uses both substitution and transposition. Three transformations will be involved. Suppose we use the ordinary alphabet, where substitutions for plaintext are first made according to Table 1.22.

That is,

A maps to AA (row A, column A)

B maps to AB

C maps to AC

...

Q maps to DB

...

Y maps to EE

Z maps to DB.

(Note that the letters Q and Z map to the same pair. When decryption is done this should not be a problem as Q and Z are very infrequent letters, and it should be easy to determine which letter was intended). Suppose we wish to encipher the following message:

TAKE ME TO YOUR LEADER.

Now, convert each letter to its letter pair equivalent.

DE AA CA AE CC AE DE CE EE CE EA DC CB AE AA AD AE DC

Take the second half of this text and place it under the first half.

DE AA CA AE CC AE DE CE EE
CE EA DC CB AE AA AD AE DC

**TABLE 1.21
Inverse
Mappings
for Sample
Table of
Homophones**

Ciphertext Pair	Letter	Ciphertext Pair	Letter	Ciphertext Pair	Letter	Ciphertext Pair	Letter
AA	E	BA	U	CA	U	DA	Y
AB	I	BB	V	CB	T	DB	T
AC	N	BC	Z	CC	T	DC	R
AD	T	BD	X	CD	S	DD	Q
AE	T	BE	E	CE	R	DE	P
AF	E	BF	O	CF	R	DF	N
AG	E	BG	M	CG	O	DG	N
AH	A	BH	L	CH	N	DH	M
AI	D	BI	I	CI	L	DI	K
AJ	L	BJ	G	CJ	I	DJ	I
AK	O	BK	C	CK	H	DK	E
AL	R	BL	E	CL	H	DL	C
AM	U	BM	E	CM	F	DM	D
AN	S	BN	E	CN	F	DN	G
AO	S	BO	E	CO	E	DO	Y
AP	S	BP	I	CP	A	DP	T
AQ	R	BQ	O	CQ	A	DQ	R
AR	L	BR	N	CR	E	DR	O
AS	H	BS	A	CS	E	DS	R
AT	B	BT	A	CT	I	DT	N
AU	C	BU	A	CU	I	DU	N
AV	A	BV	D	CV	R	DV	S
AW	E	BW	F	CW	T	DW	S
AX	I	BX	J	CX	T	DX	O
AY	M	BY	N	CY	T	DY	D
AZ	P	BZ	P	CZ	W	DZ	O

TABLE 1.22

	A	B	C	D	E
A	A	B	C	D	E
B	F	G	H	I	J
C	K	L	M	N	O
D	P	Q/Z	R	S	T
E	U	V	W	X	Y

Now, we do the second transformation. Form new pairs by associating each letter in the upper half with the letter below it; this yields

```
DC EE AE AA CD AC AC EB CA CE AA EA DA ED CA EE ED EC.
```

Now, using the same matrix given previously, map these pairs back to their single letter equivalents. This third transformation yields the final ciphertext (grouped into 5-letter blocks):

```
RYEAN     CCVKO     AUPXK     YXW
```

(If we encounter a DB pair, it doesn't matter if we map it back to a Q or a Z.) In order to decipher, an individual simply maps the ciphertext letters to their letter pair equivalents, perhaps writing them vertically to save time.

```
DE AA CA AE CC AE DE CE EE
CE EA DC CB AE AA AD AE DC
```

She then regards the pairs horizontally, and regains the plaintext

```
TAKEM     ETOYO     URLEA     DER.
```

This cipher is similar to a German wartime cipher (called the ADFGVX cipher) that perplexed the allied cryptanalysts for quite some time. It was a surprisingly simple cipher, but it was only cracked after great expenditure of time and effort.

This cipher, like the German ADFGVX cipher, uses a property called fractionation, which means a permutation on parts of a unit rather than among the units. In this cipher, this happens when we split the letter pairs. A mapping from a single character initially formed these pairs, so it is akin to moving "half" of a plaintext character. This is what confounds attempts at breaking such ciphers. Not all substitution/transposition ciphers use this property.

EXERCISES

1. Write a Java program to simulate one of the ciphers in this chapter. Prompt the user to enter a message, and then return the corresponding ciphertext. Then decrypt the message and show the user the regained plaintext. Use only uppercase English characters for your alphabet.

2. The following text was produced using a Caesar cipher on a message consisting of only uppercase English letters. Determine the shift value and recover the plaintext.

MXXFT QQHUX WMDYM QHQDO DQMFQ PNKYQ EUZOQ ARAXP AZMOO AGZFA RYKNQ

SUZZU ZSXQE ESDQQ PTMFD QPMZP USZAD MZOQN ADZAR YKOAZ PGOFE BQQOT

MZPFT AGSTF UZAIO AZRQE EABQZ XKMZP RGXXK

3. The following text was produced using a simple Vigenere cipher. Use the Kaisiski method to determine probable key length, then do a frequency analysis to determine the keyword, and recover the plaintext.

SSQYN ASXES RBFOR SOUYK VTAKO QVKSZ WOQSF VNOBB BRWKB BRCQS
QSOSF WJYSX FHKYS YGODI FSUMD BJJOD FQCWN IBSDO HSPBW XBDIL
MWQGP FZNVD DOSGO NEZSB JJSBQ FSXUW QOIOZ VLBIN TSBTP VBKUV
OXKOJ KDFMZ UCUBB DVITS PKTHC ZPZCB FWZVZ YCLMW HJOSO VBQCE
SGSSO BIWCS FDISC BZOBN DFMZU CUBBD VIORS NJHWY OBSGZ CFUTD
FSOUS BWSFV BUAOO SNOTO ZPSSR FBBCY SGQRP HDKVZ OXEJO XTHCX
FGQYU HVKOR PYPYC PBDDV JSRMS MDDPU FKQVM MSQDB FGGBP GSXLS
BXFHV OMSAO OHOBZ BIWCS FDISC BZOBN JHGKQ DZSDO HSPBG LPGHY
OORNJ GCXXS GVFMF YTWBQ NWQRB SZSND ZONSB DJBUO MZWZU WQMVF
JODFM ZUCUB BDVIH FSOOK WMIAO XOWBQ TAWDI FWMIO FNJBH OSBSD
DFMZU CUBBD VICCG DPBON EWGYO KSCMS MCUOZ VJBUC XWZVJ OAMSM
DDPUF KQVMK ORBOU KCBLG SMVFW DZBRO EWHSP BIZQS FCBRR VFFWF
FFDBF BHSDS VKMZG DFDSX TCBXF OZMSM DDPBC WJQCX OSKIP FYZFF
SXOWO VUFOZ QSKKE SOXEK OCIWB QUCBV BKFOO QSSOH FYEIQ DJCBD
PQFIQ HCQSO DRZKW DIQCN JBUDI SCBZI DZFFG KERZO SWJOS DFOOH
WMFVO VMKOI OSFZF HSBEW GKQDS KSWBQ DFMZU CUBBD VIDVS CUBID
IWZVB DDBPT SCTWC XBZ

4. The following text was produced using an auto-key Vigenere cipher. Attempt to recover the priming key, and hence the plaintext.

TVWFP VVHZD PZXLX ADBSS SSWBW KAABS DXZFG ANWTZ PWEKV AEOEA
PIOBZ TALSV XUIFW AYEMU MFWAY EMWLT AMMNL HGAHX QILIG PPXFQ
ZMEAD XUXCM RSJHZ XLXCW HKNEH YKZMB OEDXZ FGANW TZPWE MOGWO
EAPKH HRTAL SVXUI FWAYE MUMFW AYEMW LTAMM NLHGA HXQIL IGPPX
FSSSW BWKAA BS

5. The following text was produced using a monoalphabetic substitution cipher, which maps the alphabet A . . . Z to a permutation of that alphabet. Using frequency analysis, attempt to recover the plaintext.

ULNEA YTWPX TFNUR WBPHN BPEXE YRKXB PANXE YRKFX HNENW WPETF
NUULN BKRFN YZNKU LNSXW LYSUL NWNPP ETULN GXKTW YSULN PXKYZ
NKULN FXZNW UYIHY ZNKPF FULNN PKULP ETYZN KPFFU LNIKN PURKN
WULPU BYZNP FYEAU LNAKY RETWY AYTIK NPUNT BPEXE LXWYD EXBPA
NXEUL NXBPA NYSAY TLNIK NPUNT LXBBP FNPET SNBPF NLNIK NPUNT
ULNBA YTGFN WWNTU LNBPE TWPXT UYULN BGNSK RXUSR FPETX EIKNP

```
WNXEE RBGNK SXFFU LNNPK ULPET WRGTR NXUKR FNYZN KULNS XWLYS
ULNWN PPETU LNGXK TWYSU LNPXK PETYZ NKNZN KJFXZ XEAIK NPURK
NULPU BYZNW YEULN AKYRE TULNE AYTWP XTXAX ZNJYR NZNKJ WNNTG
NPKXE AMFPE UYEUL NSPIN YSULN DLYFN NPKUL PETNZ NKJUK NNULP
ULPWS KRXUD XULWN NTXEX UULNJ DXFFG NJYRK WSYKS YYTPE TUYPF
FULNG NPWUW YSULN NPKUL PETPF FULNG XKTWY SULNP XKPET PFFUL
NIKNP URKNW ULPUB YZNYE ULNAK YRETN ZNKJU LXEAU LPULP WULNG
KNPUL YSFXS NXEXU XAXZN NZNKJ AKNNE MFPEU SYKSY YTPET XUDPW
WYAYT WPDPF FULPU LNLPT BPTNP ETXUD PWZNK JAYYT PETUL NKNDP
WNZNE XEAPE TULNK NDPWB YKEXE AULNW XOULT PJ
```

6. The following ciphertext was produced from a Playfair square. Using the relative frequencies of digraphs in the English language (see Figure 1.3), attempt to recover the plaintext and the Playfair square used.

```
PK QT OX OK KR QK ZX BI OZ BZ ZO EK KQ KP ZO IB ZO KG ZS VL HR
OR HY EK RK RU PH BO OW IH KR YK FW EK OI NR KR YK FW EK AF AX
AT VA KU GX OW YH VM EI FL HT QT XG AB LO LZ RH EK KU AE MF QH
AI EK HY KY QE OW IH KR UG FT ZN AI ZS FC LO TL PH TF BZ LZ RH
EK RQ OR RH OL CI ZS XL OF VD RE IK KR HR QK OD VK RO CI EK RH
RQ LO OD VK KZ LI OL NR RL KI EK HU XZ KE AF XK SI LI OW VC KU
QE FW OR HY EK HU XZ KE MW AZ EK HY FW TB KU GX ZS VL LS DS HY
EK HU XZ KE FL FU CI EK HY FW TB KU GX KR WL SD UH IC XZ KE OW
IH KR HR AF UK PH OZ BZ OW IH KR HR AF AG AT OZ BZ EK RY FT OK
FL FU CI ZS XL OF VD RE IK KR HR QK OW KY MU BO KQ RE QR YK ON
KR AF ER KA NI UK MU WF ER AF ER WM TA RA OR RH OU ZS FV LF RE
KR YK YG OW UK OW XL QE FW OR HY EK RQ OR RH OQ YH HE KR YK YG
OW UK MW AZ EK RQ OR RH SW LZ TY RO CI ZN AF XG OU ZS VL LS DS
HY EK KY KY MU BO KU EX OW IH KR HR AF UK PH OZ BZ OW IH KR HR
AF AG AT OZ BZ EK KU HQ IO XI FL FU CI ZS XL OF VD RE IK KR AF
ER EA CI RH EK KU EX QK MS EK RH HY NI IS QT VU LW RU CI UH HI
EF MK UA CI UM YG RU WF CI ZN AF XG OU ZS VL LS DS HY EK HY EF
MK UA CI SL CI OW IH KR MS EK RH HY AF ER KA KR WL SD UH XL RU
OL CI ZS XL FA EK OR ZN AF XK SI LI EK TQ ZS XL OF VD RE IK KR
SL CI ME LI LQ HP KP RE OR ZI BO KY HY QK FW ZO ZM SL ON OL CI
EH KY KU IO EK HU OW IH RL KN RU WM EA ZN NF EK UK YK XY OZ RO
BD NL HF ZO ZK IN KR FT ML TF UA XB ZO XL OW XY RN LO GX IN KR
SL CI ME LI LQ HY PH PK RO NZ IO VU OW KO QK FW ZO KX KY HY LW
DB AT XY BZ NI EK TY HT ZO XL OW IH HR YK XS RU TF BZ MW OY RN
ZN KL KY HY ZO ZN LW DB AT XY BZ NI EK TY HT ZO XL OW XV LI OL
NR RL NZ RN LO ZS IS FL CI EK RH RQ LO HP TQ ZO MS CI EK RH RQ
LO ZA TW ZO ZK KR EK FT XI FL FU CI ZS XL OF VD RE IK KR HR QK
OD VK KO ZO EK KY KY MU BO TU IR KR XB IE UO QE FW OR RE KR FL
FD TA ZR KR OZ VK RO CI UH KI EK RP UK HM RU XG OX ZB OK AZ FW
BX RU OU BO OW XI FL XU OW XF RU KA OW VD RE IK KR GW HU XZ KE
OX ON KR YK YG OW UK AI EK KU EX NI ZX PH OD VK NI ON KR YK FW
EK OW XY RN LO GX SZ LI RF YH RN SZ HR OR OD VK KO EK KP HR OR
RH OD VK KI NI ZS PH TW EK HY UF OW IH KR UH XG UK HA XZ KE IK
SZ LZ RH ON KR OZ VK EK RU SO AZ LF RE KR OK FW XK LI UK KI EK
RP ZO EK KY KY MU BO TU IR KR XB IE SZ DZ HU XZ KE IO EK KY RU
```

```
HE KE SZ LZ RH ON KR FL FU CI EK TQ XZ KE OW IH UO QE FW OR HU
XZ KE MW AZ FL HT QT XG OL CI ZS XL FA EK OR ZN AF XK SI LI OW
IH KR HR AF UK PH OZ BZ OW IH KR HR AF AG AT OZ BZ EK RY UA HE
CV UF OW XV LI OL YX UH KI EK RQ OR RH ER YK RA ZN CD DZ ZO VB
HR OR AE KU OW VD RE NX HF AX UD SW LZ RE KR YK FW EK LW TA XG
OK KR YK YG OW UK AI EK KU EX OU ZS VL HR OR HY EK KP HR OR WH
RU EO HR OU IR KR UK SF OW YH PH EF OD ZD BZ OW FV LZ ZO ZK TD
BZ NF EK CR DN KE KR AF ER HE KY RP OL BD NL HF ZO ZK IN KR FT
TX CI OL CI HP RH FQ ZO PK XC FT FL BD NL HF ZO ZK IZ KO TX CI
OW XV LI OL NR RL NZ RN LO ZS IS XV LI CS KU GX HY EK RP OW XL
OF XC RY EA ZN YA SL CI ZO WH RU UK ZO IB AP QK WF CI DY SD OH
KR AF ER TF ON KR UK LO OW VD RE IK KR NX HF OX QB HR LO TU ON
KR YK FW EK OW IH KR HR AF UK PH OZ BZ OW IH KR HR AF AG AT OZ
BZ EK RY YD EK FL FU CI ZS XL OF VD RE IK KR SL CI ME LI LQ HU
DZ ZO VB HR OR AE KU LW DB AT XY BZ NI EK TY HT ZO XL OD PH OK
LN HB HR OR AE KU EK OR ZA PH LS IO ZK KR MK UA CI OW FC DO FL
OZ RF SO RU LC LW DB AT XY BZ NI ZN XB ZO FL CI ZN AF XG OU ZS
FV LF RE KR NF DV OW FZ LS OL BD NL HF ZO ZK IN KR FT TX CI OK
KR OD PH OK LN RS BD NL HF ZO ZK IN KR FT TX CI OL CI LS DS EK
HQ HR OR AE KU EK OR ZA PH LS IO ZK KR MK UA CI LW DB AT XY BZ
NI EK TY HT ZO XL OW XV LI OL NR RL NZ RN LO ZS IS IH KR BZ LI
OL YX UH EO AG SR RP OW ZO UA TF RF PK ZO UA HA XT TQ KU GX OW
VD RE IK KR RW AS TU PH HE KR DY LK AI EK KU RU FS CI EK KQ FT
XL AI EK RU FT LZ RH EK HU DZ KU NI BH LZ RH LS DS EK KY RU HE
RL CI LZ RH LS DS EK HQ HR OR AE KU EK OR ZA PH LS IO ZK KR MK
UA CI OU ZS VL HR OR HY RF OZ CT XO AN OZ RF PK ZO EK TY RF PK
AI ZS VC HQ HR OR HY TD GF RF UH OW XD RP LS RK HQ HR OR HY EK
RP ZS XC UH XG UK IH KR RF CI OL YX NI EK RP QK MW OY RI AS OW
XY QB HR LO TY BI QO GW RH DY SD OH KR YK FW EK OW XL SQ YL TY
EH AS TU PH HE KR DY LK AI EK KU RU FS CI EK KQ FT XL AI EK RU
FT OW IL PH HR PH EF OD ZD BZ WH RU EO HR EK OR ZA PH OU ON KR
MK UA CI EK TQ ZS XL OF XY ZX PH IU YQ PH EF UK YK XC RU TF BZ
VU OW NI ON KR MF QH AI EK RQ TL UH YK FW EK OW YH PH EF EH KY
RE RL EK LO MW OY RN ZN KL KY HY ZO ZN IK KR FQ DO DS QK IU AE
AX AT IA IS FL CI NI LS DS EK KQ RU OK OU IR KR YK FW EK OW FL
SD OH KR NX HF OU IR KR OF WF CI LS DS EK HQ HR OR AE KU EK OR
ZA PH IO EK KP TA OQ YH PH EF EK ZO ZK RL EK LO EK KQ HR OR TL
DA YD TY OZ NZ ZX PH YK PH EF MK KY TQ VU OW RI AT IA IS FL CI
ZN AF XG OU ZS XL FA LS DS EK OR KR RL FV LF RU CI ZN AF LG RH
XP SI LI OW IH KR HR AF UK PH OZ BZ OW IH KR HR AF AG AT OZ BZ
EK KU YI EK FL FI
```

CHAPTER 2

Large Integer Computing

The vast majority of modern cryptography is handled by computers, which deal very efficiently with numbers, especially integers. Thus, not surprisingly, we find that much of modern cryptography is based on arithmetic with large integers. Of course, the default integer data type for computing languages is limited in size, so programmers are often faced with producing a new data type for integers of arbitrary size. Java, however, does provide a BigInteger class, and it is very useful in cryptography. We will discuss this class later in the book, but first it would be enlightening to try to produce a similar class of our own.

So, we begin developing an Int class. It can be supplied with various methods that manipulate integers of arbitrary size; that is, it should be able to perform arithmetic with integers of hundreds or even thousands of decimal digits. Such integers are common in modern cryptography.

The Int class data fields should be able to represent an integer of arbitrary size in some way, and also be able to represent some constructors that accept parameters to initialize the data fields. We could represent the integer as an array of ints, where each int is a digit. (See Figure 2.1.) We could also have a boolean data field that records the sign of the number, as in the following code:

```
public class Int {
    //Records if Int negative/nonnegative
    boolean negative=false;

    //Digits are stored as decimal digits,
    //highest order digit first
    int[] digits;

    //Declare zero constant
    final public static Int ZERO=new Int();

    //Records position of 0 (zero) in the
    //character set
    final private static int zeroPos='0';
```

FIGURE 2.1

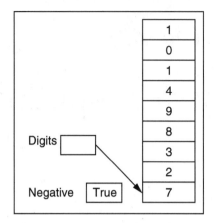

So, for example, we would store the integer -000723894101 as in Figure 2.1. Note that we disregard any leading zeros. The exception to this will be when we represent zero; the array will have the single digit 0.

2.1   CONSTRUCTORS

For constructors, we should have the following:

1. An Int constructor which can convert an atomic type int to an Int,

2. One which can convert a string into an Int,

3. One which copies an Int to a new Int, and

4. The default constructor (one which accepts no parameters). This one will set the Int to zero.

For the first constructor listed, we consider how this will be done. Suppose we want to convert the int $n = -562$ into an Int. We could set aside enough space for ten digits, since the largest int is around 2 billion and would require no more than ten decimal digits.

We first take note of the sign of the number, and then set the boolean negative field to either true or false. We could then successively divide n by ten, keeping the remainder each time and placing it in the array starting at the rear. If we have any unfilled slots in the array when we are finished, we can move forward the elements at the rear. The code to accomplish this follows:

```
public Int(int n) {
    //Produce the array-an int can not have more than 10 decimal digits
    int[] temp=new int[10];
    //zero is a special case
    if (n==0) {
        negative=false;
```

```
            digits=new int[1];
            digits[0]=0;
            return;
        }
        //Negative int n-set negative to true, take absolute value of n
        if (n<0) {
            negative=true;
            n=Math.abs(n);
        }
        int count=10;
        //Divide by 10 until nothing left
        while (n>0) {
            //Remainder is the count-th digit in the array
            temp[—count]=n%10;
            n/=10;
        }
        //Remove any leading zeros-make new array and copy
        digits=new int[temp.length-count];
        for (int i=0;i<digits.length;i++) digits[i]=temp[count+i];
    }
```

The constructor which produces a copy of an Int from another Int, and the Int() constructor which accepts no parameters, are easy to code. The Int() constructor should set the Int to zero.

```
//This one produces an array of one int containing 0
public Int() {
    negative=false;
    digits=new int[1];
    digits[0]=0;
}

public Int(Int n) {
    negative=n.negative;
    digits=new int[n.digits.length];
    for (int i=0;i<digits.length;i++) digits[i]=n.digits[i];
}
```

We now develop a constructor that produces Int objects from strings. We can arrange it so that it will parse strings to determine whether or not it can be interpreted as an Int, then place the characters (converted to ints) in the array. In case the string cannot be parsed as an Int, we can throw an IntException:

```
public class IntException extends Exception {
    public IntException() {super();}
    public IntException(String s) {super(s);}
}
```

```java
//This constructor converts a String to an Int.  May throw an
//Exception if the String cannot be converted to an Int.
public Int(String s) throws IntException {
    //Place the string into an array of characters
    char[] temp=s.trim().toCharArray();

    //Parse the array.
    //First character may be a sign
    //firstDigitLoc records index of first digit
    int firstDigitLoc=0;
    //If "-" sign symbol encountered, make negative Int, move to
    //next index
    if (temp[0]=='-') {
        negative=true;
        firstDigitLoc++;
    //If "+" just move to next symbol
    } else if (temp[0]=='+') {
        firstDigitLoc++;
    }
    int index=firstDigitLoc;

    //Check if remaining characters are digits-record # leading
    //zeros
    boolean significantDigitFound=false;
    while (index<temp.length&&Character.isDigit(temp[index])) {
        if (!significantDigitFound) {
            //Skip any leading zeros
            if (temp[index]=='0') firstDigitLoc++;
            else significantDigitFound=true;
        }
        index++;
    }

    //Throw an exception if nondigit found
    if (index<temp.length) throw new IntException("This is not a
valid integer!");

    //If no significant digit found, this was a string of all zeros
    //Make the zero Int and return
    if (!significantDigitFound) {
        negative=false;
        digits=new int[1];
        digits[0]=0;
        return;
    }
```

```
//This parsed as an integer-store it, ignoring leading zeros
char[]
c=s.trim().substring(firstDigitLoc,s.length()).toCharArray();
digits=new int[c.length];
//Subtract zeroPos from the character-this gives the
//corresponding int
for (int i=0;i<c.length;i++) digits[i]=(int)c[i]-zeroPos;
}
```

For output purposes, we should be able to convert an Int object to a string and display it. Thus, as with all good classes in Java, we will supply a toString() method.

```
//Returns the Int as a String, mainly for output purposes
public String toString() {
    //Use a StringBuffer for efficiency
    StringBuffer answer=new StringBuffer("");
    //Put a "-" symbol in front if negative
    if (negative) answer.append("-");
    //Append each digit to the StringBuffer and return it as a String
    for (int i=0;i<digits.length;i++) {
        answer.append(new Integer(digits[i]).toString());
    }
    return new String(answer);
}
```

Now that we have designed these constructors, we should test them to verify that they work. The class TestIntConstructors is a console program that simply asks the user to enter some integers and then converts them to Ints. It then turns them back to strings using the toString() method and displays them. The code can be found at the book's website, and an example run is shown in Figures 2.2(a)–(e).

FIGURE 2.2   **(a)**

(b)

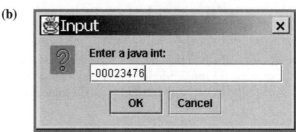

**FIGURE 2.2
(continued)**

(c)

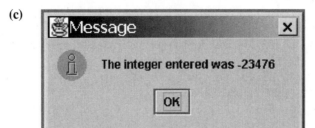

(d)

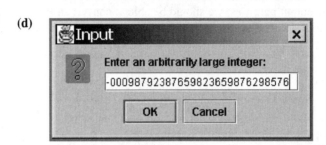

(e)

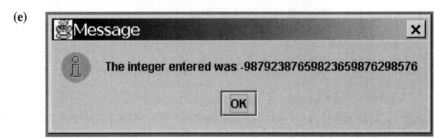

2.2 COMPARISON METHODS

We should write methods that allow us to compare Int objects; that is, methods to tell us when they are equal, and if one is less than another. To determine whether Int x is less than Int y, for example, we could do the following:

- If x and y are of different signs, the negative one is smaller. Otherwise, continue with the next step.
- If the arrays representing x and y are different lengths, and if both are negative, then the larger array is the smaller number. Otherwise the smaller array represents the lesser of the two Ints. If both arrays are the same length, continue with the next step.
- Proceed down the array until you find unequal digits. If both x and y are negative, the array containing the smaller digit is the largest. Otherwise, the array containing the larger digit represents the larger integer. If you find no unequal digits, neither integer is larger.

This is how we normally compare integers ourselves, and writing the lessThan(Int) method in Java isn't terribly difficult.

```java
public boolean lessThan(Int other) {
    //Start by assuming this is less than other
    boolean answer=false;
    //Both Ints are nonnegative here
    if (!negative&&!other.negative) {
        //If they are the same length, must compare the digits
        if (digits.length==other.digits.length) {
            int i=0;
            while (i<this.digits.length&&digits[i]==other.digits[i]) i++;
            //Each digit of this was less than each digit of other
            if (i<this.digits.length)
                if (digits[i]<other.digits[i])
                    answer=true;
        //this has smaller length than other-must be less than
        } else if (digits.length<other.digits.length) answer=true;
    //If both Ints negative, do the reverse of the above comparisons
    } else if (negative&&other.negative) {
        if (digits.length==other.digits.length) {
            int i=0;
            while (i<this.digits.length&&digits[i]==other.digits[i]) i++;
            if (i<this.digits.length)
                if (digits[i]>other.digits[i])
                    answer=true;
        } else if (other.digits.length<digits.length) answer=true;
    //If this is negative and other nonnegative, must be less than
    } else if (negative&&!other.negative) answer=true;
    //Otherwise, this is nonnegative and other negative
    //Return answer, which was initialized to false
    return answer;
}
```

The code to determine whether or not two Ints are equal should now be very simple to write.

```java
public boolean equals(Int other) {
    boolean answer=true;
    //Check if same sign
    if (negative!=other.negative) answer=false;
    //Check if different lengths
    else if (digits.length!=other.digits.length) answer=false;
    //If same length and sign, compare each digit
    else for (int i=0;i<digits.length;i++)
```

```
        //Any nonmatching digit sets answer to false
        if (digits[i]!=other.digits[i]) answer=false;
    return answer;
}
```

We now demonstrate a test program for the lessThan(Int) and equals(Int) methods. The code can be found on the book's website under the class name TestIntComparisonMethods. Screen shots of the test program are shown in Figure 2.3a–d.

(a)

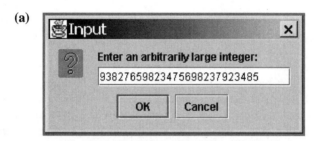

(b)

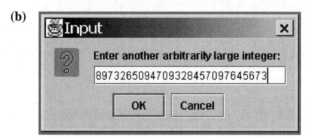

(c)

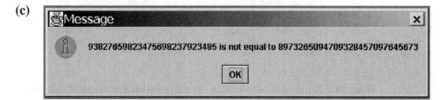

(d)

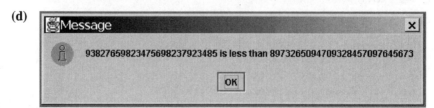

FIGURE 2.3

2.3 ARITHMETIC METHODS

Of course, we must write methods to perform arithmetic with Int objects. We must be able to add, subtract, multiply, and divide. For convenience, we should add methods to increment and decrement Int objects. First, we consider the addition of two integers a and b:

- If one is zero, return the other as the answer. Otherwise go on.
- If $a = -b$, return zero. Otherwise go on.
- If the digits are the same sign, add them beginning with the lowest digits, adding any carries in the subsequent addition. Otherwise go on.
- If the digits are of different signs, this is a subtraction; either $a - -b$ or $b - -a$. To do a subtraction, you must determine the larger of the two integers without regard to sign, then subtract the smaller integer from the larger. The sign of the answer is the same as that of the larger operand.

We shouldn't be too surprised at this addition/subtraction scheme, because it is the way humans (using base 10) normally do it. Notice that writing the add(Int) and subtract(Int) may entail using some of the methods already developed (like equals(Int) and lessThan(Int)), and may require writing a few more methods as well. For instance, in the following there is a method to negate an Int, and one to produce the absolute value. These are listed first.

```
public Int absoluteValue() {
    //Make a new Int by copying this Int
    Int answer=new Int(this);
    //Set negative to false
    answer.negative=false;
    return answer;
}

public Int negative() {
    Int answer=new Int(this);
    //Flip the negative value
    answer.negative=!this.negative;
    return answer;
}
```

The code which does most of the work is in the add(Int) method. First, it determines the sign of the two numbers; if they are the same, it is an addition problem, and the addDigits(Int) method is called. If they are not the same, it is a subtraction problem, and the subtractDigits(Int) method is called. The subtractDigits(Int) method may call the borrow(Int) method, which allows us to borrow from digits to the left for subtraction. Of course, after the numbers are added or subtracted, there may be leading zeros, which should be removed.

```
public Int add(Int other) {
    Int ans;
```

```
    //zero is a special case-nothing to do but return a copy of the
//nonzero Int
    if (this.equals(ZERO)) return new Int(other);
    else if (other.equals(ZERO)) return new Int(this);
    else if (this.equals(other.negative())) return new Int();
    //If they are the same sign, perform the addition; add carries
    else if (negative==other.negative) {
       ans=addDigits(other);
       ans.negative=negative;
    }
    //If they are of different signs, determine the larger
    //(magnitude-wise) and subtract the smaller from it.
    //Result has same sign as first (larger) operand.
    else if (this.absoluteValue().lessThan(other.absoluteValue())) {
       ans=other.subtractDigits(this);
       ans.negative=other.negative;
    } else {
       ans=this.subtractDigits(other);
       ans.negative=this.negative;
    }
    //Trim leading zeros and return
    return ans.trimZeros();
}

public Int subtract(Int other) {
    //To subtract, we add the negative
    return this.add(other.negative());
}

private Int addDigits(Int other) {
    int top1=this.digits.length-1;
    int top2=other.digits.length-1;
    int top3=Math.max(this.digits.length,other.digits.length)+1;
    Int answer=new Int();
    answer.digits=new int[top3];
    top3--;
    int carry=0; int sum=0;
    while (top1>=0&&top2>=0) {
       sum=this.digits[top1]+other.digits[top2]+carry;
       if (sum>9) {sum%=10; carry=1;} else carry=0;
       answer.digits[top3]=sum;
       top1--;top2--;top3--;
    }
    if (top1<0&&top2<0) {
       answer.digits[0]=carry;
    } else if (top1<0) {
```

```
            while (top2>=0) {
                sum=other.digits[top2]+carry;
                if (sum>9) {sum%=10; carry=1;} else carry=0;
                answer.digits[top3]=sum;
                top2--;top3--;
            }
            answer.digits[top3]=carry;
        } else {
            while (top1>=0) {
                sum=this.digits[top1]+carry;
                if (sum>9) {sum%=10; carry=1;} else carry=0;
                answer.digits[top3]=sum;
                top1--;top3--;
            }
            answer.digits[top3]=carry;
        }
        return answer;
    }

    private Int subtractDigits(Int other) {
        Int answer=new Int();
        Int copy=new Int(this);
        answer.digits=new int[this.digits.length];
        int top1=this.digits.length-1;
        int top2=other.digits.length-1;
        while (top2>=0) {
            if (copy.digits[top1]<other.digits[top2]) {
                borrow(copy,top1-1);
                copy.digits[top1]+=10;
            }
            answer.digits[top1]=copy.digits[top1]-other.digits[top2];
            top1--; top2--;
        }
        while (top1>=0) {
            answer.digits[top1]=copy.digits[top1];
            top1--;
        }
        return answer;
    }

    //Method to "borrow" for subtraction
    private void borrow(Int n,int pos) {
        while (n.digits[pos]==0) {
            n.digits[pos]=9;
            pos--;
        }
```

```
      n.digits[pos]—;
}


//Method to chop off any leading zeros
private Int trimZeros() {
   int i;
   //Look for first nonzero in the array
   for (i=0;i<this.digits.length;i++)
      if (this.digits[i]!=0)
         break;
   Int answer=new Int();
   answer.negative=this.negative;
   //Make a (possibly) smaller array for answer
   answer.digits=new int[this.digits.length-i];
   //Copy the nonzero digits over, and return answer
   for (int j=0;j<answer.digits.length;j++)
   answer.digits[j]=this.digits[j+i];
   return answer;
}
```

Methods to multiply and divide Ints should also be written. We will develop the multiply(Int) method here. When we multiply two integers, we really just multiply by a single digit at a time, then perform a total of these individual products. For example, when we do

$$\begin{array}{r} 527 \\ \times\,613 \\ \hline \end{array}$$

we actually do these separate products:

$$527 \times 6 = 3162,\ 527 \times 1 = 527,\ \text{and}\ 527 \times 3 = 1581.$$

We then add these products together, shifting some of the products to the left. That is, we append a zero to 527×1 since 1 is in the tens column, and we append two zeros to 526×6 because 6 is in the hundreds column: This gives us

$$\begin{array}{r} 527 \\ \times\quad 613 \\ \hline 1581 \\ +\quad 5270 \\ +\ 316200 \\ \hline 323051 \end{array}$$

Thus our multiplication problem actually becomes an addition problem, as long as we are able to multiply an integer by a single digit, and as long as we can append a certain number of zeros to our sub-products. Doing the latter in Java is very simple, as you can see from the following code:

```
private Int appendZeros(int places) {
//Make a new Int object
   Int result=new Int();
//If this equals 0, return 0; no need to append
   if (this.equals(ZERO)) return result;
//Make the resulting array larger
   result.digits=new int[this.digits.length+places];
//Shift the digits into the new array
   for (int i=0;i<this.digits.length;i++) {
      result.digits[i]=this.digits[i];
   }
   return result;
}
```

Now, to multiply an Int by a single digit, we simply multiply each digit in the first operand by the selected digit from the second operand. If this product is greater than 9, we use the remainder of division by 10 for the corresponding digit in the result (plus a possible carry from the previous multiplication), and we record the quotient when dividing by 10 as a carry. Take the following example:

$$\begin{array}{r} 527 \\ \times \quad 3 \\ \hline ??? \end{array}$$

We first take $7 \times 3 = 21$; 1 becomes the digit in the one's column of the result, and 2 becomes the carry.

$$\begin{array}{r} 2 \\ 527 \\ \times \quad 3 \\ \hline ??1 \end{array}$$

We then take $2 \times 3 = 6$, and add the previous carry 2, to get 8. This becomes the digit in the tens column of the result, and 0 becomes the carry.

$$\begin{array}{r} 0 \\ 527 \\ \times \quad 3 \\ \hline ?81 \end{array}$$

Now we take $5 \times 3 = 15$, and add the previous carry 0. 5 becomes the digit in the hundreds column of the result, and 1 becomes the carry.

$$\begin{array}{r} 1 \\ 527 \\ \times \quad 3 \\ \hline 581 \end{array}$$

There are no more digits to multiply, but there is the possibility of one final carry, as is the case here. This becomes the thousands digit in the result.

$$
\begin{array}{r}
527 \\
\times \quad 3 \\
\hline
1581
\end{array}
$$

Of course, this is exactly how we've done multiplication by a single digit since elementary school, but perhaps coding it seems not so elementary. Examine the following code carefully:

```
//Method to multiply an Int by a single decimal digit
//Called repeatedly by multiply(Int) method
private Int multiply(int otherDigit) {
    //Make a new Int for the answer
    Int result=new Int();
    //If digit to multiply by is 0, return 0
    if (otherDigit==0) return result;
    //Make the answer array one longer than the first operand,
    //in case there is a carry
    result.digits=new int[this.digits.length+1];
    int carry=0;
    int tempInteger;
    int i;
    for (i=this.digits.length-1;i>=0;i--) {
        //i+1th digit of result is the ith digit of the first operand
        //times the digit in the second operand.  If this is more than
        //10, we must keep only the least significant digit.
        //We also add any previous carries
        tempInteger=this.digits[i]*otherDigit+carry;
        result.digits[i+1]=tempInteger%10;
        //If the product is more than 10, we must set carry
        //for the next round
        carry=tempInteger/10;
    }
    //Possibility of one last carry; do the final digit.
    result.digits[0]=carry;
    return result;
}
```

Once we have the ability to append zeros and to multiply an Int by a single digit, multiplying two Int objects simply becomes a matter of calculating these sub-products and adding them together. This part is actually easy with the two previous methods defined, as you can see in the following code:

```
public Int multiply(Int other) {
```

```
    //Initialize the answer to 0
    Int result=new Int();
    //If either operand is 0, return 0
    if (this.equals(ZERO)||other.equals(ZERO)) return result;
    //Now, multiply the first operand by each digit in the
    //second operand, shifting left each answer by a power of ten
    //as we pass through the digits, adding each time to result.
    for (int i=0; i<other.digits.length; i++) {
        result=result.add(this.multiply(other.digits[i])
        .appendZeros(other.digits.length-1-i));
    }
    //If operands are same sign, result is positive
    //otherwise, the result is negative; 0 is already taken care of
    if (this.negative==other.negative) result.negative=false;
    else result.negative=true;
    //Return the result
    return result.trimZeros();
}
```

Note that at the end of the multiply(Int) method we remove any leading zeros which may come about. Another consideration is the sign of each operand: If they are equal, the result is a nonnegative number; otherwise, the result is negative. Zero is treated as a special case.

At this point, you should be able to write the divide(Int), and remainder(Int) methods, and will be asked to do so in the exercises. It would be prudent to write a divideAndRemainder() method, since both the quotient and remainder would probably be generated at the same time. It could return an array of two Ints, with the quotient in slot 0, and the remainder in slot 1 of the array.

Division is the most costly (in terms of computer time) to run. For now, we only consider problems where the dividend and divisor are both positive. One of the primary problems is estimating the digits in the quotient. For example, consider the following division problem:

$$6772190 \div 37658.$$

Note that 3 (the leading digit of the divisor) goes into 6 (the leading digit of the dividend) twice, but the real quotient of the previous division is 179. The estimate of the first digit of the quotient is too high. A similar problem occurs in the following problem:

$$19276 \div 273.$$

Note that the leading digit of the divisor cannot go into the leading digit of the dividend at all, and we must therefore attempt to take the divisor into the first two digits of the dividend. One way to avoid spending too much time estimating is to allow the quotient to have mixed positive and negative digits. Consider again

```
    19276 ÷ 273.
```

Number the position of each digit:

$$\underline{19276} \qquad \underline{273}$$
$$54321 \qquad\ 321$$

First, attempt to divide 1 by 2; if this fails, incorporate another digit. Here we divide 19 by 2, which yields 9. Produce the first value for the quotient:

```
90.
```

The number of zeros to add is clear when you note the position of the 9 in the dividend is 4, and the position of the 2 in the divisor is 3. Thus, we add $4 - 3 = 1$ zero. Now, subtract $90 \cdot 273$ from 19276:

```
 19276
-24570
 -5294
```

Now, attempt to divide 2 into -5; this yields -2. Since the -5 is at position 4, and 2 is still at position 3, we add a zero to get

```
-20
```

We now modify the quotient value:

```
90 + -20 = 70.
```

Now, subtract $-20 \cdot 273$ from -5294; this gives us

```
 -5294
--5460
   166
```

Note now that the value remaining is smaller than the divisor 273; thus, we have

quotient = 70, and

remainder = 166.

Here is the whole process written out; the only difference between this and the way we normally do division is that negative quantities appear in the quotient:

```
            70
           ‾‾‾
           -20
            90
       ‾‾‾‾‾‾‾‾
   273)19276
       -24570
       ‾‾‾‾‾‾‾
        -5294
       --5460
       ‾‾‾‾‾‾‾
          166
```

Here is another example for you:

$$
\begin{array}{r}
80297 \\
\hline
-3 \\
300 \\
-10000 \\
90000 \\
123\,\overline{)9876543} \\
-11070000 \\
-1193457 \\
--1230000 \\
\hline
36543 \\
-36900 \\
-357 \\
--369 \\
\hline
12
\end{array}
$$

It is entirely possible that this process could yield a negative remainder, as in the following example (the absolute value of -542 is less than the divisor, 982).

$$
\begin{array}{r}
10 \\
982\,\overline{)9278} \\
-9820 \\
\hline
-542
\end{array}
$$

When this happens, it is easy to fix: simply add the divisor to the negative remainder and subtract 1 from the quotient. In this case, this yields:

quotient = 9

remainder = 440.

Now we consider what to do when either the dividend or divisor is negative. Note that if x is the positive dividend, y is the positive divisor, q is the quotient, and r is the remainder, we can express their relationship to each other as:

$x = yq + r \qquad b > r \geq 0.$

If either x or y changes sign, we can maintain this relationship by inverting some signs. For example, we can perform calculations with all positive numbers, because:

if y is negative, change the sign of q, since

$x = yq + r \qquad$ *iff*

$x = -y(-q) + r,$

if x is negative, change the sign of both q and r, since

$x = yq + r$ *iff*

$-x = -(yq + r)$ *iff*

$-x = y(-q) - r$,

and if both x and y are negative, change the sign of r, since

$x = yq + r$ *iff*

$-x = -(-y(-q) + r)$

$-x = -yq - r$.

With this in mind, writing a division method should be a snap.

Naturally, the arithmetic methods must be tested. No programmer ever designs a class without writing a multitude of programs to wring all the bugs out of it. I've written a simple applet to do this. I ask the user to enter an Int in a text field, and then they click an operation, either "+", "−", or "*". They then enter another Int and press the "=" button. This is the beginning of a calculator; you will be asked to produce a better one in the exercises. Some screen shots follow, and the applet can be found on the book's website under the class name TestIntArithmeticMethodsApplet. (See Figure 2.4a–c.)

FIGURE 2.4   **(a)**

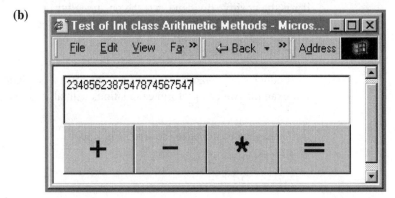

     (b)

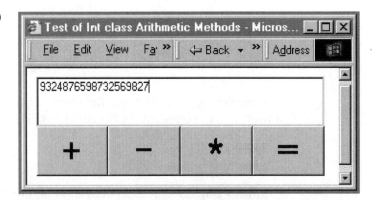

FIGURE 2.4 (c)
(continued)

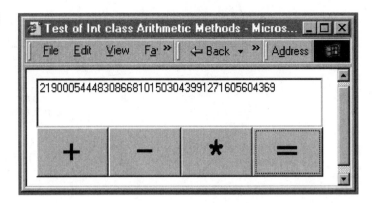

Having an Int class is a very valuable tool, for it frees us from the boundaries placed on us by the primitive integer data types of most computer languages. A Java int, for example, is only 4 bytes, which is not nearly large enough for the numbers we will need to handle in this book. However, the cost of this freedom is decreased performance, and as a result large integer packages are usually very carefully designed and optimized to yield the maximum benefit. The Int class as we have designed it here is in fact rather poor, but it is nevertheless a good introduction for someone who has never attempted the feat before. In the exercises we will discuss how to produce a much better Int class.

2.4 THE JAVA BIGINTEGER CLASS

Java provides a BigInteger class with the same functionality that we have given our Int class, and more. It is optimized for speed, and we will use it for further development. Rewriting programs for the Int class and then comparing their performances to the BigInteger class will make interesting exercises, and you are invited to do this.

2.5 CONSTRUCTORS

A partial list of the BigInteger constructors and methods follows:

- `public BigInteger(byte B[]) throws NumberFormatException`

This constructor translates a byte array containing the two's–complement representation of a signed integer into a BigInteger (see Figure 2.5). The input array is assumed to be big-endian; that is, the most significant byte is in the [0] position. The most significant bit of the most significant byte is the sign bit. The array must contain at least one byte or a Number-FormatException will be thrown.

- `public BigInteger(int signum, byte magnitude[]) throws`
  `NumberFormatException`

FIGURE 2.5

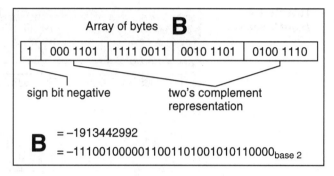

FIGURE 2.6

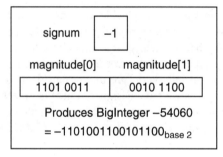

This constructor translates the sign-magnitude representation of an integer into a BigInteger (see Figure 2.6). The integer is sent in as an array of bytes, and the sign is represented as an integer signum value:

-1 for negative,

0 for zero, and

1 for positive.

The magnitude is represented as a big-endian byte array; that is, the most significant byte is in the [0] position. An invalid signum value or a 0 signum value coupled with a nonzero magnitude will result in a NumberFormatException. A zero length magnitude array is permissible and will result in a value of zero regardless of the given signum value.

• `public BigInteger(String val) throws NumberFormatException`

This translates a string containing an optional minus sign followed by a sequence of one or more decimal digits into a BigInteger. Any extraneous characters (including whitespace) will result in a NumberFormatException.

EXAMPLE. This constructor is very useful when entering large integers in decimal format from an input device. An example of how it may be called follows:

```
BigInteger m = new BigInteger("92387569832653429874569286898623498");
```

- public BigInteger(String val, int radix) throws NumberFormatException

This translates a string containing an optional minus sign followed by a sequence of one or more digits in the specified radix into a BigInteger. Any extraneous characters, including whitespace, or a radix outside the range 2 through 36, will result in a NumberFormatException.

EXAMPLE. This constructor is similar to the previous one, and is likewise very useful when entering large integers in decimal format from an input device. However, with this constructor we can specify the base of the number being entered. An example of creating a BigInteger object from the string representation of a number in base 2 follows:

```
BigInteger m = new
BigInteger("101111100001010111010000001111101010011111101",2);
```

- public BigInteger(int bitLength, int certainty, Random rnd)

This returns a randomly selected BigInteger with the specified bitLength that is probably prime. The certainty parameter is a measure of the uncertainty that the caller is willing to tolerate: the probability that the number is prime will exceed $1 - (1/2)^t$ where $t =$ certainty. The execution time is proportional to the value of the certainty parameter. The given random number generator is used to select candidates to be tested for primality. This will throw an ArithmeticException if bitLength < 2.

EXAMPLE. This BigInteger constructor will prove to be the most useful of them all for our purposes, for it can generate random (probable) primes for use in cryptosystems. To generate an integer 1024 bits long, which is prime with probability $0.875 = 1 - (0.5)^3$, we could make the following calls:

```
SecureRandom sr=new SecureRandom();
BigInteger p=new BigInteger(1024,3,sr);
```

The SecureRandom class (seen here) is a subclass of Random; if used properly, it generates random integers much more difficult to predict than those created by ordinary random number generators.

- public BigInteger(int numBits, Random rndSrc) throws
    IllegalArgumentException

This returns a random number uniformly distributed on the interval $[0, 2^{numBits} - 1]$, assuming a fair source of random bits is provided in rndSrc. Note that this constructor always returns a nonnegative BigInteger. It throws an IllegalArgumentException if numBits < 0.

EXAMPLE. This constructor just generates random positive integers without regard to primality. Again, to ensure randomness which is hard to predict, SecureRandom objects should be used, as seen here:

```
SecureRandom sr=new SecureRandom();
BigInteger p=new BigInteger(1024,sr);
```

2.6 METHODS

This is the last of the constructors; the BigInteger methods follow:

- `public static BigInteger valueOf(long val)`

Returns a BigInteger with the specified value. This factory is provided in preference to a (long) constructor because it allows for reuse of frequently used BigIntegers, such as 0 and 1, obviating the need for exported constants.

EXAMPLE. (Note that this is a static method, and so is called by the class name):

```
final BigInteger ONE=BigInteger.valueOf(1);
```

The methods following perform basic arithmetic with BigIntegers.

- `public BigInteger add(BigInteger val) throws ArithmeticException`

Returns a BigInteger whose value is (***this*** + val).

- `public BigInteger subtract(BigInteger val)`

Returns a BigInteger whose value is (***this*** − val).

- `public BigInteger multiply(BigInteger val)`

Returns a BigInteger whose value is (***this*** · val).

- `public BigInteger divide(BigInteger val) throws ArithmeticException`

Returns a BigInteger whose value is the quotient of (***this*** / val). It throws an ArithmeticException if val = 0.

- `public BigInteger remainder(BigInteger val) throws`
  `ArithmeticException`

Returns a BigInteger whose value is the remainder of (***this*** / val). It throws an ArithmeticException if val = 0.

EXAMPLE. Using these methods is elementary, as you can see from the following program fragment:

```
BigInteger op1=new BigInteger("3");
BigInteger op2=new BigInteger("2");
BigInteger sum=op1.add(op2);
BigInteger difference=op1.subtract(op2);
BigInteger product=op1.multiply(op2);
BigInteger quotient=op1.divide(op2);
BigInteger rem=op1.remainder(op2);
```

- `public BigInteger[] divideAndRemainder(BigInteger val)`
  `throws ArithmeticException`

Since most division algorithms produce the quotient and the remainder at the same time, a more efficient way of capturing both of these values is provided by the divide-AndRemainder() method.

EXAMPLE. The answers are returned in an array of two BigIntegers, as follows:

```
BigInteger op1=new BigInteger("9");
BigInteger op2=new BigInteger("2");
BigInteger[] answers=new BigInteger[2];
answers=op1.divideAndRemainder(op2);
```

When this code completes, answers[0] contains the value 4 (as a BigInteger), and answers[1] contains 1.

- `public BigInteger pow(int exponent) throws ArithmeticException`

This method returns a BigInteger whose value is $this^e$ where e = exponent and throws an ArithmeticException if $e < 0$ (as the operation would yield a noninteger value). Note that e is an integer rather than a BigInteger

EXAMPLE. Here is an example of how this method would be used (it calculates 2^{256}):

```
BigInteger base=new BigInteger("2");
BigInteger humungous=base.pow(256);
```

Clearly, care should be used with this method, for it can easily generate gigantic numbers which could exhaust the storage capacity of the computer.

- `public BigInteger gcd(BigInteger v)`

This method returns a BigInteger whose value is the greatest common divisor of |*this*| and |v|. It correctly returns (0, 0) as 0.

- `public BigInteger abs()`

This method returns a BigInteger whose value is the absolute value of *this* number.

EXAMPLE. Here is how you would call the method:

```
BigInteger test=new BigInteger("-1");
test=test.abs();
```

- `public BigInteger negate()`

This method returns a BigInteger whose value is $(-1 \cdot this)$.

- `public int signum()`

This method returns the signum function of *this* number; that is,

-1 if ***this*** **< 0,**

0 if ***this*** **= 0,**

1 if ***this*** **> 0.**

- `public BigInteger mod(BigInteger m)`

This method returns a BigInteger whose value is *this* mod m. It throws an ArithmeticException if $m \leq 0$. This method may return a negative value if the dividend is negative.

- `public BigInteger modPow(BigInteger e, BigInteger m)`

This method returns a BigInteger whose value is $(this^e)$ mod m. If $e = 1$, the returned value is *this* mod m. If $e \leq 0$, the returned value is the modular multiplicative inverse of $this^{-e}$. This method throws an ArithmeticException if $m \leq 0$.

Java Algorithm The modPow() method will be handy in the upcoming development of cryptography; b.modPow(y,n) basically returns the remainder of b^y divided by n, where b, y, and n are all positive BigIntegers. For example, if $b = 2$, $y = 3$, and $n = 5$ were all declared as BigIntegers, then b.modPow(y,n) would return the remainder of $2^3/5$, or 3. Figure 2.7 shows an applet which allows you to enter b, y, and n, and then returns and displays b.modPow(y,n).

The code for this applet can be found on the book's website under the class name TestPowApplet.

- `public BigInteger modInverse(BigInteger m) throws ArithmeticException`

This method returns the modular multiplicative inverse of *this* modulo m. (The explanation of "modular multiplicative inverse" will come later.) The method throws an ArithmeticException if $m \leq 0$ or if *this* has no multiplicative inverse mod m (that is, if *this* and m are not relatively prime).

- `public BigInteger shiftLeft(int n)`

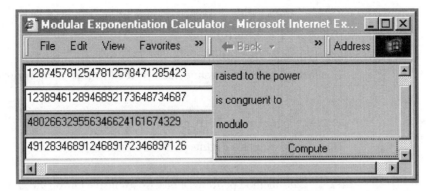

FIGURE 2.7

This method returns a BigInteger whose value is *this* << *n*; that is, it shifts the binary representation of *this* *n* bits to the left.

• `public BigInteger shiftRight(int n)`

This method returns a BigInteger whose value is *this* >> *n*; that is, it shifts the binary representation of *this* *n* bits to the right.

• `public BigInteger and(BigInteger val)`

This method returns a BigInteger whose value is (*this* & val). It performs a bitwise AND on the two BigIntegers.

EXAMPLE. If *a* and *b* are two BigIntegers, where

$$a = 1001011_{\text{base 2}}$$
$$b = 1011010_{\text{base 2}}$$

then the following call

`BigInteger c = a.and(b);`

leaves *c* with the value $1001010_{\text{base 2}}$.
This method returns a negative number iff both *this* and val are negative.

• `public BigInteger or(BigInteger val)`

This method returns a BigInteger whose value is (*this* | val).

EXAMPLE. This method performs a bitwise OR on the two operands. So if *a* and *b* are as defined previously; that is,

$$a = 1001011_{\text{base 2}}$$
$$b = 1011010_{\text{base 2}}$$

then the following call

```
BigInteger c = a.or(b);
```

leaves c with the value $1011011_{\text{base } 2}$.

This method returns a negative number iff either ***this*** or val is negative.

• **public BigInteger xor(BigInteger val)**

This method returns a BigInteger whose value is (***this*** ^ val).

EXAMPLE. This method performs a bitwise exclusive OR on the two operands. So if a and b are as defined previously; that is,

$$a = 1001011_{\text{base } 2}$$
$$b = 1011010_{\text{base } 2}$$

then the following call

```
BigInteger c = a.xor(b);
```

leaves c with the value $0010001_{\text{base } 2}$.

This method returns a negative number iff exactly one of ***this*** and val are negative.

• **public BigInteger not()**

This method returns a BigInteger whose value is ***this*** with each bit flipped. It returns a negative value iff **this** is nonnegative.

EXAMPLE. Thus, if we are using b as defined earlier; that is,

$$b = 1011010_{\text{base } 2},$$

then the following call

```
BigInteger c = b.not();
```

leaves c with the value $0100101_{\text{base } 2}$.

• **public BigInteger andNot(BigInteger val)**

This method is equivalent to and(val.not()), and is provided as a convenience for masking operations. This method returns a negative number iff ***this*** is negative and val is positive.

• **public boolean testBit(int n) throws ArithmeticException**

This method returns true iff the designated bit is set, and throws an ArithmeticException if $n < 0$.

- **public BigInteger setBit(int n) throws ArithmeticException**

This method returns a BigInteger whose value is equivalent to *this* number with the designated bit set. It throws an ArithmeticException if $n < 0$.

- **public BigInteger clearBit(int n) throws ArithmeticException**

This method returns a BigInteger whose value is equivalent to *this* number with the designated bit cleared. It throws an ArithmeticException if $n < 0$.

- **public BigInteger flipBit(int n) throws ArithmeticException**

This method returns a BigInteger whose value is equivalent to *this* number with the designated bit flipped. It throws an ArithmeticException if $n < 0$.

- **public int getLowestSetBit()**

This method returns the index of the rightmost (lowest–order) one bit in *this* number (that is, the number of zero bits to the right of the rightmost one bit). It returns -1 if **this** number contains no one bits.

- **public int bitLength()**

This method returns the number of bits in the minimal two's–complement representation of *this* number, excluding a sign bit. For positive numbers, this is equivalent to the number of bits in the ordinary binary representation.

- **public int bitCount()**

This method returns the number of bits in the two's–complement representation of *this* number that differ from its sign bit. This method is useful when implementing bit-vector style sets atop BigIntegers.

- **public boolean isProbablePrime(int certainty)**

This method returns true if *this* BigInteger is probably prime, or false if it's definitely composite. The certainty parameter is a measure of the uncertainty that the caller is willing to tolerate: the method returns true if the probability that *this* number is prime exceeds $1 - 1/2^t$ where $t = $ certainty. The execution time is proportional to the value of the certainty parameter. The test for primality here is the same one used in the constructor that generates random probable primes.

- **public int compareTo(BigInteger val)**

This method returns $-1, 0$, or 1 as *this* number is less than, equal to, or greater than val. This method is provided in preference to individual methods for each of the six boolean comparison operators:

$$==$$

$$!=$$

$$<$$

<=

>

>=

EXAMPLE.   Examples for performing these comparisons are any of the following:

```
boolean b=x.compareTo(y)<0;
b=x.compareTo(y)<=0;
b=x.compareTo(y)>0;
b=x.compareTo(y)>=0;
b=x.compareTo(y)==0;
b=x.compareTo(y)!=0;
```

• `public boolean equals(Object x)`

This method returns true iff *x* is a BigInteger whose value is equal to *this* BigInteger. It is provided so that BigIntegers can be used as hash keys.

• `public BigInteger min(BigInteger val)`

This method returns the BigInteger whose value is the lesser of *this* and val. If the values are equal, either may be returned.

• `public BigInteger max(BigInteger val)`

This method returns the BigInteger whose value is the greater of *this* and val. If the values are equal, either may be returned.

• `public int hashCode()`

This method computes a hash code for *this* object.

• `public String toString(int radix)`

This method returns the string representation of *this* number in the given radix. If the radix is outside the range from 2 through 36, it will default to 10. This representation is compatible with the (String, int) constructor.

EXAMPLE.   An example of how *this* method may be called follows:

```
BigInteger bigBoy=new BigInteger("255");
System.out.println("255 in binary is "+bigBoy.toString(2));
```

The output is:

```
255 in binary is 11111111
```

• `public String toString()`

This method returns the string representation of *this* number, radix 10. The digit-to-character mapping provided by Character.forDigit is used, and a minus sign is prepended if appropriate. This representation is compatible with the (String) constructor, and allows for string concatenation with Java's + operator.

EXAMPLE.   An example of how this method may be called follows:

```
BigInteger bigBoy=new BigInteger("255");
System.out.println(bigBoy.toString());
```

However, it is often not necessary to convert BigIntegers to Strings before printing them, for we can use implicit calls to a toString() method by concatenating a BigInteger to a String using the "+" concatenation operator:

```
BigInteger bigBoy=new BigInteger("255");
System.out.println("This # is: "+bigBoy);
```

The BigInteger will be displayed in base 10.

- `public byte[] toByteArray()`

This method converts a BigInteger into a raw array of bytes. In effect, it returns the two's–complement binary representation of *this* number in the array, which is big-endian (that is, the most significant byte is in the [0] position). The array contains the minimum number of bytes required to represent the number. For example, suppose b is a BigInteger having the value $987654321=111010110111100110100010110001_{\text{base }2}$. (You may wish to verify that this is actually the base 2 representation of 987654321.) Then we make the following call:

```
byte[] a=b.toByteArray();
```

This will produce a byteArray of 4 bytes, assign it to a, and the most significant digits of the BigInteger b will be first. That is,

$$a[0]=00111010,$$

$$a[1]=11011110,$$

$$a[2]=01101000, \text{ and}$$

$$a[3]=10110001.$$

This representation is compatible with the (byte[]) constructor.

- `public int intValue()`

This method converts *this* number to an int.

- `public long longValue()`

This method converts *this* number to a long.

- `public float floatValue()`

This method converts *this* number to a float. It is similar to the double-to-float narrowing primitive conversion defined in The Java Language Specification: If the number has too great a magnitude to represent as a float, it will be converted to infinity or negative infinity as appropriate.

- `public double doubleValue()`

This method converts *this* number to a double. It is similar to the double-to-float narrowing primitive conversion defined in The Java Language Specification: If the number has too great a magnitude to represent as a double, it will be converted to infinity or negative infinity as appropriate.

EXERCISES

1. Write the following Java methods for the Int class:

```
public Int[] divideAndRemainder(Int other);
public Int divide(Int other);
public Int remainder(Int other);
```

The first returns both the quotient and remainder of one Int object divided by another. (This is more efficient since you will probably compute both quantities at the same time anyway.) Return these two values as an array of two Ints; answer[0] could contain the quotient, and answer[1] could contain the remainder. The second and third methods return the quotient and the remainder of Int division, respectively.

2. Design a graphical calculator for Int objects, with buttons to perform addition, multiplication, subtraction, and division. If desired, write methods to perform other operations with Ints, and supply buttons for these on the calculator. Establish precedence among your operators, and include parentheses buttons to override precedence rules.

3. There are many ways to implement a class to perform arithmetic with arbitrarily large integers. The method presented in this chapter is perhaps the most intuitive for us, because it uses decimal arithmetic, and because the algorithms closely resemble what we do as humans. However, a computer does arithmetic in a different way than us. First of all, numbers are represented as a series of switches that are either on or off, or in binary.

To develop a large integer class that executes more efficiently, we want to mimic as closely as possible the way a binary computer does arithmetic. While we are at it, we might want to make the number representation more flexible, and use linked lists to hold the data instead of arrays. For example, suppose we use a doubly-linked list with a head and tail pointer. It will point at a series of ints (or bytes, or shorts, or longs), where each int represents part of the binary integer. (See the figure.)

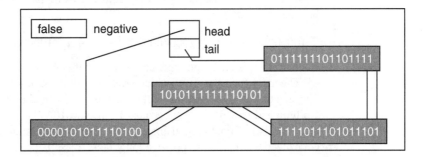

To perform addition of integers with the same sign, simply add them as binary integers the same way the computer does. If there is a carry in the high order digit of each int, carry it over to the next int. To subtract, simply add the negative, then store all negative numbers in two's–complement form, the same way a computer normally does. The two's–complement of a binary integer is where each bit is inverted, and then you add 1. For example, the byte-sized two's complement of $9 = 00001001_{base\ 2}$ is $11110111_{base\ 2}$. Thus, if you wish to compute 5 minus 9 in binary, this is

$$
\begin{array}{r}
00000101 \\
-\ \underline{00001001}
\end{array}
$$

To do a subtraction, form the two's–complement of the second integer, and add them.

$$
\begin{array}{r}
00000101 \\
+\ \underline{11110111} \\
11111100
\end{array}
$$

This answer is the two's–complement representation of -4 (you can verify this by subtracting 1 then inverting the bits), and so the answer to 5 minus 9 is -4, as it should be.

Multiplication and division in binary is particularly easy and fast to implement, since it involves mostly just shifting to the right or left, and adding. For example, to multiply 5 by 9 we take

$$00000101$$
$$\times\ \underline{00001001}$$

Which we note is simply $00000101_{\text{base 2}}$ plus $00101000_{\text{base 2}}$ (which is $00000101_{\text{base 2}}$ shifted to the left 3 places). This gives us $00101101_{\text{base 2}}$, or 45 in decimal, which is correct.

Now, with all of this in mind, rewrite the Int class.

4. If you prefer using base 10 for the Int() class (it's much easier to convert these to and from strings, for example), you may consider using base 1 billion. A number in this base can be written as

$$a_n \cdot 1000000000^n + a_{n-1} \cdot 1000000000^{n-1} + \ldots + a_1 \cdot 1000000000^1 + a_0 \cdot 1000000000^0.$$

where each a_i is an integer between 0 and 999999999.

The array (or list) of ints which hold the "digits" can store a number in this range. The size of this data structure will clearly be much smaller. Conversion between base 1 billion and base 10 is easy because 1 billion = 10^9. You may also consider using an array (or list) of type long, using as your base the maximum power of 10 which does not exceed the maximum positive long value $2^{63} - 1$.

CHAPTER 3

The Integers

In order to understand most of modern cryptography, it is necessary to understand some number theory. We begin with the divisibility properties of integers.

> ### Definition
>
> If a and b are integers with $a \neq 0$, we say that a divides b if there is an integer c such that $b = ac$. If a divides b, we also say that a is a divisor, or factor, of b, and we write $a|b$. We also write $a \nmid b$ if a does not divide b.
>
> For example, $3|27$, since $27 = 3 \cdot 9$. Likewise, $5 \nmid 32$, because there exists no integer c such that $32 = 5c$.

Using this test, we can find and list the divisors of all nonzero integers. For example, the divisors of 9 are ± 1, ± 3, and ± 9. The factors of 20 are ± 1, ± 2, ± 4, ± 5, ± 10, and ± 20. Now, we prove some properties of divisibility.

PROPOSITION 1   If x, y, and z are integers with $x|y$ and $y|z$, then $x|z$.

Proof.   Say that integer x divides integer y, and y divides integer z. Then $\exists$ (there exits) an integer c such that $y = cx$, and $\exists$ an integer d such that $z = dy$. Now, note that $z = dy = d(cx) = (dc)x$, and that dc is likewise an integer. Thus, x divides z. ∎

EXAMPLE.   Note that $3|9$, and that $9|72$. By the previous theorem, this implies that 3 also divides 72.

The next theorem is as easy to prove as the previous, and the proof is left to you.

PROPOSITION 2   If c, x, y, m, and n are integers such that $c|x$ and $c|y$, then $c|(mx + ny)$.

This proposition tells us that if an integer divides two others, it also divides any integer linear combination of the other two.

EXAMPLE. Note that 4|20 and 4|8. By the previous theorem then, 4 also divides $128 = 4 \cdot 20 + 6 \cdot 8$.

The following proposition is very useful in that it establishes that any integer can be expressed as a multiple of any other positive integer b, plus some remainder, where that remainder is nonnegative and less than b. It is called the division algorithm.

3.1 THE DIVISION ALGORITHM

PROPOSITION 3 (The Division Algorithm.) If y and b are integers such that $b > 0$, then $\exists$ unique integers q and r such that $0 \le r < b$ and $y = bq + r$. This q is called the quotient, r the remainder, b the divisor, and y the dividend.

Proof. Let S be the set of all integers of the form $y - bk$ where k is an integer. Further, let T be the set of all nonnegative members of S. T is not the empty set, since $y - bk > 0$ whenever $k < y/b$. So, T must have a smallest element; choose q to be the value of k so that $y - bq$ is the smallest member of T. Now, set $r = y - bq$. We will show that this choice of q and r are exactly those desired. First, we know that $r \ge 0$, (since $y - bq$ is nonnegative) and $r < b$, since if $r \ge b$ we would have $r > r - b = y - bq - b = y - b(q + 1) \ge 0$, which says we have a nonnegative integer smaller than r in T, a contradiction. Thus, $0 \le r < b$.

We have shown that r and q exist; now we must show that they are unique. Suppose we have two equations

$$y = bq_1 + r_1 \qquad (*)$$
$$y = bq_2 + r_2$$

with $0 \le r_1 < b$ and $0 \le r_2 < b$. Subtract the second from the first to get $0 = b(q_1 - q_2) + (r_1 - r_2)$, or $r_2 - r_1 = b(q_1 - q_2)$. Thus, $b|(r_2 - r_1)$. Since $0 \le r_1 < b$ and $0 \le r_2 < b$ we get $-b < r_2 - r_1 < b$. Because 0 is the only multiple of b between $-b$ and b (not including $-b$ and b), b divides $r_2 - r_1$ only if $r_2 - r_1 = 0$, or when $r_1 = r_2$. Replacing r_2 with r_1 in the equations in $(*)$, we easily establish that $q_1 = q_2$, and thus q and r are indeed unique. ∎

EXAMPLES. We wish to find q and r as defined in the division algorithm for all of the following equations:

- $65 = 3q + r$. Divide 65 by 3 to get $q = 21$, $r = 2$.
- $-21 = 5q + r$. If we simply divide -21 by 5, we get a quotient of -4, and a remainder of -1. To place the remainder in the proper range, simply add 5 to it, while subtracting 1 from the quotient. This yields $q = -5$, $r = 4$. This is a simple way of calculating q and r when the dividend is negative.

Prime numbers play a huge role in number theory, and in modern cryptography as well. Thus, the definition of a prime number follows.

> **Definition**
> A prime number, or a prime, is an integer greater than 1 divisible by no positive integers other than itself and 1. A positive integer greater than 1 that is not prime is said to be composite.

EXAMPLES.   All of the following integers are primes: 2, 7, 23, 29, and 163. None of these numbers has positive factors except themselves and 1. On the other hand, the following numbers are composite: $4 = 2 \times 2$, $100 = 2 \times 2 \times 5 \times 5$, and $39 = 3 \times 13$. You should be careful to note, however, that many integers are neither prime nor composite, as all primes and composite numbers are positive integers greater than 1. For example, the following integers are neither prime nor composite: 1, 0, -21, and -5.

It is important to establish that every positive integer greater than 1 has a prime divisor, for it helps us establish that there are infinitely many primes. It also helps us determine the whereabouts of a prime factor for composite numbers.

PROPOSITION 4   Every positive integer greater than 1 has a prime divisor.

Proof.   First, assume there is a positive integer greater than 1 having no prime divisors. Thus, the set of all such integers is not empty, and so has a least element, say m. Since m has no prime divisors and $m|m$, m is not prime. So m is composite, and we write $m = bc$ where $1 < b < m$ and $1 < c < m$. Now, since $b < m$, b must have a prime divisor, say p, since m is the least nonnegative integer having no prime divisors. But p then also divides m by Proposition 1, and so m has a prime divisor, a contradiction. ∎

PROPOSITION 5   There are infinitely many primes.

Proof.   Take the integer $z = n!+1$, where $n \geq 1$. Proposition 4 says z has a prime divisor, say p. Suppose $p \leq n$. Then we would have $p|n!$. This is so since

$$n! = n(n - 1)(n - 2) \ldots 3 \cdot 2 \cdot 1,$$

and if $p \leq n$, it must divide one of the numbers in the sequence. But then, by Proposition 2, we would have $p|(z - n!) = 1$, an impossibility. So the prime p must be greater than n, and since n is completely arbitrary, we have found a prime larger than n for any integer n. This establishes that there must be infinitely many primes. ∎

It is important for us to establish that there are infinitely many primes, as we must be able to freely select primes for use in cryptographic applications. The primes we choose are usually kept secret, so there must be enough primes scattered about to make finding the primes you choose very difficult for an attacker.

PROPOSITION 6   If n is composite, then n has a prime factor not exceeding the square root of n.

Proof.   Suppose n is the product of integers b and c, and say $1 < b \leq c < n$. Note that b is no greater than $\sqrt{n}$ ause if it were, c would also be greater than $\sqrt{n}$, implying that $bc > \sqrt{n} \cdot \sqrt{n} = n$, a contradiction. Proposition 4 says that b must have a prime divisor, which must also divide n by Proposition 1. Thus, a prime divisor smaller than $\sqrt{n}$ exists.   ■

The previous result tells us that if we wish to search sequentially for a prime factor of some number n, we need not exceed its square root. This can reduce our workload considerably. For example, if we wish to know whether or not 101 is prime, we need only search for factors up to 10, which is the largest integer $\leq \sqrt{101}$. We check for factors in Table 3.1.

We conclude, therefore, that 101 is prime. Proposition 6 proves it is not necessary to search for factors of 101 greater than 10, for one such factor, if it exists, must be ≤ 10.

This sequential method for determining whether or not numbers are prime is known as trial division by small primes.

Say we want to find a prime factor of an integer consisting of 500 decimal digits. (This is typical in modern cryptography.) Then the square root of that number would still be about 250 decimal digits. Asking the computer to search each number in a sequential fashion up to the square root would take an enormous amount of time. Thus, trial division is limited to integers having small prime factors. If we want to factor large integers, we must find better methods of factoring.

We can speed up trial division by noting that it isn't necessary to divide by every integer not exceeding the square root of n, but only those integers which are prime. If we make

Table 3.1

#	Factor of 101?
2	No
3	No
4	No
5	No
6	No
7	No
8	No
9	No
10	No

a table of all integers from 2 to n, we can begin by successively crossing out all multiples of 2, then multiples of 3, then multiples of 5, and so on. In this way, we can determine all primes less than or equal to any integer; they are the numbers which have not been crossed out.

For instance, we make a list of all the integers from 2 to 99, and begin by crossing out all multiples of 2 in the list, then all multiples of 3, then the multiples of 5 (because 4 and all of its multiples are already crossed out), and so on until we reach 9, the largest integer $\leq \sqrt{99} \cong 9.95$. Its multiples have already been crossed out; thus the numbers in the list which have not been crossed out are the primes ≤ 99. See Table 3.2. Integers which are multiples of 2, 3, 5, or 7 have been removed.

This method of identifying primes by crossing out multiples is known as the Sieve of Eratosthenes. Because of great storage requirements, it is not very efficient for determining large primes.

Java Algorithm We can write a Java program which sequentially searches up to $\sqrt{n}$ for the smallest prime factor of n, then returns it if found. Otherwise, we conclude n is prime, and return n. Since trial division would perform poorly for large integers, we will just write it for primitive ints.

The main method prompts the user to enter an integer n greater than 1; it then calls the sieveFactor() method, which will return the first prime divisor it finds, or n itself if n is prime.

Table 3.2

	2	3		5		7		
11		13				17		19
		23						29
31						37		
41		43				47		
		53						59
61						67		
71		73						79
		83						89
						97		

```java
import javax.swing.*;
public class TestSieveFactor {
    public static void main(String[] args) {
        boolean idiot;
        do {
            idiot=false;
            try {
                int n=new Integer(JOptionPane.showInputDialog
                                ("Enter an integer > 1:")).intValue();
                if (n<=1) {
                    idiot=true;
                    JOptionPane.showMessageDialog(null,"Invalid integer entered!");
                } else {
                    int d=sieveFactor(n);
                    if (d==n) JOptionPane.showMessageDialog(null,n+" is prime.");
                    else JOptionPane.showMessageDialog(null,d+" divides "+n+".");
                }
            } catch (NumberFormatException e) {
                idiot=true;
                JOptionPane.showMessageDialog(null,e.toString());
            }
        } while (idiot);
        System.exit(0);
    }
    private static int sieveFactor(int n) {
        int divisor; boolean prime=true;
        for (divisor=2;divisor<=Math.sqrt(n);divisor++)
            if (n%divisor==0) {prime=false; break;}
        return prime?n:divisor;
    }
}
```

If we run the previous program with some test data, we get the results shown in Figure 3.1a–h.

The ability to factor efficiently is at the heart of breaking many cryptosystems. We thus begin the study of finding divisors, or factors. In particular, we want to find the greatest common divisor of two integers.

> **Definition**
> The greatest common divisor of two integers x and y, where at least one is nonzero, is the largest integer that divides both x and y. We also call this the gcd of x and y, and write it as (x, y). We define the greatest common divisor of 0 and 0 as 0; that is, $(0, 0) = 0$.

Figure 3.1   (a)

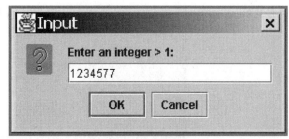

(b)

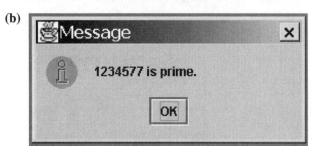

(c)

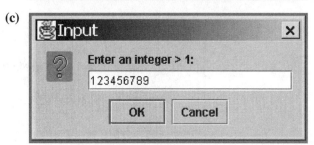

(d)

(e)

Figure 3.1 (f)

(g)

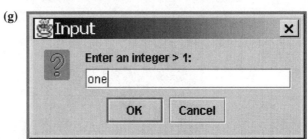

(h)

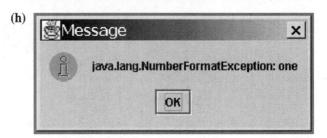

EXAMPLE. The divisors of 30 are ±1, ±2, ±3, ±5, ±6, ±10, ±15, and ±30. The divisors of 18 are ±1, ±2, ±3, ±6, ±9, ±18. The largest integer in both lists is 6, so the gcd of 30 and 18 is 6.

> *Definition*
> Two integers are said to be relatively prime if their gcd is 1.

EXAMPLES. The following pairs of integers are relatively prime. (Verify.)

a. 8 and 9

b. 23 and 44

c. 27 and 55

Note that the sign of the integers is not important when computing the gcd. This is easy to see if one simply notices that the divisors of n are exactly the same as the divisors of $-n$. So, all of the following are equal:

$$(x, y) = (x, -y) = (-x, y) = (-x, -y) = (|x|, |y|)$$

Thus, we need only concern ourselves with the gcd of positive integers.

EXAMPLE. $(18, -54) = (18, 54) = 9$.

PROPOSITION 7 Let x, y, and z be integers with $(x, y) = d$. Then

a. $(x/d, y/d) = 1$

b. $(x + cy, y) = (x, y)$.

c. An integer c divides both x and y if and only if $c|(x, y)$.

Proof. (Part a.) First, suppose there is some integer n that divides both x/d and y/d. Then $\exists$ integers j and k such that $x/d = jn$ and $y/d = kn$ or, alternatively, $x = djn$ and $y = dkn$. From this we establish that dn is a common divisor of both x and y. But d is the greatest common divisor of both x and y, so $dn \le d$, implying that $n = 1$. So the gcd of x/d and y/d is 1.

(Part b.) Let x, c, and y be integers, and suppose e is a common divisor of x and y. By Proposition 2 we know $e|(x + cy)$, so e divides both $x + cy$ and y. On the other hand, suppose f is a common divisor of $x + cy$ and y. Then f also divides $(x + cy) - cy = x$ by Proposition 2. So f is then a common divisor of x and y. Consequently, we conclude that the common divisors of x and y are identical to the common divisors of $x + cy$ and y, and so they share the same greatest common divisor.

(Part c.) The "if" part is obvious, since (x, y) divides both x and y, and because if we have $c|(x, y)$ we must have $c|x$ and $c|y$ by proposition 1. This tells us that the divisors of (x, y) is a subset of the common divisors of x and y. We can represent this with a Venn diagram, as shown in Figure 3.2.

Now we write x and y as multiples of their gcd; that is,

$$x = (x, y)e, \text{ and } y = (x, y)f.$$

and note $(e, f) = 1$ by part (a). Thus, no common divisor of x and y (except 1) can simultaneously divide e and f, and so any common divisor of x and y must also divide (x, y).

Thus, the set of divisors of (x, y) and the set of common divisors of x and y are the same set. (See Figure 3.3.) ■

EXAMPLES. To satisfy our cynical natures, we'll test the previous proposition with some data.

Figure 3.2

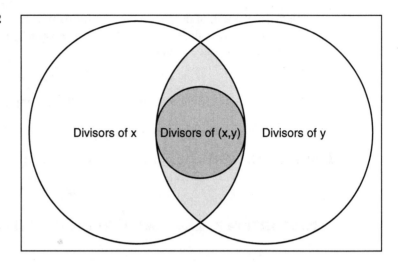

Figure 3.3

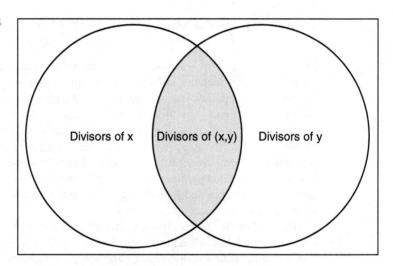

- Note that $(24, 42) = 6$, and that if we divide both 24 and 42 by 6, we can verify that $(24/6, 42/6) = (4, 7) = 1$.
- Take the same two integers, 24 and 42. Compute $= 24 + (-3)(42) = -102$, and note that $(-102, 42) = 6 = (24, 42)$.

Definition
If x and y are integers, we will say a linear combination of x and y is a sum of the form $mx + ny$ where m and n are integers.

PROPOSITION 8 The gcd of integers x and y, not both zero, is the least positive integer that is a linear combination of x and y.

Proof. Suppose d is the least positive integer that is a linear combination of x and y. We know that the set of such integers must be nonempty, as at least one of the following linear combinations must be positive:

$$x + 0 \cdot y,$$
$$-x + 0 \cdot y,$$
$$0 \cdot x + y, \text{ or}$$
$$0 \cdot x - y.$$

So, a least such element in this set, say d, exists. We must first show d is a divisor of both x and y. We have $d = mx + ny$ where m and n are integers, and by the division algorithm we can obtain

$$x = dq + r \quad \text{where } 0 \leq r < d.$$

From this equation, and because $d = mx + ny$, we can derive

$$r = x - dq = x - q(mx + ny) = (1 - qm)x - qny.$$

So we can write r also as a linear combination of x and y. Now, by construction, r is nonnegative, strictly less than d, and d is the least positive integer which may be written as a linear combination of x and y. So r must be zero. This means that d divides x, which is what we want to show. Similarly, we can show that $d|y$, and that d is therefore a common divisor of x and y, as desired.

Now, it remains to be shown that d is the gcd of x and y. Suppose c is a common divisor of x and y. Then, since $d = mx + ny$, c divides d by proposition 2. Hence, because c is arbitrary, d must be the greatest common divisor of x and y. ∎

We now turn our attention to common divisors of more than two integers.

Definition
The greatest common divisor of a set of integers $a_1, a_2, \ldots, a_n$, not all zero, is the largest divisor of all the integers in the set. We write this as $(a_1, a_2, \ldots, a_n)$.

EXAMPLE. The greatest common divisor of 20, 30, and 15 is 5.

PROPOSITION 9 $(a_1, a_2, a_3, \ldots, a_n) = ((a_1, a_2), a_3, \ldots, a_n)$.

Proof. Note that any common divisor of the n integers in the list $a_1, a_2, \ldots, a_n$ is, in particular, a common divisor of the first two, a_1 and a_2. This divisor then also divides the gcd of a_1 and a_2 by proposition 7 (part c). Now consider an integer that divides the last $n - 2$ integers in the list, and that also divides the gcd of a_1 and a_2. This divisor must then also separately divide both a_1 and a_2, and so then is a common divisor of all the n integers. We now see that the common divisors of all the n integers are exactly the same as the common divisors of the last $n - 2$ integers taken with the gcd of the first two. Hence, they also have the same greatest common divisor. ■

EXAMPLE.   The previous proposition is very handy in that it turns a large problem into a small one. It says, for example, that we can compute the gcd of 28, 126, 21, and 10 in the following way:

$$(28, 126, 21, 10)$$
$$= ((28, 126), 21, 10)$$
$$= (14, 21, 10)$$
$$= ((14, 21), 10)$$
$$= (7, 10)$$
$$= 1.$$

Note that the previous numbers, when taken together, have a gcd of 1. However, if we examine each pair from the list, we see that some pairs are not relatively prime. (For example, $(28, 21) = 7$.) This motivates us to make a distinction between these two situations, and thus make a definition.

> **Definition**
> We say that the integers $a_1, a_2, \ldots, a_n$ are mutually relatively prime if the gcd of the set of integers is 1. We say the integers are pairwise relatively prime if each pair of integers taken from the set are relatively prime.

EXAMPLE.   The numbers 18, 9, and 25 are mutually relatively prime. The largest divisor all have in common is 1. But, they are not pairwise relatively prime because $(18, 9) = 9$.

Until now, we have presented a lot of propositions about the gcd, but no really good way of finding it has been presented. We could make a list of all the divisors of our numbers, then choose the largest divisor that they have in common, but this is not really efficient. The next proposition, which you should be able to prove, leads us to the Euclidean algorithm, a lightning-fast way of finding the gcd.

PROPOSITION 10   If c and d are integers and $c = dq + r$ where q and r are integers, then $(c, d) = (d, r)$.

The previous proposition provides us with a particularly fast way of finding the gcd of two integers. We will calculate the gcd of 132 and 55. If we successively apply the division algorithm to obtain

$$132 = 2 \cdot 55 + 22$$
$$55 = 2 \cdot 22 + 11$$
$$22 = 2 \cdot 11 + 0,$$

the preceding proposition then tells us that

$$(132, 55) = (55, 22) = (22, 11) = (11, 0) = 11.$$

Note that we wisely chose q and r as the same q and r obtained by the division algorithm. The remainders are all positive, and are getting smaller after each successive division. The remainder must eventually reach 0, and the previous remainder must be the gcd. The proof that this always works follows.

3.2 THE EUCLIDEAN ALGORITHM

PROPOSITION 11 (The Euclidean Algorithm.) Let $r_0 = x$ and $r_1 = y$ be integers such that $x \geq y > 0$. If the division algorithm is successively applied to obtain $r_j = r_{j+1}q_{j+1} + r_{j+2}$ with $0 < r_{j+2} < r_{j+1}$ for $j = 0, 1, 2, \ldots, n - 2$ and $r_{n+1} = 0$, then $(x, y) = r_n$.

Proof. This follows almost immediately using proposition 10. Let $r_0 = x$, $r_1 = y$, where $x \geq y > 0$. We successively apply the division algorithm to obtain

$$r_0 = r_1q_1 + r_2 \quad \text{with } 0 \leq r_2 < r_1$$
$$r_1 = r_2q_2 + r_3 \quad \text{with } 0 \leq r_3 < r_2$$
$$\cdots$$
$$r_{i-2} = r_{i-1}q_{i-1} + r_i$$
$$\cdots$$

This process must terminate. The remainders form a strictly decreasing sequence of positive integers bounded below by zero. This sequence can certainly have no more than x terms:

$$r_0 \geq r_1 > r_2 > \ldots > r_{n-1} > r_n > r_{n+1} = 0.$$

We must eventually have $r_{n+1} = 0$ for some n, where r_n is the last nonzero remainder. Proposition 10 then tells us that

$$(x, y) = (r_0, r_1) = (r_1, r_2) = \ldots = (r_{n-1}, r_n) = (r_n, r_{n+1}) = (r_n, 0) = r_n$$

and we have the desired result. ■

EXAMPLE. Use the Euclidean algorithm to find the gcd of 252 and 198. Successively apply the division algorithm to obtain

$$252 = 1 \cdot 198 + 54$$
$$198 = 3 \cdot 54 + 36$$
$$54 = 1 \cdot 36 + 18$$
$$36 = 2 \cdot 18 + 0$$

The last nonzero remainder is 18, so $(252, 198) = 18$. We can write this process out very quickly as

$$(252, 198) = (198, 54) = (54, 36) = (36, 18) = (18, 0) = 18.$$

Java Algorithm   Once we know the Euclidean algorithm, writing a method to compute the gcd should be simple. Though the BigInteger class supplies a method to compute the gcd of two BigIntegers, it may be interesting to write our own. Here, we use a static recursive method. Recursion is natural for this algorithm, because if we have positive ints m and n in Java such that $m > n$, proposition 10 says that $(m, n) = (n, m \% n)$. This makes an easy substitution in a recursive call. The recursion is not particularly wasteful in this case since the Euclidean algorithm arrives at the gcd so quickly. The following test program simply asks the user to enter two integers, then computes and displays their gcd (see Figures 3.4a–c).

```java
import java.io.*;
import javax.swing.*;
import java.math.BigInteger;
public class TestGCD {
    public static void main(String[] args) {
        BigInteger i=new BigInteger(JOptionPane.showInputDialog("Enter an integer: "));
        BigInteger j=new BigInteger(JOptionPane.showInputDialog
                                  ("Enter another integer: "));
        JOptionPane.showMessageDialog(null,"The gcd of "+i+" and "+j+" is "+gcd(i,j));
        System.exit(0);
    }
    static BigInteger ZERO=new BigInteger("0");

    //Compute the gcd recursively using the Euclidean algorithm
    private static BigInteger gcd(BigInteger first, BigInteger second) {
    //Make sure both are nonnegative
        first=first.abs();
        second=second.abs();
    //Call the recursive method
        return recurseGCD(first,second);
    }

    private static BigInteger recurseGCD(BigInteger x, BigInteger y) {
        if (y.equals(ZERO)) return x;
        else return recurseGCD(y,x.mod(y));
    }

}
```

Figure 3.4   **(a)**

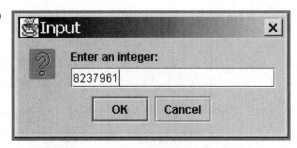

(b)

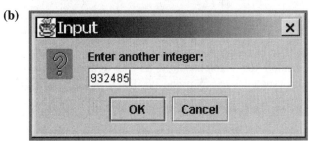

(c)

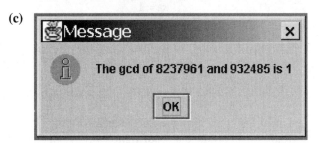

There is a test applet for computing greatest common divisors on the book's website under the class name TestGCDApplet. It uses the gcd() method supplied with the BigInteger class. Figure 3.5 shows a screen shot of a sample run.

The following development will be very useful to us later on, for it will help us solve special equations called diophantine equations, and congruences. It also reveals something interesting about the gcd. Recall that the gcd of two numbers is the least positive integer that can be expressed as a linear combination of those two numbers; that is,

$$(x, y) = mx + ny$$

for some integers m and n. What are the values of m and n? The next proposition shows us exactly how these two quantities can be computed.

PROPOSITION 12 (Extended Euclidean Algorithm). Let x and y be positive integers such that $x \geq y > 0$. Then

$$(x, y) = s_n x + t_n y$$

Figure 3.5

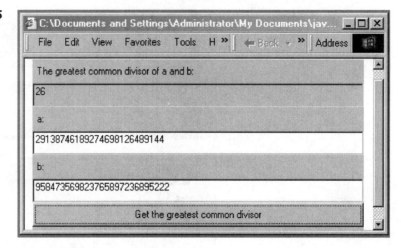

where the s_n and t_n are defined recursively as

$$s_j = s_{j-2} - q_{j-1}s_{j-1} \text{ for } j = 2, \ldots, n$$
$$s_0 = 1$$
$$s_1 = 0$$

$$t_j = t_{j-2} - q_{j-1}t_{j-1} \text{ for } j = 2, \ldots, n$$
$$t_0 = 0$$
$$t_1 = 1$$

and the q_j and r_i are as in the Euclidean algorithm.

Rather than produce a proof right away for this, we do an example to clarify what is going on. Suppose we wish to express the gcd of 252 and 198 as a linear combination of 252 and 198. We can apply the Euclidean algorithm, and while keeping track of the quotients and remainders, we shall also compute the two values s_j and t_j during the jth step. This is perhaps best done in a table. (See Table 3.3.)

The fourth remainder is the last nonzero remainder, so we need not compute the fifth row in the table. The two numbers desired are 4, and -5; that is,

$$18 = (252, 198) = 4 \cdot 252 + (-5) \cdot 198$$

Now, we can show a proof to you that this always works.

Proof. First note that $(x, y) = r_n$, where r_n is the last nonzero remainder generated in the Euclidean algorithm. If we show then that

$$r_j = s_j x + t_j y \quad (*)$$

$\forall$ (for all) $j = 0, 1, \ldots, k < n$, the result then follows by induction. First, note (*) is true when $j = 0$, and when $j = 1$, since

$$r_0 = 1 \cdot x + 0 \cdot y = s_0 x + t_0 y, \text{ and } r_1 = 0 \cdot x + 1 \cdot y = s_1 x + t_1 y.$$

Table 3.3

j	q_j	r_j	s_j	t_j
0		252	1	0
1	1	198	0	1
2	3	54	$1-0\bullet1=1$	$0-1\bullet1=-1$
3	1	36	$0-1\bullet3=-3$	$1-(-1)\bullet3=4$
4	2	18	$1-(-3)\bullet1=4$	$-1-4\bullet1=-5$
5		0		

Now, assume (*) is true for $j = 2, \ldots, k - 1$. The kth step of the Euclidean algorithm tells us that $r_k = r_{k-2} - r_{k-1}q_{k-1}$, and by using the induction hypothesis, we can then show (*) is true when $j = k$ as follows:

$$r_k = (s_{k-2}x + t_{k-2}y) - (s_{k-1}x + t_{k-1}y)q_{k-1}$$

$$= (s_{k-2} - s_{k-1}q_{k-1})x + (t_{k-2} - t_{k-1}q_{k-1})y$$

$$= s_kx + t_ky$$

Induction then says $s_nx + t_ny = r_n = (x, y)$, as desired. ∎

Java Algorithm   We should write a euclid() method to calculate the values cited in the foregoing theorem. The BigInteger class does not provide such a method, so we will write a BigIntegerMath class to place methods in. The BigInteger class will be used to house many of the methods used in this book. In particular, this class defines a euclid(BigInteger x, BigInteger y) method, which returns an array (say, arr[]) of three BigIntegers. We will set arr[0] to $(x, y) = r_n$ (from Proposition 12), arr[1] to s_n, and arr[2] to t_n. This method is not recursive; an interesting exercise for you is to write it recursively.

```
import java.math.*;
import java.security.SecureRandom;
import java.util.*;
public class BigIntegerMath {

    //Define some BigInteger constants; this is handy for comparisons
    static final BigInteger ZERO=new BigInteger("0");
    static final BigInteger ONE=new BigInteger("1");
    static final BigInteger TWO=new BigInteger("2");
    static final BigInteger THREE=new BigInteger("3");
    static final BigInteger FOUR=new BigInteger("4");
```

```
//A nonrecursive version of euclid.  It returns an array answer of 3 BigIntegers
//answer[0] is the gcd, answer[1] is the coefficient of a, answer[2] the coeff
//of b
public static BigInteger[] euclid(BigInteger a,BigInteger b) throws
IllegalArgumentException {
    //Throw an exception if either argument is not positive
    if (a.compareTo(ZERO)<=0||b.compareTo(ZERO)<=0) throw new
IllegalArgumentException("Euclid requires both arguments to be positive!");
    BigInteger[] answer=new BigInteger[3];
    //Set up all the initial table entries
    BigInteger r0=new BigInteger(a.toByteArray());
    BigInteger r1=new BigInteger(b.toByteArray());
    BigInteger s0=new BigInteger("1");
    BigInteger s1=new BigInteger("0");
    BigInteger t0=new BigInteger("0");
    BigInteger t1=new BigInteger("1");
    BigInteger q1=r0.divide(r1);
    BigInteger r2=r0.mod(r1);
    BigInteger s2,t2;
    //When r2 becomes zero, the previous table entries are the answers
    while (r2.compareTo(ZERO)>0) {
        s2=s0.subtract(q1.multiply(s1)); s0=s1; s1=s2;
        t2=t0.subtract(q1.multiply(t1)); t0=t1; t1=t2;
        r0=r1; r1=r2; q1=r0.divide(r1); r2=r0.mod(r1);
    }
    answer[0]=r1; answer[1]=s1; answer[2]=t1;
    return answer;
    }
}
```

TestEuclidApplet is on the book's website. Run it to test the algorithm (see Figure 3.6).

3.3   THE FUNDAMENTAL THEOREM OF ARITHMETIC

The following propositions lead us to the pinnacle of number theory: the Fundamental Theorem of Arithmetic, which states that every integer factors uniquely into a product of prime powers. Of course, we've been using this fact since we were children, but we rarely see the proof until after we've left high school, and most people never see it at all. But first, two other theorems:

PROPOSITION 13   If a, b, and c are positive integers with a and b relatively prime, and such that $a|bc$, then $a|c$.

Proof.   Since a and b are relatively prime, $\exists$ integers x and y such that $ax + by = 1$. Multiply both sides of the equation by c to get $acx + bcy = c$. Now, since $a|a$, and $a|bc$ by hypothesis, proposition 2 says $a|(acx + bcy)$, a linear combination of a and bc. Hence, $a|c$.   ■

Figure 3.6

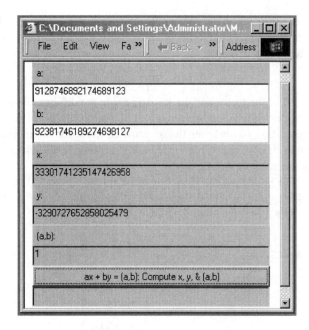

PROPOSITION 14 Suppose $a_1, a_2, \ldots, a_n$ are positive integers, and p is a prime which divides $a_1 a_2 \ldots a_n$. Then there is an integer i such that $1 \le i \le n$ and $p|a_i$.

Proof. If $n = 1$, the result is trivially true. Now suppose the theorem is true for $n = k$, and consider a product of $k + 1$ integers $a_1 a_2 \ldots a_{k+1}$ divisible by p. Since $p|a_1 a_2 \ldots a_{k+1} = (a_1 a_2 \ldots a_k) a_{k+1}$, proposition 13 says either $p|a_1 a_2 \ldots a_k$, or $p|a_{k+1}$. If $p|a_{k+1}$, we are finished. If, on the other hand $p|a_1 a_2 \ldots a_k$, our supposition says $\exists$ an integer i between 1 and n (inclusive) such that $p|a_i$. In this case, induction establishes the desired result. ∎

PROPOSITION 15 (The Fundamental Theorem of Arithmetic.) Every positive integer n greater than 1 can be written in the form $n = p_1 p_2 \ldots p_r$ where each p_r is prime, $i = 1$, $2, \ldots, n$. Furthermore, this representation is unique.

Proof. Assume some positive integer greater than 1 cannot be written as a product of primes, and let n be the smallest such integer. If n is prime, it is trivially a product of primes. So $n = ab$ is composite, where $1 < a < n$, $1 < b < n$. Since n is the smallest number greater than 1 which cannot be written as a product of primes, a and b must both be products of primes. But since $n = ab$, n is also a product of primes, contrary to our assumption. Given that this prime factorization of n exists, we must now show it is unique. Suppose n has two different factorizations

$$n = p_1 p_2 \ldots p_m = q_1 q_2 \ldots q_k$$

where each p_i and q_j is prime, $i = 1, 2, \ldots, m, j = 1, 2, \ldots, k$, and that these factors are in nondecreasing order. Remove any common primes from the two factorizations, and re-index if necessary to obtain

$$p_1 p_2 \cdots p_v = q_1 q_2 \cdots q_w, \quad \text{where } v \leq m, \; w \leq k.$$

All of the factors on the left-hand side are different from the factors on the right. Now, consider p_1, which divides $q_1 q_2 \cdots q_w$ (since $p_1 | p_1 p_2 \cdots p_v$, which is equal to $q_1 q_2 \cdots q_w$). Proposition 14 says then that p_1 must divide q_i for some i between 1 and w (inclusive), but this is clearly impossible, since each q_i is prime, and each different from p_1. Thus, the prime factorization of n is unique. ∎

The Fundamental Theorem of Arithmetic reveals that integers greater than 1 factor uniquely into primes. We often order these factors from the smallest to the largest, and group those that are equal together. We call this the prime power factorization of an integer.

EXAMPLES.

- $24 = 2^3 \cdot 3$

- $588 = 2^2 \cdot 3 \cdot 7^2$

- $450 = 2 \cdot 3^2 \cdot 5^2$

Before we move on to the next chapter, we should discuss the least common multiple of two integers. We will derive a convenient formula to compute it, based on the greatest common divisor. Proving the validity of this formula is easy with the Fundamental Theorem of Arithmetic.

Definition

The least common multiple of two integers x and y, not both zero, is the smallest positive integer that is divisible by both x and y. We denote the least common multiple, or lcm, of x and y as $\text{lcm}(x, y)$.

It isn't difficult to compute the lcm of two integers x and y if we reason in the following way: Take the prime power factorization of the two integers, and note which factors they have in common. Note that the product P of these common factors must be the gcd of x and y. To see this, note that $P | x$ and $P | y$, and furthermore:

- If we multiply P by another factor of x (or y), that product will then fail to divide y (or x), and

- if we remove a factor from P, we then have a common divisor of x and y which is smaller than P.

Thus, $P = (x, y)$. (See Figure 3.7.)

Now, remove one set of the common factors; say, from x. (See Figure 3.8.)

Figure 3.7

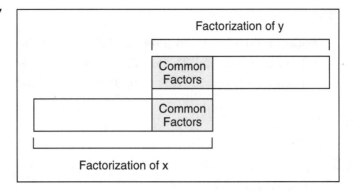

Figure 3.8

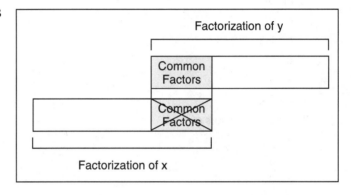

Figure 3.9

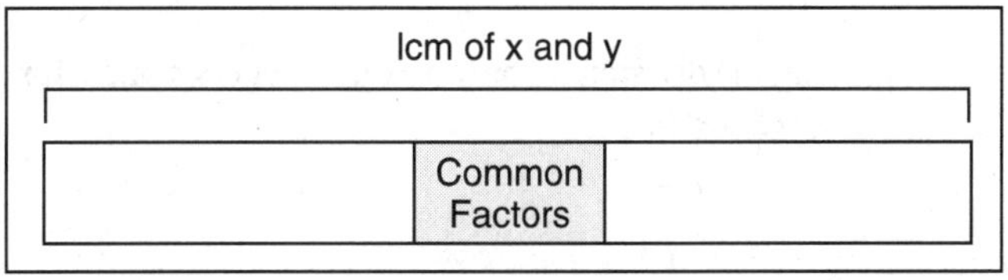

Consider now the integer formed by the product of the factors of y with the remaining factors of x. (See Figure 3.9.)

Clearly, this integer is divisible by both x and y. Furthermore, if we attempt to remove any more factors from this integer, it will no longer be divisible by either x or y (possibly neither). This is clearly the least common multiple of x and y. This yields a convenient formula for the least common multiple; that is,

$$\operatorname{lcm}(x, y) = xy/(x, y).$$

This argument doesn't really count as a proof, and you should confirm this. (Hint: Use the prime power factorization of x and y.)

EXAMPLES.

- lcm(36, 78) = 36 · 78/(36, 78) = 36 · 78/6 = 6 · 78 = 468
- lcm(21, 56) = 21 · 56/(21, 56) = 21 · 56/7 = 3 · 56 = 168
- lcm(100, 2050) = 100 · 2050/(100, 2050) = 100 · 2050/50 = 2 · 2050 = 4100

EXERCISES

1. Show that
   a. 5|20
   b. 7|42
   c. 8|8
   d. 1|55
   e. 7|0
   f. 342|0

2. Give the divisors of
   a. 72
   b. 37
   c. 30
   d. −27
   e. 0

3. Using the division algorithm, find integers q and r for the following equations. Remember, $0 \leq r < b$.
   a. $47 = 5q + r$
   b. $153 = 7q + r$
   c. $-143 = 8q + r$
   d. $-7 = 9q + r$
   e. $0 = 32q + r$
   f. $-1 = 6q + r$
   g. $-6 = 6q + r$

4. Prove proposition 2.

5. Determine which, if any, of the following integers are primes. For any that are not prime, list the positive factors.
   a. 77
   b. 78

   c. 79

   d. 1801

   e. 981

   f. 31

   g. -31

6. Find all the primes ≤ 100 using the Sieve of Eratosthenes.

7. Write a Java program to prompt the user for a positive number n, then compute and display all primes $\leq n$ using the Sieve of Eratosthenes. (Hint: Use an array of size $n + 1$ of type boolean.)

8. Find the gcd of the following sets of integers.

   a. 15, 35

   b. 21, 99

   c. 76, 24, 32

   d. 132, 64, 0

   e. 99, -100

   f. $-83, -23$

9. Determine if the following lists of integers are mutually relatively prime, pairwise relatively prime, or neither.

   a. 198, 252, 54, 18, 9

   b. 130, 65, 39, 143

   c. 14, 98, 25

   d. 32, 27, 35

10. Find a set of four integers which are mutually relatively prime, but not pairwise relatively prime.

11. Find a set of five integers which are mutually relatively prime, but not pairwise relatively prime.

12. Find the gcd of the following sets of integers using the Euclidean algorithm.

   a. 318, 3243

   b. 21, 364

   c. 102, 222

   d. 104, 24, 32

   e. 132, 64, 40

   f. 20785, 44350

   g. 99, 121

   h. 83, 23

   i. 34709, 100313

13. Prove proposition 10. (Hint: Use proposition 2 to show that the common divisors of c and d are the same as the common divisors of d and r.)

14. Write a gcd() method for the Int class without using recursion.

15. Add a gcd button to the Int calculator developed in a previous exercise. Use your own gcd() method from the previous exercise.

16. Express the gcd of each of the following pairs of integers as a linear combination of the pair.

    a. 45 and 75
    b. 121 and 32
    c. 512 and 96
    d. 10101 and 27
    e. 39 and 143
    f. 1023 and 300
    g. 25 and 26
    h. 423102 and 462
    i. 98 and 70
    j. 23984756 and 9238475

17. Write a recursive version of the euclid() method for BigIntegers.

18. Give the prime power factorization of the following integers:

    a. 10201
    b. 874
    c. 252
    d. 5250
    e. 1212
    f. 36179
    g. 4350

19. Prove that if a and b are nonzero integers, then $lcm(a, b) = ab/(a, b)$.

20. Calculate the lcm of the following pairs of integers:

    a. 104, 24
    b. 252, 198
    c. 17, 83
    d. $-123, 6$
    e. 987654321, 123456789

CHAPTER 4

Linear Diophantine Equations and Linear Congruences

LINEAR DIOPHANTINE EQUATIONS

Diophantine equations are special types of equations. What characterizes them is that their solutions must be integers. Consider the following equation:

$$12x + 27y = 32.$$

This is called a linear diophantine equation in two variables. It is diophantine because we are only interested in integer solutions for the variables, and it is linear because the highest power of any variable in the equation is 1. The preceding equation has no integer solutions for x and y (try to find one, if you like), whereas the following equation

$$12x + 27y = 30$$

has infinitely many integral solutions! One solution is $x = -20$, $y = 10$. (Try to find some more, or a formula which gives them all.) What distinguishes the first equation from the second? Proposition 16 will provide the answer to this; it will tell us which such equations have solutions, and which do not. The proof is constructive, in that it shows how to find the solutions when they exist.

PROPOSITION 16. Let a and b be nonzero integers with $d = (a, b)$. If $d|c$, the integer solutions x and y of the equation $ax + by = c$ are $x = x_0 + bn/d$, $y = y_0 - an/d$, where $x = x_0$, $y = y_0$ is a particular solution. If $d \nmid c$, the equation has no integer solutions.

Proof. Suppose x and y are integers such that

$$ax + by = c. \quad (*)$$

Then, since $d|a$ and $d|b$, by proposition 2, d also divides c. Thus, the contrapositive says if d does not divide c then there are no integral solutions. So, suppose $d|c$. Proposition 12 demonstrates the existence of integers s and t such that

$$d = as + bt.$$

Since $d|c$, there is an integer e such that $de = c$. Multiply both sides of $d = as + bt$ by e to obtain

$$c = de = (as + bt)e = a(se) + b(te)$$

and we see then that $x = x_0 = se$, $y = y_0 = te$ is a particular solution to (*). Now, let $x = x_0 + bn/d$, $y = y_0 - an/d$, where n is any integer. Note that this is also a solution:

$$ax + by = ax_0 + abn/d + by_0 - ban/d = ax_0 + by_0 = c.$$

We must show that every solution of (*) must be of this form. Suppose x and y are integers such that $ax + by = c$. Since $ax_0 + by_0 = c$, we subtract and rearrange terms to get

$$(ax + by) - (ax_0 + by_0) = 0$$

$$a(x - x_0) + b(y - y_0) = 0$$

$$a(x - x_0) = b(y_0 - y).$$

Divide both sides of the previous equation by d to get

$$(a/d)(x - x_0) = (b/d)(y_0 - y).$$

Proposition 7 tells us that $(a/d, b/d) = 1$, and we use proposition 13 to then show that $(a/d)|(y_0 - y)$. Thus, we can write $an/d = y_0 - y$ for some integer n, and so $y = y_0 - an/d$. If we insert this value of y back into

$$a(x - x_0) = b(y_0 - y)$$

we get $a(x - x_0) = b(an/d)$, and hence $x = x_0 + bn/d$, as desired.   ■

EXAMPLE.   The previous theorem allows us to find all solutions of the two equations presented at the beginning of this chapter. Consider again the equation $12x + 27y = 32$. The gcd of 12 and 27 is 3, which does not divide 32. Thus, this equation has no integer solutions. But the second equation, $12x + 27y = 30$, has infinitely many integer solutions since $3|30$. We find all the solutions by first finding a particular solution. First, note that integers s and t exist which solve $12s + 27t = (12, 27) = 3$, and proposition 12 tells us how to compute them. They are $s = -2$, $t = 1$. Thus, since $12(-2) + 27 \cdot 1 = 3$, we can multiply both sides of the equation by 10 to get $12(-20) + 27 \cdot 10 = 30$. So a particular solution to $12x + 27y = 30$ is $x_0 = -20$, $y_0 = 10$. Proposition 16 says all of the solutions to $12x + 27y = 30$ are then given by $x = -20 + 27n/3 = -20 + 9n$, and $y = 10 - 12n/3 = 10 - 4n$, $\forall$ integers n.

EXAMPLE.   Diophantine equations have real-world applications as well. Suppose you are at the grocery store with 4 dollars and 27 cents. Apples sell for 35 cents, and oranges for 49 cents. What combination of apples and oranges (if any) will exhaust your money? (Assume there is no sales tax.) We wish to find all integer solutions to the equation $35x + 49y = 427$. First, compute $(35, 49) = 7$, and note that $427 = 61 \cdot 7$, so $7|427$. Thus, the equation has infinitely many solutions. We find a particular solution by first solving $35s + 49t = 7$, and get $s = 3$, $t = -2$. Multiply both sides of $35 \cdot 3 + 49(-2) = 7$ by 61 to get $35 \cdot 183 + 49(-122)$ $= 427$, and get a particular solution to our equation; that is, $x_0 = 183$, and $y_0 = -122$. The

Table 4.1

n	Number of apples	Number of oranges	Total spent (in cents)
−26	183+7(−26)=1	−122−5(−26)=8	35•1+49•8=427
−25	183+7(−25)=8	−122−5(−25)=3	35•8+49•3=427

general solutions to the equation are then $x = 183 + 7n$, $y = -122 - 5n$ $\forall$ integers n. Since we obviously cannot buy a negative number of apples or oranges, we need to find which of these solutions are nonnegative. Thus we find that $x = 183 + 7n \geq 0$, or $n \geq -183/7 = -26\ 1/7$, and $y = -122 - 5n \geq 0$, or $n \leq -122/5 = -24\ 2/5$. Thus, n can only attain the values -26, and -25. Each of these values of n produces a satisfactory solution to our problem, which can be seen in the Table 4.1.

Note that with diophantine equations, it is only necessary to solve the equation $ax + by = c$ where a, b, and c are all positive, for if any of these are negative, the solution is still easily obtained by inverting some of the signs. For example, suppose $x = x'$ and $y = y'$ is a solution to $ax + by = c$, where a, b, and c are all positive. Then we have all of the following in case any one of the constants changes sign.

$$x = -x', y = -y' \text{ is a solution to } ax + by = -c,$$

$$x = -x', y = y' \text{ is a solution to } -ax + by = c, \text{ and}$$

$$x = x', y = -y' \text{ is a solution to } ax - by = c$$

One can easily solve for the other cases when 2 or all 3 of the constants change sign. More cases to consider are when one of a, b, or c is 0. For these cases we have

- $x = b$, $y = -a$ is a solution to $ax + by = 0$
- $x = 0$, $y = c/b$ is a solution to $0x + by = c$ (provided $b|c$)
- $x = c/a$, $y = 0$ is a solution to $ax + 0y = c$ (provided $a|c$)

Java Algorithm. We now write for the BigIntegerMath class a method to solve linear diophantine equations $ax + by = c$. Because of the previous discussion, we will allow only equations where a and b are positive, and c is nonnegative. You may wish to rewrite the method to solve equations when any of a, b, or c are negative, or zero. The method will accept the coefficients a and b, and the constant c as BigIntegers. If a or b are not positive, or if c is negative, it will throw an IllegalArgumentException. It will then compute $d = (a, b)$, and if $d \nmid c$, it will again throw an IllegalArgumentException. Otherwise, it will compute a particular solution $x = x'$, $y = y'$ to the equation, and return it in an array of BigIntegers. The element at index 1 will be x', and y' will be at index 2. For convenience, the gcd of a and b will be returned at index 0. This is useful if we want to display the general solution.

```
public static BigInteger[] solveLinearDiophantine (BigInteger a,
  BigInteger b,
```

FIGURE 4.1

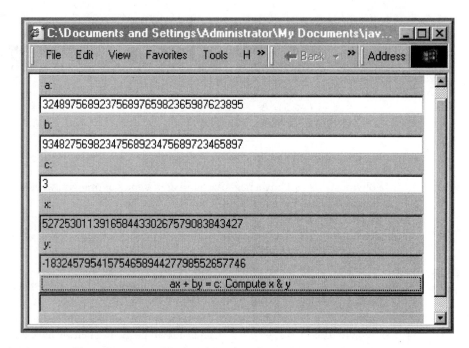

```
BigInteger c) throws IllegalArgumentException {
    if (a.compareTo(ZERO)<=0||b.compareTo(ZERO)<=0||c.compareTo(ZERO)<0)
        throw new IllegalArgumentException
        ("All constants must be positive in linear diophantine equation.");
    BigInteger[] euclidAnswers=euclid(a,b);
    if (c.mod(euclidAnswers[0]).compareTo(ZERO)!=0)
        throw new IllegalArgumentException
        ("No solution since "+euclidAnswers[0]+" does not divide "+c+".");
    BigInteger[] answer=new BigInteger[3];
    BigInteger q=c.divide(euclidAnswers[0]);
    answer[0]=euclidAnswers[0];
    answer[1]=q.multiply(euclidAnswers[1]);
    answer[2]=q.multiply(euclidAnswers[2]);
    return answer;
}
```

There is an applet called TestDiophantineApplet on the book's website you can use to solve linear diophantine equations. A screen shot of the applet solving a sample equation is shown in Figure 4.1.

4.2   LINEAR CONGRUENCES

Now we can begin the study of congruences, which are a special type of relation greatly influenced by and related to diophantine equations. They are used heavily in many cryptosystems. The definition of congruence follows.

> **Definition**
> Let m be a positive integer, and a and b integers. If $m|(a - b)$, we say that a is congruent to b modulo m, and write $a \equiv b \pmod{m}$. If $m \nmid (a - b)$, we say that a and b are incongruent modulo m (or not congruent modulo m), and write $a \not\equiv b \pmod{m}$.

EXAMPLES.   Note the following:

- $23 \equiv 2 \pmod 7$, since 7 divides $23 - 2 = 21$.
- $45 \equiv -7 \pmod{13}$, since $13|(45 - (-7) = 52)$.
- $10 \not\equiv 100$ modulo 4, since $4 \nmid (10 - 100) = -90$.

The following will help us solve linear congruences by allowing us to express them as equations.

PROPOSITION 17.   Integers a and b are congruent modulo m iff $\exists$ an integer k such that $a = b + km$.

Proof. $a \equiv b \pmod{m}$ iff $m|(a - b)$ iff $\exists$ an integer k with $a - b = km$, or $a = b + km$.
∎

EXAMPLE.

$$75 \equiv 3 \pmod 8$$

iff $8|(75 - 3)$

iff $8k = 75 - 3$ for some integer k

iff $75 = 8k + 3$ for some integer k

iff $k = 7$.

Congruences have many properties similar to equations. Some of these follow in the next proposition, and you should easily be able to prove all of them.

PROPOSITION 18.   Let a, b and c be integers, and let m be a positive integer. Then

a. $a \equiv a \pmod{m}$.

b. $a \equiv b \pmod{m}$ implies $b \equiv a \pmod{m}$.

c. $a \equiv b \pmod{m}$ and $b \equiv c \pmod{m}$ implies $a \equiv c \pmod{m}$.

EXAMPLES.

a. $7 \equiv 7 \pmod 9$ (Clearly, since $9|(7 - 7) = 0$).

b. $8 \equiv 2 \pmod 6$ and so $2 \equiv 8 \pmod 6$ (Since $6|(8 - 2) = 6$ iff $6|(2 - 8) = -6$).

c. $7 \equiv -3 \pmod 5$ and $-3 \equiv 2 \pmod 5$ implies $7 \equiv 2 \pmod 5$.

Proposition 18 tells us that congruences modulo m partition the integers into m distinct subsets modulo m, and each subset contains integers that are all congruent to each other modulo m. For example, congruences modulo 3 partition the integers into 3 subsets:

a. $\{\ldots, -9, -6, -3, 0, 3, 6, 9, \ldots\}$

b. $\{\ldots, -8, -5, -2, 1, 4, 7, 10, \ldots\}$

c. $\{\ldots, -7, -4, -1, 2, 5, 8, 11, \ldots\}$

All of the integers in set (a) are congruent to each other modulo 3. Likewise for sets (b) and (c). (Verify.) Also, there are no integers that do not belong to exactly one of these sets. Now, consider the subsets consisting of only the nonnegative members of sets (a), (b), and (c). Note that no such subset is empty, and so each will have a minimal element. For the set of nonnegative elements of set (a), this minimal element is 0. For set (b), the minimal positive element is 1, and 2 is the minimal positive element of set (c). These particular elements are often used as representatives of the congruence classes in which they reside, and a definition for them follows.

> **Definition**
> Let b be an integer, and let m be a positive integer. All integers congruent to b modulo m are called residues of b modulo m. The least nonnegative residue, or lnr, of b modulo m is the least nonnegative integer congruent to b modulo m.
>
> Again, note that such a least nonnegative residue always exists, just by noting that the least nonnegative residue r of c modulo $m > 0$ is the very same r obtained from the division algorithm
>
> $$c = dq + r \qquad 0 \le r < d$$
>
> which we already know always exists.

EXAMPLES.

a. The lnr of 29 modulo 13 is 3. That is, $3 \equiv 29 \pmod{13}$, and 3 is the smallest nonnegative integer congruent to 29 modulo 13.

b. $44 \equiv 2 \pmod 6$, and 2 is the smallest nonnegative number congruent to 44 modulo 6, hence it is the lnr of 44 modulo 6.

c. $-17 \equiv -2 \equiv 3 \pmod 5$, and 3 is the lnr of -17 modulo 5.

Note that in all of the examples, the lnr is just r from the division algorithm, for

a. $29 = 13 \cdot 2 + 3$,

b. $44 = 7 \cdot 6 + 2$, and

c. $-17 = 5 \cdot -4 + 3$.

Java Algorithm.   Since we now have the concept of the least nonnegative residue, we should write a Java method (in the BigIntegerMath class) to compute it. The BigInteger class provides a mod() method, but the Java documentation says it can return a negative remainder if the dividend is negative. We correct this by just adding the value of the modulus to the residue if it is negative. Also, recall that we do not allow negative moduli.

```
//Computes the least nonnegative residue of b mod m, where m>0.
public static BigInteger lnr(BigInteger b, BigInteger m) {
    if (m.compareTo(ZERO)<=0)
throw new IllegalArgumentException("Modulus must be positive.");
    BigInteger answer=b.mod(m);
    return (answer.compareTo(ZERO)<0)?answer.add(m):answer;
}
```

We would like to be able to form some rules of algebra for congruences. Many rules that hold for equations also hold for congruences.

PROPOSITION 19.   Let a, b, and c be integers, and let m be a positive integer. Suppose $a \equiv b \pmod{m}$. Then

a. $a + c \equiv b + c \pmod{m}$

b. $a - c \equiv b - c \pmod{m}$

c. $ac \equiv bc \pmod{m}$.

Proof.

a. We prove the first here. We have $a \equiv b \pmod{m}$, so $m|(a - b)$. But $a - b = (a + c) - (b + c)$, and this is divisible by m, hence $a + c \equiv b + c \pmod{m}$.

b. (For you to prove.)

c. (For you to prove.)   ■

We can do even better than the properties of proposition 19 when dealing with congruences. That is, we do not have to add, subtract, or multiply by the same element on both sides of a congruence to preserve it, but only by elements that are congruent modulo m. These properties are easily established, and are left to you to prove.

PROPOSITION 20.   Let a, b, c, and d be integers, and let m be a positive integer. Suppose $a \equiv b \pmod{m}$, and $c \equiv d \pmod{m}$. Then

a. $a + c \equiv b + d \pmod{m}$

b. $a - c \equiv b - d \pmod{m}$

c. $ac \equiv bd \pmod{m}$.

EXAMPLES. Note that $9 \equiv 2 \pmod 7$. Then all of the following are true:

- $(7 + 9) \equiv (-7 + 2) \pmod 7$

  Check: $(7 + 9) \equiv 16 \equiv 2 \pmod 7$ and $(-7 + 2) \equiv -5 \equiv 2 \pmod 7$

- $(3 - 9) \equiv (-4 - 2) \pmod 7$

  Check: $(3 - 9) \equiv -6 \equiv 1 \pmod 7$ and $(-4 - 2) \equiv -6 \equiv 1 \pmod 7$

- $(3 \cdot 9) \equiv (-4 \cdot 9) \pmod 7$

  Check: $(3 \cdot 9) \equiv 27 \equiv 6 \pmod 7$ and $(-4 \cdot 2) \equiv -8 \equiv 6 \pmod 7$

Note that a similar property for division does not appear in proposition 19 or proposition 20. This is because it isn't true in general. For example, note that $16 \equiv 4 \pmod{12}$, but that $16/2 = 8$ is not congruent modulo 12 to $4/2 = 2$. However, if we take the gcd of 12 and 2, note that 8 and 2 are congruent modulo $6 = 12/(12, 2)$. This is true in general, and we prove it thus:

PROPOSITION 21. Let a, b, and c be integers, and let m be a positive integer. Let $d = (c, m)$, and suppose $ac \equiv bc \pmod m$. Then $a \equiv b \pmod{m/d}$.

Proof. Since $ac \equiv bc \pmod m$, $m|(ac - bc) = c(a - b)$. Thus, there is an integer k such that $c(a - b) = km$. Divide both sides by d to get $(c/d)(a - b) = k(m/d)$. Proposition 7 says c/d and m/d are relatively prime, so $(m/d)|(a - b)$ by proposition 13. Thus, $a \equiv b \pmod{m/d}$. ∎

A special case occurs in the previous theorem when c and m are relatively prime, for then division by the integer c preserves the congruence modulo m. For example, note that $50 \equiv 15 \pmod 7$, and that $50 = 10 \cdot 5$, and $15 = 3 \cdot 5$. Since 5 is relatively prime to the modulus 7, we can factor it out on both sides of the congruence and still preserve it; that is, $10 \equiv 3 \pmod 7$.

EXAMPLES.

- $10 \equiv 4 \pmod 3$, so

  $10/2 \equiv 4/2 \pmod 3$, or

  $5 \equiv 2 \pmod 3$

- $30 \equiv 12 \pmod{18}$, so

  $30/3 \equiv 12/3 \pmod{18/3}$, or

  $10 \equiv 4 \pmod 6$.

We now have enough artillery in our arsenal to solve linear congruences. A linear congruence in one variable is of the form $ax \equiv b \pmod{m}$ where x is unknown. The following are examples of such congruences:

a. $9x \equiv 1 \pmod{45}$

b. $21z \equiv 9 \pmod{30}$

Some of these congruences have solutions, while others do not. For example, the congruence (b) has all of the following solutions for z:

$$z \equiv 9 \pmod{30}, \text{ since } 21 \cdot 9 = 189 \equiv 9 \pmod{30}$$

$$z \equiv 19 \pmod{30}, \text{ since } 21 \cdot 19 = 399 \equiv 9 \pmod{30}$$

$$z \equiv 29 \pmod{30}, \text{ since } 21 \cdot 29 = 609 \equiv 9 \pmod{30}$$

However, the congruence (a) has no solutions for x. Why? The following tells us when solutions exist, and how to find them.

PROPOSITION 22. Suppose $ax \equiv b \pmod{m}$, where b is an integer, and a and m are nonzero integers. Let $d = (a, m)$. If $d \nmid b$, the congruence has no solution for x. If $d|b$, then there are exactly d incongruent solutions modulo m, given by $x = x_0 + tm/d$, where x_0 is a particular solution to the linear diophantine equation $ax + my = b$, and $t = 0, 1, \ldots, d - 1$.

Proof. Proposition 7 says that the linear congruence $ax \equiv b \pmod{m}$ is equivalent to the linear diophantine equation $ax - mz = b$, or $ax + my = b$ where $y = -z$. The integer x is a solution of $ax \equiv b \pmod{m}$ iff $\exists$ an integer y such that $ax + my = b$. By proposition 16 we have no integer solutions to this equation if $d \nmid b$, but when $d|b$, we have infinitely many solutions given by

$$x = x_0 + mt/d, \ y = y_0 + at/d, \text{ where } x = x_0, y = y_0 \text{ is a particular solution.}$$

These values for x are then solutions to $ax \equiv b \pmod{m}$. To determine which solutions are congruent modulo m, suppose

$$x_0 + mr/d \equiv x_0 + ms/d \text{ where } r \text{ and } s \text{ are integers.}$$

Subtract x_0 from both sides to get

$$(m/d)r \equiv (m/d)s \pmod{m}$$

and note that $(m, m/d) = m/d$ since $(m/d)|m$. We then use proposition 21 to see that

$$r \equiv s \pmod{d}.$$

This says that two solutions $x_0 + mr/d$ and $x_0 + ms/d$ are congruent modulo m exactly when r and s are congruent modulo d. Thus, the complete set of incongruent solutions $x = x_0 + mt/d$ is obtained as t spans the integers $0, 1, \ldots, d - 1$. ∎

Just stating proposition 22 sounds like a mouthful, but using it to solve linear congruences is actually easy, as we'll see in the following examples. Note that for linear congruences, as with linear diophantine equations, we concern ourselves only with congruences where all the constants are positive. Congruences not in this form can easily be put so by replacing the values for a and b with their least nonnegative residues modulo m. For example, the congruence $143x \equiv -11 \pmod{121}$ yields exactly the same set of incongruent solutions as $22x \equiv 110 \pmod{121}$.

EXAMPLES.

- Find all incongruent solutions to $9x \equiv 7 \pmod{12}$. Note that $(9, 12) = 3$, and that $3 \nmid 7$. Therefore, there are no solutions.

- Find all incongruent solutions to $16x \equiv 12 \pmod{20}$. We compute $(16, 20) = 4$, and note that $4 \mid 12$. Thus, 4 incongruent solutions modulo 12 exist. We first find a particular solution by noting that solving $16x \equiv 12 \pmod{20}$ for x is the same as solving the linear diophantine equation $16x - 20y = 12$. Note that we may just as well solve the equation $16x + 20y = 12$ because we will discard the value obtained for y anyway. We find a particular solution to be $x = x_0 = -3$, $y = y_0 = 3$. The set of all incongruent solutions can be computed as

$$x = -3 + 0 \cdot (20/4) = -3 \equiv 17 \pmod{20}$$

$$x = -3 + 1 \cdot 5 \equiv 2 \pmod{20}$$

$$x = -3 + 2 \cdot 5 \equiv 7 \pmod{20}$$

$$x = -3 + 3 \cdot 5 \equiv 12 \pmod{20}.$$

The validity of each of these solutions is easily checked, and you are invited to do so.

Java Algorithm.   Surely you have noticed that solving a linear congruence simply means solving the appropriate linear diophantine equation. Therefore, writing a solveLinearCongruence() method in the BigIntegerMath class should be a snap.

```
public static BigInteger[] solveLinearCongruence(BigInteger a, BigInteger b,
BigInteger m) {
   BigInteger[] answers=solveLinearDiophantine(lnr(a,m),m,lnr(b,m));
   return answers;
}
```

I have written an applet called TestLinearCongruenceApplet which you can run from the book's website. Some screen shots are shown in Figures 4.2, 4.3, and 4.4.

Note that if there are multiple solutions, you can repeatedly press the "Next Solution" button to see the others.

4.3   MODULAR INVERSES

Congruences of the form $ax \equiv 1 \pmod{m}$ are considered special. Solutions for a to such congruences are called inverses of a, when they exist. The following definition formalizes this concept.

FIGURE 4.2

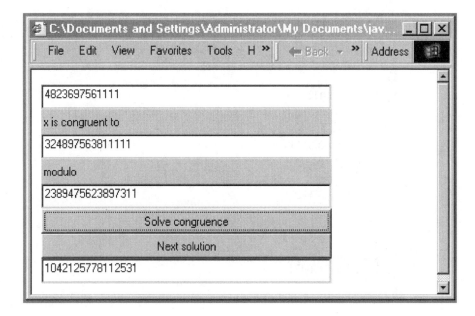

FIGURE 4.3

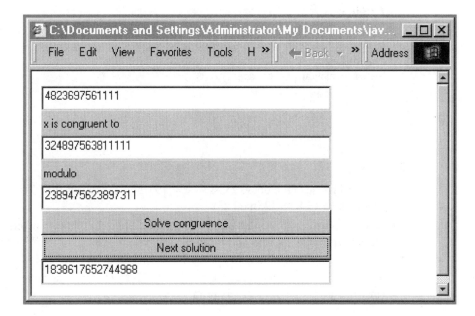

FIGURE 4.4

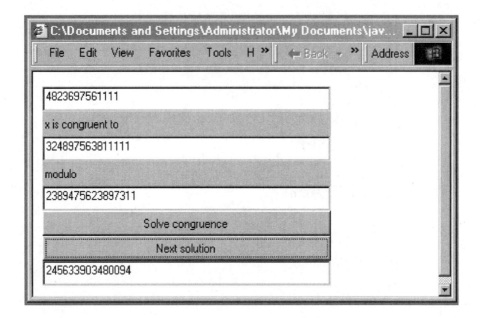

Definition

Note that the solution to $ax \equiv 1 \pmod{m}$ exists only when a is relatively prime to m, since (a, m) must divide 1. When such solutions exist, there is only one incongruent solution modulo m. A solution to such a congruence is called an inverse of a modulo m, and we write such an inverse as a'.

EXAMPLES.

- 19 is an inverse of 4 modulo 25, since $x \equiv 19 \pmod{25}$ solves $4x \equiv 1 \pmod{25}$. (Verify.) Thus, we write $4' \equiv 19 \pmod{25}$.

- A solution to $7x \equiv 1 \pmod{8}$ is $x \equiv 7 \pmod{8}$. Thus, 7 is its own inverse modulo 8, or we can write $7' \equiv 7 \pmod{8}$. This is easily checked, since $7 \cdot 7' \equiv 7 \cdot 7 \equiv 49 \equiv 1 \pmod{8}$.

- Now, consider the congruence $9x \equiv 1 \pmod{15}$. Note that 9 has no inverse modulo 15, since 9 and 15 are not relatively prime.

EXERCISES

1. Find all integer solutions to the following linear diophantine equations, if any exist:
   a. $42x + 30y = 20$

   b. $42x + 30y = 18$

   c. $252x + 198y = 90$

   d. $11x + 17y = 23$

   e. $12x + 32y = 10$

   f. $12x + 32y = 92$

   g. $36x + 81y = 117$

   h. $252x + 198y = 414$

2. Suppose for the apples and oranges example in this chapter that you have instead the following amounts of money:

   a. 2 dollars and 66 cents

   b. 3 dollars

   c. 7 dollars and 42 cents

   d. 91 cents

   Find all feasible solutions to the number of apples and oranges you should buy to exactly exhaust your money.

3. Dr. Fonebone goes to the post office to buy some 32¢ stamps and some 5¢ stamps. If the doctor spent $3.45, how many stamps of each type could he have bought?

4. Alien Commander Freenbean returns to her planet after a trip to Southeast Asia. If she exchanges her foreign currency and receives a total of 941 gznardls, where she receives 37 gznardls for each Philippine peso and 63 gznardls for each Thai baht, how much of each type of currency did she exchange? Are there multiple answers?

5. You are at a classy restaurant with only $18.17 in your pocket, and you are starving. Everything on the menu costs more than $20, except the following two items: breadsticks at $1.89 each, and large mountain oysters at $2.50 each. How much of each item should you buy to spend all your money?

6. What combination(s) of quarters and dimes totals $2.95?

7. Write a GUI or an applet to enter the values of a, b, and c for the linear diophantine equation $ax + by = c$. Display a particular solution $x = x_0$, $y = y_0$ in the window when the user presses a "compute" button. Subsequent presses of the same button should produce an alternate solution; the nth press should give the solution $x = x_0 + bn/d$, $y = y_0 - an/d$.

8. Solve all of the following congruences for x, when solutions exist. If solutions do not exist, explain why.

   a. $6x \equiv 4 \pmod{14}$

   b. $9x \equiv 7 \pmod{15}$

   c. $9x \equiv 21 \pmod{24}$

   d. $21x \equiv 9 \pmod{24}$

   e. $35x \equiv 21 \pmod{56}$

   f. $8x \equiv 7 \pmod{15}$

   g. $348975893461x \equiv 1 \pmod{9238745892364}$

    h. $46873258738754865x \equiv 3 \pmod{9283765872587542121751}$

9. Find an inverse of

    a. 10 modulo 21

    b. 5 modulo 8

    c. 6 modulo 21

    d. 13 modulo 30

    e. 13 modulo 143

    f. 14 modulo 15

    g. 33 modulo 121

    h. 985 modulo 2527

    i. 8 modulo 27

    j. 9 modulo 14

when such an inverse exists. If it does not exist, state the reason.

10. Prove proposition 18.

11. Prove proposition 19.

12. Prove proposition 20.

13. Consider how you might solve linear diophantine equations in more than two variables; for example, the equation

$$3x + 2y + 5z = 26$$

has $x = 5$, $y = 3$, $z = 1$ as a particular solution. How might you find this particular solution? Or any other? One approach you might take is to solve the equation

$$3x + 2y + 5z = 1$$

where $(3, 2, 5) = 1$, and remember that $(3, 2, 5) = ((3, 2), 5)$. That is, you can solve

$$3x + 2y = (3, 2) = 1$$

then use these values for x and y to solve the equation in three variables using the proper substitutions.

14. What combination(s) of quarters, dimes, and nickels equals 85¢?

15. How many ways can change be made for a dollar using

    a. quarters and dimes?

    b. quarters, dimes, and nickels?

16. What time does a 12-hour clock read

    a. 35 hours after 8 o'clock?

    b. 73 hours after 5 o'clock?

    c. 58 hours before 1 o'clock?

17. A satellite orbits the earth with period p hours, where $0 < p < 24$, and p is an integer. If the satellite is directly overhead at 1300 (on a 24-hour clock), then 7 orbits later is again directly overhead at 1800, what is p, the orbital period of the satellite?

18. Old Faithless is a geyser in Tibet that erupts every 5 hours. If it erupted at exactly 12 noon on June 2, 2000, when did it next erupt at exactly 12 noon?

19. The Screechids is a meteor shower through which the planet Mongo passes every 143 of its days. Mongo passed through the Screechids on its New Year's day in its year 10793. If the orbital period of Mongo is 299 of its days, when did Mongo next pass through the Screechids on New Year's day? (Mongo has no leap years, nor any other calendar adjustments.)

20. Consider now how you may solve a system of linear diophantine equations, as in the system

$$3x + 3y + 2z = 11$$

$$5x + y + 3z = 10$$

which has as a particular solution $x = 1$, $y = 2$, $z = 1$. Explain how such a solution (or any other particular solution) could be found. Does this system have infinitely many solutions?

21. Solve the following system of linear diophantine equations.

$$3x + y + 7z = 14$$

$$4x + 3z + z = 12$$

22. Solve the following system of linear diophantine equations.

$$3x + y + 7z = 14$$

$$4x + 3z + z = 12$$

$$2x + 5z + z = 10$$

23. Solve the following system of linear diophantine equations.

$$3x + y + 7z = 14$$

$$4x + 3z + z = 12$$

$$2x + 5z + z = 9$$

CHAPTER 5

Linear Ciphers

The earliest cryptosystems were simple character substitution ciphers; that is, ciphers which mapped individual characters to characters. These were the predecessors of stream ciphers. Stream ciphers may encipher characters, or they may encipher quantities as small as a single bit. What characterizes most modern stream ciphers is that the enciphering transformation enciphers quantities differently based on their position in the stream. The cipher that follows actually does not fit this definition, since its enciphering transformation always maps any particular character to the same character.

5.1 THE CAESAR CIPHER

The earliest known cipher is the Caesar cipher. This cipher simply replaces each letter in the plaintext with the letter three characters down. That is, if we are using the alphabet A thru Z, A is replaced with D, B is replaced with E, and so on, with the substitution wrapping around for letters near the end of the alphabet. (See Chapter 1, "A History of Cryptography.")

For convenience, each letter–number pair of the ordinary alphabet is shown in Table 5.1. We can represent the enciphering transformation as

$$C \equiv P + 3 \ (\text{mod } 26) \qquad 0 \leq C < 26$$

where C represents the ciphertext character, and P represents the plaintext character. To decipher, it is obvious that we solve the above congruence for P to get

$$P \equiv C - 3 \ (\text{mod } 26) \qquad 0 \leq P < 26.$$

A	B	C	D	E	F	G	H	I	J	K	L	M	N	O	P	Q	R	S	T	U	V	W	X	Y	Z
0	1	2	3	4	5	6	7	8	9	10	11	12	13	14	15	16	17	18	19	20	21	22	23	24	25

TABLE 5.1

In general, if we use an alphabet of size n, the enciphering transformation of a shift cipher is

$$C \equiv P + s \pmod{n} \qquad 0 \leq C < n.$$

We allow the shift s to be any number between 1 and $n - 1$.

EXAMPLE. Encipher the message

> THIS MESSAGE IS TOP SECRET

using the ordinary alphabet and a Caesar cipher with a shift of 3. When each letter is converted to a number, and we group into blocks of length 5, we get

> 19 7 8 18 12   4 18 18 0 6   4 8 18 19 14   15 18 4 2 17   4 19.

(Here, we group the items in blocks for readability.) After applying the enciphering transformation, each number becomes

> 22 10 11 21 15   7 21 21 3 9   7 11 21 22 17   18 21 7 5 20   7 22

and the ciphertext message is sent as

> WKLVP   HVVDI   HLVWR   SVHFU   HW.

Hopefully you can see that by shifting each of the ciphertext letters back three letters; that is, by applying the deciphering transformation

$$P \equiv C - 3 \pmod{26},$$

the plaintext is regained.

When writing programs to encipher/decipher, we will rarely use the ordinary alphabet. Computers already have a character–number association, since everything must be stored as a binary number inside a digital computer. There are various character representation schemes out there; most notable are ASCII, and EBCDIC. Java uses a character mapping called Unicode; programs using Java over the Internet usually encode characters in Unicode. The following is a partial listing of the Unicode sequence (the first 255 characters happen to be the same characters as in the ASCII sequence). The characters and their associated number code are listed. The first 32 characters (0 through 31) are nonprintable characters, and character #32 is the space. Thus, they are not shown here. (See Table 5.2.)

We will call the previous character–number association the "ASCII alphabet." In general, however, we will regard a message as merely an array of bytes, and will not concern ourselves with what the bytes represent.

Java Algorithm. To see the character encoding used by your system, the following Java program will help.

**TABLE 5.2
Partial
ASCII–Unicode
Table**

Partial ASCII - Unicode Table									
33 !	34 "	35 #	36 $	37 %	38 &	39 '	40 (	41)	42 *
43 +	44 ,	45 -	46 .	47 /	48 0	49 1	50 2	51 3	52 4
53 5	54 6	55 7	56 8	57 9	58 :	59 ;	60 <	61 =	62 >
63 ?	64 @	65 A	66 B	67 C	68 D	69 E	70 F	71 G	72 H
73 I	74 J	75 K	76 L	77 M	78 N	79 O	80 P	81 Q	82 R
83 S	84 T	85 U	86 V	87 W	88 X	89 Y	90 Z	91 [	92 \
93]	94 ^	95 _	96 `	97 a	98 b	99 c	100 d	101 e	102 f
103 g	104 h	105 i	106 j	107 k	108 l	109 m	110 n	111 o	112 p
113 q	114 r	115 s	116 t	117 u	118 v	119 w	120 x	121 y	122 z
123 {	124		125 }	126 ~						

```
public class DisplayCharacterSet {
    public static void main(String[] args) {
        for (int i=33;i<256;i++) System.out.print(i+" "+(char)i+"\t-");
    }
}
```

Here is the output of the program when I ran it:

```
-33 !   -34 "   -35 #   -36 $   -37 %   -38 &   -39 '   -40 (   -41 )   -42 *

-43 +   -44 ,   -45 -   -46 .   -47 /   -48 0   -49 1   -50 2   -51 3   -52 4

-53 5   -54 6   -55 7   -56 8   -57 9   -58 :   -59 ;   -60 <   -61 =   -62 >

-63 ?   -64 @   -65 A   -66 B   -67 C   -68 D   -69 E   -70 F   -71 G   -72 H

-73 I   -74 J   -75 K   -76 L   -77 M   -78 N   -79 O   -80 P   -81 Q   -82 R

-83 S   -84 T   -85 U   -86 V   -87 W   -88 X   -89 Y   -90 Z   -91 [   -92 \

-93 ]   -94 ^   -95 _   -96 `   -97 a   -98 b   -99 c   -100 d  -101 e  -102 f

-103 g  -104 h  -105 i  -106 j  -107 k  -108 l  -109 m  -110 n  -111 o  -112 p

-113 q  -114 r  -115 s  -116 t  -117 u  -118 v  -119 w  -120 x  -121 y  -122 z

-123 {  -124 |  -125 }  -126 ~  -127 ⌂  -128 ?  -129 ?  -130 ?  -131 ?  -132 ?

-133 ?  -134 ?  -135 ?  -136 ?  -137 ?  -138 ?  -139 ?  -140 ?  -141 ?  -142 ?
```

```
-143 ?   -144 ?   -145 ?   -146 ?   -147 ?   -148 ?   -149 ?   -150 ?   -151 ?   -152 ?

-153 ?   -154 ?   -155 ?   -156 ?   -157 ?   -158 ?   -159 ?   -160 á   -161 í   -162 ó

-163 ú   -164 ñ   -165 Ñ   -166 ª   -167 º   -168 ¿   -169 ⌐   -170 ¬   -171 ½   -172 ¼

-173 ¡   -174 «   -175 »   -176 ░   -177 ▒   -178 ▓   -179 │   -180 ┤   -181 ╡   -182 ╢

-183 ╖   -184 ╕   -185 ╣   -186 ║   -187 ╗   -188 ╝   -189 ╜   -190 ╛   -191 ┐   -192 └

-193 ┴   -194 ┬   -195 ├   -196 ─   -197 ┼   -198 ╞   -199 ╟   -200 ╚   -201 ╔   -202 ╩

-203 ╦   -204 ╠   -205 =   -206 ╬   -207 ╧   -208 ╨   -209 ╤   -210 ╥   -211 ╙   -212 ╘

-213 ╒   -214 ╓   -215 ╫   -216 ╪   -217 ┘   -218 ┌   -219 █   -220 ▄   -221 ▌   -222 ▐

-223 ▀   -224 α   -225 ß   -226 Γ   -227 π   -228 Σ   -229 σ   -230 µ   -231 τ   -232 Φ

-233 Θ   -234 Ω   -235 δ   -236 ∞   -237 φ   -238 ε   -239 ∩   -240 ≡   -241 ±   -242 ≥

-243 ≤   -244 ⌠   -245 ⌡   -246 ÷   -247 ≈   -248 °   -249 ·   -250 ·   -251 √   -252 ⁿ

-253 ²   -254 ■   -255  -
```

Java Algorithm.   Writing a program to encipher and decipher using shift transformations is very easy. In our Java programs, we will map bytes to bytes. The following is a program to encipher with shift transformations in Java. The modulus, however, is now 256. This is because the numeric range of a single byte is 0 through 255.

I have written an applet called TestCaesarCipherApplet which shows how the Caesar cipher operates. It can be found on, and run from, the book's website. Two pictures are shown in Figures 5.1 and 5.2.

FIGURE 5.1

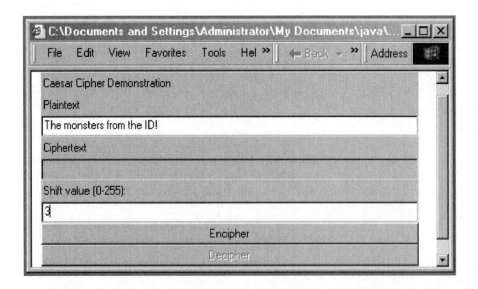

FIGURE 5.2

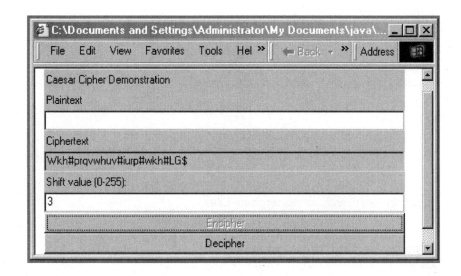

The code for this applet follows:

```java
import java.math.*;
import java.applet.*;
import java.awt.*;
import java.awt.event.*;
public class TestCaesarCipherApplet extends Applet implements ActionListener {

    int shift=0;
    byte[] msgArray=null;
    byte[] encmsgArray=null;

    Label titleLabel=new Label("Caesar Cipher Demonstration");
    Label Label1=new Label("Plaintext");
    TextField msg=new TextField(40);
    Label Label2=new Label("Ciphertext");
    TextField encmsg=new TextField(40);
    Label shiftLabel=new Label("Shift value (0-255):");
    TextField entryShiftValue=new TextField(40);
    Button encipherButton=new Button("Encipher");
    Button decipherButton=new Button("Decipher");

    public void init() {
        setLayout(new GridLayout(9,1));
        add(titleLabel);
        add(Label1);
        add(msg);
        add(Label2);
        add(encmsg);
        encmsg.setEditable(false);
        add(shiftLabel);
```

```
        add(entryShiftValue);
        add(encipherButton);
        encipherButton.addActionListener(this);
        add(decipherButton);
        decipherButton.addActionListener(this);
        decipherButton.setEnabled(false);
    }

    public void actionPerformed(ActionEvent e) {
        if (e.getSource()==encipherButton) {
            try {
                shift=Integer.parseInt(entryShiftValue.getText());
            } catch (NumberFormatException nfe) {
                shift=0;
            }
            msgArray=msg.getText().getBytes();
            encmsgArray=caesarEncipher(msgArray,shift);
            encmsg.setText(new String(encmsgArray));
            msg.setText("");
            encipherButton.setEnabled(false);
            decipherButton.setEnabled(true);
        } else if (e.getSource()==decipherButton) {
            msgArray=caesarDecipher(encmsgArray,shift);
            msg.setText(new String(msgArray));
            encmsg.setText("");
            decipherButton.setEnabled(false);
            encipherButton.setEnabled(true);
        }
    }

//The enciphering method.
    private static byte[] caesarEncipher(byte[] message,int shift) {
        byte[] m2=new byte[message.length];
        for (int i=0;i<message.length;i++) {
            m2[i]=(byte)((message[i]+shift)%256);
        }
        return m2;
    }

//The deciphering method.
    private static byte[] caesarDecipher(byte[] message,int shift) {
        byte[] m2=new byte[message.length];
        for (int i=0;i<message.length;i++) {
            m2[i]=(byte)((message[i]+(256-shift))%256);
        }
        return m2;
    }

}
```

Note that in this program, the BigInteger class (or the Int class) is not used. This is because it isn't necessary to use large integers when we are only shifting a single byte up or down by a maximum of 255. Regular Java ints work just fine. In the program, the user enters a shift value, and then the plaintext. It enciphers this as an array of bytes, and then converts the enciphered byte array back to a string and displays the ciphertext. Next it reverses the process and recovers the plaintext.

Note also that the message need not be text. Any type of data can be enciphered and deciphered, as long as it is first converted into an array of bytes.

5.2 WEAKNESSES OF THE CAESAR CIPHER

The Caesar Cipher is a secret key cryptosystem; that is, revealing the enciphering key makes decryption simple. In the Caesar cipher, the shift value is the enciphering key. Anyone knowing it can immediately decrypt, so it must be protected from unauthorized persons.

Ciphertext Only Attack. Whenever a cryptosystem can be broken by examining only the ciphertext, we call this a ciphertext only attack. As discussed previously, frequency analysis of the ciphertext can be used to break the Caesar cipher. Any cipher vulnerable to ciphertext only attack is considered completely insecure and should never be used.

Exhaustive Key Search. There is yet another method for breaking the Caesar cipher: simply try all the possible keys! After all, there are only 25 viable keys in the ordinary alphabet, and only 255 useful keys in the ASCII alphabet! This kind of attack is called an exhaustive search. An exhaustive search is rarely effective against all but the simplest of cryptosystems.

Seeing that the Caesar cipher is so vulnerable, we endeavor to develop stronger cryptosystems.

5.3 AFFINE TRANSFORMATION CIPHERS

After the Caesar cipher, the simplest type of enciphering transformation is the affine transformation, which multiplies each plaintext value by another number and then adds a shift. This may be represented by the congruence

$$C \equiv mP + b \pmod{n}$$

where n is the size of the alphabet. The multiplier m in the above congruence must be relatively prime to n, otherwise decryption is not possible. For in order to decrypt, we must solve the above congruence for P. A unique solution exists only if an inverse of m modulo n (denoted m') exists, which further only exists when $(m, n) = 1$. The inverse m' of m modulo n is easily obtained by using the extended Euclidean algorithm, and hence we have the deciphering transformation

$$P \equiv m'(C - b) \pmod{n}.$$

EXAMPLE.   Encipher

WAR LOST

using an affine transformation with the ordinary alphabet. Use 7 as the multiplier, and 10 as the shift. Then recover the plaintext. The ordinary alphabet associations are shown in Table 5.3:

A	B	C	D	E	F	G	H	I	J	K	L	M	N	O	P	Q	R	S	T	U	V	W	X	Y	Z
0	1	2	3	4	5	6	7	8	9	10	11	12	13	14	15	16	17	18	19	20	21	22	23	24	25

TABLE 5.3

The plaintext message, when the letters are converted to their numerical equivalents, yields

22 0 17 11 14 18 19

We then compute the following congruences:

$$C \equiv 7P + 10 \equiv 7 \cdot 22 + 10 \equiv 8 \ (\text{mod } 26)$$

$$C \equiv 7P + 10 \equiv 7 \cdot 0 + 10 \equiv 10 \ (\text{mod } 26)$$

$$C \equiv 7P + 10 \equiv 7 \cdot 17 + 10 \equiv 25 \ (\text{mod } 26)$$

$$C \equiv 7P + 10 \equiv 7 \cdot 11 + 10 \equiv 9 \ (\text{mod } 26)$$

$$C \equiv 7P + 10 \equiv 7 \cdot 14 + 10 \equiv 4 \ (\text{mod } 26)$$

$$C \equiv 7P + 10 \equiv 7 \cdot 18 + 10 \equiv 6 \ (\text{mod } 26)$$

$$C \equiv 7P + 10 \equiv 7 \cdot 19 + 10 \equiv 13 \ (\text{mod } 26)$$

The results of these calculations produce the ciphertext (in numbers)

8 10 25 9 4 6 13

or, the corresponding letters,

IKZJE   GN

To recover the plaintext, we must solve the congruence

$$C \equiv 7P + 10 \ (\text{mod } 26)$$

for P. Since 7 is relatively prime to 26, an inverse of it exists modulo 26, and it can be found solving the congruence

$$7x \equiv 1 \ (\text{mod } 26)$$

for x. Quick calculations using the extended Euclidean algorithm yield

$$x \equiv 15 \ (\text{mod } 26).$$

This value for x is an inverse of 7 modulo 26, and this is easily verified:

$$7x = 7(15) = 105 \equiv 1 \text{ (mod 26)}.$$

Thus, to recover the plaintext from the ciphertext, we crank it through the deciphering transformations:

$$C \equiv 15P - 10 \equiv 15 \cdot (8 - 10) \equiv 15 \cdot -2 \equiv 22 \text{ (mod 26)}$$

$$C \equiv 15P - 10 \equiv 15 \cdot (10 - 10) \equiv 15 \cdot 0 \equiv 0 \text{ (mod 26)}$$

$$C \equiv 15P - 10 \equiv 15 \cdot (25 - 10) \equiv 15 \cdot 15 \equiv 17 \text{ (mod 26)}$$

$$C \equiv 15P - 10 \equiv 15 \cdot (9 - 10) \equiv 15 \cdot -1 \equiv 11 \text{ (mod 26)}$$

$$C \equiv 15P - 10 \equiv 15 \cdot (4 - 10) \equiv 15 \cdot -6 \equiv 14 \text{ (mod 26)}$$

$$C \equiv 15P - 10 \equiv 15 \cdot (6 - 10) \equiv 15 \cdot -4 \equiv 18 \text{ (mod 26)}$$

$$C \equiv 15P - 10 \equiv 15 \cdot (13 - 10) \equiv 15 \cdot 3 \equiv 19 \text{ (mod 26)}$$

which gives us

22 0 17 11 14 18 19

or

WARLO   ST.

5.4 WEAKNESSES OF AFFINE TRANSFORMATION CIPHERS

Clearly, affine ciphers are secret key ciphers, since if m and b in the enciphering transformation $C \equiv mP + b$ (mod n) are revealed, it is easy to compute the inverse of m modulo n, and then decipher.

Ciphertext Only Attack–Frequency Analysis.   As with the Caesar cipher, breaking affine ciphers is easy. We may proceed as follows:

1. Suppose the message is English text, and we are using the ordinary alphabet A = 00, B = 01, ... , Z = 25. (Of course, the message may not be English text, or even text at all, but the principle remains the same.)

2. Note that the most common letter appearing in English text is "E"(= 4), followed by "T"(= 19).

3. Examine as much ciphertext as possible. The character appearing most often is probably the character "E" enciphered, and the second most frequent character is probably "T" enciphered.

4. Knowing what "E" and "T" map to allows us to calculate a and $b,$ and thus the mapping of all the other letters.

This can be easily seen with an example. Suppose the letter appearing most frequently in a large amount of ciphertext is "V," followed by "E." Then "E"(= 4) probably maps to "V"(= 21), and "T"(= 19) probably maps to "E"(= 4). We can then form the two congruences

$$21 \equiv 4a + b \ (\text{mod } 26) \quad (*)$$

$$4 \equiv 19a + b \ (\text{mod } 26).$$

Now, subtract the first congruence in (*) from the second (we can do this by proposition 20) to obtain

$$-17 \equiv 9 \equiv 15a \ (\text{mod } 26)$$

Solving this congruence (for a) yields:

$$a \equiv 11 \ (\text{mod } 26).$$

We can then replace a with 11 in one of the congruences in (*), then calculate the value for b. For example, solving $21 \equiv 4(11) + b \ (\text{mod } 26)$ for b yields

$$b \equiv 21 - 44 = -23 \equiv 3 \ (\text{mod } 26).$$

We can then calculate $11'$, an inverse of 11 modulo m. This we determine quickly to be

$$11' \equiv 19 \ (\text{mod } 26)$$

We can use this value along with b to decrypt a message. If it works, congratulations! If not, then our guesses for the mappings of "E" and "T" were incorrect.

Exhaustive Key Search.   Note that using ciphers which map single characters to characters in this way are simply not practical. If we are using a Caesar cipher with the ordinary alphabet, there are only 25 choices for the shift value b, and if we know that an affine cipher with the ordinary alphabet is being used, there are only 12 choices for the multiplier and 25 choices for the shift. A computer could test all of the possible combinations very quickly.

Monoalphabetic substitution ciphers should never be used. Even if we allow every possible character to character mapping in the ordinary alphabet, there are 25! = 15,511,210,043,330,985,984,000,000 such mappings. (To see this, note that when we map the letter "A" to another letter, we have 25 choices, assuming we want to map no letter to itself). When we map "B" we have 24 choices remaining (the mapping must be one-to-one; no two letters may map to the same letter), and so on. This makes a total of $25 \cdot 24 \ldots 2 \cdot 1 = 25!$ mappings. (See Table 5.4.)

TABLE 5.4

Choices for:																									
A	B	C	D	E	F	G	H	I	J	K	L	M	N	O	P	Q	R	S	T	U	V	W	X	Y	Z
2	2	2	2	2	2	1	1	1	1	1	1	1	1	1	1	9	8	7	6	5	4	3	2	1	0
5	4	3	2	1	0	9	8	7	6	5	4	3	2	1	0										

Certainly, 25! seems like a huge number (and it is), but even these generalized character-to-character mappings are vulnerable to the same frequency analysis used on Caesar ciphers. If enough ciphertext is examined, we can determine what most letters map to, then can fill out the rest of the letters by simply guessing.

5.5   THE VIGENERE CIPHER

As described in Chapter 1, the Vigenere cipher maps characters to characters based on a key which specifies multiple shifts. A key of length n represents a series of shifts $s_0, s_1, \ldots, s_{n-1}$. The enciphering transformation maps the ith character of the plaintext message $P = p_0, p_1, \ldots, p_{t-1}$ to the ith ciphertext character of the ciphertext message $C = c_0, c_1, \ldots, c_{t-1}$ in this way:

$$c_i \equiv p_i + s_r \pmod{m} \qquad\qquad (0 \le c_i < m, 0 \le i < t)$$

where

$$r \equiv i \pmod{n} \qquad\qquad (0 \le r < n).$$

EXAMPLE.   For convenience in the following example, we provide a table of character-to-number associations for the ordinary alphabet. (See Table 5.5.)

We will use the ordinary alphabet, and the keyword SPACE representing the shifts $s_0 = 18$, $s_1 = 15$, $s_2 = 0$, $s_3 = 2$, and $s_4 = 4$. The plaintext message is

DANGER WILL ROBINSON.

So using the Vigenere transformation, we compute the following (see Table 5.6). Thus, the ciphertext message (grouped in blocks of 5 characters) is

VPNII   JLINP   JDBKR   KDN

Vigenere ciphers fall prey to frequency analysis, just like monoalphabetic substitution ciphers. See Chapter 1 to see how this is done.

To get around the weaknesses posed by ciphers which map single characters to single characters, we may wish to construct mappings that deal with entire blocks of characters. There are certainly many more ways to construct such a mapping; these are called block ciphers.

A	B	C	D	E	F	G	H	I	J	K	L	M	N	O	P	Q	R	S	T	U	V	W	X	Y	Z
0	1	2	3	4	5	6	7	8	9	10	11	12	13	14	15	16	17	18	19	20	21	22	23	24	25

TABLE 5.5   Table of character-to-number associations for the ordinary alphabet

TABLE 5.6

i	r	s_r	p_i	c_i
0	0	18	3	21
1	1	15	0	15
2	2	0	13	13
3	3	2	6	8
4	4	4	4	8
5	0	18	17	9
6	1	15	22	11
7	2	0	8	8
8	3	2	11	13
9	4	4	11	15
10	0	18	17	9
11	1	15	14	3
12	2	0	1	1
13	3	2	8	10
14	4	4	13	17
15	0	18	18	10
16	1	15	14	3
17	2	0	13	13

5.6 BLOCK AFFINE CIPHERS

We construct an affine transformation that maps four-letter blocks to other four-letter blocks. We will call this a block affine cipher. Suppose we are using the numerical alphabet 00, 01, ..., 99, and suppose the numerals 00 through 25 represent the letters A through Z, respectively. (For now, we'll just say that 26 through 99 are unassigned; the reason we've extended the ordinary alphabet in this way will become clear soon.) The message to send (in characters) is

HOWDY DOO

First, regroup the letters into blocks of size four,

HOWD   YDOO

and convert each letter into its numerical equivalent, grouping the digits together to form a large integer. Each character gets two digits; A = 00, B = 01, and so on. Leading zeros are significant.

07142203   24031414

Note that the largest integer which can appear in a block of size four in the ordinary alphabet is ZZZZ = 25252525. Thus, we will choose 25252526 as our modulus. To construct an affine cipher mapping,

$$C \equiv mP + b \pmod{25252526}$$

we choose any shift b between 1 and 25252525, and any multiplier m relatively prime to 25252526. Say we choose $b = 23210025$ and $m = 21035433$. (Verify that this choice of m is relatively prime to 25252526.) We use these values to map each block to another. For the first block we get

$$C \equiv 21035433 \cdot 7142203 + 23210025 = 150239355888924 \equiv 8007496 \pmod{25252526}$$

and for the second we compute

$$C \equiv 21035433 \cdot 24031414 + 23210025 = 505511222302287 \equiv 20470469 \pmod{25252526}.$$

This gives us the enciphered message

08007496   20470469

and this is the message that is sent. Note that no digit pair greater than 25 has an equivalent in the ordinary alphabet, and the digit pairs 74, 96, 47, and 69 all appear in the above message. (Now you can see why we took 00, 01, ... , 99 as our alphabet.) Note that if there are less than eight digits in the block, we add leading zeros. To decrypt, we must find an inverse modulo 25252526 of $m = 21035433$. A quick computation with the extended Euclidean algorithm reveals $m' = 5174971$. Using this value and the congruence

$$P \equiv m'(C - b) \pmod{n}$$

we can convert the first enciphered block back to its plaintext form,

$$P \equiv 5174971(8007496 - 23210025) \equiv 7142203 \pmod{25252526}$$

and then the second

$$P \equiv 5174971(20470469 - 23210025) \equiv 24031414 \pmod{25252526}$$

which returns us to our plaintext message

HOWD YDOO

5.7 WEAKNESSES OF THE BLOCK AFFINE CIPHER–KNOWN PLAINTEXT ATTACK

This cipher, though not vulnerable to frequency analysis, is vulnerable to a different kind of attack, called a known plaintext attack. This is when the cryptanalyst has both the ciphertext and the corresponding plaintext for a particular message. (This is not so unlikely; one plaintext message getting into enemy hands is good enough for this to work. We always assume that the cryptanalyst has easy access to every ciphertext message.) Say the analyst has ciphertext blocks C_1 and C_2, and their corresponding plaintext blocks P_1 and P_2. These values are known, and it is only left to calculate m and b from the two congruences

$$C_1 \equiv mP_1 + b \;(\text{mod } n)$$

$$C_2 \equiv mP_2 + b \;(\text{mod } n).$$

We assume that the block size, and hence the value of the modulus, is also known to the cryptanalyst. (If not, it shouldn't be hard to figure out simply by trying different values.)

EXAMPLE. Suppose we use the message HOWDY DOO, as previously presented, with the same values for the multiplier $m = 21035433$ and shift $b = 23210025$. Suppose someone eavesdrops on our transmission and easily gets the ciphertext

08007496   20470469.

But somehow, through devious means he also gets the plaintext message

HOWDY DOO

or

07142203   24031414.

To obtain the values for m and b, he must simply solve the two congruences

$$8007496 \equiv 7142203\,m + b \;(\text{mod } 25252526)$$

$$20470469 \equiv 24031414\,m + b \;(\text{mod } 25252526)$$

for m and b. He subtracts the first congruence from the second to get

$$12462973 \equiv 16889211\,m \;(\text{mod } 25252526)$$

which he can solve quickly to get $m \equiv 21035433 \;(\text{mod } 25252526)$. Replacing m in the first congruence with 21035433, he gets

$$8007496 \equiv 7142203 \cdot 21035433 + b \;(\text{mod } 25252526),$$

which is then easily solved for b to yield

$$b \equiv 23210025 \;(\text{mod } 25252526).$$

Though a known plaintext attack may be thought unlikely, especially by egomaniacs running a "secure" facility, it is dangerous to use block affine ciphers for this reason, even though they are used in many applications today. Thus, we continue to develop better enciphering methods. However, before we move on to the next topic, we need to address the topic of padding.

5.8   PADDING METHODS

Note that when we use block ciphers, the size of the message we are sending may not be a multiple of the block size. For example, when we are using a block size of four,

    HOWDY DOO   =   HOWD   YDOO

is a perfect multiple of the block size, but

    HOWDY FOLKS   =   HOWD   YFOL   KS

is not. When this happens, we must pad the end of the message so that it becomes a perfect block. We may choose to pad with some character, such as the letter X, as in

    HOWD   YFOL   KSXX

or we may pad with zeros once we have converted the message into its numerical equivalent, like

    07142203   24051411   10180000.

This is not really satisfactory, as the characters or digits that we choose to pad with may well be a valid part of the message, and not padding at all. This might possibly create confusion at the receiving end. One solution to this problem is PKCS#5, a proposed standard method of padding.

PKCS#5 Padding.   This type of padding works like this: suppose the block size is 64 bytes, and the message is 125 bytes long. This makes 1 complete block, plus 61 bytes, 3 bytes short of a full block. To complete the block, we append 3 bytes, each containing the number 3, as seen in Figure 5.3 (in binary):

FIGURE 5.3

The message is now encrypted, and sent. On the receiving end, the message is decrypted. The last block is inspected, and the last 3 bytes, each containing the number 3, are removed. In general, if our message is N bytes short of a full block, we append N blocks, each containing the number N.

What if our last block is complete? With PKCS#5, we add padding anyway! If our block size is 64 bytes, and our message is 128 bytes, we will still append 64 bytes (each byte containing the number 64) to the message! Why is this done? Suppose the message being sent is an exact multiple of the block size. Now, suppose the last 6 bytes of the message happen to contain the number 6. How is the receiver to know whether this is padding or part of the message? She doesn't. This is why we append an entire block to messages that are already perfect multiples of the block size.

Note that PKCS#5 padding has a limitation: It cannot be used for ciphers in which the ciphertext block size exceeds 255 bytes. This should be simple to see if you note that each byte of padding in PKCS#5 contains a binary number revealing the number of bytes of padding. Clearly, $11111111_{(base\ 2)} = 255$ is the largest number we can write in a byte, so a complete block of 255 bytes would be padded as shown in Figure 5.4.

FIGURE 5.4

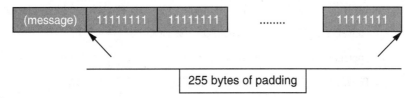

255 bytes of padding

Java Algorithm.   Block ciphers are difficult to write, not because the enciphering transformations are any more difficult, but because you must pad/unpad and block/unblock the messages. To do all this, we will write a Ciphers class; it will contain methods to do all the blocking and padding activities, and methods to encipher and decipher using various transformations. The first will be the block affine transformation. For better readability (hopefully), the explanation for the code is interspersed with the code:

```
import java.math.*;
public class Ciphers {
```

The following is the padding method. You pass in the message and the block size. It computes the number of blocks, then pads using the PKCS#5 scheme. This means padding is added even if the message is a perfect multiple of the block size. It also means that any ciphers using this method are effectively limited to a maximum block size of 255 bytes.

```
private static byte[] pad(byte[] msg,int blockSize) {
    //Check that block size is proper for PKCS#5 padding
    if (blockSize<1||blockSize>255) throw new
IllegalArgumentException("Block size must be between 1 and 255.");
    //Pad the message
    int numberToPad=blockSize-msg.length%blockSize;
    byte[] paddedMsg=new byte[msg.length+numberToPad];
    System.arraycopy(msg,0,paddedMsg,0,msg.length);
    for (int i=msg.length;i<paddedMsg.length;i++) paddedMsg[i]=(byte)numberToPad;
    return paddedMsg;
}
```

This method takes a padded message, then converts it to a 2-dimensional byte array. Each "vector" in this 2D array is a block. The enciphering methods will work with this 2D array.

```
private static byte[][] block(byte[] msg,int blockSize)  {
    //Create a 2D array of bytes corresponding to the message-all blocks should be
    //full
    int numberOfBlocks=msg.length/blockSize;
    byte[][] ba=new byte[numberOfBlocks][blockSize];
    for (int i=0;i<numberOfBlocks;i++)
        for (int j=0;j<blockSize;j++)
            ba[i][j]=msg[i*blockSize+j];
    return ba;
}
```

This method "unblocks" the message; that is, after the enciphering or deciphering transformation, it takes the 2D array of blocks, then converts it back to a linear array of bytes. The method must be careful to take into account that the enciphering or deciphering transformation may produce an integer smaller than the block size. In that case, it fills in the linear array from the rear of the block.

```
private static byte[] unBlock(byte[][] ba,int blockSize) {
    //Create the 1D array in which to place the enciphered blocks
    byte[] m2=new byte[ba.length*blockSize];
    //Place the blocks in the 1D array
    for (int i=0;i<ba.length;i++) {
        int j=blockSize-1;
        int k=ba[i].length-1;
        while (k>=0) {
            m2[i*blockSize+j]=ba[i][k];
            k--;
            j--;
        }
    }
    return m2;
}
```

This method removes the padding. All it has to do is examine the numerical value in the last block, then remove exactly that many blocks.

```
private static byte[] unPad(byte[] msg,int blockSize) {
    //Determine the amount of padding-just look at last block
    int numberOfPads=(msg[msg.length-1]+256)%256;
    //Chop off the padding and return the array
    byte[] answer=new byte[msg.length-numberOfPads];
    System.arraycopy(msg,0,answer,0,answer.length);
    return answer;
}
```

Finally, here are the enciphering and deciphering methods for the block affine cipher. Each accepts a message, the block size, and the values of *a* and *b* from the enciphering transformation

$$C \equiv aP + b.$$

```
public static byte[] affineEncipher(byte[] msg,int blockSize,BigInteger a,BigInteger
b) {
    //Compute the modulus
    BigInteger modulus=BigInteger.valueOf(2).pow(8*blockSize);
    //Check the multiplier
    if (!(modulus.gcd(a).equals(BigIntegerMath.ONE))) throw new
        IllegalArgumentException("Enciphering key is not relatively prime to the
        modulus.");
    byte ba[][]=block(pad(msg,blockSize),blockSize);
    //Begin the enciphering
    for (int i=0;i<ba.length;i++)
      ba[i]=getBytes(a.multiply(new BigInteger(ba[i])).add(b).mod(modulus));
    return unBlock(ba,blockSize);
}


public static byte[] affineDecipher(byte[] msg,int blockSize,BigInteger a,BigInteger
b) {
    //Compute the modulus
    BigInteger modulus=BigInteger.valueOf(2).pow(8*blockSize);
    //Check the multiplier
    if (!(modulus.gcd(a).equals(BigIntegerMath.ONE))) throw new
        IllegalArgumentException("Enciphering key is not relatively prime to the
        modulus.");
    //Compute inverse of a
    BigInteger ainv=a.modInverse(modulus);
    byte[][] ba=block(msg,blockSize);
    //Begin the deciphering
    for (int i=0;i<ba.length;i++)
        ba[i]=getBytes(BigIntegerMath.lnr(ainv.multiply(new
        BigInteger(ba[i]).subtract(b)),modulus));
    //Go from blocks to a 1D array, and remove padding; return this
    return unPad(unBlock(ba,blockSize),blockSize);
}
```

This following method is necessary. In order to encipher or decipher, at some point we convert BigIntegers back into an array of bytes using the toByteArray() method from the BigInteger class. This method, in addition to returning the binary representation of the Big-Integer, also returns a sign bit in the high order bit position. This can screw up everything if the BigInteger already fills up the block; in this case the extra sign bit forces another byte to be created. When this happens, we must remove the forward byte. This is never a problem for us, as all of the BigIntegers we use are positive; thus the sign bit is always 0.

```
//Method to rectify the extra bit problem of the toByteArray() method
private static byte[] getBytes(BigInteger big) {
   byte[] bigBytes=big.toByteArray();
   if (big.bitLength()%8!=0) return bigBytes;
   else {
      byte[] smallerBytes=new byte[big.bitLength()/8];
      System.arraycopy(bigBytes,1,smallerBytes,0,smallerBytes.length);
      return smallerBytes;
   }
}
```
}

This is the end of the Ciphers class. More methods will be added later, as we develop more cryptosystems.

}

I have written an applet called TestBlockAffineCipherApplet to test this cipher. The applet can be viewed online at the book's website. Two screen shots are shown in Figures 5.5 and 5.6.

FIGURE 5.5

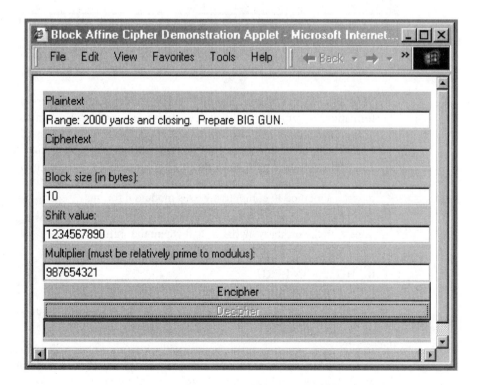

FIGURE 5.6

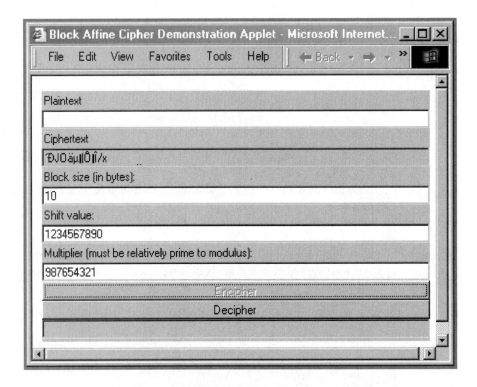

EXERCISES

1. Writing a program to encipher and decipher individual characters using affine transformations is very easy. All you need do is use a method that computes inverses mod *n*, and the rest is as easy as writing the Caesar cipher. Write a TestAffineCipherApplet class which tests the two static methods affineEncipher(), and affineDecipher(). These last two methods should accept an array of bytes (a message), along with the enciphering key(s), and return an array of bytes. You must use primitive ints, so you need to write a method to compute inverses modulo *n* for ints.

2. Encipher, and then decipher, the following messages using Caesar shift transformations with the ordinary alphabet, and where the shift *b* = 23.

   a. KENNEDY IS DEAD

   b. HITLER IN PERU

   c. BIG BROTHER

3. Repeat the previous exercise but use a single character affine cipher with a multiplier of 15 and a shift of 6.

4. Repeat the previous exercise, but use a block affine cipher with a block size of 4 characters per block. Use 25252526, the appropriate value for the modulus (using the ordinary alphabet), and use 1542327 for the multiplier, and 9923411 for the shift. Pad messages that are not multiples of the block size with the letter X.

CHAPTER 6

Systems of Linear Congruences—Single Modulus

In this chapter we will discuss systems of linear congruences. The systems we consider will be of two types:

1. Multiple linear congruences consisting of several variables, modulo a single modulus.

2. Multiple linear congruences consisting of a single variable, modulo different moduli.

Here, we discuss systems of type 1. For these types of systems, you should know how to handle systems of equations, as well as matrices. Take the following example of a system of linear congruences with multiple variables modulo a single modulus:

$$5x + 3y + 2z \equiv 2 \ (\text{mod } 7)$$

$$3x + 4y + 6z \equiv 1 \ (\text{mod } 7) \qquad (*)$$

$$2x + y + z \equiv 4 \ (\text{mod } 7)$$

6.1 MODULAR MATRICES

Note that we can write this in matrix notation as $AX \equiv B \ (\text{mod } 7)$ where A is

$$\begin{vmatrix} 5 & 3 & 2 \\ 3 & 4 & 6 \\ 2 & 1 & 1 \end{vmatrix}$$

X is the column vector

$$\begin{vmatrix} x \\ y \\ z \end{vmatrix}$$

and B is the vector

$$\begin{vmatrix} 2 \\ 1 \\ 4 \end{vmatrix}$$

where congruence for matrices and matrix multiplication are defined as follows:

Definition
We say two $k \times p$ matrices A and B are congruent to each other modulo n if each entry $a_{i,j} \equiv b_{i,j} \pmod n$ for $i = 1, \ldots, k, j = 1, \ldots, p$.

EXAMPLES.   Here are some examples of congruent matrices.

$$\begin{vmatrix} 3 & 4 \\ 1 & -8 \end{vmatrix} \equiv \begin{vmatrix} 13 & -6 \\ 21 & 2 \end{vmatrix} \pmod{10}$$

$$\begin{vmatrix} 0 & 1 & 2 \\ 1 & 1 & 1 \\ 2 & 0 & 0 \end{vmatrix} \equiv \begin{vmatrix} 6 & 7 & 8 \\ -2 & -5 & 1 \\ 11 & 9 & 15 \end{vmatrix} \pmod 3$$

$$\begin{vmatrix} 6 & 5 & 4 & 3 \\ 0 & 0 & 6 & 4 \\ 1 & 2 & 3 & 3 \\ 0 & 0 & 1 & 7 \end{vmatrix} \equiv \begin{vmatrix} 0 & -1 & -2 & -3 \\ 0 & -6 & 0 & -2 \\ 7 & 2 & -3 & -9 \\ 6 & 0 & -5 & 1 \end{vmatrix} \pmod 6$$

Definition
If A is an $m \times n$ matrix, and B is an $n \times p$ matrix, the matrix product $C = AB$ is the $m \times p$ matrix

$$\begin{vmatrix} c_{1,1} & c_{1,2} & \cdots & c_{1,p} \\ c_{2,1} & c_{2,2} & \cdots & c_{2,p} \\ \cdots & \cdots & & \cdots \\ c_{m,1} & c_{m,2} & \cdots & c_{m,p} \end{vmatrix}$$

where the i, jth entry of C is $\Sigma a_{i,k} b_{k,j}$ $k = 1, 2, \ldots, n$.

This simply means we multiply the entries of the ith row of A by the entries of the jth column of B, then sum them up to get the i, jth entry of $C = AB$. This also means, of course, that the number of columns of the first matrix must be the same as the number of rows in the second matrix. An example illustrating this process is shown in Table 6.1.

To use matrices to solve linear systems of congruences, we must determine whether or not the operations we use for ordinary matrices representing systems of equations still hold

TABLE 6.1

$$\begin{vmatrix} 1 & 2 & 5 & 1 \\ 2 & 4 & 0 & 0 \end{vmatrix} \bullet \begin{vmatrix} 3 & 1 & 3 \\ 1 & 7 & 0 \\ 0 & 1 & 1 \\ 0 & 2 & 1 \end{vmatrix} = \begin{vmatrix} 5 & 1 \bullet 1 + 2 \bullet 7 + 5 \bullet 1 + 1 \bullet 2 = 22 & 9 \\ 10 & 30 & 6 \end{vmatrix}$$

for matrices when used for congruences. Recall from linear algebra the three basic row operations that are permitted on matrices; we will modify these rules slightly:

1. Any two rows may be exchanged.

2. Any row may be multiplied by a nonzero scalar.

3. A multiple of any row may be added to another row.

We redefine the three elementary row operations for matrices used to represent a system of congruences:

Definition
The three elementary row operations for matrices modulo n are:

1. Any two rows may be exchanged.
2. Any row may be multiplied by an integer scalar relatively prime to the modulus. (Call this a multiple of a row.)
3. A multiple of a row may be added to another row.

We will show now that when the elementary operations are defined this way, they do not affect the solutions to a system of congruences.

PROPOSITION 23. When matrices are used to represent a system of linear congruences, the three elementary row operations for matrices do not affect the solution(s) of the corresponding system of congruences modulo n.

Proof. Operation 1 clearly still holds if the matrices are representing congruences, for switching the order of the congruences in a system does not affect the solution. If scalars are always understood to be integers, then multiplying both sides of a congruence by a scalar that is relatively prime to the modulus will not alter the solution. To see this, consider the congruence

$$acx + bcy \equiv dc \;(\text{mod } n) \quad (\$)$$

where c is relatively prime to n. Suppose $x = x'$, $y = y'$ is a solution to this congruence; that is,

$$acx' + bcy' \equiv dc \;(\text{mod } n).$$

Then we have

$$ax' + by' \equiv d \;(\text{mod } n)$$

by Proposition 21, and so $x = x'$, $y = y'$ is also a solution to the congruence

$$ax + by \equiv d \;(\text{mod } n). \quad (\$\$)$$

Clearly, the reverse is also true: If $x = x_0$, $y = y_0$ is a solution to ($\$\$$), then it is also a solution to ($\$$). So, the solutions to ($\$$) and ($\$\$$) are identical when $(c, n) = 1$, so operation 2 also holds for matrices representing congruences, provided the scalar multiple is relatively prime to the modulus. Lastly, it is clear from proposition 20 that operation 3 is still valid for matrices when they are used to represent congruences. Proposition 20 says we can add congruent items to both sides of a congruence without changing the congruence.   ■

Thus, we can solve the previous system (*) using elementary row operations on the augmented matrix. We will attempt to produce an upper triangular matrix, then use back substitution to obtain values for the variables. When this is done using matrices defined over the real numbers it is called Gaussian elimination; we may as well call it that in this setting, too.

$$\begin{vmatrix} 5 & 3 & 2 & 2 \\ 3 & 4 & 6 & 1 \\ 2 & 1 & 1 & 4 \end{vmatrix}$$

The augmented matrix $A|B$.

$$\begin{vmatrix} 5 & 3 & 2 & 2 \\ 6 & 1 & 5 & 2 \\ 2 & 1 & 1 & 4 \end{vmatrix}$$

Multiply second row by 2; all operations are done modulo 7 and the least nonnegative residue is retained.

$$\begin{vmatrix} 5 & 3 & 2 & 2 \\ 0 & 5 & 2 & 4 \\ 2 & 1 & 1 & 4 \end{vmatrix}$$

Subtract 3 times third row from second row.

$$\begin{vmatrix} 5 & 3 & 2 & 2 \\ 0 & 5 & 2 & 4 \\ 5 & 6 & 6 & 3 \end{vmatrix}$$

Multiply third row by 6.

$$\begin{vmatrix} 5 & 3 & 2 & 2 \\ 0 & 5 & 2 & 4 \\ 0 & 3 & 4 & 1 \end{vmatrix}$$

Subtract first row from third row.

$$\begin{vmatrix} 5 & 3 & 2 & 2 \\ 0 & 5 & 2 & 4 \\ 0 & 5 & 2 & 4 \end{vmatrix}$$

Multiply third row by 4.

$$\begin{vmatrix} 5 & 3 & 2 & 2 \\ 0 & 5 & 2 & 4 \\ 0 & 0 & 0 & 0 \end{vmatrix}$$

Subtract second row from third row. Here we obtain a row of all zeros (mod 7), so we cannot get a unique solution in this case. (Here, of course, we take a unique solution to mean that all other solutions are congruent to it).

$$\begin{vmatrix} 1 & 2 & 6 & 6 \\ 0 & 1 & 6 & 5 \\ 0 & 0 & 0 & 0 \end{vmatrix}$$

Multiply both the first and second rows by 3, an inverse of 5 modulo 7. This gives the following solutions for the system:

$y \equiv -6z + 5 \equiv z + 5 \pmod 7$, and

$x \equiv -2y - 6z + 6 \equiv 5y + z + 6 \equiv 5(z + 5) + z + 6 \equiv 6z + 25 + 6 \equiv 6z + 3 \pmod 7$.

If we allow z to range from 0 through 6, we can list all of the incongruent solutions to this system. They are presented in Table 6.2, and you are asked to recompute each solution and to verify each of them.

The preceding example teaches us an important lesson: that systems of congruences may have multiple solutions due to linear dependence, as it is in linear algebra. Of course, when dealing with congruences, we have finitely many incongruent solutions, rather than infinitely many solutions as when dealing with systems of equations defined over the real numbers.

6.2 MODULAR MATRIX INVERSES

Later on it will be useful for us to be able to obtain the inverse of a square $m \times m$ matrix A modulo n. That is, we will wish to find the matrix M such that $MA \equiv AM \equiv I \pmod n$, where I is the $m \times m$ identity matrix.

$$\begin{vmatrix} 1 & 0 & 0 & \cdots & 0 \\ 0 & 1 & 0 & \cdots & 0 \\ 0 & 0 & 1 & \cdots & 0 \\ \cdots & \cdots & \cdots & \cdots & \cdots \\ 0 & 0 & 0 & 0 & 1 \end{vmatrix}$$

Of course, an inverse modulo n of a matrix A may not exist, but when it does, we denote it as A'. We should be able to find it by forming the augmented matrix $A|I$, and using Gauss–Jordan elimination with elementary row operations. We illustrate how this will be done with an example; we will attempt to find an inverse modulo 5 of the 2×2 matrix A, which is

$$\begin{vmatrix} 1 & 4 \\ 2 & 2 \end{vmatrix}$$

TABLE 6.2

x	3	2	1	0	6	5	4
y	5	6	0	1	2	3	4
z	0	1	2	3	4	5	6

Specifically, we are looking for a matrix A' such that

$$A'A \equiv AA' \equiv I \,(\text{mod } 5).$$

We begin by joining the matrix A with the 2×2 identity matrix.

$$\begin{vmatrix} 1 & 4 & 1 & 0 \\ 2 & 2 & 0 & 1 \end{vmatrix}$$

The augmented matrix $A|I$.

$$\begin{vmatrix} 1 & 4 & 1 & 0 \\ 0 & 4 & 3 & 1 \end{vmatrix}$$

Subtract twice the first row from the second row. All operations are done modulo 5, and the least nonnegative residue is retained.

$$\begin{vmatrix} 1 & 0 & 3 & 4 \\ 0 & 4 & 3 & 1 \end{vmatrix}$$

Subtract the second row from the first row.

$$\begin{vmatrix} 1 & 0 & 3 & 4 \\ 0 & 1 & 2 & 4 \end{vmatrix}$$

Multiply the second row by 4, an inverse of 4 modulo 5. Now, we have A', an inverse of A modulo 5; it is the matrix

$$\begin{vmatrix} 3 & 4 \\ 2 & 4 \end{vmatrix}$$

To verify that this is an inverse of A modulo 5, take the product AA' (you could also take $A'A$), and verify that you get the 2×2 identity matrix. We do this here:

$$\begin{vmatrix} 1 & 4 \\ 2 & 2 \end{vmatrix}\begin{vmatrix} 3 & 4 \\ 2 & 4 \end{vmatrix} \equiv \begin{vmatrix} 1 & 0 \\ 0 & 1 \end{vmatrix} (\text{mod } 5)$$

Now that we have discussed finding inverses, we discuss how they may be used. When an inverse modulo n of a square matrix A exists, it is quite useful in solving linear systems of congruences, for if

$$AX \equiv B \,(\text{mod } n),$$

then by finding A', an inverse of A modulo n, we can find the solutions by multiplying both sides of the congruence by A':

$$A'AX \equiv A'B \,(\text{mod } n).$$

The left-hand side of the above simplifies to

$$A'AX \equiv IX \equiv X \,(\text{mod } n),$$

which then yields

$$X \equiv A'B \,(\text{mod } n).$$

The matrices A' and B are both known; we simply take the product $A'B$ modulo n to get our solutions for X. (Note: Linear algebra says that when I is the identity matrix, $IX = X$, so certainly $IX \equiv X \pmod{n}$.)

EXAMPLE. Find the solutions to $AX \equiv B \pmod 5$ by finding A' where A is the matrix

$$\begin{vmatrix} 1 & 4 \\ 2 & 2 \end{vmatrix}$$

X is the vector

$$\begin{vmatrix} x \\ y \end{vmatrix}$$

and B is the vector

$$\begin{vmatrix} 3 \\ 2 \end{vmatrix}.$$

We already found the inverse A' of A modulo 5 earlier; it is the matrix

$$\begin{vmatrix} 3 & 4 \\ 2 & 4 \end{vmatrix}$$

and to use it to find X, we simply take the product $A'B$:

$$\begin{vmatrix} 3 & 4 \\ 2 & 4 \end{vmatrix}\begin{vmatrix} 3 \\ 2 \end{vmatrix} \equiv \begin{vmatrix} 17 \\ 14 \end{vmatrix} \equiv \begin{vmatrix} 2 \\ 4 \end{vmatrix} \pmod 5$$

We now verify that $x \equiv 2 \pmod 5$ and $y \equiv 4 \pmod 5$ is actually a solution to the system of congruences

$$x + 4y \equiv 3 \pmod 5$$
$$2x + 2y \equiv 2 \pmod 5.$$

Substitution reveals

$$2 + 4 \cdot 4 = 18 \equiv 3 \pmod 5$$
$$2 \cdot 2 + 2 \cdot 4 = 12 \equiv 2 \pmod 5$$

and the solution checks.

You may have noticed something amiss in multiplying both sides of the congruence $AX \equiv B \pmod n$ by some matrix A' in order to solve for X. Namely, how do we know that multiplying both sides of a matrix congruence by a matrix preserves the congruence? That is, if two $n \times k$ matrices A and B are such that $A \equiv B \pmod m$, is it true that $AC \equiv BC \pmod m$ for any $k \times p$ matrix C, and that $DA \equiv DB \pmod m$ for any $q \times n$ matrix D? The next proposition shows that this is the case, and thus vindicates our seeming recklessness.

PROPOSITION 24. Suppose two $n \times k$ matrices A and B are such that $A \equiv B \pmod m$. Then $AC \equiv BC \pmod m$ for any $k \times p$ matrix C, and $DA \equiv DB \pmod m$ for any $q \times n$ matrix D.

Proof.   Suppose the matrices are as stated. Note that the i, jth entries in the product matrices AC and BC are $\Sigma a_{i,t} c_{t,j}$ and $\Sigma b_{i,t} c_{t,j}$, respectively. Since $A \equiv B$ (mod m), we have $a_{i,t} \equiv b_{i,t}$ (mod m) $\forall$ i and t, and so

$$\Sigma a_{i,t} c_{t,j} \equiv \Sigma b_{i,t} c_{t,j} \pmod{m}$$

by proposition 20, which says congruent items (mod m) can be added to both sides of a congruence (mod m) and preserve the congruence. Thus, $AC \equiv BC$ (mod m). The proof that $DA \equiv BA$ (mod m) is nearly identical to the previous; you are invited to do it.   ∎

Java Algorithm.   In this chapter we discussed modular arithmetic and congruences for matrices. This is a perfect opportunity to define a useful class for these purposes. We can call it the ModMatrix class; it represents a matrix whose elements are all taken modulo m.

ModMatrix objects need not be square; we will define how to add, subtract, and multiply them. There will be exceptions thrown if the matrices are of the improper size. Of course, matrices are not invertible unless they are square (and sometimes not even then), so we will develop a subclass of ModMatrix called ModSquareMatrix. It will have the appropriate methods for inverting matrices. Finally, we will also define a ModIdentityMatrix class, which extends ModSquareMatrix.

First, the ModMatrix class: its data items will consist of a two dimensional array of BigIntegers, a BigInteger representing the modulus, and ints to record the number of rows and number of columns in the matrix.

```
import java.math.BigInteger;
import java.security.*;
public class ModMatrix {
  //A ModMatrix is a 2D array of BigIntegers
  BigInteger[][] array;

  //Number of columns/rows recorded here
  int numRows, numCols;

  //The modulus of the ModMatrix
  BigInteger modulus;
```

The ModMatrix constructors are of different types. The first produces either a matrix of all zeros or of random entries, the second reads a one-dimensional array into a two-dimensional matrix, and the third simply copies another matrix. The last constructor is the default constructor, which accepts no arguments. It does nothing, but is used by the subclasses we define.

```
//Creates a matrix with random entries having r rows, c columns,
//Or, it creates a matrix of all zeros
//Matrices start indexing at 1,1.  Zeroth column and row are not used.
public ModMatrix(int r,int c,BigInteger m,boolean makeZero) {
      SecureRandom sr=new SecureRandom();
      modulus=m;
      array=new BigInteger[r+1][c+1];
```

```
        numRows=r;
        numCols=c;
        for (int i=0;i<r;i++) {
            for (int j=0;j<c;j++) {
                //If makeZero set to true, make the zero matrix
                if (makeZero) array[i+1][j+1]=new BigInteger("0");
                //otherwise, make matrix with random entries
                else array[i+1][j+1]=new
BigInteger(modulus.bitLength(),sr).mod(modulus);
            }
        }
    }


    //Creates a matrix getting its values from the 1D array a.
    //If array is not long enough to fill matrix, zeros are used.
    public ModMatrix(int r,int c,BigInteger[] a, BigInteger m) {
        modulus=m;
        //Make the 2D array larger than specified-indices start at 1,1
        array=new BigInteger[r+1][c+1];
        numRows=r;
        numCols=c;
        for (int i=0;i<r;i++) {
            for (int j=0;j<c;j++) {
                int pos=i*c+j;
                //Set values for the matrix from the array
                if (pos<a.length&&a[pos]!=null)
                    array[i+1][j+1]=BigIntegerMath.lnr(a[pos],m);
                //If we have run out of input from the array, fill rest of matrix
                //with zeros
                else array[i+1][j+1]=new BigInteger("0");
            }
        }
    }


    //Makes a copy of another ModMatrix
    public ModMatrix(ModMatrix m) {
        array=new BigInteger[m.numRows+1][m.numCols+1];
        numRows=m.numRows;
        numCols=m.numCols;
        modulus=m.modulus;
        for (int i=1;i<=m.numRows;i++) {
            for (int j=1;j<=m.numCols;j++) {
                array[i][j]=new BigInteger(m.array[i][j].toString());
            }
        }
    }
```

```
//This is the default constructor; it does nothing-required for subclass
public ModMatrix() {}
```

The methods of this class must provide us with the ability to retrieve the number of rows or columns, the modulus, and individual elements in the matrix. We should also be able to set entries in the matrix. Thus, the following methods are provided.

```
//Methods declared here-get rows or columns or modulus of the ModMatrix
public int rows() {return numRows;}
public int columns() {return numCols;}
public BigInteger getModulus() {return modulus;}

//Allows one to retrieve an element.
public BigInteger getElement(int row,int column) {return array[row][column];}

//Allows one to set the value of an element-least nonnegative residue always used
public void setElement(int row,int column,BigInteger value) {
        array[row][column]=BigIntegerMath.lnr(value,modulus);
}
```

These are the methods that will be most useful; those that add, subtract, and multiply two matrices. The least nonnegative residue modulo *m* is always maintained.

```
//Adds two matrices together and returns result.
public ModMatrix add(ModMatrix m) throws MatricesNonConformableException {
        ModMatrix result;
        //Matrices must be the same dimensions and have same modulus to be added
        //together
        if (!modulus.equals(m.modulus)) throw new MatricesNonConformableException
            ("These matrices cannot be added; different moduli.");
        if (numRows==m.numRows&&numCols==m.numCols) {
                //Make a new ModMatrix for the sum-start with zero matrix
                result=new ModMatrix(numRows,numCols,modulus,true);
                //Add i,j-th entries of each to get i,j-th entry of result
                for (int i=1;i<=numRows;i++) {
                    for (int j=1;j<=numCols;j++) {

result.array[i][j]=BigIntegerMath.lnr(array[i][j].add(m.array[i][j]),modulus);
                    }
                }
        } else throw new MatricesNonConformableException
        ("These matrices cannot be added; different dimensions.");
        return result;
}

//Subtracts 2nd matrix from 1st and returns result.
```

```
public ModMatrix subtract(ModMatrix m) throws MatricesNonConformableException {
    //Multiply the 2nd matrix by the scalar -1 then add them-see
    //multiply(BigInteger) method
    return this.add(m.multiply(new BigInteger("-1")));
}


//Multiplies two matrices.
public ModMatrix multiply(ModMatrix m) throws MatricesNonConformableException {
    ModMatrix result;
    //Both matrices must be using the same modulus
    if (!modulus.equals(m.modulus)) throw new MatricesNonConformableException
("These matrices cannot be multiplied; different moduli.");
    //If # rows in 2nd matrix = # columns in 1st matrix, they can be multiplied
    //together
    if (m.numRows==numCols) {
            result=new ModMatrix(numRows,m.numCols,modulus,true);
            //Move down the rows in outer loop
            for (int i=1;i<=numRows;i++) {
                //Multiply i-th row of 1st by j-th column of 2nd
                for (int j=1;j<=m.numCols;j++) {
                    //Start the i,j-th entry of result at zero
                    result.array[i][j]=new BigInteger("0");
                    //i,j-th entry is sum of i,k-th entry of 1st times k,j-th
                    //entry of 2nd for all k
                    for (int k=1;k<=m.numRows;k++)
                        result.array[i][j]=BigIntegerMath.lnr
(result.array[i][j].add(array[i][k].multiply(m.array[k][j]))),modulus);
                }
            }
    } else throw new MatricesNonConformableException
    ("These matrices cannot be multiplied!");
    return result;
}


//Multiplies a matrix by a scalar.
public ModMatrix multiply(BigInteger scalar) {
    ModMatrix result=new ModMatrix(numRows,numCols,modulus,true);
    for (int i=1;i<=numRows;i++)
        for (int j=1;j<=numCols;j++)
            //Multiply i,j-th entry by the scalar

result.array[i][j]=BigIntegerMath.lnr(array[i][j].multiply(scalar),modulus);
    return result;
}
```

Many of the methods of ModMatrix throw a MatricesNonConformableException; this means the matrices were simply of the wrong dimensions to do the operation.

```
public class MatricesNonConformableException extends Exception {
  public MatricesNonConformableException() {super();}
  public MatricesNonConformableException(String s) {super(s);}
}
```

The following test applet, called TestModMatrixCalculatorApplet, just verifies that the arithmetic methods as we have defined them actually work. It is a calculator for modular matrices. The applet and its source code can be found on the book's website. A screen shot is shown in Figure 6.1.

The ModSquareMatrix inherits all methods from the ModMatrix class, and supplies other methods to do Gaussian elimination modulo n. It also uses these same methods to produce an inverse modulo n. Of course, if the Gaussian elimination fails an exception will be thrown; namely, either a SingularMatrixException or an ArithmeticException. The gaussianSolve() method I have written here only works when the modulus is prime; you will be asked in the exercises to modify the method so that it works with a composite modulus.

```
public class SingularMatrixException extends Exception {
  public SingularMatrixException() {super();}
  public SingularMatrixException(String s) {super(s);}
}
```

The ModSquareMatrix class definition follows:

```
import java.math.BigInteger;
import java.security.*;
import java.util.*;
//ModSquareMatrix objects inherit all methods from ModMatrix
public class ModSquareMatrix extends ModMatrix {

  //Creates a square matrix with random entries
  //Or, it creates a matrix with all zeros
```

FIGURE 6.1

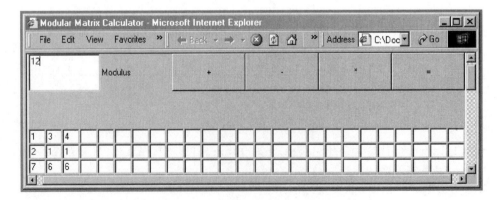

```
    //Another parameter specifies whether or not you wish the random
    //matrix to be invertible; if NOT, matrix may still be invertible by accident
    public ModSquareMatrix(int s,BigInteger m,boolean makeZero,boolean
makeInvertible)
    throws MatricesNonConformableException {

//Call a superconstructor from ModMatrix-make the zero matrix,
        // or a matrix with random entries
        super(s,s,m,makeZero);

        //Zero matrix is not invertible
        if (makeZero&&makeInvertible) throw new IllegalArgumentException
          ("Zero matrix cannot be inverted!");

        //A random invertible matrix is desired
        if (makeInvertible) {
          Random r=new Random();
          SecureRandom sr=new SecureRandom();
          boolean done=false;
          //Do this until the matrix inverts
          while (!done) {
            try {
                //Try to take the inverse-may throw an exception if not
                //invertible
                this.inverse();
                done=true;
            } catch (SingularMatrixException sme) {
                //Change a random entry in the matrix
                int row=Math.abs(r.nextInt())%numRows+1;
                int col=Math.abs(r.nextInt())%numCols+1;
                BigInteger value=new
                    BigInteger(modulus.bitLength(),sr).mod(modulus);
                this.setElement(row,col,value);
            } catch (ArithmeticException ae) {
                //Change a random entry in the matrix
                int row=Math.abs(r.nextInt())%numRows+1;
                int col=Math.abs(r.nextInt())%numCols+1;
                BigInteger value=new
                    BigInteger(modulus.bitLength(),sr).mod(modulus);
                this.setElement(row,col,value);
            }
          }
        }
    }
```

```
//Makes a square matrix from a 1D array of values
public ModSquareMatrix(int s,BigInteger[] a,BigInteger m) {
    super(s,s,a,m);
}

//Makes a copy of a matrix
public ModSquareMatrix(ModSquareMatrix m) {
    array=new BigInteger[m.numRows+1][m.numCols+1];
    numRows=m.numRows;
    numCols=m.numCols;
    modulus=m.modulus;
    for (int i=1;i<=m.numRows;i++) {
        for (int j=1;j<=m.numCols;j++) {
            array[i][j]=new BigInteger(m.array[i][j].toString());
        }
    }
}

//Method which uses Gaussian elimination to solve AX=B mod m for X
//A is the ModSquarematrix calling the method
//B is the Modmatrix constants - need not be a Vector
//X is the ModMatrix returned
public ModMatrix gaussianSolve(ModMatrix constants) throws
   MatricesNonConformableException,SingularMatrixException {
   //This method only works when the modulus is prime
   if (!modulus.isProbablePrime(16)) throw new IllegalArgumentException
      ("Gaussian elimination method currently requires modulus to be prime!");
   //Copy the matrices and modify the copies
   ModSquareMatrix mat=new ModSquareMatrix(this);
   ModMatrix b;

   //If the ModMatrix constants is square, the answer should also be a
   //ModSquareMatrix object
   //(not just a ModMatrix)
   //Check for this here
   if (constants instanceof ModSquareMatrix)
       b=new ModSquareMatrix((ModSquareMatrix)constants);
   else b=new ModMatrix(constants);

   //Check if matrices are of compatible size first
   if (b.numRows!=mat.numRows) throw new MatricesNonConformableException
   ("Matrix of coefficients and matrix of constants have different # of rows!");

   //Work the rows, starting with the first row
   int currentRow=1;
   while (currentRow<=mat.numRows) {
```

```
        int i=currentRow;
        //Make sure diagonal element is nonzero, if possible, by swapping
        while
            (i<=mat.numRows&&mat.array[i][currentRow].equals(BigIntegerMath.ZERO))
            i++;
        if (i>mat.numRows) throw new SingularMatrixException
            ("Linear dependence exists here!");
        //Swap with a row not having zero in diagonal position
        if (currentRow!=i) swapRows(mat,b,currentRow,i);
        //Now, you must produce all zeros below and above the diagonal element
        i=1;
        //Multiply each row by the proper scalar
        while (i<=mat.numRows) {
            if (i!=currentRow) {
                BigInteger scalar=mat.array[i][currentRow];
                if (!scalar.equals(BigIntegerMath.ZERO)) {
                    multiplyRow(mat,b,i,mat.array[currentRow][currentRow]);
                    multiplyRow(mat,b,currentRow,scalar);
                    //Replace row i with row i minus diagonal row
                    subtractRow(mat,b,i,currentRow);
                }
            }
            i++;
        }
        currentRow++;
    }
    //Now, produce 1's along main diagonal by multiplying by an inverse
    for (int index=1;index<=mat.numRows;index++) {
        multiplyRow(mat,b,index,mat.array[index][index].modInverse(modulus));
    }
    //Remember, b may be a square matrix-polymorphism takes care of this here
    return b;
}


//This method exists in case the answer is actually a square matrix
public ModSquareMatrix gaussianSolve(ModSquareMatrix constants)
    throws MatricesNonConformableException,SingularMatrixException {
    return (ModSquareMatrix) gaussianSolve((ModMatrix)constants);
}


//Used by gaussianSolve to multiply a row by some scalar
private void multiplyRow(ModSquareMatrix mat,ModMatrix b,int i,BigInteger
scalar) {
    //Multiplies row i by scalar-answer replaces i-th row
    for (int k=1;k<=mat.numCols;k++)
mat.array[i][k]=BigIntegerMath.lnr(mat.array[i][k].multiply(scalar),mat.modulus);
```

```
        for (int k=1;k<=b.numCols;k++)
b.array[i][k]=BigIntegerMath.lnr(b.array[i][k].multiply(scalar),mat.modulus);
    }


    //Used by gaussianSolve to subtract one row from another
    private void subtractRow(ModSquareMatrix mat,ModMatrix b,int i,int j) {
        //Subtracts row j from row i; answer replaces row i
        for (int k=1;k<=mat.numCols;k++)
mat.array[i][k]=BigIntegerMath.lnr(mat.array[i][k].subtract(mat.array[j][k]),mat.
modulus);
        for (int k=1;k<=b.numCols;k++)
b.array[i][k]=BigIntegerMath.lnr(b.array[i][k].subtract(b.array[j][k]),mat.modulus)
;
    }


    //Used by gaussianSolve to swap two rows
    private void swapRows(ModSquareMatrix mat,ModMatrix b,int r1,int r2) {
        BigInteger temp;
        for (int j=1;j<=mat.numCols;j++) {
            temp=mat.array[r1][j];
            mat.array[r1][j]=mat.array[r2][j];
            mat.array[r2][j]=temp;
        }
        for (int j=1;j<=b.numCols;j++) {
            temp=b.array[r1][j];
            b.array[r1][j]=b.array[r2][j];
            b.array[r2][j]=temp;
        }
    }


    //Method produces an inverse of A (if possible) by using gaussianSolve on AX=I
    //mod m
    //where I is an identity matrix
    public ModSquareMatrix inverse() throws
MatricesNonConformableException, SingularMatrixException {
        //See the ModIdentityMatrix class-subclass of ModSquareMatrix
        return gaussianSolve(new ModIdentityMatrix(numRows,modulus));
    }
}
```

Finally, we define a ModIdentityMatrix class, which is a subclass of the ModSquare-Matrix class. We use it in the inverse() method of ModMatrix, by generating the augmented matrix AII to produce an inverse of A.

```
import java.math.BigInteger;
//ModIdentityMatrix objects inherit all methods from ModSquareMatrix, and from
ModMatrix
```

FIGURE 6.2

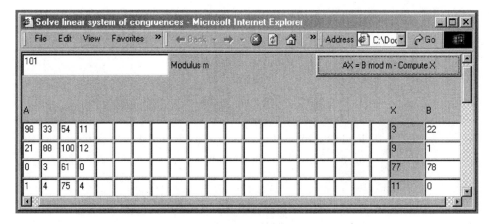

```java
public class ModIdentityMatrix extends ModSquareMatrix {

   //Make a ModSquareMatrix whose diagonal elements are all 1, zeros elsewhere
   public ModIdentityMatrix(int n,BigInteger mod) throws
                        MatricesNonConformableException {
      //Call a super constructor first, making zero matrix
      super(n,mod,true,false);
      //Set the diagonal elements to 1
      for (int i=1;i<=n;i++) array[i][i]=new BigInteger("1");
   }

}
```

I have written a test applet called TestLinearSystemSolveApplet to test Gaussian elimination modulo m. Consider the congruence $AX \equiv B$ (mod m). The user enters the modulus m, the square matrix of coefficients A, and a vector of constants B. If a unique solution X exists modulo m, the applet will compute and display it. The applet and its source code can be found on the book's website. A screen shot is shown in Figure 6.2.

EXERCISES

1. Solve the following systems of linear congruences, if any solutions exist. For any systems that have multiple solutions, report all the solutions.

    a. $2x + 5y \equiv 1$ (mod 11)

        $3x + 2y \equiv 7$ (mod 11)

    b. $2x + 5y \equiv 1$ (mod 11)

        $3x + 2y \equiv 6$ (mod 11)

    c. $4x + 3y + z \equiv 2$ (mod 7)

        $y + 3z \equiv 5$ (mod 7)

        $2x + 6y + 3z \equiv 0$ (mod 7)

    d. $11x + 12y + z \equiv 1 \pmod{23}$

        $15x + 20y + 22z \equiv 11 \pmod{23}$

        $3x + 9y \equiv 12 \pmod{23}$

    e. $11x + 12y + z \equiv 1 \pmod{23}$

        $15x + 20y + 22z \equiv 11 \pmod{23}$

        $3x + 9y \equiv 10 \pmod{23}$

2. Find an inverse of the matrix A modulo n, if such an inverse exists.

    a. $n = 26$, and matrix A follows:

$$\begin{vmatrix} 2 & 7 \\ 5 & 1 \end{vmatrix}$$

    b. $n = 25$, and matrix A follows:

$$\begin{vmatrix} 1 & 2 & 0 \\ 3 & 0 & 1 \\ 4 & 3 & 2 \end{vmatrix}$$

    c. $n = 7$, and matrix A follows:

$$\begin{vmatrix} 2 & 0 & 0 \\ 3 & 3 & 0 \\ 6 & 1 & 2 \end{vmatrix}$$

    d. $n = 13$, and matrix A follows:

$$\begin{vmatrix} 1 & 0 & 9 & 0 \\ 0 & 2 & 3 & 0 \\ 3 & 4 & 0 & 1 \\ 10 & 1 & 2 & 1 \end{vmatrix}$$

3. Write a transpose() method for the ModMatrix class which returns the transpose of a matrix. The transpose of a matrix is simply the matrix "flipped over"; that is, the $m \times n$ matrix becomes an $n \times m$ matrix where the i, jth element in the transpose is just the j, ith element of the original. For example, the transpose of

$$\begin{vmatrix} 1 & 2 \\ 3 & 4 \\ 5 & 6 \end{vmatrix}$$

is

$$\begin{vmatrix} 1 & 3 & 5 \\ 2 & 4 & 6 \end{vmatrix}$$

4. Modify the gaussianSolve() method so that it works for matrices whose modulus is not prime.

CHAPTER 7

Matrix Ciphers

Matrices offer us an alternative way to implement a linear block cipher. We will call such a matrix-based cryptosystem a matrix cipher. In the matrix ciphers, we use an enciphering transformation

$$C \equiv AP + B \pmod{n}$$

but now A is a $m \times m$ matrix (called the enciphering matrix), P is a column vector of numbers corresponding to a block of plaintext letters of length m, and B is a column vector of length m. (When B is the zero vector, these are called Hill ciphers.) To decipher, we must again solve for P:

$$AP + B \equiv C \pmod{n}$$

$$AP \equiv C - B \pmod{n}$$

$$P \equiv IP \equiv A'AP \equiv A'(C - B) \pmod{n}.$$

(Proposition 24 allows us to multiply both sides of a congruence by a matrix and preserve the congruence.) A' represents an inverse of A modulo n; that is, A' must satisfy the congruence

$$A'A \equiv I \pmod{n}$$

where I represents the identity matrix. A must be chosen, of course, so that it has an inverse modulo n.

EXAMPLE. We use the ordinary alphabet, so $n = 26$. Let the enciphering matrix A be

$$\begin{vmatrix} 5 & 17 \\ 4 & 15 \end{vmatrix}$$

let the shift vector B be

$$\begin{vmatrix} 5 \\ 2 \end{vmatrix}$$

and the message is THE END, which we split into blocks of size 2 to get TH EE ND. To encipher the plaintext TH, we use the vector P, which is

$$\begin{vmatrix} 19 \\ 7 \end{vmatrix}$$

and crank it through the transformation $AP + B \equiv C \pmod{26}$.

$$\begin{vmatrix} 5 & 17 \\ 4 & 15 \end{vmatrix} \begin{vmatrix} 19 \\ 7 \end{vmatrix} + \begin{vmatrix} 5 \\ 2 \end{vmatrix} \equiv \begin{vmatrix} 11 \\ 1 \end{vmatrix} \pmod{26}$$

The number pair 11, 1 corresponds to the letter pair LB, and so this is the ciphertext. We now encipher the pair EE

$$\begin{vmatrix} 5 & 17 \\ 4 & 15 \end{vmatrix} \begin{vmatrix} 4 \\ 4 \end{vmatrix} + \begin{vmatrix} 5 \\ 2 \end{vmatrix} \equiv \begin{vmatrix} 15 \\ 0 \end{vmatrix} \pmod{26}$$

which yields the ciphertext PK. Finally, we encipher the pair ND

$$\begin{vmatrix} 5 & 17 \\ 4 & 15 \end{vmatrix} \begin{vmatrix} 13 \\ 3 \end{vmatrix} + \begin{vmatrix} 5 \\ 2 \end{vmatrix} \equiv \begin{vmatrix} 17 \\ 21 \end{vmatrix} \pmod{26}$$

to get the ciphertext RV. Thus, the message sent is

LB   PA   RV.

To decipher, compute an inverse A' of A modulo 26; verify that the following is such a matrix.

$$\begin{vmatrix} 17 & 5 \\ 18 & 23 \end{vmatrix}$$

To decipher, crank the ciphertext through the inverse transformation $P \equiv A'(C - B)$ (mod 26). If we send the letter pair LB back through,

$$\begin{vmatrix} 17 & 5 \\ 18 & 23 \end{vmatrix} \begin{vmatrix} 11 - 5 \\ 1 - 2 \end{vmatrix} \equiv \begin{vmatrix} 19 \\ 7 \end{vmatrix} \pmod{26}$$

we note that we have the pair 19, 7 corresponding to the letter pair TH, the original plaintext. You are invited to do the subsequent letter pairs.

Note that we can make the block size m as large as desired by choosing large $m \times m$ encryption matrices. When $m \geq 10$, cryptanalysis of such systems is quite difficult.

7.1 WEAKNESSES OF MATRIX CRYPTOSYSTEMS

Matrix cryptosystems, like the block affine system, are resistant to frequency analysis. In general, when using the ordinary alphabet with blocks of size n, there are 26^n different ways to map an n-block of text to another. Maintaining a frequency table of these blocks when n is large quickly becomes infeasible. For example, when the enciphering matrix is 10 by 10, that is, the block size $n = 10$, there are $26^{10} \cong 1.4 \times 10^{14}$ possible blocks. A table of that size

would quickly exhaust the space and exceed the search time of even the greatest computers. For this reason, matrix ciphers (where the size of the block is reasonably large) are still
used today, and are relatively secure for most purposes.

Of course, these matrix cryptosystems are secret key. The enciphering matrix A is the enciphering key, and must be given only to authorized users, since anyone in possession of it
can quickly compute the inverse deciphering matrix A' and decipher messages.

Known Plaintext Attack.   You will notice that the matrix ciphers are vulnerable to
a known plaintext attack, for if a cryptanalyst manages to acquire enough plaintext $P = p_1$,
$p_2, \ldots, p_m$ corresponding to known ciphertext $C = c_1, c_2, \ldots, c_m$, she can compute the
inverse A' of the enciphering matrix A, and the shift vector B, by solving the matrix congruence $AP + B \equiv C \pmod{n}$ for A and B, or equivalently, by solving the corresponding system of congruences

$$a_{1,1}p_1 + a_{1,2}p_2 + \ldots + a_{1,m}p_m + b_1 \equiv c_1 \pmod{n}$$

$$a_{2,1}p_1 + a_{2,2}p_2 + \ldots + a_{2,m}p_m + b_2 \equiv c_2 \pmod{n}$$

$$\ldots$$

$$a_{m,1}p_1 + a_{m,2}p_2 + \ldots + a_{m,m}p_m + b_m \equiv c_m \pmod{n}$$

using different plaintext to ciphertext mappings.

EXAMPLE.   Suppose a cryptanalyst knows we are using a matrix cipher of block length 2, with
the ordinary alphabet. She has some ciphertext,

   BT GT HM

and its corresponding plaintext

   AT TA CK.

The job of the cryptanalyst is to get what she doesn't know, namely A and B. Suppose
she denotes the enciphering matrix A as

$$\begin{vmatrix} a & b \\ c & d \end{vmatrix}$$

and the shift vector B as

$$\begin{vmatrix} s \\ t \end{vmatrix}$$

The first mapping takes the pair AT to BT, or

$$0a + 19b + s \equiv 1 \pmod{26}$$

$$0c + 19d + t \equiv 19 \pmod{26}$$

and the second and third mappings follow:

$$19a + 0b + s \equiv 6 \ (\text{mod } 26)$$

$$19c + 0d + t \equiv 19 \ (\text{mod } 26)$$

$$2a + 10b + s \equiv 7 \ (\text{mod } 26)$$

$$2c + 10d + t \equiv 12 \ (\text{mod } 26)$$

She then rearranges the congruences to get two systems

$$0a + 19b + s \equiv 1 \ (\text{mod } 26)$$

$$19a + 0b + s \equiv 6 \ (\text{mod } 26)$$

$$2a + 10b + s \equiv 7 \ (\text{mod } 26)$$

and

$$0c + 19d + t \equiv 19 \ (\text{mod } 26)$$

$$19c + 0d + t \equiv 19 \ (\text{mod } 26)$$

$$2c + 10d + t \equiv 12 \ (\text{mod } 26).$$

She solves the first system to obtain values for a, b, and s, and the second system to get the values for c, d, and t. Since the coefficients of the two systems are the same, she can solve them simultaneously.

$$\begin{vmatrix} 0 & 19 & 1 & 1 & 19 \\ 19 & 0 & 1 & 6 & 19 \\ 2 & 10 & 1 & 7 & 12 \end{vmatrix}$$

She then proceeds to reduce the matrix, say first by multiplying row 2 by 11, an inverse of 19 modulo 26, then by swapping row 2 with row 1, then by subtracting row 1 from row 3. This yields

$$\begin{vmatrix} 1 & 0 & 11 & 14 & 1 \\ 0 & 19 & 1 & 1 & 19 \\ 0 & 10 & 5 & 5 & 10 \end{vmatrix}.$$

She then multiplies row 2 by 11, then subtracts 10 times row 2 from row 3

$$\begin{vmatrix} 1 & 0 & 11 & 14 & 1 \\ 0 & 1 & 11 & 11 & 1 \\ 0 & 0 & 25 & 25 & 0 \end{vmatrix}.$$

She then multiplies row 3 by 25 (which is its own inverse mod 26), then subtracts 11 times row 3 from both row 1 and row 2. This gives the desired solutions.

$$\begin{vmatrix} 1 & 0 & 0 & 3 & 1 \\ 0 & 1 & 0 & 0 & 1 \\ 0 & 0 & 1 & 1 & 0 \end{vmatrix}$$

She now knows that

$a \equiv 3 \pmod{26}$ $c \equiv 1 \pmod{26}$

$b \equiv 0 \pmod{26}$ $d \equiv 1 \pmod{26}$

$s \equiv 1 \pmod{26}$ $t \equiv 0 \pmod{26}$

and so an enciphering matrix A is

$$\begin{vmatrix} 3 & 0 \\ 1 & 1 \end{vmatrix}$$

and its corresponding shift vector B is

$$\begin{vmatrix} 1 \\ 0 \end{vmatrix}.$$

(You should test these values to ensure that A and B actually map the given plaintext to the ciphertext.) Once our cryptanalyst has A, it is simple to compute the inverse A' modulo 26 to obtain

$$\begin{vmatrix} 9 & 0 \\ 17 & 1 \end{vmatrix}.$$

EXAMPLE.   Earlier we enciphered the message

    TH EE ND

to the ciphertext

    LB PA RV.

Suppose the cryptanalyst knows we are using matrix ciphers of block size $m = 2$ with the ordinary alphabet. She acquires both the plaintext message and the ciphertext message. Now,

"TH"(=19 7) corresponds with "LB"(=11 1),

"EE"(=4 4) corresponds with "PA"(=15 0),

"ND"(=13 3) corresponds with "RV"(=17 21).

Using the same procedure described above, she solves the first system to obtain values for a, b, and s, and the second system to get the values for c, d, and t. You should be able to do this, and to verify that an enciphering matrix A is

$$\begin{vmatrix} 5 & 17 \\ 4 & 15 \end{vmatrix}$$

and the corresponding shift vector B is

$$\begin{vmatrix} 5 \\ 2 \end{vmatrix}$$

It is now a simple matter for her to compute A', an inverse of A modulo 26.

$$\begin{vmatrix} 17 & 5 \\ 18 & 23 \end{vmatrix}$$

In these examples we have chosen the block size to be artificially small to simplify the computations. In reality larger block sizes would be used; the computations involved are the same, there are only more of them.

Java Algorithm.   You will be asked in the exercises to develop some classes to perform encryption and decryption with matrices, but before you do that, we review a couple of constructors, one from ModMatrix, and the other from ModSquareMatrix. I refer to the constructors which produce a ModMatrix or a ModSquareMatrix with random entries; here is the code for review:

```
//Creates a matrix with random entries having r rows, c columns,
//Or, it creates a matrix of all zeros
//Matrices start indexing at 1,1.  Zeroth column and row are not used.
public ModMatrix(int r,int c,BigInteger m,boolean makeZero) {
    SecureRandom sr=new SecureRandom();
    modulus=m;
    array=new BigInteger[r+1][c+1];
    numRows=r;
    numCols=c;
    for (int i=0;i<r;i++) {
        for (int j=0;j<c;j++) {
            //If makeZero set to true, make the zero matrix
            if (makeZero) array[i+1][j+1]=new BigInteger("0");
            //otherwise, make matrix with random entries
            else array[i+1][j+1]=new
                        BigInteger(modulus.bitLength(),sr).mod(modulus);
        }
    }
}


//Creates a square matrix with random entries
//Or, it creates a matrix with all zeros
//Another parameter specifies whether or not you wish the random
//matrix to be invertible; if NOT, matrix may still be invertible by accident
```

```java
public ModSquareMatrix(int s,BigInteger m,boolean makeZero,boolean makeInvertible)
    throws MatricesNonConformableException {
        //Call a superconstructor from ModMatrix-make the zero matrix,
        //or a matrix with random entries
        super(s,s,m,makeZero);

        //Zero matrix is not invertible
        if (makeZero&&makeInvertible) throw new IllegalArgumentException
            ("Zero matrix cannot be inverted!");

        //A random invertible matrix is desired
        if (makeInvertible) {
            Random r=new Random();
            SecureRandom sr=new SecureRandom();
            boolean done=false;
            //Do this until the matrix inverts
            while (!done) {
                try {
                    //Try to take the inverse-may throw an exception if not invertible
                    this.inverse();
                    done=true;
                } catch (SingularMatrixException sme) {
                    //Change a random entry in the matrix
                    int row=Math.abs(r.nextInt())%numRows+1;
                    int col=Math.abs(r.nextInt())%numCols+1;
                    BigInteger value=new
                                        BigInteger(modulus.bitLength(),sr).mod(modulus);
                    this.setElement(row,col,value);
                } catch (ArithmeticException ae) {
                    //Change a random entry in the matrix
                    int row=Math.abs(r.nextInt())%numRows+1;
                    int col=Math.abs(r.nextInt())%numCols+1;
                    BigInteger value=new
                                        BigInteger(modulus.bitLength(),sr).mod(modulus);
                    this.setElement(row,col,value);
                }
            }
        }
}
```

The ModSquareMatrix constructor has an additional boolean variable to allow the user to specify whether or not they wish to enforce invertibility on the new matrix. If so, we can use this to generate random invertible square matrices modulo n; perfect for use as keys with this cryptosystem.

FIGURE 7.1

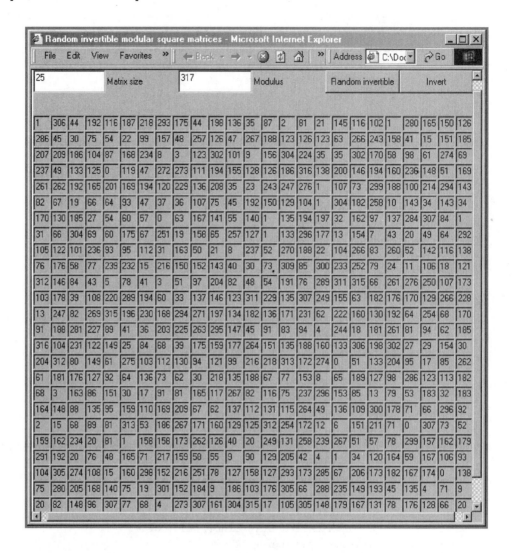

There is an applet called TestRandomModSquareMatrixApplet which can be found on the book's website. It generates random invertible matrices for a specified size, and modulus. Pressing a button allows you to invert the matrix. A screen shot of this applet is shown in Figure 7.1.

7.2 TRANSPOSITION CIPHERS

As you recall, transposition ciphers simply permute the characters in a plaintext message. Matrices provide us with a convenient way of specifying permutations for this purpose. Thus, we make the following definition:

> **Definition**
> A square matrix A is a transposition matrix if each column and row of A contain a single 1; all other entries are 0.

EXAMPLE.

$$A = \begin{vmatrix} 0 & 0 & 1 & 0 \\ 0 & 0 & 0 & 1 \\ 0 & 1 & 0 & 0 \end{vmatrix}.$$

Note that an identity matrix is a transposition matrix (but one which we would never use). These types of matrices do exactly what we want. Note that if we take the product

$$V = AX$$

where V and B are column vectors, and A is a transposition matrix, then

- since each row of A contains a single 1, each entry in V will merely be an entry from X, and

- since each column of A contains a single 1, each entry of V will be a different entry from X.

Thus, the entries of V are merely a permutation of the entries of X.

EXAMPLE. Suppose we have the following:

$$A = \begin{vmatrix} 0 & 1 & 0 & 0 & 0 \\ 0 & 0 & 0 & 0 & 1 \\ 1 & 0 & 0 & 0 & 0 \\ 0 & 0 & 1 & 0 & 0 \\ 0 & 0 & 0 & 1 & 0 \end{vmatrix}$$

$$B = \begin{vmatrix} 12 \\ 5 \\ 23 \\ 8 \\ 6 \end{vmatrix}$$

and we take $V = BX$. Then we see that

$$V = \begin{vmatrix} 0 & 1 & 0 & 0 & 0 \\ 0 & 0 & 0 & 0 & 1 \\ 1 & 0 & 0 & 0 & 0 \\ 0 & 0 & 1 & 0 & 0 \\ 0 & 0 & 0 & 1 & 0 \end{vmatrix} \begin{vmatrix} 12 \\ 5 \\ 23 \\ 8 \\ 6 \end{vmatrix} = \begin{vmatrix} 5 \\ 6 \\ 12 \\ 23 \\ 8 \end{vmatrix}.$$

We can now specify in terms of matrices what we mean by a transposition cipher. A transposition cipher having block length n maps a plaintext block P (as a column vector) to a ciphertext block C (also a column vector) by the transformation

$$C = AP.$$

EXAMPLE. Suppose we wish to encrypt the message THIS IS NIRVANA using the transposition matrix

$$A = \begin{vmatrix} 0 & 0 & 1 & 0 & 0 \\ 0 & 0 & 0 & 0 & 1 \\ 0 & 0 & 0 & 1 & 0 \\ 0 & 1 & 0 & 0 & 0 \\ 1 & 0 & 0 & 0 & 0 \end{vmatrix}$$

and the ordinary alphabet. First, we group the plaintext into blocks of length 5,

THISI SNIRV ANAXX

and, if necessary, pad with X's (or random letters, if desired). This corresponds to the message

19 7 8 18 8 18 13 8 17 21 0 13 0 23 23.

If we consider each block as a column vector, we derive each enciphered block by multiplying A by each plaintext vector. So we get this for the first, second, and third blocks:

$$\begin{vmatrix} 0 & 0 & 1 & 0 & 0 \\ 0 & 0 & 0 & 0 & 1 \\ 0 & 0 & 0 & 1 & 0 \\ 0 & 1 & 0 & 0 & 0 \\ 1 & 0 & 0 & 0 & 0 \end{vmatrix} \begin{vmatrix} 19 \\ 7 \\ 8 \\ 18 \\ 8 \end{vmatrix} = \begin{vmatrix} 8 \\ 8 \\ 18 \\ 7 \\ 19 \end{vmatrix}$$

$$\begin{vmatrix} 0 & 0 & 1 & 0 & 0 \\ 0 & 0 & 0 & 0 & 1 \\ 0 & 0 & 0 & 1 & 0 \\ 0 & 1 & 0 & 0 & 0 \\ 1 & 0 & 0 & 0 & 0 \end{vmatrix} \begin{vmatrix} 18 \\ 13 \\ 8 \\ 17 \\ 21 \end{vmatrix} = \begin{vmatrix} 8 \\ 21 \\ 17 \\ 13 \\ 18 \end{vmatrix}$$

$$\begin{vmatrix} 0 & 0 & 1 & 0 & 0 \\ 0 & 0 & 0 & 0 & 1 \\ 0 & 0 & 0 & 1 & 0 \\ 0 & 1 & 0 & 0 & 0 \\ 1 & 0 & 0 & 0 & 0 \end{vmatrix} \begin{vmatrix} 0 \\ 13 \\ 0 \\ 23 \\ 23 \end{vmatrix} = \begin{vmatrix} 0 \\ 23 \\ 23 \\ 13 \\ 0 \end{vmatrix}.$$

Thus, the enciphered message is

8 8 18 7 19 8 21 17 13 18 0 23 23 13 0

or

IISHT   IVRNS   AXXNA

Of course, we must ensure that transpositions are reversible. It seems natural to think that they are, but how do we do this in the setting of matrices? Of course, what we seek is an inverse A' of the transposition matrix A so that

$$P = A'C.$$

Transposition matrices are easily invertible using Gauss–Jordan elimination with the augmented matrix $A|I$. Since a transposition matrix is chosen so that each row and column contains a single 1, and nothing else, any such matrix can be reduced to an identity matrix simply by swapping rows! Thus, an inverse A' of any transposition matrix A always exists.

EXAMPLE. Let A be defined as the same matrix used in our transposition cipher example; that is

$$A = \begin{vmatrix} 0 & 0 & 1 & 0 & 0 \\ 0 & 0 & 0 & 0 & 1 \\ 0 & 0 & 0 & 1 & 0 \\ 0 & 1 & 0 & 0 & 0 \\ 1 & 0 & 0 & 0 & 0 \end{vmatrix}.$$

To find an inverse A' of A, first form the augmented matrix $A|I$.

$$\begin{vmatrix} 0 & 0 & 1 & 0 & 0 & 1 & 0 & 0 & 0 & 0 \\ 0 & 0 & 0 & 0 & 1 & 0 & 1 & 0 & 0 & 0 \\ 0 & 0 & 0 & 1 & 0 & 0 & 0 & 1 & 0 & 0 \\ 0 & 1 & 0 & 0 & 0 & 0 & 0 & 0 & 1 & 0 \\ 1 & 0 & 0 & 0 & 0 & 0 & 0 & 0 & 0 & 1 \end{vmatrix}$$

By simply swapping the rows so that we obtain the identity matrix on the left hand side, we get

$$\begin{vmatrix} 1 & 0 & 0 & 0 & 0 & 0 & 0 & 0 & 0 & 1 \\ 0 & 1 & 0 & 0 & 0 & 0 & 0 & 0 & 1 & 0 \\ 0 & 0 & 1 & 0 & 0 & 1 & 0 & 0 & 0 & 0 \\ 0 & 0 & 0 & 1 & 0 & 0 & 0 & 1 & 0 & 0 \\ 0 & 0 & 0 & 0 & 1 & 0 & 1 & 0 & 0 & 0 \end{vmatrix}.$$

Thus, the inverse A' of A that we seek is

$$A' = \begin{vmatrix} 0 & 0 & 0 & 0 & 1 \\ 0 & 0 & 0 & 1 & 0 \\ 1 & 0 & 0 & 0 & 0 \\ 0 & 0 & 1 & 0 & 0 \\ 0 & 1 & 0 & 0 & 0 \end{vmatrix}.$$

We will use this inverse to regain the plaintext of our ciphertext example. We get for the first block

$$
\begin{vmatrix}
0 & 0 & 0 & 0 & 1 \\
0 & 0 & 0 & 1 & 0 \\
1 & 0 & 0 & 0 & 0 \\
0 & 0 & 1 & 0 & 0 \\
0 & 1 & 0 & 0 & 0
\end{vmatrix}
\begin{vmatrix} 8 \\ 8 \\ 18 \\ 7 \\ 19 \end{vmatrix}
=
\begin{vmatrix} 19 \\ 7 \\ 8 \\ 18 \\ 8 \end{vmatrix}
$$

for the second we get

$$
\begin{vmatrix}
0 & 0 & 0 & 0 & 1 \\
0 & 0 & 0 & 1 & 0 \\
1 & 0 & 0 & 0 & 0 \\
0 & 0 & 1 & 0 & 0 \\
0 & 1 & 0 & 0 & 0
\end{vmatrix}
\begin{vmatrix} 8 \\ 21 \\ 17 \\ 13 \\ 18 \end{vmatrix}
=
\begin{vmatrix} 18 \\ 13 \\ 8 \\ 17 \\ 21 \end{vmatrix}
$$

and for the third we get

$$
\begin{vmatrix}
0 & 0 & 0 & 0 & 1 \\
0 & 0 & 0 & 1 & 0 \\
1 & 0 & 0 & 0 & 0 \\
0 & 0 & 1 & 0 & 0 \\
0 & 1 & 0 & 0 & 0
\end{vmatrix}
\begin{vmatrix} 0 \\ 23 \\ 23 \\ 13 \\ 0 \end{vmatrix}
=
\begin{vmatrix} 0 \\ 13 \\ 0 \\ 23 \\ 23 \end{vmatrix}.
$$

This produces the plaintext blocks

19 7 8 18 8   18 13 8 17 21   0 13 0 23 23

or

THISI   SNIRV   ANAXX.

7.3   COMBINATION SUBSTITUTION/TRANSPOSITION CIPHERS

When substitution ciphers are combined with transposition ciphers, the resulting cipher can be very hard to crack, especially when the block sizes are different. Now that we have a convenient vehicle (matrices) for representing these ciphers, we will discuss how this is done.

Suppose we use a matrix cipher to map blocks of n characters from the plaintext P to the ciphertext C'. Then we regroup this ciphertext into blocks of size m and apply a transposition cipher to these blocks to produce another ciphertext C''. This, of course, permutes the characters in each m character block, and since the first encryption was done for n character blocks, some characters find themselves in different blocks. Finally, to put another nail in the coffin, we can encrypt C'' again using the first matrix cipher to produce the final ciphertext C. For many ciphers, multiple encryption does not strengthen the cipher; hence it is often just a waste of time, but in this case, it strengthens the cipher considerably. This type of cryptosystem confounds any attempt at frequency analysis, and even makes a known plaintext attack more difficult.

Note that if we are using this type of cipher, we must be careful about how we pad the message. We must pad enough characters so that the message is divisible by both n and m (the block size of the first and second ciphers, respectively.) Thus, we wish to ensure the size of the message is divisible by the least common multiple of m and n.

EXAMPLE.   Suppose we are using the ordinary alphabet, and we wish to encipher the following message

SCOOBY DOO WHERE ARE YOU

using first the matrix cipher transformation $C' \equiv AP + B \pmod{26}$ where the enciphering matrix A is

$$\begin{vmatrix} 5 & 17 \\ 4 & 15 \end{vmatrix}$$

and the shift vector B is

$$\begin{vmatrix} 5 \\ 2 \end{vmatrix}$$

Secondly, we wish to perform a transposition $C'' = TC'$, where the transposition matrix T is

$$\begin{vmatrix} 0 & 0 & 0 & 1 & 0 \\ 1 & 0 & 0 & 0 & 0 \\ 0 & 0 & 0 & 0 & 1 \\ 0 & 1 & 0 & 0 & 0 \\ 0 & 0 & 1 & 0 & 0 \end{vmatrix}.$$

Note that the substitution cipher uses a block size of 2 characters, whereas the transposition cipher uses a block size of 5 characters. Thus, the length of the plaintext needs to be divisible by lcm(2, 5) = 10. Finally, we apply once again the previous matrix substitution to get the final ciphertext.

$$C \equiv AC'' + B \pmod{26}.$$

We will first group the plaintext P into letter pairs:

SC OO BY DO OW HE RE AR EY OU

and note that in this case, no padding is necessary. (See Table 7.1.)

A	B	C	D	E	F	G	H	I	J	K	L	M	N	O	P	Q	R	S	T	U	V	W	X	Y	Z
0	1	2	3	4	5	6	7	8	9	10	11	12	13	14	15	16	17	18	19	20	21	22	23	24	25

TABLE 7.1

Converted to numbers (using Table 7.1) the message is

18 2   14 14   1 24   3 14   14 22   7 4   17 4   0 17   4 24   14 20.

When we apply the matrix transformation $C' \equiv AP + B \pmod{26}$, we get the results shown in Table 7.2.

Now, we regroup the ciphertext into blocks of length 5.

25 0 1 8 2   2 24 16 7 24   4 12 2 0 8   23 17 14 25 20

We apply the transposition cipher $C'' = TC'$. (See Table 7.3.)

Finally, we regroup the ciphertext into blocks of length 2, and reapply the first matrix transformation. (See Table 7.4.)

The final ciphertext is

CT PK ZH HG HA VK PG YV SE QU.

What makes ciphers like this so difficult for anyone doing frequency analysis is that the blocks are split up by the enciphering transformation. You should verify that the plaintext is regained by applying the inverse matrix transformation (at the beginning and the end) using

$$A' = \begin{vmatrix} 17 & 5 \\ 18 & 23 \end{vmatrix}$$

P	18 2	14 14	1 24	3 14	14 22	7 4	17 4	0 17	4 24	14 20
C'	25 0	1 8	2 2	24 16	7 24	4 12	2 0	8 23	17 14	25 20

TABLE 7.2

C'	25 0 1 8 2	2 24 16 7 24	4 12 2 0 8	23 17 14 25 20
C''	8 25 2 0 1	7 2 24 24 16	0 4 8 12 2	25 23 20 17 14

TABLE 7.3

C''	8 25	2 0	1 7	2 24	24 16	0 4	8 12	2 25	23 20	17 14
C	2 19	15 10	25 7	7 6	7 0	21 10	15 6	24 21	18 4	16 20

TABLE 7.4

and

$$T' = \begin{vmatrix} 0 & 1 & 0 & 0 & 0 \\ 0 & 0 & 0 & 1 & 0 \\ 0 & 0 & 0 & 0 & 1 \\ 1 & 0 & 0 & 0 & 0 \\ 0 & 0 & 1 & 0 & 0 \end{vmatrix}$$

the inverse of the transposition matrix T.

EXAMPLE. Here we encipher the message

   BLOW ME DOWN

using the ordinary alphabet, a 3×3 substitution matrix, and a 4×4 transposition matrix. Here, though, the transposition is done by taking $C'' = C'T$, instead of $C'' = TC'$.

Enciphering matrix:

```
            7   19   22

a   =      15   11    1

            0   21   17
```

The inverse of the enciphering matrix modulo 26:

```
           14   23    5

ainv =      7   21    5

           25   23    0
```

The transposition matrix:

```
          0   1   0   0

          0   0   0   1
t =
          1   0   0   0

          0   0   1   0
```

The inverse of the transposition matrix:

```
0   0   1   0

1   0   0   0

0   0   0   1

0   1   0   0
```

The plaintext "BLOW ME DOWN," padded with X's:

```
        1   22    3   13

p  =   11   12   14   23

       14    4   22   23
```

Do the first substitution:

```
   4    2   17   20

  20   24   13    3

   1    8   18   16
```

Do the transposition:

```
  17    4   20    2

  13   20    3   24

  18    1   16    8
```

Do the second substitution.
The final ciphertext is "IAH OVV DLX WQQ".

```
   8   14    3   22

   0   21   11   16

   7   21   23   16
```

Begin decryption—reverse second substitution:

```
  17    4   20    2

  13   20    3   24

  18    1   16    8
```

Reverse the transposition:

```
   4    2   17   20

  20   24   13    3

   1    8   18   16
```

Now reverse the first substitution, and the recovered plaintext is "BLO WME DOW NXX."

```
   1   22    3   13

  11   12   14   23

  14    4   22   23
```

EXERCISES

1. Using the ordinary alphabet and a block size of 2, encipher and decipher the following messages:

   a. GREY LADY DOWN

   b. WHERE EAGLES DARE

   c. TOKYO IN FLAMES

   Pad with the letter X if necessary. Use the enciphering matrix

   $$\begin{vmatrix} 2 & 7 \\ 5 & 4 \end{vmatrix}$$

   and shift vector

   $$\begin{vmatrix} 21 \\ 19 \end{vmatrix}$$

2. Repeat the previous exercise, but use a block size of 3 with the enciphering matrix

   $$\begin{vmatrix} 12 & 21 & 9 \\ 7 & 8 & 18 \\ 3 & 23 & 6 \end{vmatrix}$$

   and the shift vector

   $$\begin{vmatrix} 19 \\ 5 \\ 6 \end{vmatrix}$$

3. Repeat the previous exercise, but use a block size of 5 with the enciphering matrix

   $$\begin{vmatrix} 20 & 15 & 3 & 1 & 5 \\ 4 & 23 & 16 & 4 & 3 \\ 3 & 8 & 13 & 10 & 8 \\ 12 & 15 & 4 & 3 & 2 \\ 5 & 6 & 7 & 8 & 9 \end{vmatrix}$$

   and the following shift vector

   $$\begin{vmatrix} 14 \\ 12 \\ 13 \\ 9 \\ 21 \end{vmatrix}$$

4. Suppose that you are a cryptanalyst trying to find the enciphering matrices used in the previous exercises. Recover the enciphering matrix A and shift vector B from each of

the exercises using only knowledge of the modulus, the block size, and the plain-text–ciphertext message pairs. If you are unable to obtain these matrices, state why.

5. Show that if T is a transposition matrix, then the inverse of T is the same as the transpose of T.

6. Encipher and decipher the following messages:

   a. GREY LADY DOWN

   b. WHERE EAGLES DARE

   c. TOKYO IN FLAMES

Pad with the letter X if necessary. Use the transposition matrix

$$
\begin{vmatrix}
0 & 0 & 0 & 1 & 0 & 0 & 0 \\
0 & 1 & 0 & 0 & 0 & 0 & 0 \\
1 & 0 & 0 & 0 & 0 & 0 & 0 \\
0 & 0 & 0 & 0 & 1 & 0 & 0 \\
0 & 0 & 0 & 0 & 0 & 1 & 0 \\
0 & 0 & 0 & 0 & 0 & 0 & 1 \\
0 & 0 & 1 & 0 & 0 & 0 & 0
\end{vmatrix}
$$

7. Repeat the previous exercise, but first encrypt with matrix A, given by

$$
\begin{vmatrix}
20 & 15 & 3 & 1 & 5 \\
4 & 23 & 16 & 4 & 3 \\
3 & 8 & 13 & 10 & 8 \\
12 & 15 & 4 & 3 & 2 \\
5 & 6 & 7 & 8 & 9
\end{vmatrix}
$$

then with the transposition matrix, then again with matrix A.

8. Implement a matrix cipher program by adding a matrixEncipher() method and a matrixDecipher() method to the Ciphers class.

CHAPTER 8

Systems of Linear Congruences—Multiple Moduli

Now we proceed with the next type of linear systems of congruences. These systems involve a single variable with multiple moduli, as in the following example:

$$x \equiv 3 \pmod 4$$

$$x \equiv 0 \pmod 5 \ (*)$$

$$x \equiv 0 \pmod 7$$

$$x \equiv 8 \pmod 9.$$

We wish to find all integers x which solve all four of the congruences in (*). We can go about finding solutions as follows: first, rewrite the first congruence as an equality

$$x = 4t + 3$$

where x is an integer (proposition 17 allows this). Insert this expression into the second congruence to get

$$4t + 3 \equiv 0 \pmod 5,$$

then solve for t to get

$$t \equiv 3 \pmod 5.$$

We can now rewrite the previous as an equation

$$t = 5u + 3$$

which we can then substitute for x in the next congruence, since

$$x = 4t + 3 = 4(5u + 3) + 3 = 20u + 15.$$

Doing this, we see that

$$20u + 15 \equiv 6u + 1 \equiv 0 \pmod 7$$

161

or that

$$u \equiv 1 \pmod 7.$$

Again, rewrite this congruence as an equation; namely

$$u = 7v + 1$$

which we can then substitute for x in the last congruence since

$$x = 20u + 15 = 20(7v + 1) + 15 = 140v + 35.$$

Replace x with this expression in the last congruence

$$140v + 35 \equiv 5v + 8 \equiv 8 \pmod 9$$

to obtain solutions for v, which are all v such that

$$v \equiv 0 \pmod 9.$$

Finally, rewrite this congruence as an equation

$$v = 9w + 0.$$

Once we back substitute this value for x, we get

$$x = 140v + 35 = 140(9w) + 35 = 1260w + 35$$

or, written as a congruence,

$$x \equiv 35 \pmod{1260}.$$

These are exactly the solutions desired, for note that if $x \equiv 35 \pmod{1260}$, we certainly have all of the following:

$$x \equiv 35 \equiv 3 \pmod 4$$
$$x \equiv 35 \equiv 0 \pmod 5$$
$$x \equiv 35 \equiv 0 \pmod 7$$
$$x \equiv 35 \equiv 8 \pmod 9.$$

8.1   THE CHINESE REMAINDER THEOREM

This method of solving these types of congruences is very effective, but we can develop an even faster method of solving such systems if we only require that the moduli be pairwise relatively prime. Note, however, that the previous method has no such requirement. The proof of proposition 27 describes the new method; it is called the Chinese Remainder Theorem, since the Chinese have known its results since ancient times. However, we must first establish the two following facts:

PROPOSITION 25.   Suppose integers $a_1, a_2, \ldots, a_n$ are pairwise relatively prime. Then $(a_1 a_2 \ldots a_n)|c$ if and only if $a_1|c, a_2|c, \ldots, a_n|c$.

Proof. Clearly, if the product $p = (a_1 a_2 \ldots a_n)$ divides c, then each a_i, $i = 1, 2, \ldots, n$ likewise divides c, since each $a_i | p$, and $p | c$. Conversely, suppose each a_i divides c. Then the prime factorization of c must contain the prime factorization of each a_i, and since these are pairwise relatively prime, no a_i can have a prime factor in common with any other. Thus, the prime factorization of c contains the prime factorization of the product p, and so $p | c$. ■

The next proposition is what we really need for the Chinese Remainder Theorem, and using the previous result makes its proof very simple. You are requested to do this.

PROPOSITION 26. Let $a \equiv b \pmod{m_1}$, $a \equiv b \pmod{m_2}, \ldots, a \equiv b \pmod{m_n}$ where $a_1, a_2, \ldots, a_n$ are pairwise relatively prime. Then we have $a \equiv b \pmod{m_1 m_2 \ldots m_n}$.

PROPOSITION 27. (THE CHINESE REMAINDER THEOREM.)
Suppose $m_1, m_2, \ldots, m_n$ are pairwise relatively prime. Then the system of congruences

$$x \equiv a_1 \pmod{m_1}$$

$$x \equiv a_2 \pmod{m_2}$$

$$\ldots$$

$$x \equiv a_n \pmod{m_n}$$

has a unique solution modulo $M = m_1 m_2 \ldots m_n$; namely,

$$x \equiv a_1 M_1 M_1' + a_2 M_2 M_2' + \ldots + a_n M_n M_n' \pmod{M}$$

where $M_i = M/m_i$ and M_i' is an inverse of M_i modulo m_i $\forall$ $i = 1, 2, \ldots, n$.

Proof. Let all the quantities be defined as stated in the proposition. First, note that $M_i = m_1 m_2 \ldots m_{i-1} m_{i+1} \ldots m_n$ and m_i are relatively prime for any i. To see this, note that each m_i is relatively prime to m_k $\forall$ $i \neq k$, and so if we have an integer p greater than 1 which divides m_i, it cannot divide any other m_k, and hence cannot divide the product $m_1 m_2 \ldots m_{i-1} m_{i+1} \ldots m_n = M_i$. Thus, proposition 22 says that an inverse M_i' of M_i modulo m_i exists. Then the integer given by

$$x = a_1 M_1 M_1' + a_2 M_2 M_2' + \ldots + a_n M_n M_n'$$

simultaneously solves the system of congruences

$$x \equiv a_1 \pmod{m_1}$$

$$x \equiv a_2 \pmod{m_2}$$

$$\ldots$$

$$x \equiv a_n \pmod{m_n}.$$

To see this, note that $m_k | M_i$ when $i \neq k$, hence giving us $M_i \equiv 0 \pmod{m_k}$. Thus, all terms of x modulo m_k vanish except the kth term, and so we have

$$x \equiv a_k M_k M_k' \equiv a_k \cdot 1 \equiv a_k \pmod{m_k}$$

for any k. That is, x is also a solution to the individual congruences of the system. To show this solution is unique (in the sense that all other solutions are congruent to it modulo M), let x and y both be simultaneous solutions to the previous system. Note now that we have $x \equiv y \equiv a_k$ $(\bmod\ m_k) \ \forall \ k$, and proposition 26 tells us then that $x \equiv y \ (\bmod\ M)$, as desired.   ■

EXAMPLE.   We'll use the Chinese Remainder Theorem (CRT) to solve the same system (*); that is, the system

$$x \equiv 3 \ (\bmod\ 4)$$

$$x \equiv 0 \ (\bmod\ 5)$$

$$x \equiv 0 \ (\bmod\ 7)$$

$$x \equiv 8 \ (\bmod\ 9).$$

(Note that the moduli are pairwise relatively prime.) The proof of CRT shows us how to get our solutions very quickly by computing $M = 4 \cdot 5 \cdot 7 \cdot 9 = 1260$, and

$$M_1 = 1260/4 = 315, M_2 = 1260/5 = 252, M_3 = 1260/7 = 180, M_4 = 1260/9 = 140.$$

We then compute inverses y_i of each M_i modulo m_i:

$$M_1' = 3 \ \text{(an inverse of 315 modulo 4)}$$

$$M_2' = 3 \ \text{(an inverse of 252 modulo 5)}$$

$$M_3' = 3 \ \text{(an inverse of 180 modulo 7)}$$

$$M_4' = 2 \ \text{(an inverse of 140 modulo 9)}$$

To get our solution, we now simply form the sum

$$x = a_1 M_1 M_1' + a_2 M_2 M_2' + a_3 M_3 M_3' + a_4 M_4 M_4'$$

$$= 3 \cdot 315 \cdot 3 + 0 \cdot 252 \cdot 3 + 0 \cdot 180 \cdot 7 + 8 \cdot 140 \cdot 2$$

$$= 5075$$

$$\equiv 35 \ (\bmod\ 1260).$$

This is exactly the same solution we obtained earlier, only perhaps less directly but certainly more quickly. (Note that computing M_2, M_3, y_2 and y_3 isn't even necessary in this example, because they vanish in the final computation.)

Java Algorithm.   Suppose we write a static method in the BigIntegerMath class to solve such sets of congruences; we can call it solveCRT(). We can make it solve systems of the form

$$x \equiv a_1 \pmod{m_1}$$

$$x \equiv a_2 \pmod{m_2}$$

...

$$x \equiv a_n \pmod{m_n}.$$

If any individual congruence does not have a unique solution, we will throw an exception; likewise if the moduli are not pairwise relatively prime. We will pass in the values of a_i and m_i as arrays of BigIntegers, and the solution will be returned as an array of two BigIntegers, say answer[]. Then answer[0] will contain the residue solution, and answer[1] will contain M, the product of the individual moduli.

Here is the program:

```
//Finds simultaneous solutions to a linear system of congruences
//involving only one variable and multiple moduli.
public static BigInteger[] solveCRT(BigInteger[] residue, BigInteger[] modulus) {

  //See if the number of moduli and residues match
  if (residue.length!=modulus.length) throw new IllegalArgumentException
("Residues and moduli are in different amounts.");

  //See if the moduli are pairwise relatively prime
  for (int i=0; i<modulus.length-1; i++) {
    for (int j=i+1; j<modulus.length; j++) {
      if (!(modulus[i].gcd(modulus[j]).equals(ONE)))
        throw new IllegalArgumentException
        ("Moduli are not pairwise relatively prime.");
    }
  }

  //Form the product of the individual moduli
  BigInteger M=new BigInteger("1");
  for (int i=0; i<modulus.length; i++)
    M=M.multiply(modulus[i]);

  //Form the solution as in the Chinese Remainder Theorem
  BigInteger solution=new BigInteger("0");
  for (int i=0;i<modulus.length; i++) {
    BigInteger Mi=M.divide(modulus[i]);
      solution=solution.add(residue[i].multiply(Mi).multiply
      (Mi.modInverse(modulus[i])));
  }
  solution=lnr(solution,M);
```

FIGURE 8.1

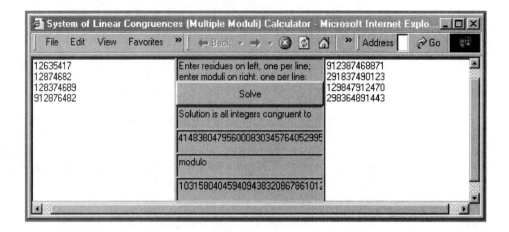

```
//Answer must be returned as a two dimensional array.
BigInteger[] result=new BigInteger[2];
result[0]=solution;
result[1]=M;
return result;
}
```

I have written an applet called TestCRTApplet which allows you to solve these types of systems using the Chinese Remainder Theorem. It can be run from the book's website, and a screen shot follows (see Figure 8.1). The Chinese Remainder Theorem has many important applications in cryptography, and it is equally useful to both the cryptographer and the cryptanalyst. We will investigate many of these applications in upcoming chapters.

EXERCISES

1. Solve the following systems of linear congruences using the Chinese Remainder Theorem (CRT).

   a. $x \equiv 23 \pmod{26}$

   $x \equiv 2 \pmod{31}$

   $x \equiv 5 \pmod{17}$

   b. $x \equiv 1 \pmod{26}$

   $x \equiv 1 \pmod{33}$

   $x \equiv 1 \pmod{35}$

   c. $5x \equiv 3 \pmod{18}$

   $3x \equiv 4 \pmod{7}$

   $2x \equiv 5 \pmod{25}$

   $6x \equiv 10 \pmod{11}$

2. Solve the previous systems of linear congruences without using the Chinese Remainder Theorem.

3. Willie the woodchuck is building a dam for his family. After gnawing down trees all day he stacks the logs in the mud in rows of 5, and notices he has 1 left over. Disgruntled, he stacks them in rows of 6 and notices he has 2 logs remaining. Highly upset now, Willie chews one of the logs to bits in a fit of rage (so he has 1 less log now), then stacks the logs in rows of 7 and has none remaining. What is the minimum number of logs Willie produced that day?

4. Francine the dancing gorilla is dividing up coconuts for her family. If she divides them up equally among all her 46 children, she has 3 coconuts left over, but if she divides them up only among her 25 favorite children, she has 2 coconuts remaining. What is the minimum number of coconuts Francine has?

5. Redneck Slim is planting petunias for his sweetheart Daisy Mae. If he places them in 9 rows, he has 2 plants left over. If he puts them in 10 rows, he has 3 plants left over, but if he puts them in 11 rows he has exactly 1 plant left over for his date Saturday night. What is the minimum number of petunia plants?

6. Show that the system of congruences

$$x \equiv a_1 \;(\text{mod } m_1)$$

$$x \equiv a_2 \;(\text{mod } m_2)$$

$$\vdots$$

$$x \equiv a_n \;(\text{mod } m_n)$$

has a solution iff the gcd of m_i and m_k divides $a_i - a_k$ where $1 \leq i < k \leq n$. This can serve as a check for systems which do not have moduli that are pairwise relatively prime.

7. Solve the following systems of linear congruences:

   a. $x \equiv 7 \;(\text{mod } 24)$

   $x \equiv 23 \;(\text{mod } 56)$

   b. $x \equiv 80 \;(\text{mod } 95)$

   $x \equiv 4 \;(\text{mod } 38)$

   $x \equiv 50 \;(\text{mod } 60)$

8. Write a static solveMultipleModuli() method in the BigIntegerMath class to find a particular solution to linear systems of congruences with multiple moduli that need not be pairwise relatively prime. (Thus, you cannot use the Chinese Remainder Theorem.)

CHAPTER 9

Quadratic Congruences

QUADRATIC CONGRUENCES MODULO A PRIME

The type of congruences we will first investigate here are those of the form

$$x^2 \equiv a \pmod{p}$$

where p is prime. (Later on, we will allow the modulus to be composite.) Not all such congruences have solutions; for example,

$$x^2 \equiv 5 \pmod{11}$$

has two solutions, $x \equiv 4 \pmod{11}$, and $x \equiv -4 \equiv 7 \pmod{11}$. (Verify.) But the congruence

$$x^2 \equiv 2 \pmod 5$$

has no solutions. (Verify by trying all values from 0 through 4.) It turns out that such congruences either have no solutions, or exactly two, as the next theorem shows.

PROPOSITION 28. If p is an odd prime and $p \nmid a$, then the congruence $x^2 \equiv a \pmod p$ has either no solutions or exactly two incongruent solutions modulo p.

Proof. Suppose the congruence has a solution, say $x = z$; that is, $z^2 \equiv a \pmod p$. Then clearly, $x = -z$ is also a solution, since $(-z)^2 = z^2 \equiv a \pmod p$. Also, $z \not\equiv -z \pmod p$, because if $z \equiv -z \pmod p$, this would imply that $2z \equiv 0 \pmod p$, which cannot be because p is odd and does not divide z (since $z^2 \equiv a \pmod p$ and $p \nmid a$).

Now we must show these two solutions (when they exist) are the only solutions. Suppose $x = z$, $x = y$ are two solutions to this quadratic congruence, hence $z^2 \equiv y^2 \equiv a \pmod p$ and so $z^2 - y^2 = (z + y)(z - y) \equiv a - a \equiv 0 \pmod p$. This says that $p|(z + y)$ or $p|(z - y)$, which further implies then that $z \equiv -y \pmod p$ or $z \equiv y \pmod p$. Either way, we are left with only two distinct solutions, $x \equiv z \pmod p$ and $x \equiv -z \pmod p$. ∎

Note that the previous only applies to odd primes, so quadratic congruences modulo 2 (the only even prime) are handled somewhat differently. We will not have occasion to do this.

169

9.2 FERMAT'S LITTLE THEOREM

How do we find solutions to quadratic congruences? When the modulus is a prime of the form $4k + 3$, that is, congruent to 3 modulo 4, these solutions are easily obtained. But before we do this, we must first prove Fermat's Little Theorem, an extremely useful result.

PROPOSITION 29. (FERMAT'S LITTLE THEOREM.) Let p be prime and b an integer such that $p \nmid b$. Then $b^{p-1} \equiv 1 \pmod{p}$.

Proof. Note first that p divides none of the integers $b, 2b, \ldots, (p - 1)b$, for if $p|kb$ for some k between 1 and $p - 1$ (inclusive), then by proposition 13, $p|k$ since $p \nmid b$, and this is impossible. Now we want to show that no two of the integers $b, 2b, \ldots, (p - 1)b$ are congruent modulo p. Assume two of them are; that is,

$$jb \equiv kb \pmod{p} \text{ where } 1 \leq j < k \leq p - 1.$$

Then proposition 21 says $j \equiv k \pmod{p}$ since b and p are relatively prime. But this cannot be since j and k are positive integers both less than $p - 1$.

Thus, the sequence of integers $1, 2, \ldots, p - 1$ has the same number of members as the sequence $b, 2b, \ldots, (p - 1)b$, and the least nonnegative residues of the latter (modulo p) must therefore be a permutation of $1, 2, \ldots, p - 1$. Thus we must have

$$1 \cdot 2 \ldots (p - 1) \equiv b \cdot 2b \ldots (p - 1)b \pmod{p}, \text{ or}$$

$$(p - 1)! \equiv b^{p-1}(p - 1)! \pmod{p}.$$

Since $(p - 1)!$ is relatively prime to p, we can divide it out and preserve the congruence by proposition 21. This yields the desired result; namely,

$$b^{p-1} \equiv 1 \pmod{p}. \qquad \blacksquare$$

Now we can find the solutions to $x^2 \equiv a \pmod{p}$ when p is a prime congruent to 3 modulo 4. These solutions are in the next proposition, which you can prove quickly with the aid of Fermat's Little Theorem. Solutions to quadratic congruences when the modulus is a prime of the form $4k + 1$ are more difficult to obtain, and we will not cover such congruences here.

PROPOSITION 30. Let p be a prime congruent to 3 modulo 4, and a an integer such that $p \nmid a$. Then if the congruence $x^2 \equiv a \pmod{p}$ has solutions, they are $x \equiv a^{(p+1)/4} \pmod{p}$, and $x \equiv -a^{(p+1)/4} \pmod{p}$.

(Hint: First show that $a^{(p-1)/2} \equiv 1 \pmod{p}$; this is called Euler's criterion. It may not be clear to you when proving proposition 30 why p must be congruent to 3 modulo 4; it is simply the only way $(p + 1)/4$ can be an integer.)

EXAMPLES. We will solve all of the following congruences. Note that the modulus is prime and congruent to 3 modulo 4.

- $x^2 \equiv 2 \pmod{23}$

  Solutions: $x \equiv \pm 2^{(23+1)/4} = \pm 2^6 = \pm 64 \equiv \pm 5 \pmod{23}$

  If you prefer to always use least nonnegative residues, the solutions are:

  $x \equiv 5 \pmod{23}$, and $x \equiv -5 \equiv 18 \pmod{23}$
- $x^2 \equiv 17 \pmod{19}$

  Solutions: $x \equiv \pm 17^{(19+1)/4} = \pm 17^5 \equiv \pm 6 \pmod{19}$
- $x^2 \equiv 2 \pmod{7}$

  Solutions: $x \equiv \pm 2^{(7+1)/4} = \pm 2^2 \equiv \pm 4 \pmod{7}$

9.3 QUADRATIC CONGRUENCES MODULO A COMPOSITE

We are now ready to attempt solving congruences when the modulus is not prime. Let $n = pq$, where p and q are distinct primes of the form $4k + 3$, and consider the congruence

$$x^2 \equiv a \pmod{n} \quad (*)$$

where $0 < a < n$. Suppose (*) has a solution, say $x = y$. Then it has four solutions, according to the following proposition.

PROPOSITION 31. Let $n = pq$ where p and q are primes congruent to 3 modulo 4, and let a be an integer such that $0 < a < n$. Suppose the equation $x^2 \equiv a \pmod{n}$ has a solution. Then all the solutions are given by

$$x \equiv \pm(zqq_p{}' \pm wpp_q{}') \pmod{n}$$

where $z = a^{(p+1)/4}$, $w = a^{(q+1)/4}$, $q_p{}'$ is an inverse of q modulo p, and $p_q{}'$ is an inverse of p modulo q.

Proof. We will show it has exactly four solutions as follows. Note that $x = \pm y$ are solutions to $x^2 \equiv a \pmod{n}$ iff they are solutions to both $x^2 \equiv a \pmod{p}$ and $x^2 \equiv a \pmod{q}$. This is easy enough to see if you use the definition of congruence:

y is a solution to $x^2 \equiv a \pmod{n}$

iff $y^2 \equiv a \pmod{n}$

iff $n|(y^2 - a)$

iff $p|(y^2 - a)$ and $q|(y^2 - a)$ (since $n = pq$ and clearly $p|n$ and $q|n$)

iff $y^2 \equiv a \pmod{p}$ and $y^2 \equiv a \pmod{q}$

iff y is a solution to both $x^2 \equiv a \pmod{p}$ and $x^2 \equiv a \pmod{q}$

Now let z be the least nonnegative residue of y modulo p, and let w be the least nonnegative residue of y modulo q. So $x = \pm z$ are solutions to $x^2 \equiv a \pmod{p}$, and $x = \pm w$ are solutions to $x^2 \equiv a \pmod{q}$. We can combine these solutions in four different ways to get four sets of simultaneous congruences:

1. $x \equiv z \pmod{p}$ and $x \equiv w \pmod{q}$
2. $x \equiv p - z \pmod{p}$ and $x \equiv q - w \pmod{q}$
3. $x \equiv p - z \pmod{p}$ and $x \equiv w \pmod{q}$
4. $x \equiv z \pmod{p}$ and $x \equiv q - w \pmod{q}$.

Using the Chinese Remainder Theorem (CRT) on each of sets 1 through 4, we can find the value for x which solves the two congruences simultaneously, and these four values are thus solutions to (*). For congruences 1 and 2, we use CRT to construct the two solutions

$$x \equiv \pm(zqq_p' + wpp_q') \pmod{n}$$

where q_p' is an inverse of q modulo p, and p_q' is an inverse of p modulo q. Similarly, using CRT on congruences 2 and 3 we arrive at the other pair of solutions

$$x \equiv \pm(zqq_p' - wpp_q') \pmod{n}.$$

We then can write the four solutions quickly as

$$x \equiv \pm(zqq_p' \pm wpp_q') \pmod{n}.$$

and the proof is complete. ∎

EXAMPLE. Suppose we wish to solve

$$x^2 \equiv 23 \pmod{77}.$$

Note that the prime factorization of 77 is $7 \cdot 11$, and both of these primes are congruent to 3 modulo 4. We first obtain the solutions to

a. $x^2 \equiv 23 \equiv 2 \pmod{7}$, and
b. $x^2 \equiv 23 \equiv 1 \pmod{11}$.

The solutions to (a) are $x \equiv \pm 3 \pmod{7}$, and the solutions to (b) are $x \equiv \pm 1 \pmod{11}$. Using the Chinese Remainder Theorem, we then separately solve the four sets of congruences

1. $x \equiv 3 \pmod{7}$ and $x \equiv 1 \bmod 11$)
2. $x \equiv -3 \pmod{7}$ and $x \equiv -1 \bmod 11$)
3. $x \equiv -3 \pmod{7}$ and $x \equiv 1 \bmod 11$)
4. $x \equiv 3 \pmod{7}$ and $x \equiv -1 \bmod 11$).

Each yields a solution to $x^2 \equiv 23 \pmod{77}$. We can do all of these at once, as denoted in the formula of proposition 31:

$$x = \pm(3 \cdot 11 \cdot 2 \pm 1 \cdot 7 \cdot 8) \pmod{77}$$

which yields the four solutions

$$x \equiv \pm 122 \equiv \pm 45 \ (\text{mod } 77),$$

or

$$x \equiv \pm 10 \ (\text{mod } 77).$$

(Here 2 is an inverse of 11 mod 7, and 8 is an inverse of 7 mod 11.) If you prefer to have the solutions in terms of least nonnegative residues modulo n, they are

$$x \equiv 45 \ (\text{mod } 77),$$

$$x \equiv 32 \ (\text{mod } 77),$$

$$x \equiv 10 \ (\text{mod } 77),$$

$$x \equiv 67 \ (\text{mod } 77).$$

You should verify that each solution satisfies the congruence $x^2 \equiv 23 \ (\text{mod } 77)$.

We see from the previous development that solving quadratic congruences when the modulus is not prime involves obtaining the prime factorization of n, solving the congruences for the prime moduli, and then recombining the solutions using CRT. This will work even when the solutions we seek are for quadratic congruences more complicated than the simple congruence $x^2 \equiv a \ (\text{mod } p)$.

To continue with this, we will now consider quadratic congruences of the form

$$ax^2 + bx + c \equiv 0 \ (\text{mod } p)$$

where p is a prime of the form $4k + 3$, and a is not divisible by p. Solving such a congruence can go quickly by completing the square, almost the same way we do in algebra. First, multiply both sides by an inverse of a modulo p. This inverse exists because $(a, p) = 1$:

$$x^2 + a'bx + a'c \equiv 0 \ (\text{mod } p).$$

Now move $a'c$ to the RHS:

$$x^2 + a'bx \equiv -a'c \ (\text{mod } p).$$

Next, add the exact quantity to both sides to make the LHS a perfect square:

$$x^2 + a'bx + (2'a'b)^2 \equiv -a'c + (2'a'b)^2 \ (\text{mod } p).$$

The value desired is $2'a'b$, where $2'$ is an inverse of 2 modulo p, which exists since p is an odd prime. Now, rewrite the LHS as a square, and factor the RHS:

$$(x + 2'a'b)^2 \equiv a'((2'b)^2a' - c) \ (\text{mod } p).$$

Proposition 30 now tells us the solutions to the previous congruence:

$$x + 2'a'b \equiv \pm(a'((2'b)^2a' - c))^{(p+1)/4} \ (\text{mod } p).$$

Thus, we finally arrive at our solutions for x:

$$x \equiv \pm(a'((2'b)^2a' - c))^{(p+1)/4} - 2'a'b \ (\text{mod } p).$$

The previous formula can be used to solve these types of quadratic congruences, but often it is easier to complete the square yourself and simplify as you proceed.

EXAMPLE. We wish to solve the congruence

$$3x^2 + 10x + 7 \equiv 1 \pmod{19}.$$

Move the 7 to the RHS:

$$3x^2 + 10x \equiv -6 \equiv 13 \pmod{19}.$$

Multiply both sides by 13, an inverse of 3 modulo 19:

$$x^2 + 10 \cdot 13x \equiv 13 \cdot 3x^2 + 13 \cdot 10x \equiv 13 \cdot 13 \equiv 169 \equiv 17 \pmod{19}.$$

Now, add $(10 \cdot 13 \cdot 2')^2$ to both sides. 10 is an inverse of 2 modulo 19:

$$x^2 + 10 \cdot 13x + (10 \cdot 13 \cdot 10)^2 \equiv 17 + (16 \cdot 10)^2 \equiv 17 + 8^2 \equiv 5 \pmod{19}.$$

Write the LHS as a square:

$$(x + 10 \cdot 13 \cdot 10)^2 \equiv (x + 8)^2 \equiv 5 \pmod{19}.$$

Proposition 30 gives us the solutions to $(x + 8)^2 \equiv 5 \pmod{19}$; they are

$$x + 8 \equiv \pm 5^{(19+1)/4} \equiv \pm 5^5 \equiv \pm 9 \pmod{19}, \text{ or}$$

$$x \equiv \pm 9 - 8 \pmod{19}.$$

This yields the two solutions

$$x \equiv 1 \pmod{19}, \text{ and } x \equiv -17 \equiv 2 \pmod{19}.$$

You should verify that each of the solutions is correct. We will solve this congruence once again however, this time using the quadratic formula:

$$x \equiv \pm(a'((2'b)^2a' - c))^{(p+1)/4} - 2'a'b \pmod{p}.$$

The congruence to solve is

$$3x^2 + 10x + 7 \equiv 1 \pmod{19},$$

or in standard form,

$$3x^2 + 10x + 6 \equiv 0 \pmod{19},$$

so $a = 3$, $b = 10$, $c = 6$, $a' = 13$, and $2' = 10$.

Substituting these values into (††) we get

$$x = \pm(13((10 \cdot 10)^2 \cdot 13 - 6))^{(19+1)/4} - 10 \cdot 13 \cdot 10$$

$$\equiv \pm(13(10000 \cdot 13 - 6))^5 - 8$$

$$\equiv \pm(13(15))^5 - 8$$

$$\equiv \pm 5^5 - 8$$

$$\equiv \pm 9 - 8 \pmod{19}.$$

This yields $x \equiv 1 \pmod{19}$, and $x \equiv -17 \equiv 2 \pmod{19}$, the same solutions obtained by completing the square.

We are finally ready to solve the type of congruence which we will find most useful; those of the type

$$ax^2 + bx + c \equiv 0 \pmod{n}$$

where $(a, n) = 1$, $n = pq$, and where p and q are both primes congruent to 3 modulo 4.

PROPOSITION 32. Let $n = pq$, where p and q are primes congruent to 3 modulo n. Suppose a is an integer relatively prime to n, and that the congruence

$$ax^2 + bx + c \equiv 0 \pmod{n}$$

has a solution. Then all the solutions are given by

$$x \equiv (\pm(a'((2'b)^2 a' - c))^{(p+1)/4}) q q_p' + (\pm(a'((2'b)^2 a' - c))^{(q+1)/4}) p p_q' - 2'a'b \pmod{n}.$$

(Again, q_p' means an inverse of q modulo p, and p_q' is an inverse of p modulo q.)

Proof. Most of the work involved in finding the solutions has already been done. As before, use some algebra to rewrite the congruence as

$$(x + 2'a'b)^2 \equiv a'((2'b)^2 a' - c) \pmod{n}.$$

As before, this splits up into two congruences

$$(x + 2'a'b)^2 \equiv a'((2'b)^2 a' - c) \pmod{p}, \text{ and}$$

$$(x + 2'a'b)^2 \equiv a'((2'b)^2 a' - c) \pmod{q},$$

and proposition 30 tells us the solutions:

$$x + 2'a'b \equiv \pm(a'((2'b)^2 a' - c))^{(p+1)/4} \pmod{p}, \text{ and}$$

$$x + 2'a'b \equiv \pm(a'((2'b)^2 a' - c))^{(q+1)/4} \pmod{q}$$

We then use CRT to recombine these solutions and obtain solutions to $ax^2 + bx + c \equiv 0 \pmod{n}$:

$$x + 2'a'b \equiv (\pm(a'((2'b)^2 a' - c))^{(p+1)/4}) q q_p' + (\pm(a'((2'b)^2 a' - c))^{(q+1)/4}) p p_q' \pmod{n},$$

or

$$x \equiv (\pm(a'((2'b)^2 a' - c))^{(p+1)/4}) q q_p' + (\pm(a'((2'b)^2 a' - c))^{(q+1)/4}) p p_q' - 2'a'b \pmod{n}.$$

Here q_p' is an inverse of q modulo p, and p_q' is an inverse of p modulo q. These are the values claimed in the proposition. ∎

The formula may appear quite horrifying at first, but it provides the solutions we seek very nicely. We demonstrate this now:

EXAMPLE. We solve the congruence

$$2x^2 + 3x + 16 \equiv 0 \pmod{21}.$$

Note that $21 = 3 \cdot 7$. The congruence is already in standard form, so we have $a = 2$, $b = 3$, $c = 16$, $a' = 11$, and $2' = 11$. We first calculate the quantities $\pm(a'((2'b)^2a' - c))^{(3+1)/4}$ (mod 3), $\pm(a'((2'b)^2a' - c))^{(7+1)/4}$ (mod 7), and $2'a'b$ (mod 3 and mod 7):

$$\pm(a'((2'b)^2a' - c))^{(3+1)/4}$$

$$\equiv \pm(11((11 \cdot 3)^2 11 - 16))^{(3+1)/4}$$

$$\equiv \pm(2((2 \cdot 0)^2 2 - 1))^{(3+1)/4}$$

$$\equiv \pm 2 \ (\text{mod } 3).$$

$$\pm(a'((2'b)^2a' - c))^{(7+1)/4}$$

$$\equiv \pm(11((11 \cdot 3)^2 11 - 16))^{(7+1)/4}$$

$$\equiv \pm(4((4 \cdot 3)^2 4 - 2))^{(7+1)/4}$$

$$\equiv \pm 0 \ (\text{mod } 7).$$

$$2'a'b$$

$$\equiv 11 \cdot 11 \cdot 3$$

$$\equiv 2 \cdot 2 \cdot 0$$

$$\equiv 0 \ (\text{mod } 3)$$

$$2'a'b$$

$$\equiv 11 \cdot 11 \cdot 3$$

$$\equiv 4 \cdot 4 \cdot 3$$

$$\equiv 6 \ (\text{mod } 7)$$

The four solutions we seek (actually two, because of ± 0 below) are then

$$x \equiv (\pm 1 - 0) \cdot 7 \cdot 1 + (\pm 0 - 6) \cdot 3 \cdot 5 \ (\text{mod } 21).$$

Here, 1 is an inverse of 7 mod 3, and 5 is an inverse of 3 mod 7. If we provide the answers in terms of least nonnegative residues, we get

$$x \equiv 7 - 6 \equiv 1 \ (\text{mod } 21),$$

$$x \equiv -7 - 6 \equiv -13 \equiv 8 \ (\text{mod } 21).$$

The methods we have discussed here can be easily extended to solve quadratic congruences modulo $n = p_1 p_2 \ldots p_n$ where the factors are all distinct primes congruent to 3 modulo 4. You may wish to attempt this.

Java Algorithm. We should write a solveQuadratic() method (in the BigIntegerMath class, of course) to solve quadratic congruences of the forms described above. That is, the modulus must be a product of distinct primes of the form $4k + 3$. If we are going to deal with truly large integers, then we must take many things into consideration:

- We cannot send in the modulus n as a parameter directly; rather, we must send in the prime factorization $n = pq$. This is because factoring n when n has large prime factors is an intractable problem. (We will discuss this more later.)

- We must test each factor of n first to see if each one is a probable prime, using the isProbablePrime() method of the BigInteger class. (This method of determining primality does not involve attempted factoring and will execute quickly.) If the factor is probably prime, we must also test whether it is congruent to 3 modulo 4. If either is not the case, our method is unusable and we must throw an exception.

- We must check that no factor of the modulus n is repeated; that is, the two primes p and q must be unique if we are to use the Chinese Remainder Theorem to produce the solutions. (CRT requires that the moduli be pairwise relatively prime; if any two moduli are equal this condition is certainly violated.) If $p = q$, we throw an exception.

- We must check the solutions we obtain. It is possible the quadratic congruence we are trying to solve has, in fact, no solutions! Thus, any values we obtain must be checked against the original congruence. If any solution fails to check, we must again throw an exception.

The method as we have outlined has many rules to follow, but if we take the proper precautions, this method can produce very satisfactory results. The code follows:

```
import java.math.BigInteger;
import java.security.SecureRandom;
public class BigIntegerMath {
    //Define zero as a BigInteger; this is handy for comparisons
    static final BigInteger ZERO=new BigInteger("0");
    static final BigInteger ONE=new BigInteger("1");
    static final BigInteger TWO=new BigInteger("2");
    static final BigInteger THREE=new BigInteger("3");
    static final BigInteger FOUR=new BigInteger("4");

//Other methods......

    //Solves quadratic congruences ax^2+bx+c congruent to 0 mod n=pq
    //Returns four solutions when they exist
    public static BigInteger[] solveQuadratic(BigInteger a, BigInteger b, BigInteger
c,
        BigInteger p, BigInteger q, int primeTolerance) {
        //Check that the factors of the modulus are distinct
        if (p.equals(q))
            throw new IllegalArgumentException("The modulus factors are not unique!");
        //Check that the factors are congruent to 3 modulo 4
        BigInteger n=p.multiply(q);
        if (!lnr(p.mod(FOUR),n).equals(THREE))
```

```
        throw new IllegalArgumentException(p+" is not of form 4k+3!");
    if (!lnr(q.mod(FOUR),n).equals(THREE))
        throw new IllegalArgumentException(q+" is not of form 4k+3!");
    //Check that the factors of the modulus are prime
    if (!p.isProbablePrime(primeTolerance))
        throw new IllegalArgumentException(p+" is not prime!");
    if (!q.isProbablePrime(primeTolerance))
        throw new IllegalArgumentException(q+" is not prime!");
    //Create the array of solutions
    BigInteger[] result=new BigInteger[4];
    //Start forming the terms
    BigInteger aInv=a.modInverse(n);
    BigInteger pInv=p.modInverse(q);
    BigInteger qInv=q.modInverse(p);
    BigInteger twoInv=TWO.modInverse(n);
    BigInteger term1=
      aInv.multiply(twoInv.multiply(b).modPow(TWO,n).multiply(aInv).subtract(c));
    BigInteger term2=twoInv.multiply(aInv).multiply(b);
    BigInteger t1=
      lnr(term1.modPow(p.add(ONE).divide(FOUR),n)
      .subtract(term2).multiply(q).multiply(qInv),n);
    BigInteger t2=
      lnr(term1.modPow(q.add(ONE).divide(FOUR),n)
      .subtract(term2).multiply(p).multiply(pInv),n);
    BigInteger t3=
      lnr(term1.modPow(p.add(ONE).divide(FOUR),n).negate()
      .subtract(term2).multiply(q).multiply(qInv),n);
    BigInteger t4=
      lnr(term1.modPow(q.add(ONE).divide(FOUR),n).negate()
      .subtract(term2).multiply(p).multiply(pInv),n);
    //Form the solutions
    result[0]=lnr(t1.add(t2),n);
    result[1]=lnr(t1.add(t4),n);
    result[2]=lnr(t3.add(t2),n);
    result[3]=lnr(t3.add(t4),n);
    //Check the solutions; if any are bad, throw an exception
    BigInteger x;
    for (int i=0;i<4;i++) {
        x=result[i];
        if (!lnr(a.multiply(x.multiply(x)).add(b.multiply(x)).add(c),n).
           equals(ZERO))
            throw new IllegalArgumentException("Solution x="+x+" does not check!");
    }
    return result;
  }
}
```

FIGURE 9.1

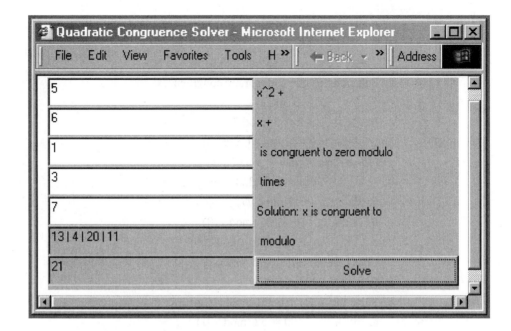

I have written an applet test program of the solveQuadratic() method, which can be run from the book's website. You enter the values a, b, c, p, and q for the quadratic congruence $ax^2 + bx + c \equiv 0 \pmod{pq}$. The primes p and q must both be congruent to 3 modulo 4. A screen shot of the applet, called TestSolveQuadraticApplet, is shown in Figure 9.1.

EXERCISES

1. Solve the following quadratic congruences:
   a. $x^2 \equiv 1 \pmod 7$
   b. $x^2 \equiv -2 \pmod{11}$
   c. $x^2 \equiv 6 \pmod{19}$
   d. $x^2 \equiv -3 \pmod{19}$
   e. $x^2 \equiv 3 \pmod{23}$
   f. $x^2 \equiv 7 \pmod{31}$

   Check the solution(s) you obtain.

2. Solve the following quadratic congruences:
   a. $x^2 \equiv 7 \pmod{93}$
   b. $x^2 \equiv -17 \pmod{33}$
   c. $x^2 \equiv -8 \pmod{57}$
   d. $x^2 \equiv 23 \pmod{77}$

    e. $x^2 \equiv 12 \pmod{69}$

    f. $x^2 \equiv 8 \pmod{217}$

    Check the solution(s) you obtain.

3. Solve the following quadratic congruences:

    a. $3x^2 + 2x \equiv 0 \pmod 7$

    b. $2x^2 + 3x + 9 \equiv 5 \pmod 7$

    c. $5x^2 + 10x + 13 \equiv 18 \pmod{23}$

    Check the solution(s) you obtain.

4. Solve the following quadratic congruences:

    a. $3x^2 + 2x \equiv 12 \pmod{77}$

    b. $2x^2 + 3x + 9 \equiv 106 \pmod{133}$

    c. $5x^2 + 10x + 13 \equiv 101 \pmod{209}$

    Check the solution(s) you obtain.

5. Prove proposition 30.

6. Solve the following quadratic congruences:

    a. $4x^2 + 2x + 100 \equiv 58 \pmod{231}$

    b. $2x^2 + 3x + 182 \equiv 0 \pmod{1463}$

    Check the solution(s) you obtain.

7. The solveQuadratic() method can be written in a much "cleaner" way. First, write a method to solve quadratic congruences of the form

$$x^2 \equiv a \pmod p$$

where p is a prime congruent to 3 modulo 4. Use this method in conjunction with the solveCRT() method, and use the Chinese Remainder Theorem to produce the solutions.

8. Suppose the quadratic congruence $ax^2 + bx + c \equiv 0 \pmod n$ has solutions, and that $n = p_1 p_2 \ldots p_m$, where each prime factor p_i is unique, and each congruent to 3 modulo 4. Explain how you would find the solutions.

9. Revise the solveQuadratic() method to compute and return solutions of quadratic congruences as described in the previous exercise.

CHAPTER 10

Quadratic Ciphers

The cryptosystems we are about to cover in this chapter are called public key cryptosystems. All the cipher systems we've looked at so far have been secret key schemes. This is the classical view of cryptography; it means that both the enciphering key and deciphering key must be kept secret, for knowing one is equivalent to knowing the other. For example, consider a block affine transformation

$$C \equiv aP + b \pmod{m}$$

where $(a, m) = 1$. The enciphering key are the numbers a, m, and b. If an unauthorized user captured these values, she could certainly encrypt messages to you, but even worse (obviously), she can easily derive the decryption key a' (where a' is an inverse of a modulo m) and decrypt any messages.

With public key cryptography, the situation is somewhat different. Public key means that two keys are involved: a public key used for enciphering, and a private key used for deciphering. But knowing the encryption key is not equivalent to knowing the decryption key, and this is the crucial difference. With public key cryptography, each user generates a public key, which they distribute to everyone, and a private key, which they do not divulge to anyone. Anyone who wants to send a message to some user must look up their public encryption key and use it to encrypt the message. On the receiving end, the user decrypts the message with their private key. No one else can decrypt because only the intended recipient knows the private key, and the private key is very difficult to calculate from the encryption key.

10.1 THE RABIN CIPHER

The encryption process of the following cipher, known as the Rabin cipher, involves producing ciphertext C from plaintext P as follows:

$$C \equiv P^2 \pmod{n}. \quad (0 \le P < \text{n}, 0 \le C < \text{n}) \quad (\dagger)$$

Here n is the product of two distinct large primes, say p and q, both congruent to 3 modulo 4. At current levels of computing power, n should be at least 1024 bits in length. The public key in this cipher is n. What is not made public is the prime factorization of n; that is, the two primes p and q are kept secret. These two values are necessary for decryption; thus, they are the private key.

The enciphering process is described in (†). Anyone knowing the value of n can send messages. Now, in order to decipher, we must solve the congruence

$$C \equiv P^2 \pmod{n}$$

for the plaintext P. We know from previous work that these solutions are obtained by forming the two congruences

$$C \equiv P^2 \pmod{p}$$

$$C \equiv P^2 \pmod{q}$$

and solving them. We then combine these solutions using CRT to obtain solutions for P. Thus, we can only solve (†) for P by factoring the modulus $n = pq$ (at least, no other way to solve these congruences is known). This is why the prime factors of n are kept secret. Only the individual possessing them can decipher. From proposition 31, we get the solution(s) to (†) as

$$P \equiv \pm(zqq_p{}' \pm wpp_q{}') \pmod{n}$$

where $z = C^{(p+1)/4}$, $w = C^{(q+1)/4}$, $q_p{}'$ is an inverse of q modulo p, and $p_q{}'$ is an inverse of p modulo q.

The obvious drawback to this method is that solving such congruences can produce four distinct square roots P for C. That is, it reports four possible plaintext messages during the decryption phase. If the message is text, it is easy to identify the correct one; it's the one that doesn't look like garbage! However, if the message is some type of binary stream, for example, the messages must be tagged in some way so this tag will reappear in the decryption process.

Why is it that we can reveal the value of n to everyone? We know that if someone manages to factor n into its prime factors p and q, our cryptosystem and we will be, metaphorically, up the creek without a paddle! Anyone knowing p and q can decrypt; the question is, how easy is it to factor n? If n is the product of two sufficiently large primes (say a few hundred digits each), then it is nearly impossible to factor n in a reasonable period of time. In fact, it will take somewhere on the order of a few billion years! We may find this hard to believe since we routinely factor integers in our math classes, but we simply don't appreciate the size of the numbers involved here. Indeed, factoring has become a huge study involving many techniques, some of which we shall study in upcoming chapters.

EXAMPLE.   To see how the Rabin cipher works, we use the ordinary alphabet A = 00, B = 01, ..., Z = 25. We will use a block size of four characters. With our choice of alphabet and block size, the largest possible block corresponds to ZZZZ = 25252525. We must pick a modulus n greater than this, and furthermore, n must be the product of 2 primes congruent to 3 modulo 4. Let $p = 6911$ and $q = 6947$. (You may wish to verify that p and q are both primes of the form $4k + 3$.) These two values are the private key, and must not be made public. We then compute $n = 6911 \cdot 6947 = 48010717$. The value of n can be made known to anyone, and in fact is necessary for encryption.

We wish to encipher the message

SHOOT NOW GEEK

which we will regroup into blocks of four letters each,

SHOO   TNOW GEEK

then convert the characters into their numerical equivalents. Leading zeros are important:

18071414 19131422   06040410.

Notice that should our messages not be evenly divisible into blocks of size 4, we should use some type of padding scheme. We proceed to encrypt the first block:

$$C \equiv 18071414^2$$

$$\equiv 1339280 \ (\text{mod } 48010717)$$

This residue is the first ciphertext block. The second block we encrypt as follows:

$$C \equiv 19131422^2$$

$$\equiv 22338923 \ (\text{mod } 48010717)$$

and the third as:

$$C \equiv 6040410^2$$

$$\equiv 40412478 \ (\text{mod } 48010717)$$

The transmitted enciphered message is the sequence of numbers

01339280   22338923   40412478.

Now, if you have done the job right and haven't told anyone about the two secret numbers, $p = 6911$, and $q = 6947$, you should be the only individual able to decrypt. (Of course, in this example, $n = 48010717$ is easily factorable into $n = 6911 \cdot 6947$; in reality we would use a much larger block size, and much larger primes.) To decrypt the first enciphered block, you must solve the congruence

$$1339280 \equiv P^2 \ (\text{mod } 48010717)$$

for P. Using the Chinese Remainder Theorem, we derive the four roots

$$\rightarrow \quad P \equiv 18071414 \ (\text{mod } 48010717)$$

$$P \equiv 16274554 \ (\text{mod } 48010717)$$

$$P \equiv 29939303 \ (\text{mod } 48010717)$$

$$P \equiv 31736163 \ (\text{mod } 48010717).$$

The correct root is marked. We decrypt the second block by solving

$$22338920 \equiv P^2 \pmod{48010717}$$

for P. We get the following roots, with the correct one again marked:

$$P \equiv 39784853 \pmod{48010717}$$

$$P \equiv 28879295 \pmod{48010717}$$

$$P \equiv 8225864 \pmod{48010717}$$

$$\rightarrow \quad P \equiv 19131422 \pmod{48010717}.$$

We solve this third congruence

$$40412478 \equiv P^2 \pmod{48010717}$$

for P to decrypt the third block. The roots we obtain are:

$$P \equiv 36711428 \pmod{48010717}$$

$$\rightarrow \quad P \equiv 6040410 \pmod{48010717}$$

$$P \equiv 11299289 \pmod{48010717}$$

$$P \equiv 41970307 \pmod{48010717}.$$

You can surely see the problem of deciding between four roots during decryption. In this case, deciding was easy because of our alphabet (no character ≥ 26). In general, how do we know which solution for P is the correct one? The answer is, if we didn't write the message, we don't know. The correct root may be any of the four roots, and there is no way of knowing in advance which one it will be. This poses a problem for this cryptosystem: What if two (or more) roots could both be construed as a valid message? One solution may be to tag the blocks with special character(s) which do not otherwise appear in the messages. For instance, in our example we use only the characters A = 00 through Z = 25; we could use the number 26 to tag the beginning of each block, as in:

SHOO   TNOW   GEEK

converts to

28705651   20676817   47296051.

Now, in front of each block, we place the tag, 26:

2628705651   2620676817   2647296051

and encipher this message. Thus, the block size of the enciphered message is greater than that of the plaintext. This is not a problem; many cipher systems exhibit different plaintext/ciphertext block sizes. When we decrypt, the tags will reappear, which we then remove from the message and convert back to characters. Similar tagging schemes can be used for messages that use ASCII character encoding and Unicode. You should remember that some messages, however, are not text at all, but may be any type of binary stream whatsoever.

Careful planning is necessary to ensure that a tagging scheme will work properly; that is, will not cause confusion on the receiving end. We will soon discuss a type of tagging which is most often employed with Rabin cipher implementations.

We actually have been rather presumptuous throughout this chapter, and we should correct this now. The Rabin cipher says both primes p and q must be of the form $4k + 3$. A natural question to ask now is, "OK, we know there are infinitely many primes, but are there infinitely many primes of the form $4k + 3$?" This is important because we must be able to freely select such primes for this cipher. But what if such primes eventually "run out," and we are left only with primes of the form $4k + 1$? The next result assures us that this does not happen.

PROPOSITION 33 There are infinitely many primes of the form $4k + 3$.

Proof. First note that if we have any two integers both of the form $4k + 1$, their product is also of the form $4k + 1$, since if $m = 4j + 1$ and $n = 4i + 1$ we have

$$mn = (4j + 1)(4i + 1) = 16ji + 4i + 4j + 1 = 4(4ji + i + j) + 1. \quad (*)$$

Hence, mn is also of the form $4k + 1$ (where k here is equal to $4ji + i + j$). Given this, we now assume there are finitely many primes congruent to 3 modulo 4. Thus, we can list them in a finite sequence starting with the smallest prime congruent to 3 modulo 4, and progressing through them in order to the largest, say $p_0 = 3$, $p_1 = 7$, $p_2 = 11$, ..., p_n. Now, consider the integer

$$N = 4p_1p_2 \ldots p_n + 3$$

which must contain a prime factor of the form $4k + 3$, for if not, its prime factors would all be congruent to 1 modulo 4, and hence their product N would also be congruent to 1 modulo 4, a contradiction. However, now note that $3 \nmid N$; for if $3|N$, we also have $3|(N - 3) = 4p_1p_2 \ldots p_n$, another contradiction (since $p_0 = 3$ does not appear in the sequence $4p_1p_2 \ldots p_n$). Likewise, none of the other primes p_i ($1 \le i \le n$) divides N, since if we have some $p_i|N$, we then also have $p_i|(N - 4p_1p_2 \ldots p_n) = 3$, which is ridiculous because all of the primes p_i ($i = 1, 2, \ldots, n$) are larger than 3. Since no prime of the form $4k + 3$ in the list $p_1, p_2, \ldots, p_n$ can divide N, and N must have such a prime as a factor, we can only conclude that our assumption is incorrect. There must be infinitely many primes congruent to 3 modulo 4. ∎

10.2 WEAKNESSES OF THE RABIN CIPHER

The Rabin cipher is quite secure, provided the proper precautions are taken. (Of course, the necessity of taking the proper precautions is true of any cipher.) As presented here, the Rabin cipher has certain weaknesses which can be exploited. We describe these weaknesses below.

Chosen Ciphertext Attack A chosen ciphertext attack is when an adversary has the ability to pass a single ciphertext message (of his choice) through an individual's decryption machine. The adversary may even have access to the decryption machine himself, but this does not necessarily mean he has access to the private key; these values may be secured inside the hardware in such a way that their retrieval by unauthorized means is not possible.

Suppose the Rabin decryption machine returns all 4 plaintext message values, and leaves it up to the application to decide which message is correct. If the Rabin decryption machine works this way, the analyst can factor n. To see this, suppose the analyst chooses a random integer, say z, and encrypts it using the public key value n:

$$C \equiv z^2 \pmod{n}.$$

He then runs this ciphertext C back through the decryption machine, and receives 4 messages in return. One of the returned values will be congruent to z modulo n, and another will be congruent to $-z$ modulo n. However, the other 2 roots, say r and r', are congruent to neither z nor $-z$ modulo n. Take either root, say r; he can derive one of the prime factors of n by simply noting that since $z \not\equiv r \pmod{n}$, $n \nmid (z - r)$, and so

$$(z - r, n) \neq n.$$

But if he can also show that $z - r$ and n are not relatively prime, he will then have found a nontrivial divisor of n; that is, p or q. He can do this in the following way; note that n cannot divide $z + r = z - (-r)$ since $z \not\equiv -r \pmod{n}$. Hence, n divides neither $z + r$ nor $z - r$. However, since $z^2 \equiv r^2 \pmod{n}$ he has

$$n \mid (z^2 - r^2), \text{ or } n \mid (z + r)(z - r)$$

which implies n is not relatively prime to $z - r$. Thus, $(z - r, n)$ yields a nontrivial divisor of n; namely, p or q.

EXAMPLE. Here we show a chosen ciphertext attack on Rabin. The adversary does not know the first two values p and q listed here; she only knows n, the product of p and q. She submits a message m to the decryption machine and gets four roots: x_1, x_2, x_3, and x_4. She is interested only in a root congruent to neither m nor $-m$ modulo n. The first root, x_1, is such a root. She calculates $(m - x_1, n)$, and in this case, obtains the factor q. She then derives p by taking $p = n/q$.

p is unknown to adversary:

$p =$
17976931348623159077293051907890247336179769789423065727343008115773267580550096313270847732240753602112011387987139335765878976881441662249284743063947412437776789342486548527630221960124609411945308295208500576883815068234246288147391311054082723716335051068458629823994724593847971630483535363296242241378590

q is unknown to adversary:

$q =$
3595538626972463181545861038157804946723595395788461314546860162315465351611001926265416954644815072042240227759742786715317579537628833244985694

86127894824875553578684973097055260443920249218823890616590417001153767630136468492576294782622108165447432670102136917259647989449187695943260967071265924844827668

$n = pq$ is public:

$n =$
6463401214262201460142975337733990392088820533943096806426069085504931027773578178639440282304582692737743592184379603898823911830098184219017630477289656624126175473460199218350039550077930421359211527676813513655358443728523951232367618867695234094116329170407261008577515178308213161721510479824786077168039180583408274776831691763152279716383800031412340152137152869819345741269583108122123538437343928423821045606152759418497127367645255205598014712084444888413036198687032378283647381146628192392272381849431882332598356071136706057555737475784812146651136260498654127694383482536657973180910847042149686379313.

Here is the bogus plaintext message that the adversary creates:

$m =$
3275628365082365092375902375908237509238750982759082375908273590823759087230958732098750932857903287509328750932487509832750983275098327590823750983709573092875093287509238587236589723658923659302750943275903428573265897265982356982365982356892658923650957809367239856892365982365982365982365982569825698235698265398236598269852732095689236589237932865982365982365987263986598236589726895698236598236598723658972.

The adversary computes the ciphertext by squaring the plaintext modulo n, and submits this to the decryption machine:

$C =$
6331175258121749631417265114115696135106929549214134339048342167588542966331248766247258033892260246598725326407852329339166212242715216615917798050568061328748253191898375248108531756400401814998101752286977535117697331996441847867733097013770907208558443347717410328642926548315542628348301060991597524541220743388252142331519414064269685864227740398688035009584408779834318823189112044751015402539264247086185192099845255539683212695374135696330442931169690006410634311794364957784418800457585030758560064753995190942293115578955198138212298271399040518748965782046565242764022176873403735774342171966051684944586280.

The decryption machine calculates and returns four roots to the adversary (knowing p and q you should be able to do this yourself and verify these calculations):

$x_1=$
136581210291743377386869067901142217233939214683424267658172999911458881

10137179133489858739056377014955418116065393138128994017463206572086498416070571705314011152928769000337192325260392980183091752907203123930659804070075336579450565751392922651569168633266576075065719636416845690282320305062507791085558639787903229521445899140687090636607917511898693341093723894495064925648985272373453897181107526432386664734934015786718196492608859495803424734018651372280238610767355931554987185888155655449267702884073996502716760099810207722110516129854911652071870793729691216695506923066755098517382626285867590850161814

$x_2 =$
646340121426220146014297533773399039208882053394309680642606908550493102777357817863944028230458269273774359218437960389882391183009818421901763047728965662412617547346019921835003955007793042135921120011397700541884920613828636040861669499259695818587873834304817863266879208243500328662822468949603514429294593183242499967850418193039319734128542907410305264280840194596062208229721721575619326334301633808096371901642616118279889076940956593970564961630350816442734696208879578004704914454839159413528981202586205579277469624415143284798681381686101886005289966226205540129572365887768528361108718721848981401341614

$x_3 =$
509758911134476768627428465872256821974942838710885412984433908639034221675986026529045440839894499124220178057784029008592451008377752701036778887023248609272506018058329918463080702403863240305003623695650112058937803672099029328731104372840296893719946584374965350200555153662364413348947997357400696861217520179308532263224177769444321605559204884154300604276476342031285317637105587077673382032659128518515457211275118074667747810675930562525554131021930766038917512195143922278492879233106264746550209344203223206092234609011593384650412449029364693946405688752953245814369117586114812144264821845539060013631319

$x_4 =$
327562836508236509237590237590823750923875098275908237590827359082375908723095873209875093285790328750932875093248750983275098327509832759082375098370957309287509328750923858723658972365892365930275094327590342857326589726598235698236598235689265892365095780936723985689236598236598236598236598236598256982569823569826539823659826985273209568923658923793286598236598236598726398659823658972689569823659823659872365897 2.

Two of these roots will yield a nontrivial divisor of n. We begin with x_1 by calculating $(m - x_1, n)$.

$(m - x_1, n) =$
359538626972463181545861038157804946723595395788461314546860162315465351
611001926265416954644815072042240227759742786715317579537628833244985694
861278948248755535786849730970552604439202492188238906165904170011537676
301364684925762947826221081654474326701021369172596479894491876959432609
670712659248448276687.

This is certainly not a trivial divisor of n. We have found one of its prime factors, and in this case, we found q. To find p, the adversary simply divides n by q (of course).

$p = n/q =$
179769313486231590772930519078902473361797697894230657273430081157732675
805500963132708477322407536021120113879871393357658789768814416622492847
430639474124377767893424865485276302219601246094119453082952085005768838
150682342462881473913110540827237163350510684586298239947245938479716304
83535632962424224137859.

You will be asked to write a program to execute such attacks in Java. A slight modification to the chosen ciphertext attack yields the adaptive chosen ciphertext attack, described below.

Homomorphic Property—Adaptive Chosen Ciphertext Attack   Note that the Rabin cipher has the following behavior: If we encrypt a plaintext message P to C, note that if we separate P into 2 parts, say m and m^*, which individually encrypt to c and c^*, respectively, we have

$$P^2 \equiv (mm^*)^2 \equiv m^2 m^{*2} \equiv cc^* \equiv C \pmod{n}.$$

This is referred to as the homomorphic property of the Rabin transformation. This can be exploited to employ an adaptive chosen ciphertext attack on this cipher. This attack is when a cryptanalyst has access to the decryption machine, as in the chosen ciphertext attack, but does not have total freedom to choose any message. That is, suppose the analyst chooses an integer z and computes

$$C \equiv z^2 \pmod{n},$$

but the decryption machine has been instructed to reject this message. The analyst must then "adapt" by trying to disguise the message C as another message. She can do this by selecting a random integer x relatively prime to n, and then computing

$$C^* \equiv Cx^2 \pmod{n}$$

and submitting the message C^* to the decryption machine. Now, note that

$$Cx^2 \equiv z^2 x^2 \equiv (zx)^2 \pmod{n}$$

by the homomorphic property, and so

$$C^* \equiv (zx)^2 \pmod{n}.$$

Thus, the decryption machine will return 4 square roots modulo n of C^*, say s_1, s_2, s_3, s_4. One of these 4 values will be congruent to zx modulo n, and another will be congruent to $-zx$ modulo n. However, the remaining 2 roots will be congruent to neither zx nor $-zx$ modulo n. Choose one from the latter category, say s_i, and compute $s_i x'$ where x' is an inverse of x modulo n. This value $s_i x'$ is congruent to neither z nor $-z$ modulo n, and can be used in the same manner as the chosen ciphertext attack described previously to obtain a prime factor of n.

Redundancy One solution to the chosen ciphertext problem and the adaptive chosen ciphertext problem is to ensure that the decryption machine returns only the correct plaintext message and withholds the other 3 roots. We can do this by padding with redundancy. For example, we can pad each block with 8 characters, where these characters are the first 8 characters of that block. Using this, the decryption machine will be able to distinguish the correct root from the other roots, as (with very high probability) only one root will possess the required redundancy.

Another form of redundancy is to append a "digest" of each block. A digest, in this case, is a fixed-size compressed version of the block. See Chapter 16 on cryptographic applications for more information about message digests/hashes.

Now, if an adversary computes an enciphered message from some random plaintext message z to the decryption machine, it will only return the correct root z, giving him no new information. This is also the case even if he attempts to disguise the message in the manner described using an adaptive chosen plaintext attack.

Weak Primes If the primes p and q for the Rabin cipher are not chosen carefully, the Pollard $p - 1$ method can be used to factor n (see Chapter 12 on factorization techniques). Specifically, p (also q) must be chosen so that $p - 1$ does not consist entirely of small factors.

For example, consider the prime $p = 10888869450418352160768000001 = 27! + 1$. Then $p - 1 = 27!$, and so the largest factor of $p - 1$ is 27—a very small integer when compared to p. The Pollard $p - 1$ method of factorization uses this fact to find the prime p. One solution to this problem is to choose p so that $p = 2t + 1$, where t is prime. Then we have $p - 1 = 2t$, and so $p - 1$ has a large prime factor, namely t.

For similar reasons, we also want to avoid primes p such that $p + 1$ consists entirely of small factors. When we generate primes with the intent of avoiding these weaknesses to factoring methods, we call such primes strong primes.

10.3 STRONG PRIMES

Definition
A prime number p is said to be a strong prime if integers r, s, and t exist such that:

(a) $p - 1$ has a large prime factor r

(b) $p + 1$ has a large prime factor s

(c) $r - 1$ has a large prime factor t.

Prime Generator—Gordon's Algorithm This algorithm produces strong primes. When we produce integers that are the product of large strong primes, these integers are highly resistant to factoring methods.

1. Generate two large random primes s and t of approximately the same size. (Use an appropriate random number generator and primality test; see Chapter 11 on primality testing.)

2. Choose an integer i^*, then find the first prime $r = 2it + 1$, where $i = i^*, i^* + 1, i^* + 2, \ldots$.

3. Compute $z =$ the lnr of $s^{r-2} \pmod{r}$.

4. Calculate $p^* = 2zs - 1$.

5. Choose an integer k^*, then find the first prime $p = p^* + 2krs$, where $k = k^*, k^* + 1, k^* + 2, \ldots$.

6. p is a strong prime.

To see that p is indeed a strong prime, note that by FLT we have $s^{r-1} \equiv 1 \pmod{r}$. Thus,

$$p^* = 2zs - 1 \equiv 2s^{r-2} \cdot s - 1 \equiv 2 \cdot 1 - 1 \equiv 1 \pmod{r}, \text{ and}$$

$$p^* = 2zs - 1 \equiv -1 \pmod{s}.$$

This immediately gives us what we need:

(a) $p - 1 = p^* + 2krs - 1 \equiv 0 \pmod{r}; \to r = 2it + 1$ is a large prime factor of $p - 1$

(b) $p + 1 = p^* + 2krs + 1 \equiv 0 \pmod{s}; \to s$ is a large prime factor of $p + 1$

(c) $r - 1 = 2it \equiv 0 \pmod{t}; \to t$ is a large prime factor of $r - 1$.

and we establish that p is a strong prime.

EXAMPLE. The following demonstrates finding a strong prime using Gordon's algorithm. First we generate s and t, two primes of about the same size.

$s =$
6492577451237557645642982325831833581050183984929252961827522302197958133156067177304138810373895137395987048195563277386549407088209816417448217
01213543

$t =$
4592298163519361454094076722068713720462656850623927447620392828239988008622089493892324339945089295059259438905626017010589364279547337054858511
046387127

Now, we look for the first prime r of the form $2it + 1$, where i begins at 1. In this case, we get:

$r =$
5969987612575169890322299738689327836601453905811105681906510676711984411208716342060021641928616083577037270577313822113766173563411538171316063
6030326511

Now, we compute z, the lnr of s^{r-2} modulo r:

$z =$
665230492072090237201496662581252085144747143014640731643715847110536584
592217084417720567412260139505217601163389933696724796030966764997614576
5260549183

We compute p^* as $2zs - 1$:

$p^* =$
346084307903560664425684232051486131077315397498633595581688753937826631
433322997849280623926140157753141972793817951619368163028361404889048627
525470705306956391991968534559962944356650024630432157045548591633214550
857822086145412115926942830031833676001801967113277394757571799217642094
28697654507474370737

We search now for the first prime p of the form $p^* + 2krs$, where here k starts with the value 1. This yields a strong prime, and, in this case, we get:

$p =$
136859550991023357674233837751193444637145211672745580838508211454534324
823686210424604005719046718052981484190707562992713417956940416543355152
315219159854859002395777579635185385039269578229009584384066590554210488
182334714799737615710384650453125076807810092764555005612188062536100529
7295821927389722213180427

Java Algorithm I have created a PrimeGenerator class for the purpose of generating strong primes. One creates a PrimeGenerator object, then calls a getStrongPrime() method. The primes generated by this method are of sufficient size and quality to thwart modern factorization methods.

```
import java.security.*;
import java.math.*;
import java.util.*;
public class PrimeGenerator {

    //To find primes, we first specify the minimum bit length
    //The methods will produce primes 1 to 3 bits larger than requested, but never
    // smaller
    int minBitLength;

    //certainty is the number of primality tests to pass
    int certainty;

    SecureRandom sr;

    public PrimeGenerator(int minBitLength, int certainty, SecureRandom sr) {
        //The bit length of the prime will exceed minBitLength
```

```
   if (minBitLength<512) throw new IllegalArgumentException
      ("Strong/Safe primes must be at least 64 bytes long.");
   //Set the values
   this.minBitLength=minBitLength;
   this.certainty=certainty;
   this.sr=sr;
}


//This method finds and returns a strong prime
public BigInteger getStrongPrime() {
   //The strong prime p will be such that p+1 has a large prime factor s
   BigInteger s=new BigInteger(minBitLength/2-8,certainty,sr);
   //t will be a large prime factor of r, which follows
   BigInteger t=new BigInteger(minBitLength/2-8,certainty,sr);
   BigInteger i=BigInteger.valueOf(1);
   //p-1 will have a large prime factor r
   //r is the first prime in the sequence 2t+1, 2*2t+1, 2*3t+1,...
   BigInteger r;
   do {
      r=BigIntegerMath.TWO.multiply(i).multiply(t).add(BigIntegerMath.ONE);
      i=i.add(BigIntegerMath.ONE);
   } while (!r.isProbablePrime(certainty));
   BigInteger z=s.modPow(r.subtract(BigIntegerMath.TWO),r);
   BigInteger pstar=BigIntegerMath.TWO.multiply(z).multiply(s).
      subtract(BigIntegerMath.ONE);
   BigInteger k=BigInteger.valueOf(1);
   //The strong prime p is the first prime in the sequence 2rs+p*, 2*2rs+p*,
   //2*3rs+p*,...
   BigInteger p=BigIntegerMath.TWO.multiply(r).multiply(s).add(pstar);
   while (p.bitLength()<=minBitLength) {
      k=k.multiply(BigIntegerMath.TWO);
      p=BigIntegerMath.TWO.multiply(k).multiply(r).multiply(s).add(pstar);
   }
   while (!p.isProbablePrime(certainty)) {
      k=k.add(BigIntegerMath.ONE);
      p=BigIntegerMath.TWO.multiply(k).multiply(r).multiply(s).add(pstar);
   }
   return p;
}

}
```

An applet that tests the getStrongPrime() method follows; it is called TestPrimeGenerator Applet, and can be run from the book's website. A screen shot of the applet is shown in Figure 10.1.

FIGURE 10.1

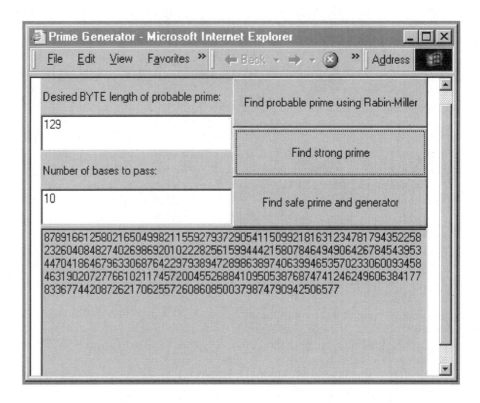

This applet also allows you to generate a probable prime using what is called the Rabin–Miller test. We have been using the constructor provided in Java from the BigInteger class:

`public BigInteger(int bitLength, int certainty, Random r).`

This constructor generates random BigIntegers of the specified bitlength, until one passes a primality test for a certain number of trials. The probability that this number is prime is

$$1 - (1/2)^{\text{certainty}}.$$

This constructor does not use the Rabin Miller primality test. However, we will cover the Rabin–Miller test in the chapter on primality testing. This applet also allows you to generate what are called safe primes, suitable for other types of cryptosystems. The PrimeGenerator class has a getSafePrimeAndGenerator() method, and a getSafePrime() method. Look in the chapter on exponential congruences for the definitions of safe prime, and generator.

There are other properties a prime may have that would make it vulnerable to certain factoring algorithms; see the chapter on factorization techniques for more information.

Square Root Problem The Chinese Remainder Theorem can help an adversary if Rabin is used to send the same message to multiple entities. Suppose someone wants to send the same message P to 2 entities, having moduli n, and n^*. They would compute the lnr's of

$$C \equiv P^2 \pmod{n}$$

$$C^* \equiv P^2 \pmod{n^*}.$$

Since it is very likely that these 2 moduli are pairwise relatively prime, one can easily compute a simultaneous solution modulo $M = n \cdot n^*$ for x to the set of congruences

$$x \equiv C \pmod{n}$$

$$x \equiv C^* \pmod{n^*}.$$

Since $P^2 < n \cdot n^*$, by CRT we must have $x = P^2$. Thus, by merely taking the normal positive square root of x, one can obtain P.

EXAMPLE. In this example, we will use parameters which would be feasible in actual practice. I think this is important for examples in cryptanalysis, to give you an idea of the scope of the problem. Suppose we wish to send the message

$m =$
3275628365082365092375902375908237509238750982759082375908273590827359082375908
7230958732098750932857903287509328750932487509832750983275098327509832759082375
0983709573092875093287509238587236589723658923659302750943275903428573326
5897265982356982365982356892658923650957809367239856892365982365982365982
36598236598256982569823569826539823659826985273209568923658923793286598
2365982365987263986598236589726895698236598236598723658972

to two different entities using Rabin. The first entity uses the public modulus

$n =$
6463401214262201460142975337733990392088820533943096806426069085504931027773578178639440282304582692737743592184379603898823911830098184219017630477289656624126175473460199218350039550077930421359211527676813513655358443728523951232367618867695234094116329170407261008577515178308213161721510479824786077168039180583408274776831691763152279716383800031412340152137152869819345741269583108122123538437343928423821045606152759418497127367645255205598014712084444888413036198687032378283647381146628192392272381849431882332598356071136706057555737475784812146651136260498654127694383482536657973180910847042149686379313,

and the second uses the modulus

$n^* =$
8273153554255617868983008432299507701873690283447163912225368429446311715550180068654843561349865846704311797996005892990494607142525675800342567010930760478881504606029054999488050624099750939339790755426321297478

880797251065757743055215064989964046890133812129409097921942823451284700
353341417572617870433870197661339699702384692398942940091526767537122407
294622549228222879740566332018250812637451109162228995890265099106862175
129783360538190048124955153727405933205488194213497935668384446131585719
769748108125895563260802289655241774630887967226547180792062432701705774
92531681313372190101243642764049531447613 57.

To compute the ciphertext $C \equiv m^2 \pmod{n}$ for the first entity, we obtain

$C =$
6331175258121749631417265114115696135106929549214134339048342167588542966
3312487662472580338922602465987253264078523293391662122427152166159177980
5056806132874825319189837524810853175640040181499810175228697753511769
7331996441847867733097013770907208558443347717410328642926548315542628348
3010609915975245412207433882521423315194140642696858642277403986880350095
8440877983431882318911204475101540253926424708618519209984525553968321269
5374135696330442931169690064106343117943649577844188004575850307585600
6475399519094229311557895519813821229827139904051874896578204656524276402
21768734037357743421719660516849445862 8,

and we apply the transformation $C^* \equiv m^2 \pmod{n^*}$ to obtain the ciphertext for the second entity:

$C^* =$
3941352481138538372399957853781551196604361615857999427246124872978844046
3274593948461368414816925248743452817906095698609011802587047997316541580
7243287982752578261206149474414115340822662855315835762700720048234558712
4445436173302993730573641691027524602521410239805865116914059082680835881
3845938845685753507638064949141815142059552740316792545972052346571502
1500179306273478205638799251490159856470610252397459099946884001280830252
6293997995433520872686198772934353510189079623471030356200252593323482754
8252338675726208932120378745263183500781730485201288929913901582666475013
6364110090814992374452422470738855529 1.

An eavesdropper captures both messages C and C^*, and knows their plaintext equivalents are the same. He has access to the public moduli n, and n^*, so he simply needs to find the simultaneous solution x to

$$x \equiv C \pmod{n}$$

$$x \equiv C^* \pmod{n^*}.$$

CRT tells him exactly how to compute this solution; it is

$$x \equiv Cn^*(n^*)' + C^*nn' \pmod{n \cdot n^*}$$

where $(n^*)'$ is an inverse of n^* modulo n, and n' is an inverse of n modulo n^*. Both of these values are easily computable using the extended Euclidean algorithm. The values he obtains for n' and $(n^*)'$ are

$n' =$
10326346198188286106278666375277746217509428904279382607377766093206423942144277412814817995614938363035147210138390141622243773942812053749684424519907944266801715470297606284208984156893807147900142799454318855422111527608872856745568456504296455743142110722243624901987860926610817585812436119775538111493797357218154871261340974722791358131905698539485239808448712497071606494742647212424537822328497746829005320358815225934851562504693598724428080017454027279791775824817125434120769029806248121616752833393483612189478992538808158575248060806679999874054991522413565923459124721094404114303310867579290716115560 82,

and

$(n*)' =$
56566554175287416080899545271654164688458964007962700402246811094731791572935565057632826263971656331256227163923178740845861169908159925198235348116718484782822914523431987273962126628206017379295128714694448530755059806340807592991200832032970734891833517702319778131097135434167430378299139079673221622006870266072664522352582560120446228078279495683635612334814283069639639862157145772648106454297779887455123091323597837218971005951984101784453710492197728649973835310310037026756532369889853010873417058831288556992474301830840735542637086756837432269125547112274951609967399232498190089468651608956593592819968.

He then combines these values using the CRT formula to obtain

$m^2 \equiv x \equiv$
10729741186132168090751486138433921776529508280820611432512308938113601552470163534116187137700755514858033641955553287115260998301783661256348759132743774366383284560564102604339402201257843418730131489454745672773025762558645181799141125144647706451385286054059130038030219812839835009500851733782082168283397027174188977082936677404101086293986515413621558357654715433800322268202523317566636248645872692814603306522649698809934494650124568337229990238047506736305336578039069199643720801446427858423431494496251334843683955033588783462031210961173064409003525561616658995829043690359792989228205096905554990386422720017648540054636940319995601981711146412020022705260733414365487655596963988531201706888881566574323508450455164381314320646382473907820579509784259428257082354155105865745256509992538572757424398951566596819756096784 (mod $n \cdot n*$).

Since he knows m^2 is less than $n \cdot n*$, x must in fact equal m^2 (rather than some residue of m^2). He merely needs to compute the positive square root of x to regain the plaintext:

$m = \sqrt{x} =$
3275628365082365092375902375908237509238750982759082375908273590823759087230958732098750932857903287509328750932487509832750983275098327590823750983709573092875093287509238587236589723658923659302750943275903428573 26

58972659823569823659823568926589236509578093672398568923659823659823 6598 236598236598256982569823569826539823659826985273209568923658923793286598 23659823659872639865982365897268956982365982365982365982365 98723658972.

Note that nowhere did the eavesdropper have to use any private information of either of the intended recipients! You will be asked to program this attack in Java.

A similar situation to the repeated message problem occurs if the message P is small when compared to a modulus n. For, in this case, it may turn out that P^2 is still less than n. Thus, the ciphertext $C = P^2$, and one can derive the plaintext P by simply taking the positive square root of C.

EXAMPLE.   Suppose we want to send the message

$P =$
23901847921064892176487658947562193452175401245010052134527164521635472 1 6457821534782157845217845872165478215472647656865871571612897687926489 47 56345234

to someone using Rabin. Their public modulus is

$n =$
64634012142622014601429753377339903920888205339430968064260690855049310 2 77735781786394402823045826927377435921843796038988239118300981842190176 3 04772896566241261754734601992183500395500779304213592115276768135136553 5 84437285239512323676188676952340941163291704072610085775151783082131617 2 15104798247860771680391805834082747768316917631522797163838000314123401 5 21371528698193457412695831081221235384373439284238210456061527594184971 2 73676452552055980147120844448884130361986870323782836473811466281923922 7 23818494318823325983560711367060575557374757848121466511362604986541276 9 43834825366579731809108470421496863793133.

By applying the enciphering transformation, we obtain the ciphertext

$C = P^2 =$
57129833404171410810834564319046222864290102685679534605553542566727844 1 85093482479373648715096810249263252142814012618230814162356131531112779 7 09370554551198208809716900499519364062878130971869830920199036515601548 7 81451800443153014386698801077033223603401131208051992795393900468762857 2 888504994514756.

The ciphertext is still smaller than the modulus; thus, all one needs to do is take the square root of the ciphertext message to derive P:

$P = \sqrt{C} =$
23901847921064892176487658947562193452175401245010052134527164521635472 1

6457821534782157845217845872165478215472647656865871571611289768792648947
56345234.

A remedy to this problem, called salt, is described shortly.

Forward Search Attack This attack is useful when the number of possible messages is small or predictable in some way. If this is the case, an adversary simply needs to encrypt all suspected messages (using public information) until a result is obtained that matches some ciphertext.

10.4 SALT

Salt simply refers to adding random data to the end of each block. This helps solve certain problems; in the case of the Rabin cipher, it certainly foils the forward search attack, as the messages are no longer predictable. It also solves the square root problem for small messages, if enough salt is used. To solve the square root problem posed by using the Chinese Remainder Theorem, we simply salt each block of each message differently (randomly) every time the message is sent. Thus, no 2 entities will receive the same message because of the random data tagged on the end. One who has the decrypting keys knows how much salt has been added (this is agreed on beforehand), and so removes it after decryption. At current levels of computing power, at least 64 bits of salt should be used (per block).

EXAMPLE. To foil a small message attack, we will add some salt to the small message in the previous example. We will encipher using the same modulus.

$P =$
2390184792106489217648765894756219345217540124501005213452716452163547216457821534782157845217845872165478215472647656865871571611289768792648947563452343204985729038750923487509238750932759063428568293658792658926502345732904573029875903245790234592437590279023457902709270927908270927309827032198749812648917264891276489127648912764982136489721634897126984621894

By applying the enciphering transformation, we now obtain the ciphertext

$P^2 \equiv C \equiv$
3625531511499322906933703974285568163096128607972134719990213013639705325077597371770057423230207092443868430969638304376282186862788123507880619656193981989034375448324101281488059228003612934060466521289183903297756948365559041013027893319386299837209113452803406506711065305279911090074924907807682653104133732672741651640093283311957222738321914700404068958189360537124686459716740458640058331351448073568441798525411772983418548115205243573204500080422545899827434427159516688812254174134167123563900005334919291034911308665083036791884013458868738314676627120908783947099134485738813532993131205259794448205485 9 (mod n).

The plaintext is now large enough so that when squared modulo n, we obtain a residue different from P^2. An attacker is now forced to compute the modular square root.

Java Algorithm   I have written methods to encrypt and decrypt using Rabin. To ensure only the correct message is returned out of the four possible roots obtained in the decryption phase, I add 4 bytes of redundancy to the beginning of each block; that is, before a block is encrypted, the first 4 bytes of the blocks are repeated at the front. (See Figure 10.2.)

Then, to protect against attacks commonly used on Rabin ciphers, I add 4 bytes of salt to the head of each block before encrypting it. This means a different ciphertext will be produced each time the message is encrypted. (See Figure 10.3.)

Of course, after decrypting, the receiver knows these bytes are simply random data, and throws them out.

I also use PKCS#5 padding, and so that the addition of redundancy and salt does not further restrict the block size, I do not include it in the padding. Thus, the maximum plaintext block size (including salt and redundancy) is $255 + 8 = 263$ bytes. (See Figure 10.4.)

FIGURE 10.2

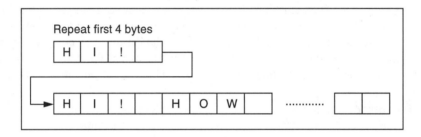

FIGURE 10.3

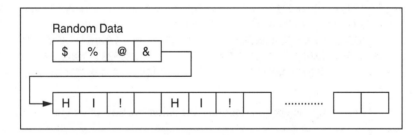

FIGURE 10.4

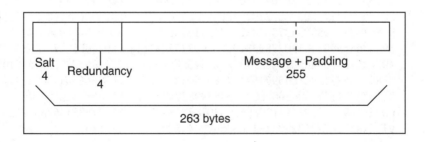

```
public class Ciphers {

    public static byte[] rabinEncipherWSalt(byte[] msg,BigInteger n,SecureRandom sr)
{
        //Compute the plaintext block size-take 4 bytes salt and 4 bytes redundancy
        //into account
        int blockSize=(n.bitLength()-1)/8;
        if (blockSize<12) throw new IllegalArgumentException
            ("Block size must be >= 12 bytes");
        byte[][] ba=block(pad(msg,blockSize-8),blockSize-8);
        //Begin the enciphering
        for (int i=0;i<ba.length;i++) {
            ba[i]=addRedundancyAndSalt(ba[i],sr);
            ba[i]=getBytes(new BigInteger(1,ba[i]).modPow(BigIntegerMath.TWO,n));
        }
        //Return to a 1D array.  The ciphertext block size is one byte greater than
        //plaintext block size.
        return unBlock(ba,blockSize+1);
    }

    public static byte[] rabinDecipherWSalt(byte[] msg,BigInteger p,BigInteger q) {
        //Compute inverse of p mod q, and of q mod p
        BigInteger n=p.multiply(q);
        BigInteger pinv=p.modInverse(q);
        BigInteger qinv=q.modInverse(p);
        BigInteger pexp=(p.add(BigIntegerMath.ONE)).divide(BigIntegerMath.FOUR);
        BigInteger qexp=(q.add(BigIntegerMath.ONE)).divide(BigIntegerMath.FOUR);
        //Compute the ciphertext block size
        int blockSize=(n.bitLength()-1)/8+1;
        byte[][] ba=block(msg,blockSize);
        //Begin the deciphering
        for (int i=0;i<ba.length;i++) {
            //Get the four roots
            BigInteger term1=new BigInteger(1,ba[i])
                .modPow(pexp,n).multiply(q).multiply(qinv);
            BigInteger term2=new BigInteger(1,ba[i]).
                modPow(qexp,n).multiply(p).multiply(pinv);
            byte[][] msgroot=new byte[4][0];
            BigInteger sum=term1.add(term2);
            BigInteger difference=term1.subtract(term2);
            msgroot[0]=getBytes(BigIntegerMath.lnr(sum,n));
            msgroot[1]=getBytes(BigIntegerMath.lnr(sum.negate(),n));
            msgroot[2]=getBytes(BigIntegerMath.lnr(difference,n));
            msgroot[3]=getBytes(BigIntegerMath.lnr(difference.negate(),n));
            boolean[] isCorrectRoot=new boolean[4];
            for (int k=0;k<4;k++) {
                isCorrectRoot[k]=true;
```

```
            for (int j=4;j<8;j++) if (msgroot[k][j]!=msgroot[k][j+4]) {
                isCorrectRoot[k]=false;
                break;
            }
        }
        boolean correctFound=false;
        for (int k=0;k<4;k++) if (isCorrectRoot[k]) {
            if (!correctFound) {
                correctFound=true;
                ba[i]=msgroot[k];
            } else {
                ba[i]=null;
                throw new IllegalArgumentException
                    ("Multiple messages satisfied redundancy requirement!");
            }
        }
        if (!correctFound) throw new NoSuchElementException
            ("No message satisfied redundancy requirement!");
        ba[i]=removeRedundancyAndSalt(ba[i]);
    }
    //Go from blocks to a 1D array, and remove padding; return this
    return unPad(unBlock(ba,blockSize-9),blockSize-9);
}


//Method to add redundancy and salt to blocks using Rabin
private static byte[] addRedundancyAndSalt(byte[] b,SecureRandom random) {
    byte[] answer=new byte[b.length+8];
    byte[] salt=new byte[4];
    random.nextBytes(salt);
    //Put salt in front
    System.arraycopy(salt,0,answer,0,4);
    //Follow with 1st 4 bytes of message-redundancy
    System.arraycopy(b,0,answer,4,4);
    //Copy the message over
    System.arraycopy(b,0,answer,8,b.length);
    return answer;
}


private static byte[] removeRedundancyAndSalt(byte[] b) {
    byte[] answer=new byte[b.length-8];
    //Copy the message over
    System.arraycopy(b,8,answer,0,answer.length);
    return answer;
}


//Other methods...


}
```

Following is an applet called TestRabinCipherApplet, which demonstrates the Rabin cipher. It can be found on, and run from, the book's website. (See Figure 10.5.) The applet requests you to enter a desired size for the modulus. Two strong primes are found, and the modulus is their product.

FIGURE 10.5

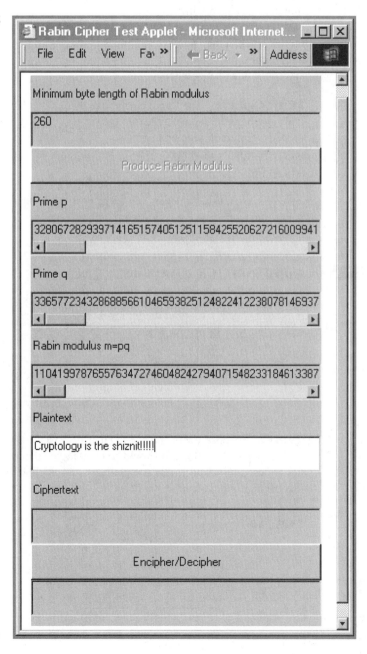

You first type a plaintext message in the plaintext area, then click a button to encipher. Clicking this button again regains the plaintext. If you encipher again, you will see that an entirely different ciphertext is generated. This is, of course, because salt is used.

Take note of the block sizes with Rabin; that is, the ciphertext block size is one byte greater than the plaintext block size. Why? This is easy to see if you recall that the message (as an integer) in a block must be less than the modulus. Suppose, for example, that the modulus (as a binary integer) is 26 bits long. We would then choose the plaintext block size as the largest byte smaller than 26 bits, or 3 bytes. However, once the encryption takes place on this block, it may produce a number as long as 26 bits (certainly greater than 3 bytes) in length; thus, the ciphertext block size needs to be one byte greater than the plaintext block size, or in this case, 4 bytes.

Static Ciphers   The Rabin cipher, like many other block ciphers, has a weakness in that it always maps the same plaintext to the same ciphertext. We call these ciphers memoryless, or static. Common plaintext in these cryptosystems can expose itself by appearing often (encrypted) in the ciphertext. When a block cipher is being used in this way, we say it is running in electronic code book, or ECB, mode.

A solution to this is to modify these ciphers so that a particular plaintext maps to different ciphertexts, usually depending on its position in the data. When a cipher is modified to behave this way, it is called a stream cipher. There are many ways to do this; the standard method for public key ciphers is called chaining.

10.5   CIPHER BLOCK CHAINING (CBC)

Cipher block chaining refers to a method of enhancing block enciphering. It employs a mask using exclusive–or at the bit level. You should be familiar with how an exclusive–or works, but we will review it here in Table 10.1. Suppose x and y are bits, and we represent the exclusive–or operation with the symbol $\oplus$.

One should note that the $\oplus$ operation is commutative, and reversible, in the sense that if x, y, and z are bits, then

$$z = x \oplus y \text{ iff } x = y \oplus z \text{ iff } y = x \oplus z.$$

EXAMPLE.   Suppose $x = 0$, and $y = 1$. Then $z = x \oplus y = 0 \oplus 1 = 1$. We can recover x by taking $z \oplus y = 1 \oplus 1 = 0 = x$. It should be clear to you that this is possible no matter what values are used for x and y. For completeness, all possible values are in the Table 10.2; note that the appropriate columns match.

TABLE 10.1

x	y	$x \oplus y$
0	0	0
0	1	1
1	0	1
1	1	0

TABLE 10.2

x	$y \oplus z$	y	$x \oplus z$	$z = x \oplus y$
0	0	0	0	0
0	0	1	1	1
1	1	0	0	1
1	1	1	1	0

We will also use the $\oplus$ operator to denote the exclusive–or operation on quantities larger than a bit; for example, if $X = x_0 x_1 \ldots x_n$, $Y = y_0 y_1 \ldots y_n$ are two bit sequences of length n, then

$$X \oplus Y$$

denotes

$$x_i \oplus y_i \quad i = 0, 1, 2, \ldots, n.$$

Now we can describe CBC, which uses exclusive–or in its operation. It can be used with any block cipher to change how enciphering is done. This is how it works:

Before the first plaintext block P_1 is enciphered, it is $\oplus$-ed with a block of random bits called an initialization vector, or IV. The IV does not need to be secret. The result of this plus operation is then enciphered; this produces the first ciphertext block C_1.

$$C_1 = E(P_1 \oplus \text{IV})$$

We do not specify which block enciphering transformation to use, because it doesn't matter; CBC is intended to work with any block cipher.

Subsequent plaintext blocks are $\oplus$-ed with the previous ciphertext block, then enciphered to produce the next ciphertext block. That is,

$$C_2 = E(P_2 \oplus C_1)$$

$$C_3 = E(P_3 \oplus C_2)$$

$$\vdots$$

$$C_n = E(P_n \oplus C_{n-1})$$

It should be clear to anyone that this avoids the problem of identical plaintext blocks always mapping to the same ciphertext blocks, for any particular block will be enciphered differently depending on whether it is first, second, . . . , or last.

Since $\oplus$ is reversible, and since enciphering transformations are intended to be reversible, we can recover the plaintext by simply doing what we did earlier in reverse. To decrypt the first ciphertext block, we run it through the deciphering transformation, then $\oplus$ it with the IV; this yields the first plaintext block $P_1 = D(C_1) \oplus \text{IV}$, since

$$D(C_1) \oplus \text{IV}$$

$$= D(E(P_1 \oplus \text{IV})) \oplus \text{IV}$$

$$= P_1 \oplus \text{IV} \oplus \text{IV}$$

$$= P_1 \oplus 0$$

$$= P_1$$

We can then regain each subsequent plaintext block P_i, because we just use the decryption transformation, and the previous ciphertext block C_{i-1},

$$D(C_2) \oplus C_1 = D(E(P_2 \oplus C_1)) \oplus C_1 = P_2 \oplus C_1 \oplus C_1 = P_2 \oplus 0 = P_2$$

$$D(C_3) \oplus C_2 = P_3$$

$$\vdots$$

$$D(C_n) \oplus C_{n-1} = P_n$$

Figure 10.6 shows a diagram showing CBC encryption:

It should be clear that by reversing this operation, decryption coupled with CBC regains the plaintext. (See Figure 10.7.)

FIGURE 10.6

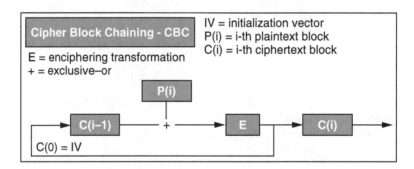

FIGURE 10.7

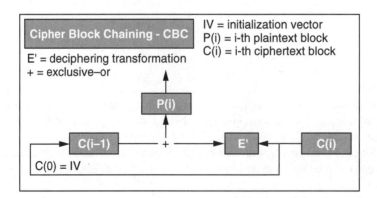

EXAMPLE.   For simplicity's sake, we'll do an example of CBC using a simple shift Vigenere cipher with a block size of one byte. Since we are using a bitwise operation (namely, exclusive–or), we will be mapping bytes. Some numbers will be in base 2.

The plaintext message is

$$p = \text{I LOVE YOU} = [73, 76, 79, 86, 69, 89, 79, 85] = [01001001, 01001100, 01001111,$$
$$01010110, 01000101, 01011001, 01001111, 01010101].$$

(The last quantity is the binary representation.) The key is

$$k = \text{CROAK} = [67, 82, 79, 65, 75] =$$

$$[01000011, 01010010, 01001111, 01000001, 01001011],$$

and the initialization vector is one byte long, given in binary by

$$\text{iv} = 10110010.$$

(Throughout the rest of this example, all numbers will be represented in binary.) The first ciphertext block is enciphered as

$$c_1 = E(p_1 \oplus \text{iv})$$

$$= E(01001001 \oplus 10110010)$$

$$= E(11111011)$$

$$\equiv 11111011 + 01000011 \pmod{100000000}$$

$$\equiv 00111110 \pmod{100000000}$$

where we represent the enciphering transformation as E. The resulting ciphertext block is used as input for enciphering the next ciphertext block. This yields

$$c_2 = E(p_2 \oplus c_1)$$

$$= E(01001100 \oplus 00111110)$$

$$= E(01110010)$$

$$\equiv 01110010 + 01010010 \pmod{100000000}$$

$$\equiv 11000100 \pmod{100000000}.$$

The enciphering continues, with each block's value dependent on the previous ciphertext block.

$$c_3 = 11011010$$

$$c_4 = 11001101$$

$$c_5 = 11010011$$

$$c_6 = 11001101$$

$$c_7 = 11010100$$

$$c_8 = 11010000$$

Some ciphers do not need to use chaining, for they are already stream ciphers. The following public key cipher is a perfect example.

10.6 BLUM–GOLDWASSER PROBABILISTIC CIPHER

This is another public key cipher based on quadratic congruences, which uses a mask at the bit level with an exclusive–or operation. This cipher qualifies as a stream cipher, which encrypts the same block differently depending on its position in the plaintext. Note that Rabin and most of the other block ciphers presented thus far do not have this property; that is, they always map a particular plaintext to the same ciphertext, unless we employ some type of chaining.

To generate keys for Blum–Goldwasser, one must choose two large primes, p and q, both congruent to 3 modulo 4, and let $n = pq$. At current levels of computing power, n should be at least 1024 bits in length. Then, using the extended Euclidean algorithm, find two integers a and b such that

$$ap + bq = 1.$$

The public key is the integer n, and the private key is the 4 values a, b, p, and q.

To encrypt a message (anyone can do this with the public key n), one does the following.

1. Let k be the largest integer not exceeding $\log_2 n$, and let h be the largest integer not exceeding $\log_2 k$. Represent the plaintext message P as an array $m_1 m_2 \ldots m_t$ of length t where each m_i is a binary number of length h.

2. Select a random square x_0 modulo n. One can do this by selecting a random integer r between 1 and $n - 1$, then setting

$$x_0 \equiv r^2 \ (\text{mod } n) \ \ (0 < x_0 < n)$$

3. Now, for $i = 1$ to t (in order) do
   - Let $x_i \equiv x_{i-1}^2 \ (\text{mod } n) \ \ (0 < x_i < n)$
   - Let p_i be the h least significant bits of x_i.
   - Let $c_i = p_i \oplus m_i$.

4. Compute $x_{t+1} \equiv x_t^2 \ (\text{mod } n) \ \ (0 < x_{t+1} < n)$

5. Send the ciphertext message $C = c_1 c_2 \ldots c_t$ and the integer x_{t+1}.

Note that only knowledge of n is required to encrypt. Now, to decrypt, the individual possessing the private key values a, b, p, and q proceeds as follows.

1. Let $d \equiv ((p + 1)/4)^{t+1} \ (\text{mod } p - 1) \ \ (0 \leq d < p - 1)$

2. Let $e \equiv ((q + 1)/4)^{t+1} \ (\text{mod } q - 1) \ \ (0 \leq e < q - 1)$

3. Let $u \equiv x_{t+1}^d \ (\text{mod } p) \ \ (0 \leq u < p)$

4. Let $v \equiv x_{t+1}^e \ (\text{mod } q) \ \ (0 \leq v < q)$

5. Retrieve x_0 by taking $x_0 \equiv vap + ubq \ (\text{mod } n) \ \ (0 < x_0 < n)$

6. Now, for i from 1 to t do:

- Let $x_i \equiv x_{i-1}^2 \pmod{n}$ $(0 < x_i < n)$
- Let p_i be the h least significant bits of x_i.
- Compute $m_i = p_i \oplus c_i$.

and the plaintext message $P = m_1 m_2 \ldots m_t$ is regained.

Why does this scheme work? In particular, how does the recipient retrieve the random value x_0 chosen by the sender? Decryption hinges on this, for once the receiver computes x_0, she can compute each successive x_i, and consequently compute each $m_i = p_i \oplus c_i$. First, observe that since x_t is a square modulo n, that is, $x_t \equiv x_{t-1}^2 \pmod{n}$, has a solution, then $x_t \equiv x_{t-1}^2 \pmod{p}$ also has a solution (see the proof of proposition 31). Thus, we have

$$x_t^{(p-1)/2} \equiv 1 \pmod{p}.$$

(This is called Euler's criterion; you were asked to prove this in order to prove proposition 30). Given this, note that

$$x_{t+1}^{(p+1)/4} \equiv (x_t^2)^{(p+1)/4} \equiv x_t^{(p+1)/2} = x_t^{(p-1)/2+1} \equiv x_t^{(p-1)/2} x_t \equiv x_t \pmod{p}$$

In the same way, $x_t^{(p+1)/4} \equiv x_{t-1} \pmod{p}$ and hence

$$(x_{t+1}^{(p+1)/4})^2 \equiv x_{t-1} \pmod{p}.$$

Continuing in this way, we obtain

$$u \equiv x_{t+1}^d \equiv (x_{t+1}^{(p+1)/4})^{t+1} \equiv x_0 \pmod{p}.$$

We obtain a similar result for v:

$$v \equiv x_{t+1}^e \equiv (x_{t+1}^{(q+1)/4})^{t+1} \equiv x_0 \pmod{q}.$$

Note that we have not yet obtained x_0; only 2 residues of x_0 congruent to u and v modulo p and q, respectively. We need the lnr of x_0 modulo n, for this is x_0 itself. To achieve this, we note that since

$$ap + bq = 1$$

we have both of the following:

$$bq \equiv 1 \pmod{p}$$

$$ap \equiv 1 \pmod{q}.$$

Thus, using the above two congruences, we derive the two congruences

$$vap + ubq \equiv x_0 \pmod{p}$$

$$vap + ubq \equiv x_0 \pmod{q}$$

and hence, by proposition 26, we know that

$$vap + ubq \equiv x_0 \pmod{n}$$

and hence the random seed x_0 is discovered, making decryption possible.

Since the intended recipient is the only one with knowledge of a, b, p, and q, she should be the only individual able to compute x_0. For without these values, it appears necessary to obtain x_0 by computing the sequence $x_t, \ldots, x_2, x_1$ by taking successive square roots modulo n beginning with x_{t+1}. As we have mentioned, this is an intractable problem without knowledge of the prime factors of n.

Why is this called a "probabilistic" cipher? It has to do with the apparent "randomness" of successive squares modulo n. Note that encryption is done by taking successive squares modulo n, and "masking" (via $\oplus$) the h least significant bits of the ith square with the ith plaintext unit. This produces a ciphertext that appears random, in the same sense that squares modulo n appear random. That is, if we could examine a square modulo n and notice some pattern in its binary digits, we could use this information to help us find the square root modulo n. We know of no other way to find solutions to quadratic congruences modulo n without factoring n into its prime factors; thus, a square modulo n looks merely like random data.

EXAMPLE.   We will do an example of this type of encryption using small values for p and q; in practice we would use primes hundreds of digits long. Say the recipient chooses two primes, $p = 503$, and $q = 563$. (Note that both p and q are congruent to 3 modulo 4). Using the extended Euclidean algorithm, she computes two values a and b such that $ap + bq = 1$. These are $a = -122$, and $b = 109$. She computes $n = pq = 503 \cdot 563 = 283189$, and makes public the value of n.

Now suppose someone wishes to send the message (seen as a binary integer)

$$P = 10011100001011111010$$

to this recipient. He knows the value $n = 283189$, and so uses it to select a random square $x_0 = 258507 \equiv 736^2 \pmod{283189}$. (The value 736 was chosen randomly.) Now, to block the message, he computes $\log_2 n \cong 18.11140570189$, and so chooses $k = 18$. He then computes $\log_2 k \cong 4.169925001442$, and then chooses $h = 4$. (Note the recipient can also compute these values, so she also knows the appropriate block size.) He then splits the message up into 4 bit blocks, to get

$$m_1 = 1001$$
$$m_2 = 1100$$
$$m_3 = 0010$$
$$m_4 = 1111$$
$$m_5 = 1010.$$

Now he must compute the successive squares x_1, x_2, x_3, x_4, x_5 modulo n, and mask (via $\oplus$) the h least significant bits of the ith square with the ith plaintext unit to get the ith ciphertext unit. We show this in Table 10.3.

Finally, the sender must compute $x_6 \equiv x_5^2 \equiv 67738 \pmod{n}$. He then sends to the recipient the ciphertext message

$$C = (1000, 1101, 0001, 1010, 0100, 67738).$$

TABLE 10.3

i	x_i	x_i (in binary)	p_i	m_i	$c_i = p_i \oplus m_i$
1	61585	1111000010010001	0001	1001	1000
2	245137	111011110110010001	0001	1100	1101
3	9347	10010010000011	0011	0010	0001
4	144197	100011001101000101	0101	1111	1010
5	188862	101110000110111110	1110	1010	0100

TABLE 10.4

i	x_i	x_i (in binary)	p_i	c_i	$m_i = p_i \oplus c_i$
1	61585	1111000010010001	0001	1000	1001
2	245137	111011110110010001	0001	1101	1100
3	9347	10010010000011	0011	0001	0010
4	144197	100011001101000101	0101	1010	1111
5	188862	101110000110111110	1110	0100	1010

To decrypt the message, the recipient must retrieve the random seed that the sender chose. Then she can compute the same sequence of squares x_1, x_2, x_3, x_4, x_5 and retrieve the plaintext by $\oplus$-ing the 4 least significant bits of the squares with the ciphertext. She does this by computing

$$d \equiv ((503 + 1)/4)^6 \equiv 302 \pmod{502}$$

$$e \equiv ((563 + 1)/4)^6 \equiv 101 \pmod{562}$$

$$u \equiv 67738^{302} \equiv 468 \pmod{503}$$

$$v \equiv 67738^{101} \equiv 90 \pmod{563}.$$

Finally, she obtains x_0, the lnr of $vap + ubq$ modulo n.

$$x_0 \equiv 90 \cdot -122 \cdot 503 + 468 \cdot 109 \cdot 563 \equiv 258507 \pmod{283189}$$

For completeness, Table 10.4 shows the recovery process.
Thus, the plaintext $P = 1001\ 1100\ 0010\ 1111\ 1010$ is regained.

10.7 WEAKNESSES OF THE BLUM–GOLDWASSER PROBABILISTIC CIPHER

This cipher can be broken if the following weaknesses are not dealt with. First, the primes must be chosen carefully; for example, we must avoid primes p for which the factorization of $p - 1$ consists entirely of small factors. Also, as with Rabin, Blum–Goldwasser is vulnerable to a chosen ciphertext attack. You should consider how such an attack may be posed.

EXERCISES

1. Use Rabin to encipher the following messages:

   a. TORPEDO AWAY

   b. FIRE AT WILL

   c. WILL GONE BELAY MY LAST

   Use $p = 11027$, $q = 10859$, and the ordinary alphabet. Use a tagging scheme for the sake of decryption. Block and pad as necessary, but do not use salt. Then decipher.

2. Explain how Blum–Goldwasser probabilistic encryption is vulnerable to a chosen ciphertext attack.

3. Write a Java program to execute a chosen ciphertext attack on Rabin.

4. Write a Java program to execute a square root attack on an unsalted enciphered message sent to multiple recipients using the Rabin transformation.

5. Write a rabinEncipherWCBC() method and a rabinDecipherWCBC() method for the Ciphers class.

6. Write enciphering and deciphering methods for the Blum–Goldwasser cipher.

CHAPTER 11

Primality Testing

Note that we are now using cryptosystems that require us to find and use large prime numbers. How do we find large prime numbers? Do we pick a large random odd integer and try to factor it? No. Factoring takes a lot of time, and is not a good way of determining whether or not an integer is prime. In fact, this is exactly what makes the Rabin cipher and others like it secure. If factoring the public key n was not extremely difficult, anyone could factor n and obtain the private key values p and q (the factors of n). You may have assumed that attempted factoring is the only way to determine whether or not a number is prime. It isn't. We develop alternative methods to do this now.

First recall Fermat's Little Theorem (FLT): If p is prime and $p \nmid a$, $a^{p-1} \equiv 1 \pmod{p}$. (Note that the contrapositive of FLT says that if $a^{p-1} \not\equiv 1 \pmod{p}$, p must be composite.) What about the converse of FLT? That is, if $a^{p-1} \equiv 1 \pmod{p}$, can we conclude that p is prime? Surprisingly, this is often true. We can see this if we raise 2 to some integer powers, as shown in Table 11.1.

It appears that when n is prime, we always get a value congruent to 1, and when n is composite, we get a value not congruent to 1. However, this doesn't always hold. There are composite integers n for which $2^{n-1} \equiv 1 \pmod{n}$. Take the composite number $341 = 11 \cdot 31$. When we raise 2 to the 340 power, we get a least nonnegative residue of 1 modulo 341. (Verify.) If the converse of FLT were true, we could conclude that 341 is prime; but it obviously isn't, so the converse of FLT is not true.

There isn't anything special about the choice of 2 as our base, so we might want to simply try another base. For example, we apply "Fermat's test" on 341 using 3 as the base. We get

$$3^{340} \equiv 56 \pmod{341}.$$

This establishes immediately that 341 is composite. So, we might think we can get around the failure of Fermat's test by just trying different bases modulo n until we either

1. Obtain a least nonnegative residue not equal to 1, and conclude that n is composite.
2. Do not obtain a residue congruent to 1 modulo n after many tries with different bases, and conclude that n is probably prime since we can't prove it isn't using this test.

TABLE 11.1

n	$2^{n-1} \equiv x \pmod{n}$	Is n prime?
3	$2^2 \equiv 1 \pmod 3$	Yes
4	$2^3 \equiv 0 \pmod 4$	No
5	$2^4 \equiv 1 \pmod 5$	Yes
6	$2^5 \equiv 2 \pmod 6$	No
7	$2^6 \equiv 1 \pmod 7$	Yes
8	$2^7 \equiv 0 \pmod 8$	No
9	$2^8 \equiv 4 \pmod 9$	No
10	$2^9 \equiv 2 \pmod{10}$	No
11	$2^{10} \equiv 1 \pmod{11}$	Yes

This isn't a bad idea, actually, if it weren't for the existence of Carmichael numbers; these are very rare composite integers that fool Fermat's test for any base b relatively prime to n. The integer $561 = 3 \cdot 11 \cdot 17$ is a Carmichael number, and we can prove it in this way: Take any base b relatively prime to 561; so $(b, 3) = (b, 11) = (b, 17) = 1$. FLT tells us then that $b^2 \equiv 1 \pmod 3$, $b^{10} \equiv 1 \pmod{11}$, and $b^{16} \equiv 1 \pmod{17}$. This tells us then that

$$b^{560} = (b^2)^{280} \equiv 1 \pmod 3,$$

$$b^{560} = (b^{10})^{56} \equiv 1 \pmod{11}, \text{ and}$$

$$b^{560} = (b^{16})^{35} \equiv 1 \pmod{17}.$$

Proposition 26 now implies that $b^{560} \equiv 1 \pmod{561}$ for any base b such that $(b, 561) = 1$, and so 561 is a Carmichael number.

Though Carmichael numbers are very rare (much rarer than primes), there are still infinitely many of them. However, we will not prove this. The fact that they exist at all is enough to avoid using Fermat's test for primality, especially when we can develop better tests which Carmichael numbers cannot fool. An example of such a test is Miller's test. Miller's test is based on Fermat's test, but carries it a bit further. In order to prove that it works, we will need the following, which you should easily be able to prove.

PROPOSITION 34 Let p be prime, and suppose $x^2 \equiv 1 \pmod p$. Then $x \equiv 1 \pmod p$ or $x \equiv -1 \pmod p$.

Proposition 34 says the only square roots of 1 modulo a prime are 1 and -1. This fact will be immensely helpful. Now we can discuss Miller's test, which is based on proposition 34.

11.1 MILLER'S TEST

> **Definition** (Miller's Test.)
> Let n be a positive integer with $n - 1 = 2^s t$ where s is a nonnegative integer, and t is an odd positive integer. We say that n passes Miller's test for the base b if either $b^t \equiv 1$ (mod n) or $b^{kt} \equiv -1$ (mod n) for some $k = 2^j$, $0 \leq j \leq s - 1$.

Let's discuss in detail how Miller's test works. Suppose you are testing the integer n for primality, and obtain $b^{n-1} \equiv 1$ (mod n). This doesn't tell you if n is prime or not, so consider the quantity $y = (n - 1)/2$, and evaluate $x \equiv b^y$ (mod n). If n is prime we must have $x \equiv 1$ (mod n), or $x \equiv -1$ (mod n), since $x^2 = x \cdot x = (b^{(n-1)/2})(b^{(n-1)/2}) = b^{(n-1)} \equiv 1$ (mod n) by Fermat's Little Theorem, and Proposition 34 says the only square roots of 1 modulo a prime are 1 and -1. So, when we compute x we have the following cases to consider:

1. x is congruent to neither 1 nor -1 modulo n. In this case, x has a square root that is congruent to neither 1 nor -1; hence n cannot be prime by Proposition 34 and so fails the test.

2. $x \equiv -1$ (mod n). This case says that n may be prime. We can go no further with the test once we obtain a residue of -1, so we conclude that n passes the test.

3. $x \equiv 1$ (mod n) This also says that n may be prime, and furthermore we can continue to test n for primality in this way:

    a. If $2 | y$, divide y by 2 (again) and evaluate $x \equiv b^y$ (mod n). Then consider as before the three cases above.

    b. If y is not divisible by 2, the last value for x was congruent to 1 modulo n. We can go no further with the test, and conclude that n passes the test for primality.

Note that the previous procedure must eventually terminate, since

- we must eventually obtain a residue not equal to 1, or
- during each iteration we divide the value of y in half, and at some point y must fail to be divisible by 2.

It should be clear to you that if you run a prime number through Miller's test, it will pass.

PROPOSITION 35 If n is prime and b is a positive integer such that $n \nmid b$, then n passes Miller's test for the base b.

Proof. If n is prime in the algorithm described above, you must eventually

1. Obtain a value for $x \equiv -1$ (mod n), or

2. Fail to be able to divide y by 2 any further

Either way, the prime n passes the test. At no point can you generate a square root of 1 that is congruent to neither 1 nor -1 modulo n, for this is demanded by Proposition 34. ∎

EXAMPLES.

1. Take the prime $n = 29$ and a base $b = 5$; we will see that n passes Miller's test. Start with the exponent $y = (n - 1)/2 = (29 - 1)/2 = 14$ and compute $5^{14} \equiv 1 \pmod{29}$. So far, this is a pass; divide y by 2 to get $y = 7$ and compute $5^7 \equiv 28 \equiv -1 \pmod{29}$. This is also a pass, and we can continue no further since we obtained a residue of -1. (Had we obtained a residue of 1, we still could not have proceeded since y cannot be halved any further; regardless, $n = 7$ passes Miller's test for the base 5.)

2. Take the prime $n = 257$, and the base $b = 22$, and note the progression of Miller's test in Table 11.2.

   TABLE 11.2

Exponent y	$22^y \equiv ?\pmod{257}$	Conclusion
128	1	Pass–continue
64	1	Pass–continue
32	−1	Pass–STOP

3. We repeat the above test for $n = 257$, but using a different base $b = 17$. (See Table 11.3.)

   TABLE 11.3

Exponent y	$17^y \equiv ?\pmod{257}$	Conclusion
128	1	Pass–continue
64	1	Pass–continue
32	1	Pass–continue
16	−1	Pass–STOP

4. We repeat the test one more time for $n = 257$, but using a base $b = 4$. (See Table 11.4.)

   TABLE 11.4

Exponent y	$4^y \equiv ?\pmod{257}$	Conclusion
128	1	Pass–continue
64	1	Pass–continue
32	1	Pass–continue
16	1	Pass–continue
8	1	Pass–continue
4	−1	Pass–STOP

You are invited to verify the values obtained here. When an integer n fails Miller's test, n is definitely composite, but if it passes, we still don't know for sure whether or not it is prime. However, there exist no composite integers that can fool Miller's test to every base b; even Carmichael numbers must eventually fail Miller's test for some base b. We will not prove this, but will state a proposition to this effect. The proposition actually says something much stronger; it puts an upper bound on the number of bases for which a composite integer can fool Miller's test.

PROPOSITION 36   Suppose n is an odd, composite positive integer. Then n fails Miller's test for at least 75 percent of the test bases b where $1 \leq b \leq n - 1$.

For example, take the Carmichael number 561; it passes Fermat's test, but fails Miller's test for the base 2. (See Table 11.5.)

The failure of Miller's test establishes definitely that 561 is composite. Note that Proposition 36 says that there can be nothing akin to Carmichael numbers for Miller's test. In fact, Proposition 36 allows us to establish a "probability" that an integer is prime. Suppose, for example, that we take a very large integer n and it passes Miller's test for some base b between 1 and $n - 1$. Since n can pass Miller's test for at most 75 percent of such bases, there is no more than a 25 percent chance that n is composite, or equivalently, no less than a 75 percent chance that n is prime.

11.2   THE RABIN–MILLER TEST

If we then repeat Miller's test on n with different bases, we can either discover that n is composite, or force the probability that it is prime as close to 1 as desired. This is in fact what modern computers do when searching for large primes, and this particular method of finding "probable" primes is called the Rabin–Miller test.

Succinctly: if an integer n passes Rabin–Miller for q different bases, then the probability that n is prime is no less than $1 - (1/4)^q$. It is important to note that the bases used for the Rabin–Miller test be chosen as randomly as possible. The study of pseudo-random number generation is a broad topic of great interest to cryptographers; see Chapter 16 on cryptographic applications.

Java Algorithm   The Java BigInteger class provides a constructor to generate probable primes. The test used is different than Rabin–Miller as we have presented it; their version establishes after q passes that n is prime with probability $1 - (1/2)^q$. (Most likely, they are

TABLE 11.5

Test	Status
$2^{560} \equiv 1 \pmod{561}$	Passes Fermat's test
$2^{280} \equiv 1 \pmod{561}$	Pass
$2^{140} \equiv 67 \pmod{561}$	FAIL–STOP

using the Solovay–Strassen primality test, which uses what are called Jacobi symbols; there is no reason for us to learn it, since Rabin–Miller does just as well, and provides higher probability with fewer trials.) We will write a method called primeProbability() to perform Rabin–Miller's test on an integer *n*. It will return the probability that *n* is prime, given a certain number of passes requested. If *n* fails any pass, primeProbability() will return 0.

```java
import java.math.BigInteger;
import java.security.SecureRandom;
public class BigIntegerMath {
//. . .
static final BigInteger TWO=new BigInteger(929);
//. . .
   //Implements the Rabin-Miller test.
   //Number of different bases to try is passed in as an int
   //If the BigInteger passes all tests, returns the probability it is prime as a
   //double.
   //Returns zero if the BigInteger is determined to be composite.
   public static double primeProbability(BigInteger n,int numPasses) {
      if (numPasses<=0) throw new IllegalArgumentException
         ("Number of bases must be positive!");
      BigInteger b,x;
      SecureRandom sr=new SecureRandom();
      BigInteger nMinusOne=n.subtract(ONE);
      for (int i=0;i<numPasses;i++) {
         //Choose a random base smaller than n
         b=new BigInteger(n.bitLength()-1,sr);
         //Check Fermat's condition first
         x=b.modPow(nMinusOne,n);
         if (!x.equals(ONE)) return 0.0;//not prime
         //Divide n-1 by 2
         BigInteger[] dr=nMinusOne.divideAndRemainder(TWO);
         //Perform the root tests
         while (dr[1].equals(ZERO)) {
            x=b.modPow(dr[0],n);
            //if you get -1, this is a PASS; get out
            if (x.equals(nMinusOne)) break;//pass
            //Now, if its not -1 or 1, this is a FAIL, return 0
            if (!x.equals(ONE)) return 0.0;//not prime
            //If its 1, so far its a pass
            //We can continue with the test; divide by 2
            dr=dr[0].divideAndRemainder(TWO);
         }
      }
      //Only way to get here is by passing all tests
      return 1.0-Math.pow(0.25,numPasses);
   }
}
```

FIGURE 11.1

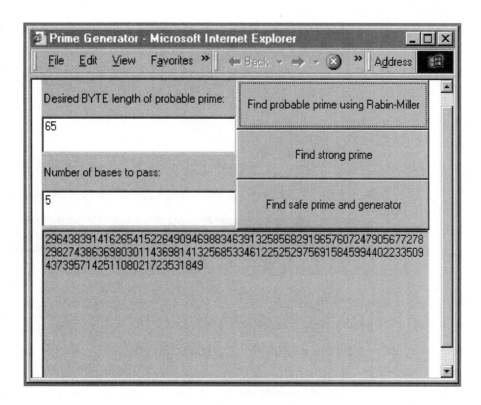

The applet called TestPrimeGeneratorApplet generates probable primes of a specified byte length. It generates random numbers of the requested length, and tests each for primality until one passes, using the number of tests specified. The screen shot in Figure 11.1 is of the applet generating a probable prime using Rabin–Miller.

This particular prime is just a probable prime. It was not constructed to be a strong prime, or a safe prime, though it may be either purely by accident. See the chapters on quadratic ciphers (Chapter 10) and on exponential congruences (Chapter 13) for an explanation of the terms strong prime and safe prime.

EXERCISES

1. Using the Rabin–Miller primality test, determine the probability that the integer is prime for each of the following numbers. Choose your own bases (as randomly as you can). You should be able to do the calculations without the aid of a computer.

Integer to test	Number of random bases to use
19	3
101	5
103	4
97	3

2. Repeat the previous exercise using these larger numbers. A program may be used.

Integer to test	Number of random bases to use
118691349287502432650127495149\1498649	10
52398765725747654376124333864\78252751	15
88438883512725438948586054071\9510049	20
93094086628069060728503686809\6531589	30
89947644004209235508303308904\0210287	33

3. Test the following number for primality; use 5 different random bases:

1358298529049385849277351428359266778603493846931744549748519669727813
0927542418487205392083207560592298578262953847383475038725543234929971
1555483428006287218857634994063903317828641441646807307668371605262231
7651279843577212995655335528603220308038077575973232019898509488400406
9116123084147875437183658467465148948790552744167567.

CHAPTER **12**

Factorization Techniques

The Rabin cipher, like some other modern ciphers, is believed secure because breaking it seems to involve factoring a huge integer having two large prime factors. This certainly appears to be the case; finding large prime factors is an intractable problem. Hence, research into better factorization techniques is a very serious endeavor now, often involving fair sums of money.

Many factorization methods have been developed over the years, but unfortunately, they are not widely known to the public. In fact, it is likely that trial division is the only method of factoring most people will learn in their lives.

Recall how the trial division method works; to factor an integer n, do trial divisions of n by integers between 2 and the square root of n. A factor, say d, of n is guaranteed to lie in this range by proposition 6. We can then take $n_1 = n/d$, then continue to factor n_1 by looking for factors between 2 and the square root of n_1. We continue in this way, reducing the size of n by producing a smaller number n_i to factor, at iteration i. We will eventually obtain the full factorization of n. The trial division method is quite simple, but is very inefficient when n has only large prime factors, since it may be necessary to try factors very near $\sqrt{n}$. When n is very large, its square root is also very large; a loop passing through all the primes less than $\sqrt{n}$ could take virtually an eternity. However, it is important to note that when n does have small prime factors, this sequential search for factors is quite efficient, and often finds small factors well before an alternative factoring method would.

We will cover a few alternative methods of factoring here; many are quite innovative, and the fact that they actually work may seem surprising to you. Though none of the methods covered here are nearly fast enough to break ciphers based on the factoring problem, investigating them is undoubtedly worthwhile, for they may provide insight into even better factorization methods.

12.1 FERMAT FACTORIZATION

This method is named after Pierre de Fermat. Though it can be even more inefficient than the trial division method, it is valuable in that it provides you with an alternative view of factoring.

To see how it works, consider an odd positive integer n, and suppose that

$$n = ab$$

where a and b are integers. (Note that since n is odd, both a and b must be odd.) Now, note that we can write n as the difference of two squares

$$n = s^2 - t^2$$

if we have

$$s = (a + b)/2, \text{ and}$$

$$t = (a - b)/2.$$

Note that both s and t are integers, since both a and b are odd. Similarly, if we have an odd positive integer n that is the difference of two squares, say

$$n = x^2 - y^2$$

then we can factor this integer into

$$n = cd$$

where

$$c = (x + y), \text{ and}$$

$$d = (x - y).$$

Thus, we can approach the problem of factoring an odd positive integer n by looking for squares whose difference is n, rather than looking directly for factors of n. That is, we look for integer solutions of the equation

$$n = x^2 - y^2.$$

We can do this by rewriting the previous equation in this way:

$$y^2 = x^2 - n.$$

and search for perfect squares of the form $x^2 - n$. We can do this sequentially; we start with m, the smallest integer greater than the square root of n, and look for perfect squares in the sequence

$$m^2 - n, (m + 1)^2 - n, (m + 2)^2 - n, \ldots.$$

This search is guaranteed to end, since m will have to go no further than $m = (n + 1)/2$, since:

$$((n + 1)/2)^2 - n = ((n - 1)/2)^2$$

and all the terms are integers. To see that the previous equation is true, note that

$$((n + 1)/2)^2 - ((n - 1)/2)^2 = (n^2 + 2n + 1)/4 - (n^2 - 2n + 1)/4 = 4n/4 = n.$$

(However, if we do go this far, note that we have only obtained the trivial factorization $n = n \cdot 1$.)

EXAMPLES.   We will use Fermat factorization to factor the following integers:

a) 3811. We begin with $m = 62 > 61.73 \cong \sqrt{3811}$ and look for perfect squares in the sequence

$62^2 - 3811 = 3844 - 3811 = 33$

$63^2 - 3811 = 3969 - 3811 = 158$

$64^2 - 3811 = 4096 - 3811 = 285$

$65^2 - 3811 = 4225 - 3811 = 414$

$66^2 - 3811 = 4356 - 3811 = 545$

$67^2 - 3811 = 4489 - 3811 = 678$

$68^2 - 3811 = 4624 - 3811 = 813$

$69^2 - 3811 = 4761 - 3811 = 950$

$70^2 - 3811 = 4900 - 3811 = 1089 = 33^2$

Thus we obtain a factorization of 3811 by noting that

$3811 = 70^2 - 33^2 = (70 + 33)(70 - 33) = 103 \cdot 37.$

b) 6077

Begin with $m = 78 > 77.95 \cong \sqrt{6077}$ and examine the sequence

$78^2 - 6077 = 6084 - 6077 = 7$

$79^2 - 6077 = 6241 - 6077 = 164$

$80^2 - 6077 = 6400 - 6077 = 323$

$81^2 - 6077 = 6561 - 6077 = 484 = 22^2$

And we see that $6077 = 81^2 - 22^2 = (81 + 22)(81 - 22) = 103 \cdot 59.$

c) 11

Begin with $m = 4 > 3.32 \cong \sqrt{11}$ and examine the sequence

$4^2 - 11 = 16 - 11 = 5$

$5^2 - 11 = 25 - 11 = 14$

$6^2 - 11 = 36 - 11 = 25 = 5^2$

And here we obtain the trivial factorization $11 = 6^2 - 5^2 = (6 + 5)(6 - 5) = 11 \cdot 1.$

Hopefully you can see how inefficient this method of factoring can be. It can be even worse than the trial division method, for trial division never has to test more than $\sqrt{n}$ integers, but with the Fermat method it may be necessary to search as many as $(n + 1)/2 - \sqrt{n}$ integers before the procedure is guaranteed to terminate. As the integer n gets larger, the quantity $(n + 1)/2 - \sqrt{n}$ becomes much larger than $\sqrt{n}$. (See Table 12.1.)

The Fermat factorization method is most efficient when the two factors of n, say

$$n = ab = x^2 - y^2 = (x + y)(x - y)$$

TABLE 12.1

n	s = square root of n	(n+1)/2−s
101	10.04987562	40.95012438
1001	31.63858404	469.361416
10001	100.0049999	4900.995
100001	316.2293472	49684.77065
1000001	1000.0005	499000.9995
10000001	3162.277818	4996838.722
100000001	10000.00005	49990001
1000000001	31622.77662	499968378.2
10000000001	100000	4999900001

are close together (thereby making x and y close together). This keeps the search of the sequence

$$m^2 - n, (m + 1)^2 - n, (m + 2)^2 - n, \ldots$$

relatively short.

Java Algorithm   To develop a method to extract factors of n using Fermat factorization, we need to be able to compute $\sqrt{n}$. The BigInteger class contains no square root method, so we must write our own. We wish this method to return the largest integer whose square does not exceed n. To compute the integer square root of a positive number, we will approach the real root using a numerical algorithm known as Newton's method. Suppose we wish to find the square root of n; i.e., a solution to

$$x^2 = n.$$

We will do this by trying to find a root (or a zero) of the function

$$f(x) = x^2 - n.$$

To use Newton's method, we need the derivative of $f(x)$, which, in this case is

$$f'(x) = 2x.$$

We begin with an initial guess for the root, say r_0. Suppose, for convenience, that this guess overestimates the true root. (See Figure 12.1.) We compute subsequent guesses by computing

$$r_k = r_{k-1} - f(r_{k-1})/f'(r_{k-1}) \qquad k = 1, 2, 3, \ldots$$

These guesses approach a true root of $f(x)$ rather quickly. If the root we seek is irrational, we truncate the result to produce the integer square root. I have written a sqrt() method and

FIGURE 12.1

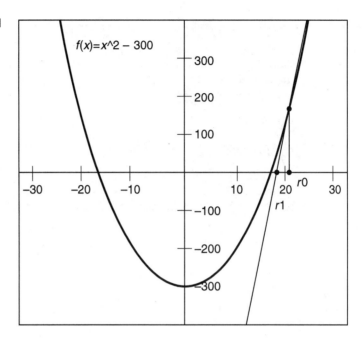

placed it in the BigIntegerMath class. It makes use of the BigDecimal class, which allows us to compute with arbitrarily large numbers using arbitrary precision.

```
public static BigInteger sqrt(BigInteger m) {
    //Uses the Newton method to find largest integer whose square does not exceed m
    //We search for a zero of f(x)=x^2-p ==> note that derivative f'(x)=2x

    int diff=m.compareTo(ZERO);
    //Throw an exception for negative arguments
    if (diff<0) throw new IllegalArgumentException
        ("Cannot compute square root of a negative integer!");
    //Return 0 in case m is 0
    if (diff==0) return BigInteger.valueOf(0);

    BigDecimal two=new BigDecimal(TWO);
    //Convert the parameter to a BigDecimal
    BigDecimal n=new BigDecimal(m);

    //Begin with an initial guess-the square root will be half the size of m
    //Make a byte array at least that long, & set bits in the high order byte
    byte[] barray=new byte[m.bitLength()/16+1];
    barray[0]=(byte)255;
    //This is the first guess-it will be too high
    BigDecimal r=new BigDecimal(new BigInteger(1,barray));
```

FIGURE 12.2

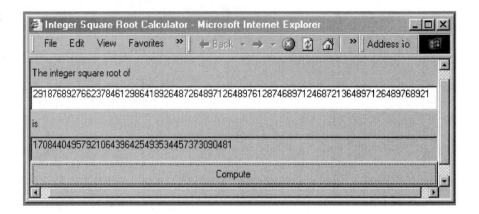

```
The integer square root of

2918768927662378461298641892648726489712648976128746897124687213648971264897689921

is

170844049579210643964254935344573373090481

                           Compute
```

```
//Next approximation is computed by taking r-f(r)/f'(r)
r=r.subtract(r.multiply(r).subtract(n).divide
    (r.multiply(two),BigDecimal.ROUND_UP));
//As long as our new approximation squared exceeds m, we continue to approximate
while (r.multiply(r).compareTo(n)>0) {
    r=r.subtract(r.multiply(r).subtract(n).divide
        (r.multiply(two),BigDecimal.ROUND_UP));
}

return r.toBigInteger(); //Method truncates any fractional part of a BigDecimal
}
```

We will test the method with the following applet, TestSQRTApplet, from the book's website. (See Figure 12.2.)

Once we have this square root finding method, writing a program to find factors using Femat's method should be simple.

12.2   MONTE CARLO FACTORIZATION

Another method of factoring was developed by J. M. Pollard, who called it the Monte Carlo method, due to the type of numbers generated in the method. Here we will not prove that this works; we will only describe the algorithm.

Say n is composite, and that p is its smallest prime divisor. We wish to choose a sequence of integers, say $m_0, m_1, m_2, \ldots, m_k$ such that their lnr's are distinct modulo n, but not all distinct modulo p. Though we will not prove the following, this happens when

- k is large compared to $\sqrt{p}$,
- k is small compared to $\sqrt{n}$, and
- the m_i (where $0 \le i \le k$) are chosen randomly.

Suppose we generate a sequence of random integers as mentioned, and we come across a pair m_q, m_r such that

$$m_q \equiv m_r \,(\text{mod } p)$$

but

$$m_q \not\equiv m_r \,(\text{mod } n).$$

It follows then that the gcd of $m_q - m_r$ and n; that is, $(m_q - m_r, n)$, is a nontrivial divisor of n, since

$$p | (m_q - m_r)$$

but

$$n \nmid (m_q - m_r).$$

The question is, how quickly can we find such a pair of numbers? As mentioned earlier, this pair will surface relatively quickly if we generate the sequence randomly. We do this in the following way:

- Start with an initial, randomly generated integer, m_0.
- Generate successive terms in the sequence by computing

$$m_i \equiv m_{i-1}^2 + 1 \,(\text{mod } n), \quad 0 \le m_i < n$$

This, of course, is not a random sequence, but it "appears to be," and for our purposes it will suffice. (See the chapter on cryptographic applications.) Once we have generated m_{2i} in the sequence, we check the greatest common divisor of $m_{2i} - m_i$ and n; if we have

$$(m_{2i} - m_i, n) = d, \qquad\qquad\qquad 1 < d < n,$$

then, as we mentioned before, we have found a nontrivial divisor of n.

EXAMPLE. We will attempt to factor $n = 356659679$. Start with an initial value for m_0, say 1260345256, and proceed to generate numbers in the sequence.

$$m_1 = 1260345256^2 + 1 \equiv 72342499 \,(\text{mod } 356659679)$$

$$m_2 = 72342499^2 + 1 \equiv 278250477 \,(\text{mod } 356659679)$$

Now we can compute

$$(m_2 - m_1, 356659679) = 1.$$

This fails to help us, so we continue to compute numbers in our sequence.

$$m_3 = 278250477^2 + 1 \equiv 66447814 \,(\text{mod } 356659679)$$

$$m_4 = 66447814^2 + 1 \equiv 333376938 \,(\text{mod } 356659679)$$

Now we compute $(m_4 - m_2, n)$, which again is 1. This gives us nothing, so we continue to compute the next two values, m_5 and m_6, then m_7 and m_8, and so on. We obtain a nontrivial divisor when we compute $(m_8 - m_4, n) = 359$. A complete listing of these values can be seen in Table 12.2.

TABLE 12.2

i	m_i	$(m_i - m_{i/2}, n)$
0	1260345256	
1	72342499	
2	278250477	1
3	66447814	
4	333376938	1
5	52340019	
6	274018250	1
7	212607484	
8	181355157	359

EXAMPLE.   Let $n = 72133$. We apply the Monte Carlo method to obtain the values shown in Table 12.3.

TABLE 12.3

i	m_i	$(m_i - m_{i/2}, n)$
0	1868187221	
1	71909	
2	50177	1
3	1098	
4	51477	1
5	3642	
6	63826	1
7	47102	
8	3724	53

EXAMPLE.   Let $n = 9090909091$. We apply the Monte Carlo method to obtain the values shown in Table 12.4.

TABLE 12.4

i	m_i	$(m_i - m_{i/2}, n)$
0	44016065	
1	4887155761	
2	4763918935	1
3	842766808	
4	1750315397	11

EXAMPLE.   Let $n = 992387659879678689176986897665716567855813467857777$. We apply the Monte Carlo method to obtain the values shown in Table 12.5.

TABLE 12.5

i	m_i	$(m_i - m_{i/2}, n)$
0	169995877	
1	28898598196999130	
2	835128977751601367248137220756901	57

Java Algorithm   The monteCarloFactor() method will be quite interesting to write. We will make an array of integers to hold the generated sequence, and compute gcd's at every other iteration of the number–generating loop. The code to do this is elementary. (This method is in the BigIntegerMath class):

```
//Monte Carlo factorization method returns a Monte Carlo factor.
//An array holds a sequence of random numbers; must specify max
//size of this array.
//This puppy returns null if no factor is found.
public static BigInteger monteCarloFactor(BigInteger n,int maxArraySize)
throws IllegalArgumentException, ArrayIndexOutOfBoundsException {
   if (n.compareTo(THREE)<=0)
     throw new IllegalArgumentException("Number to factor must be > 3");
   BigInteger[] m=new BigInteger[maxArraySize];
   m[0]=BigInteger.valueOf(new Random().nextInt());
   BigInteger g;
   for (int i=1;i<maxArraySize;i++) {
     m[i]=m[i-1].multiply(m[i-1]).add(ONE).mod(n);
```

```
    if (i%2==0) {
        g=m[i].subtract(m[i/2]).gcd(n);
        if (g.compareTo(ONE)>0&&g.compareTo(n)<0) return g;
    }
  }
}
return null;
}
```

This method is unsatisfactory for integers having truly "large" factors (say, greater than 10^{15}). You can verify this by testing the method with numbers having factors of this size; the method starts to fail at around this point. Recall that the length of the sequence k should be large compared to $\sqrt{p}$. In the previous case, $k = 100000$, and $\sqrt{p} = \sqrt{900383347} \cong$ 30006.39, which is why the method succeeded in finding the factor. But for factors exceeding, say, 2^{40}, k would need to be at least as high as 2^{20}, and will thus require storage space for around a million BigIntegers. This is already beginning to test the capacity of some machines, and factors of much larger size are common in modern cryptography.

12.3   THE POLLARD $p - 1$ METHOD OF FACTORIZATION

This method of factorization was also developed by J. M. Pollard. It can be effective in finding large factors p if the choice of p is such that the integer $p - 1$ consists of only small prime factors. This is certainly not unusual, and in fact is quite common. It may seem strange to you that the factorization of $p - 1$ can help us find the factor p, but it can.

Suppose n is a large composite integer, and that n has a factor p such that $(p - 1)|k!$ for some k. Now, if the prime factorization of $p - 1$ consists entirely of small prime factors, this number k will not be excessively large (and $k!$ will be computable).

Now, by Fermat's Little Theorem (FLT), we have

$$2^{p-1} \equiv 1 \pmod{p}$$

and since $(p - 1)|k!$ for some integer k, we have $k! = (p - 1)q$ for some integer q. This then yields

$$2^{k!} = 2^{(p-1)q} = (2^{(p-1)})^q \equiv 1^q = 1 \pmod{p}. \quad \text{(FLT is used here.)}$$

This says that $p|(2^{k!} - 1)$. Now, let Z be the least nonnegative residue of $2^{k!} - 1$ modulo n.

$$\text{If } n \nmid (2^{k!} - 1)$$

we have

$$Z = (2^{k!} - 1) - ni, \text{ for some integer } i.$$

Note, now that $p|Z$, since it divides both $2^{k!} - 1$, and n. Thus, we see that a divisor of n can be found simply by computing (Z, n). Should Z and n not be relatively prime; that is, $(Z, n) = d > 1$, then d is a nontrivial factor of n.

Note that if $n|(2^{k!} - 1)$, the $p - 1$ method will fail, since then we would have $Z \equiv 0 \pmod{n}$, and computing the gcd of Z and n would only yield the trivial factor n since (Z, n)

$= (0, n) = n$. It turns out that this is unlikely when n has large prime factors (we will not prove this), but should it happen, we can simply choose a base b other than 2 when computing $b^{k!} - 1$, and start over.

EXAMPLE.   We will attempt to find a factor of $n = 632887$. (Note that $632887 = 769 \cdot 823$, and that $768 = 2^8 \cdot 3$, so that the smallest value of k for which $768|k!$ is $k = 10$. (To see this, note that $10! = 10 \cdot 9 \cdot 8 \cdot 7 \cdot 6 \cdot 5 \cdot 4 \cdot 3 \cdot 2 \cdot 1 = (2 \cdot 5) \cdot 9 \cdot (2^3) \cdot 7 \cdot (2 \cdot 3) \cdot 5 \cdot (2^2) \cdot 3 \cdot 2 \cdot 1 = 4275 \cdot 2^8 \cdot 3 = 4275 \cdot 768.$)

We start by choosing a random base, say $b = 261482$. We then proceed to compute the least nonnegative residue $r_i \equiv b^{i!}$ modulo n, for $i = 1, 2, 3, \ldots$. When we have found a nontrivial gcd of $(r_i - 1, n)$, we have found a nontrivial divisor of n.

$$r_1 = 261482 \pmod{632887}$$

$$r_2 = r_1{}^2 \equiv 155053 \pmod{632887} \quad (r_2 - 1, n) = 1$$

$$r_3 = r_2{}^3 \equiv 386889 \pmod{632887} \quad (r_3 - 1, n) = 1$$

$$r_4 = r_3{}^4 \equiv 181843 \pmod{632887} \quad (r_4 - 1, n) = 1$$

$$r_5 = r_4{}^5 \equiv 293940 \pmod{632887} \quad (r_5 - 1, n) = 1$$

$$r_6 = r_5{}^6 \equiv 630444 \pmod{632887} \quad (r_6 - 1, n) = 1$$

$$r_7 = r_6{}^7 \equiv 249467 \pmod{632887} \quad (r_7 - 1, n) = 1$$

$$r_8 = r_7{}^8 \equiv 234544 \pmod{632887} \quad (r_8 - 1, n) = 1$$

$$r_9 = r_8{}^9 \equiv 422180 \pmod{632887} \quad (r_9 - 1, n) = 1$$

$$r_{10} = r_9{}^{10} \equiv 582903 \pmod{632887} \quad (r_{10} - 1, n) = 769$$

In the 10th step, we find that 769 is a nontrivial divisor of 632887, exactly as we expected, since 768 divides 10!, but no smaller value of the factorial function.

EXAMPLE.   Here we try to factor $n = 559374799933$ starting with the base $b = 557566181343$. The values have been placed in Table 12.6.

This says a factor of 559374799933 is found; namely, 740279. Apparently, this also says 559374799933 divides 23!, but no smaller value of the factorial function.

Java Algorithm   A method to extract factors using the $p - 1$ method follows. It is also in the BigIntegerMath class.

```java
public static BigInteger pMinusOneFactor(BigInteger n)
throws IllegalArgumentException {
    if (n.compareTo(THREE)<=0)
        throw new IllegalArgumentException("Integer must be larger than three!");
    Random rand=new Random();
    BigInteger power=BigInteger.valueOf(1);
```

TABLE 12.6

i	$b^{i!}$	$(b^{i!}-1, n)$
1	557566181343	1
2	436541389360	1
3	155204284985	1
4	538254521186	1
5	224074559848	1
6	556398555479	1
7	461773086408	1
8	524373376099	1
9	528286461332	1
10	257084687919	1
11	553469773152	1
12	378473232758	1
13	281899611802	1
14	377823757725	1
15	263895130902	1
16	262689042015	1
17	286305785793	1
18	489134478513	1
19	96491246483	1
20	194503288400	1
21	141727500886	1
22	97401438906	1
23	173399991845	740279

```
BigInteger residue=lnr(BigInteger.valueOf(rand.nextInt()),n);
BigInteger test=residue.subtract(ONE);
BigInteger gcd=test.gcd(n);
while (true) {
    while (gcd.equals(ONE)) {
        power=power.add(ONE);
        residue=residue.modPow(power,n);
        test=residue.subtract(ONE);
        gcd=test.gcd(n);
    }
    if (gcd.equals(n)) {
        power=BigInteger.valueOf(1);
        residue=lnr(BigInteger.valueOf(rand.nextInt()),n);
        test=residue.subtract(ONE);
        gcd=test.gcd(n);
    } else return gcd;
}
}
```

The Pollard $p - 1$ method can be used to break cryptosystems based on factoring numbers having large prime factors if the primes are chosen carelessly. To prevent this method from factoring quickly, one must make sure that the choice of a prime p must be such that $p - 1$ has at least one large prime factor. For example, consider the following prime:

p = 16008630711655973815586992579875751462675645756500739864671111485700599292229670785906961966186581616907358764375896420271207454072087935880724049716170074948433541353770954060661548558807676156108125377861121677226656934787295293329889991101773874178363226192550806087278026993983201987753863431668129069694725023377440941427581587582883491337467096707834838006093447039446697876577964675654567542454935015745756327147824586540568076139584880189902876325559021702608324313798713168608058109667487105601058149951387902658985594240349807979283515964749134492536956801651580054344868002580339156153452269485576149340174891898959024039678782478455571644644887340404413620113305501956454600212109103897807363568846200889593629505668975015349890036398801531802798229526258122752000000000000000000000000000000000000000000000000000000000000000000000000000000000000000000000001.

If you run the Pollard $p - 1$ method on a large integer having this prime p as a factor, p will be found in only 399 iterations! Why? It turns out that this particular prime $p = 399! + 1$. Though these primes are rare, there many other primes q not specifically of this form such that $q - 1$ divides $k!$ for a relatively small value of k. To ensure this does not happen, we must choose such primes such that $q - 1$ has a large prime factor, forcing k to also be large.

 I have written an applet (called TestFactorApplet), which demonstrates both the Monte Carlo method, and the Pollard $p - 1$ method of factorization. You enter an integer, then

FIGURE 12.3

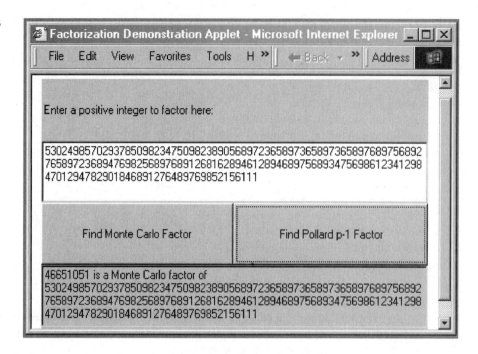

press a button to find a factor. You may choose either method, and the applet is threaded so that you can search for a Monte Carlo factor and a Pollard $p - 1$ factor at the same time. (See Figure 12.3.)

EXERCISES

1. Write a fermatFactor() method and place it in the BigIntegerMath class.
2. Write a trialDivisionFactor() method in the BigintegerMath class to work with BigIntegers.
3. Write a test program to compare the performance of the factoring methods for numbers having factors of small, intermediate, and large sizes. How does the trial division method compare to the other methods when factors are small?

CHAPTER **13**

Exponential Congruences

This chapter involves solving congruences of the form

$$a^x \equiv b \pmod{n}$$

for x. If there is a solution for x, we call x a discrete logarithm modulo n of a to the base b, and we write

$$x = \log_{b,n} a.$$

When the modulus n is clear from the context, we often simply write

$$x = \log_b a.$$

If p is a large prime, these congruences can be very difficult to solve; this is formally known as the discrete logarithm problem, or DLP. To help us understand the nature of these problems, we'll need to do some development. As a review, recall Fermat's Little Theorem:

If p is prime, and b is an integer such that $p \nmid b$, then
$b^{p-1} \equiv 1 \pmod{p}$.

However, could b^z be congruent to 1 modulo p for some value z smaller than $p - 1$? We can see this is possible just from the following simple example: let $p = 7$, and examine the powers of each integer greater than 0 but less than 7. (See Table 13.1.)

Note that the integers 2, 4, and 6 (and also 1, obviously), yield powers which are congruent to 1 modulo 7 for values smaller than 6.

TABLE 13.1

b	b^2	b^3	b^4	b^5	b^6
1	1	1	1	1	1
2	4	1	2	4	1
3	2	6	4	5	1
4	2	1	4	2	1
5	4	6	2	3	1
6	1	6	1	6	1
All operations done mod 7; Inr is retained					

13.1 ORDER OF AN INTEGER

Definition
Let n be a positive integer and b an integer. Then the least positive integer z for which $b^z \equiv 1 \pmod{n}$ is called the order of b modulo n. We denote this as $|b|_n$. If the modulus n is clear from the context, we simply write $|b|$.

EXAMPLES. From the previous table, we see that

$$|2|_7 = 3, |3|_7 = 6, |4|_7 = 3, |5|_7 = 6, \text{ and } |6|_7 = 2.$$

Using this property, we can derive the following propositions:

PROPOSITION 37 If p is prime and b an integer such that $p \nmid b$, then

a) the positive integer x is a solution to $b^x \equiv 1 \pmod{p}$ iff $|b|_p$ divides x.

b) $|b|_p$ divides $p - 1$.

Proof.

a) Suppose $|b|$ divides x; then $x = k|b|$ for some positive integer k. Thus,

$b^x = b^{k|b|} = (b^{|b|})^k \equiv 1 \pmod{p}$.

On the other hand, suppose $b^x \equiv 1 \pmod{p}$. Then, if

$x = q|b| + r \quad 0 \le r < |b|$

we see that

$$b^x = b^{q|b|+r} = (b^{|b|})^{qb}b^r \equiv b^r \pmod{p}.$$

Now, since $b^x \equiv 1 \pmod{p}$, $b^r \equiv 1 \pmod{p}$ also. But since $0 \le r < |b|$, we must have $r = 0$ since $|b|$ is the least positive integer k such that $b^k \equiv 1 \pmod{p}$. Hence, $|b|$ divides x.

b) (Exercise. Hint: use FLT and part (a).)   ∎

PROPOSITION 38   Suppose p is prime and b an integer such that $p \nmid b$. Then, if i and j are nonnegative integers, $b^i \equiv b^j \pmod{p}$ iff $i \equiv j \pmod{|b|_p}$.

Proof.   Suppose $i \equiv j \pmod{|b|}$ and $0 \le j \le i$. Then $i = j + k|b|$ for some positive integer k. Thus,

$$b^i = b^{j+k|b|} = b^j(b^{|b|})^k \equiv b^j \pmod{p}.$$

On the other hand, if $b^i \equiv b^j \pmod{p}$, where $i \ge j$, we have $p \nmid b^j$ since $p \nmid b$. Then, note that since

$$b^i \equiv b^j b^{i-j} \equiv b^j \pmod{p}$$

we can divide this congruence by b^j using proposition 21 to obtain

$$b^{i-j} \equiv 1 \pmod{p}.$$

By proposition 27, we then know that $|b|$ divides $i - j$, or $i \equiv j \pmod{|b|}$.   ∎

13.2   GENERATORS

> **Definition**
> An integer g such that the prime p does not divide g is called a generator modulo p if $|g|_p = p - 1$.

EXAMPLE.   Note from the previous example that 3 and 5 are generators modulo 7; 1, 2, 4, and 6 are not.

Most cryptosystems that depend on the difficulty of DLP use generators. Thus, we prove some important facts about generators.

PROPOSITION 39   If g is a generator modulo p, then the sequence of integers $g, g^2, \ldots, g^{p-1}$ is a permutation of $1, 2, \ldots, p - 1$.

Proof.   To show this, we need only show that none of the $p - 1$ members of the former sequence are congruent to 0 modulo p, and that none are congruent to each other modulo

p. Note that since $p \nmid g$, p likewise does not divide g^k for any positive integer k. So, none of the integers $g, g^2, \ldots, g^{p-1}$ are congruent to 0 modulo p. Now, suppose

$$g^i \equiv g^j \pmod{p}$$

for some positive integers i and j, where $0 < i \leq j < p$. By proposition 38, we then have $i \equiv j \pmod{|g|}$. But since i and j are both no greater than $|g| = p - 1$ (recall that g is a generator), we must have $i = j$. Thus, no two members of $g, g^2, \ldots, g^{p-1}$ are congruent modulo p, and so these integers must simply be a permutation of the positive integers not exceeding $p - 1$. ∎

It is important to be able to find generators, since the discrete logarithm problem is most intractable when generators are used as the base. Note that proposition 39 says that when we have $g^x \equiv b \pmod{p}$ for prime p and generator g, the solution (when it exists) is unique, and, it turns out, harder to find.

PROPOSITION 40   If $|b|_p = t$ and u is a positive integer, then $|b^u|_p = t/(t, u)$.

Proof.   Let $s = |b^u|$, $v = (t, u)$, $t = t'v$ for some integer t', and $u = u'v$ for some integer u'. By proposition 7 we have

$$(t', u') = 1.$$

Thus, we have

$$(b^u)^{t'} = (b^{u'v})^{t/v} = (b^t)^{u'} \equiv 1 \pmod{p}$$

since $|b| = t$. Then, by proposition 37, $s|t'$. But since

$$(b^u)^s = b^{us} \equiv 1 \pmod{p}$$

we have $t|us$, which is equivalent to $t'v|u'vs$. Thus we derive the fact that $t'|u's$, and since t' and u' are relatively prime, we have $t'|s$ by proposition 13. Now, since $s|t'$, and since $t'|s$, we have
$|b^u| = s = t' = t/(t, u)$. ∎

We will now prove that if a prime p has a generator, then it has many generators. This is important, since if there are too few generators (or none at all) to choose from when picking a generator for a cipher, one may be hard (or impossible) to find.

PROPOSITION 41   Let r be the number of positive integers not exceeding $p - 1$ which are relatively prime to $p - 1$. Then, if the prime p has a generator, it has r of them.

Proof.   Let g be a generator modulo p. By proposition 40, we know that

$$|g^u|_p = |g|_p/(u, |g|_p) = (p - 1)/(u, p - 1)$$

for any positive integer u. Furthermore, from the previous equation, we can say that

g^u is a generator modulo p iff $|g^u|_p = p - 1$ iff u and $p - 1$ are relatively prime. (*)

Now, from proposition 39 we know that the sequence

$$g, g^2, \ldots, g^{p-1}$$

is simply a permutation of $1, 2, \ldots, p - 1$. Since there are exactly r integers in the first set that are relatively prime to $p - 1$, there are exactly r integers in the former sequence of the form g^i where i is relatively prime to $p - 1$. But, from the previous development (*), these are exactly the generators modulo p. ∎

This tells us that when a prime has a generator, it has quite a few, since there are always many positive integers smaller than p which are relatively prime to $p - 1$.

EXAMPLE.   Consider the prime $p = 101$; since $p - 1 = 100 = 2^2 \cdot 5^2$, any positive integer smaller than 100 not having a 2 or a 5 in its factorization will be relatively prime to 100. There are clearly many such integers.

Note that proposition 41 does not tell us that every prime has a generator; it only says that if it has a generator, it has a certain number of them. We need this fact, but will not prove it.

PROPOSITION 42   Every prime has a generator.

Proposition 41 also says that if we find a generator g modulo p, we can find another by simply calculating the lnr of g^i modulo p for some i relatively prime to $p - 1$. But how do we find a generator in the first place? This isn't difficult to do in practice, since we will choose our primes carefully. For example, if prime p is such that $p - 1$ consists entirely of small factors, such a prime p is susceptible to some discrete logarithm finding algorithms (like Pohlig–Hellman). If we choose p so that $p - 1$ has at least one large prime factor, we call it a safe prime.

A solution is to choose primes of the form $p = 2Rt + 1$ where t is prime, and R is a relatively small positive integer. We first select integers t at random, and subject them to primality testing, until a particular value of t passes. We then select small values of R (say, $\leq$ 1 billion) at random and submit $p = 2Rt + 1$ to primality testing, until p passes with some value of R. Since R is small, it can be easily factored, and since $p - 1 = 2Rt$, the factorization of $p - 1$ is known. Thus, we present a method of finding generators.

13.3   GENERATOR SELECTION

Suppose p is prime, and $p_1^{e_1} \cdot p_2^{e_2} \cdot \ldots \cdot p_n^{e_n}$ is the prime factorization of $p - 1$. To find a generator g modulo p, do the following:

1. Choose a random integer x between 2 and $p - 2$.

2. For $i = 1$ to n do

   a) Compute $z = p/p_i$

b) Calculate the lnr of x^2 modulo p. If the least nonnegative residue is 1 modulo p, x is not a generator. Return to step 1.

3. x is a generator modulo p.

EXAMPLE.   Here we generate a safe prime p, and then a generator for p. This will be simple because we will know the factorization of $p - 1$ by our method of construction. We begin by finding a large random prime t:

$t = 10613489717292810394391885407329587981421015305407018531630560566764811516728531826831958668100515002060747248367157674837403135189116674601954897381846728211246036708099048606601439297700504038644255829445960865866815893376000131118992625844138529556165370800654724945516246034477594900028893324777956849747479$.

We will now search for the first prime of the form $2rt + 1$, where r begins with the value 1, and increments by 1 for each iteration. It turns out that this happens when r reaches the value 362, and the target safe prime p is

$p = 76841665553199947255397250349066216985488150811146814169005258503377235381114570426263380757047728614919810078178221565822798698769204724118153457044570312249421305766637111911794420515351649239784412205188756668875747068042240949301506611111562953986637284596740208605537621289617787076209187671392407592174797$.

(You may wish to verify that p is, indeed, $2 \cdot 362 \cdot t + 1$, and is prime.) Since $r = 362$ is a relatively small integer, it can be easily factored. The prime factorization of r is:

$$r = 362 = 2 \cdot 181$$

Now we generate another random integer x between 2 and $p - 2$. Let us choose $x = 2$. We test if x is a generator by raising it to all of the following powers modulo p:

$x^{(p-1)/2} \equiv$

$76841665553199947255397250349066216985488150811146814169005258503377235381114570426263380757047728614919810078178221565822798698769204724118153457044570312249421305766637111911794420515351649239784412205188756668875747068042240949301506611111562953986637284596740208605537621289617787076209187671392407592174796 \pmod{p}$

$x^{(p-1)/181} \equiv$

$75961007803309281954916800954202975856273255230222909507970057868500650978178717535081069957567655567271159163468578626357231867357218835033537842274188279129834353226435343666816052031148960948571253534290735720617145777499086762998290123253430178908008007905852345568862289297440888836496564879035543972034961 \pmod{p}$

$$x^{(p-1)/t} \equiv$$
88250436209631796779659651318894620729729809745361797646356310339459182198787453122058560031100937405340558296821374893066353027058699717113329784015217065825962377858834878767894752265396985241367417483713579073929216 \pmod{p}.

None of these yield a residue of 1, so we conclude 2 is a generator of this safe prime p.

Java Algorithm   In my PrimeGenerator class, there is a method called getSafePrime-AndGenerator(), which finds a safe prime p and a corresponding generator. There is also a method called getSafePrime(), which finds and returns a safe prime but does not find a generator for it.

```java
import java.security.*;
import java.math.*;
import java.util.*;
public class PrimeGenerator {

    int minBitLength;
    int certainty;
    SecureRandom sr;

    public PrimeGenerator(int minBitLength, int certainty, SecureRandom sr) {
        //The bit length of the prime will exceed minBitLength
        if (minBitLength<512) throw new IllegalArgumentException
            ("Strong/Safe primes must be at least 64 bytes long.");
        this.minBitLength=minBitLength;
        this.certainty=certainty;
        this.sr=sr;
    }

    //This method returns a safe prime of form 2rt+1 where t is a large prime,
    //and the factorization of r is known
    //It also returns a generator for the safe prime
    //The zero-th slot in the resulting array is the safe prime
    //Slot 1 of the result is the generator
    public BigInteger[] getSafePrimeAndGenerator() {
        BigInteger[] p=new BigInteger[2];
        BigInteger r=BigInteger.valueOf(0x7fffffff);
        BigInteger t=new BigInteger(minBitLength-30,certainty,sr);
        //p is the first prime in the sequence 2rt+1, 2*2rt+1, 2*3rt+1,...
        do {
            r=r.add(BigIntegerMath.ONE);
            p[0]=BigIntegerMath.TWO.multiply(r).multiply(t).add(BigIntegerMath.ONE);
```

```
   } while (!p[0].isProbablePrime(certainty));

//We must get the prime factors of p-1=2rt
//Put the prime factors in a Vector-list each prime factor only once
Vector factors=new Vector();

//Add t to the vector, since t is a prime factor of p-1=2rt
factors.addElement(t);

//We know 2 is a factor of p-1=2rt, so add 2 to the Vector
factors.addElement(BigInteger.valueOf(2));

//r may be prime-don't factor it if you don't have to
if (r.isProbablePrime(10)) factors.addElement(r);
//otherwise, find the factors of r and add them to the Vector
else {
   //Divide all the 2's out of r, since 2 is already in the Vector
   while (r.mod(BigIntegerMath.TWO).equals(BigIntegerMath.ZERO)) {
      r=r.divide(BigIntegerMath.TWO);
   }

   //We now get the prime factors of r, which should be small enough to
   //factor
   //Start with 3 - 2 is already in the Vector
   BigInteger divisor=BigInteger.valueOf(3);
   //Do not search for factors past the square root of r
   //Square the divisor for comparison to r
   BigInteger square=divisor.multiply(divisor);
   while (square.compareTo(r)<=0) {
      //If this divisor divides r, add it to the Vector
      if (r.mod(divisor).equals(BigIntegerMath.ZERO)) {
         factors.addElement(divisor);
         //Divide r by this divisor until it no longer divides
         while (r.mod(divisor).equals(BigIntegerMath.ZERO))
            r=r.divide(divisor);
      }
      divisor=divisor.add(BigIntegerMath.ONE);
      //Do not search for factors past the square root of r
      //Square the divisor for comparison to r
      square=divisor.multiply(divisor);
   }
}
```

```
//Now, start looking for a generator
boolean isGenerator;
BigInteger pMinusOne=p[0].subtract(BigIntegerMath.ONE);
BigInteger x,z,lnr;
do {
    //Start by assuming the test # is a generator
    isGenerator=true;
    //Pick a random integer x smaller than the safe prime p
    x=new BigInteger(p[0].bitLength()-1,sr);
    for (int i=0;i<factors.size();i++) {
        //Compute z as p-1 divided by the i-th prime factor in the Vector
        z=pMinusOne.divide((BigInteger)factors.elementAt(i));
        //Raise x to the z power modulo p
        lnr=x.modPow(z,p[0]);
        //If this equals 1, x is not a generator
        if (lnr.equals(BigIntegerMath.ONE)) {
            isGenerator=false;
            //break-no reason to try the other prime factors for this failed x
            break;
        }
    }
    //While x is not a generator, go back and pick another random x
} while (!isGenerator);
//If we get here, we found a generator-set it and return it
p[1]=x;
return p;
}

//getSafePrime() is identical to this, but does not search for a generator.

}
```

 The TestPrimeGeneratorApplet class allows us to retrieve safe primes. Here is a shot of it, displaying a safe prime and its generator. (See Figure 13.1.)

13.4   CALCULATING DISCRETE LOGARITHMS

There are a variety of discrete log finding algorithms known; however, none of them are fast enough to break the cryptosystems based on DLP. However, those implementing such ciphers should take care that the primes they use do not have certain weaknesses, which some of these algorithms exploit.

FIGURE 13.1

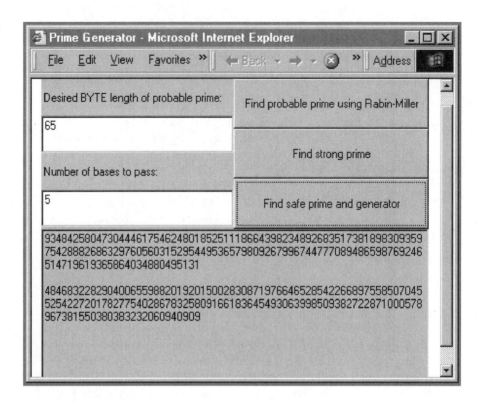

Exhaustive Search for Discrete Logs   The most obvious solution to finding a discrete logarithm (and by far the slowest) is to search by taking successive powers. For example, to solve

$$b^x \equiv z \ (\text{mod } n) \qquad 0 < z < n$$

for x, we simply calculate the lnr's of the sequence

$$b, b^2, b^3, \ldots$$

until we derive z.

EXAMPLE.   Suppose we wish to solve the congruence

$$257^x \equiv 369 \ (\text{mod } 1009)$$

for x. We calculate the successive powers until we obtain a least nonnegative residue of 369 modulo 1009. (See Table 13.2.)

(The successive powers of 257^x go across from left to right.) There are 10 columns in the table; the last entry (369) is the 104th entry, so

$$257^{104} \equiv 369 \ (\text{mod } 1009).$$

TABLE 13.2

	Column									
Row	1	2	3	4	5	6	7	8	9	10
1	257	464	186	379	539	290	873	363	463	938
2	924	353	920	334	73	599	575	461	424	1005
3	990	162	265	502	871	858	544	566	166	284
4	340	606	356	682	717	631	727	174	322	16
5	76	361	958	10	552	604	851	763	345	882
6	658	603	594	299	159	503	119	313	730	945
7	705	574	204	969	819	611	632	984	638	508
8	395	615	651	822	373	6	533	766	107	256
9	207	731	193	160	760	583	499	100	475	995
10	438	567	423	748	526	985	895	972	581	994
11	181	103	237	369						

This example alone should suggest to you that exhaustive search is obviously not the way we want to go about finding discrete logs. However, an exhaustive search may be worthwhile if the base is an integer of low order modulo n.

Java Algorithm   I have written a method to calculate discrete logs using exhaustive search. The code is in the BigIntegerMath class:

```
public static BigInteger logExhaustiveSearch
(BigInteger base, BigInteger residue, BigInteger modulus) {
   //This algorithm solves base^x = residue (mod modulus) for x using exhaustive
   //search
   BigInteger basePow=BigInteger.valueOf(1);
   BigInteger j;
   for (j=BigInteger.valueOf(1);j.compareTo(modulus)<0;j=j.add(ONE)) {
      basePow=basePow.multiply(base).mod(modulus);
      if (basePow.equals(residue)) break;
   }
   if (j.equals(modulus)) throw new NoSuchElementException("No solution");
   return j;
}
```

Baby-step Giant-step Algorithm   The next algorithm is an improvement of exhaustive search in that it doesn't cycle through all exponents. It is based on the fact that if m is the smallest integer no less than $\sqrt{n}$, where n is the modulus, and

$$a^x \equiv b \pmod{n}$$

we can write

$$x = im + j$$

where $0 \le i$ and $j < m$. This yields

$$a^x = a^{im} \cdot a^j,$$

implying that

$$b((a^m)')^i \equiv a^j \pmod{n},$$

where $(a^m)'$ is an inverse of a^m modulo n (if this inverse exists). The baby-step giant-step algorithm exploits this: The algorithm finds a discrete log (if one exists) of

$$a^x \equiv b \pmod{n}$$

1. Let b be an integer between 1 and $n-1$.
2. Let m be the smallest integer no less than $\sqrt{n}$.
3. Make a table whose entries are (j, g^j) for $j = 0, 1, 2, \ldots, m-1$. The entries for g^j should be the least nonnegative residues modulo n.

   Compute $(g^m)'$, an inverse of g^m modulo n. (Of course, this assumes g^m is invertible modulo n; if not, this method will fail. Of course, if the modulus is prime, this will not be a problem.)
5. Set $y = b$.
6. For i from 0 to $m-1$ do:

   - Search the second components in the table for a g^j such that $g^j = y$ for some index j.
   - If such an entry is found, compute and return $x = im + j$.
   - If no such entry is found, set y equal to the lnr of $y(g^m)'$.

This algorithm will usually be superior in running time to exhaustive search because it only checks a maximum of $m = \sqrt{n}$ exponents (whereas exhaustive search may cycle through n exponents). However, the table required can be quite large, obviously, if n is very large. Also, the method we use to search the table is important. A sequential search is out of the question, and a binary search on a sorted table will also be time-consuming; a much preferable alternative is to use a hash table.

EXAMPLE.   We'll use baby-step giant-step to solve the congruence

$$43^x \equiv 140 \pmod{307}.$$

(Note 43 is a generator modulo the prime 307.) First, since $\sqrt{307} \cong 17.5214$, we'll set $m = 18$. Hence, Table 13.3 will have 18 entries:

TABLE 13.3

j	lnr of 43^j mod 307
0	1
1	43
2	7
3	301
4	49
5	265
6	36
7	13
8	252
9	91
10	229
11	23
12	68
13	161
14	169
15	206
16	262
17	214

(We will not sort the table by second component; we will assume that an efficient method is being used to search the table.) Now, we must compute an inverse of 43^{18} modulo 307:

$$(43^{18})' \equiv 299' \equiv 115 \;(\text{mod } 307).$$

We now set $y = 140$, and begin the loop. We show the iterations in the following table. At each iteration y is set equal to the lnr of its old value times 115 modulo 307. (See Table 13.4.)

We now compute and return the value of $x = 4(18) + 15 = 87$. You should check that indeed,

$$43^{87} \equiv 140 \;(\text{mod } 307).$$

TABLE 13.4

i	y	y in table?
0	140	No
1	136	No
2	290	No
3	194	No
4	206	Yes (index 15)

Java Algorithm   The BigIntegerMath class also contains a method to compute discrete logs using baby-step giant-step. The code follows:

```
public static BigInteger logBabyStepGiantStep
(BigInteger base, BigInteger residue, BigInteger modulus) {
    //This algorithm solves base^x = residue (mod modulus) for x using baby step
    //giant step
    BigInteger m=sqrt(modulus).add(ONE);
    //Use a hash table to store the entries-use Java Hashtable class
    Hashtable h=new Hashtable();
    BigInteger basePow=BigInteger.valueOf(1);
    //Build the hash table base^j is the key, index j is the value
    for (BigInteger j=BigInteger.valueOf(0);j.compareTo(m)<0;j=j.add(ONE)) {
        h.put(basePow,j);
        basePow=basePow.multiply(base).mod(modulus);
    }
    //Compute an inverse of base^m modulo p
    BigInteger basetotheminv=base.modPow(m,modulus).modInverse(modulus);
    BigInteger y=new BigInteger(residue.toByteArray());
    //Search the hashtable for a base^j such that y=base^j for some j
    BigInteger target;
    for (BigInteger i=BigInteger.valueOf(0);i.compareTo(m)<0;i=i.add(ONE)) {
        target = (BigInteger)h.get(y);
        if (target!=null) return i.multiply(m).add(target);
        y=y.multiply(basetotheminv).mod(modulus);
    }
    throw new NoSuchElementException("No solution");
}
```

I have written TestDiscreteLogApplet to test these log finding methods. It can be run from the book's website. Figures 13.2 and 13.3 show two screen shots.

FIGURE 13.2

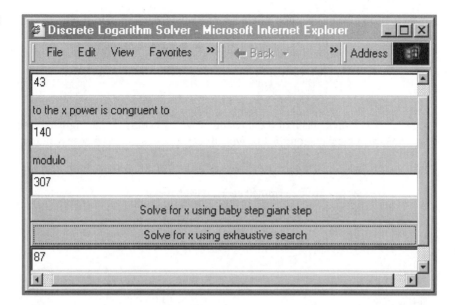

FIGURE 13.3

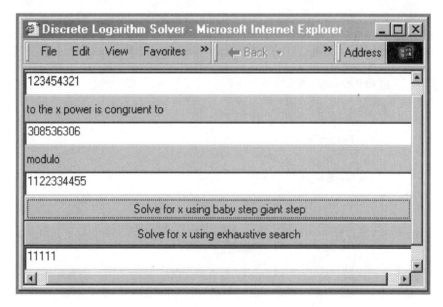

Pohlig–Hellman Algorithm for Discrete Logs   The Pohlig–Hellman algorithm is only effective when a prime modulus p is such that $p - 1$ consists entirely of small factors. But in this case, it is very effective. Consider the prime p, and let the prime factorization of $p - 1$ be given by

$$p - 1 = p_1^{e_1} \cdot p_2^{e_2} \cdot \ldots \cdot p_n^{e_n}.$$

Let g be a generator modulo p, and suppose we wish to solve

$$g^x \equiv b \pmod{p}$$

for x. To do this, we will first determine each residue x_i such that

$$x \equiv x_i \pmod{p_i^{e_i}} \ \forall \ i.$$

To compute each of these residues, we will compute the digits of each x_i in terms of its p_i-ary representation; that is, we will construct each x_i as a base p_i number:

$$x_i = d_{ei}-_1 \cdot p_i^{ei-1} + d_{ei}-_2 \cdot p_i^{ei-2} + \ldots + d_2 \cdot p_i^2 + d_1 \cdot p_i + d_0. \ (^*)$$

Once we have determined each x_i, we have a system

$$x \equiv x_1 \pmod{p_1^e 1}$$

$$x \equiv x_2 \pmod{p_2^e 2}$$

$$\ldots$$

$$x \equiv x_n \pmod{p_n^e n}$$

which we can then solve for $x = \log_g b$ using the Chinese Remainder Theorem (notice the moduli are pairwise relatively prime). The trick, of course, is to obtain the representation given by $(^*)$; this is described in the following algorithm.

Suppose p, g, and the prime factorization of $p - 1$ are as described previously. We wish to find $x = \log_{g,p} b$:

1. For $i = 1$ to n do:

    (a) Let $q = p_i$, $e = e_i$, $c = 1$, and $d_{-1} = 0$.

    (b) Compute $g^* = g^{(p-1)/q}$.

    (c) For $k = 0$ to $e - 1$ do:

        I.   Set $c = cg^d k - 1^{qk-1}$

        II.   Set $b^* = (bc')^{n/(qk-1)}$ (where c' is an inverse of c modulo p)

        III. Compute $d_k = \log_{g*} b^*$

    (d) Let $x_i = d_{e-1} \cdot q^{e-1} + d_{e-2} \cdot q^{e-2} + \ldots + d_2 \cdot q^2 + d_1 \cdot q + d_0$

2. Use CRT to compute a simultaneous solution x to the system

$$x \equiv x_1 \pmod{p_1^{e_1}}$$

$$x \equiv x_2 \pmod{p_2^{e_2}}$$

$$\ldots$$

$$x \equiv x_n \pmod{p_n^{e_n}}$$

One step may require clarification; namely, step 1.(a).III: How do we know that

$$d_k = \log_{g^*} b^*$$

is indeed the kth digit in the p_i-ary representation of x_i? Note first that if $q = p_i$ and $e = e_i$ as in the algorithm, we have $|g^*| = q$. During the kth loop of step 1.(a).III, we have

$$c = g^d_{k-1}k^{-1+\cdots+d_1q+d_0}$$

and so

$$b^* = (b/c)^{n/q^{k+1}}$$

$$= (g^{x-d}k - 1^{q^{k-1}-d}1^{q-d_0})^{n/q^{k+1}}$$

$$= (g^{n/q^{k+1}})^{x}i^{-d}k - 1^{q^{k-1-d}}1^{q-d_0} \quad \text{(switch order of exponents)}$$

$$= (g^{n/q^{k+1}})^{d_e} - 1^{q^{e-1}+\cdots+d}k^{q^k}$$

$$= (g^{n/q})^{d_e} - 1^{q^{e-1-k}+\cdots+d}k \quad \text{(divide and multiply by } q^j)$$

$$= (g^*)^{d_k} \quad \text{(since } |g^*| = q)$$

Thus, we indeed have $d_k = \log_{g^*} b^*$.

Note that in order for us to compute a logarithm with Pohlig–Hellman, we need to know the prime factorization of $p - 1$, and to compute other logarithms (specifically, step 1.(c).III.). We must use another algorithm to compute these logs; for example, baby-step giant-step. If one of the factors of $p - 1$ is large, then computing this "sublogarithm" is also an intractable problem.

Admittedly, the notation in this algorithm looks virtually labyrinthine; however (as usual), an example will show how straightforward it really is. We will use small parameters.

EXAMPLE. Let the prime $p = 41$. We can easily obtain the prime power factorization of $p - 1$:

$$p - 1 = 40 = 2^3 \cdot 5$$

We want to find $\log_{6,41} 5$; that is, the solution to $6^x \equiv 5 \pmod{41}$.
To do this, we must compute each of the following:

1. $x_1 \equiv x \pmod{2^3} \rightarrow x_1 = d_0 + d_1 2 + d_2 2^2$
2. $x_2 \equiv x \pmod{5} \rightarrow x_2 = d_0$

We begin with x_1:

$$g^* = 6^{40/2} \equiv 40 \pmod{41}.$$

Let $c = 1$ and compute $b^* = (5 \cdot 1')^{40/2} \equiv 1 \pmod{41}$.

Compute $d_0 = \log_{40} 1 = 2$ (by using, for example, baby-step giant-step).

Now, let $c = 1 \cdot 6^2 \equiv 36 \pmod{41}$ and compute $b^* = (5 \cdot 36')^{40/4} \equiv 1 \pmod{41}$.

Compute $d_1 = \log_{40} 1 = 2$ (by using, for example, baby-step giant-step).

Now, let $c = 1 \cdot 6^{1 \cdot 2} \equiv 36 \pmod{41}$ and compute $b^* = (5 \cdot 36')^{40/8} \equiv 1 \pmod{41}$.

Compute $d_2 = \log_{40} 1 = 2$ (by using, for example, baby-step giant-step).

This yields

$$x_1 = 2 + 2 \cdot 2 + 2 \cdot 2^2 = 14.$$

Now, to compute x_2:

$$g^* = 6^{40/5} \equiv 10 \pmod{41}$$

Let $c = 1$ and compute $b^* = (5 \cdot 1')^{40/5} \equiv 18 \pmod{41}$.

Compute $d_0 = \log_{10} 18 = 2$ (by using, for example, baby-step giant-step).

This immediately yields

$$x_2 = 2.$$

Thus, we seek a solution to the system of congruences

$$x \equiv 14 \equiv 6 \pmod{2^3}$$

$$x \equiv 2 \pmod 5.$$

By using the Chinese Remainder Theorem, we derive the solution

$$x \equiv 22 \pmod{40}.$$

Thus, $\log_{6,\, 41} 5 = 22$. (Verify!)

Now, to the index-calculus algorithm. But before we describe it, we should cover some properties which discrete logarithms possess; they are very similar to properties of logarithms of real numbers.

PROPOSITION 43   Let p be prime, and let g be a generator modulo p. Suppose a and b are positive integers not divisible by p. Then we have all of the following:

a) $\log 1 \equiv 0 \pmod{p - 1}$

b) $\log(ab) \equiv \log a + \log b \pmod{p - 1}$

c) $\log(a^k) \equiv k \cdot \log a \pmod{p - 1}$

where all logarithms are to the base g modulo p.

Proof.

a) From FLT, we have $g^{p-1} \equiv 1 \pmod{p}$. Since g is a generator modulo p, no smaller power of g is congruent to 1 modulo p, and thus $\log 1 = p - 1 \equiv 0 \pmod{p-1}$.

b) Note that from the definition of discrete logarithms,

$$g^{\log(ab)} \equiv ab \pmod{p},$$

and

$$g^{\log a \,\cdot\, \log b} \equiv g^{\log a} \cdot g^{\log b} \equiv ab \pmod{p}.$$

Thus,

$$g^{\log(ab)} \equiv g^{\log a \,\cdot\, \log b} \pmod{p},$$

and by using proposition 38, we conclude that

$$\log(ab) \equiv \log a + \log b \pmod{p-1}$$

c) Exercise. ∎

EXAMPLES. Take the prime $p = 13$, and note that 2 is a generator modulo 13 (this is easily checked). Note that since $2^0 \equiv 2^{12} \equiv 1 \pmod{13}$ by FLT, we have

$$\log_{2,13} 1 = 12 \equiv 0 \pmod{12}.$$

Also, note that

$$\log_{2,13} 12 = 6,$$

$$\log_{2,13} 9 = 8, \text{ and}$$

$$\log_{2,13}(9 \cdot 12) = \log_{2,13}(108) = \log_{2,13}(4) = 2.$$

(Since $108 \equiv 4$ modulo 13.)

This gives us

$$\log_{2,13}(9 \cdot 12) = 2 \equiv 6 + 8 = \log_{2,13} 12 + \log_{2,13} 9 \pmod{12}.$$

Also, note that

$$10 \cdot \log_{2,13} 12 = 10 \cdot 6 = 60,$$

and

$$\log_{2,13} 12^{10} = \log_{2,13} 61917364224 = \log_{2,13} 1 = 12.$$

(Since $61917364224 \equiv 1$ modulo 13.)
This yields

$$\log_{2,13} 12^{10} = 12 \equiv 0 \equiv 60 = \log_{2,13} 12^{10} \pmod{12}.$$

Index–Calculus Algorithm   An optimized variant of this algorithm is the fastest known algorithm to date for computing discrete logarithms to the base g modulo a prime p, where g is a generator.

To compute $\log_{g,\,p} b$ where $g^x \equiv b \pmod{p}$ using the index–calculus algorithm:

1. Select from the numbers $2, 3, \ldots, p - 2$, a subset of the first t primes $S = \{p_1, p_2, \ldots, p_t\}$ such that "many" of the elements g^i where $1 \le i < p - 1$ can be written as a product of elements from S.

2. Select a random integer j such that $0 \le j \le p - 2$ and compute the lnr of g^j modulo p.

3. Attempt to write g^j as a product of elements from S:

$$g^j = p_1^{c_1} \cdot p_2^{c_2} \cdot \ldots \cdot p_t^{c_t}, \quad c_i \ge 0 \ \forall i.$$

If this is not successful, return to step 2; otherwise, continue.

4. Take the logarithm modulo p of both sides to produce a congruence;

$$j \cdot \log(g) \equiv j \equiv c_1 \cdot \log(p_1) + c_2 \cdot \log(p_2) + \ldots + c_t \cdot \log(p_t) \pmod{p - 1}.$$

(Simplify using the properties of discrete logarithms, as shown.)

5. Repeat steps 2 through 4 to make a system of at least t such congruences. Attempt to find a unique solution for each logarithm by solving the system. If the system is linearly dependent, go back to step 2 and generate new congruences to replace those that are linearly dependent on the others.

6. Select a random integer k such that $0 \le k \le p - 2$, and compute the lnr of $b \cdot g^k$ modulo p.

7. Attempt to write $b \cdot g^k$ as a product of elements from S:

$$b \cdot g^k = p_1^{d_1} \cdot p_2^{d_2} \cdot \ldots \cdot p_t^{d_t}, \quad d_i \ge 0 \ \forall i.$$

If this attempt is not successful, return to step 6; otherwise, continue.

8. Take the logarithm to the base g of both sides; this yields

$$\log(b \cdot g^k)$$
$$\equiv \log(b) + k \cdot \log(g)$$
$$\equiv \log(b) + k$$
$$\equiv d_1 \cdot \log(p_1) + d_2 \cdot \log(p_2) + \ldots + d_t \cdot \log(p_t) \pmod{p - 1}.$$

which we then solve for $\log_{g,\,p} b$:

$$\log(b) \equiv d_1 \cdot \log(p_1) + d_2 \cdot \log(p_2) + \ldots + d_t \cdot \log(p_t) - k \pmod{p - 1}.$$

EXAMPLE.   We will use the index–calculus algorithm to find a solution to $6^x \equiv 57 \pmod{107}$. Note that 107 is prime, and that 6 is a generator modulo 107 (verify). So, the parameters are $p = 107$, $g = 6$, and $b = 57$. We will choose $S = \{2, 3, 5, 7\}$. Now, we generate some random integers, and attempt to write powers of $g = 6$ as products of elements from S.

$$\text{lnr of } 6^{24} \text{ modulo } 107: \quad 42 = 2 \cdot 3 \cdot 7$$

$$\text{lnr of } 6^{6} \text{ modulo } 107: \quad 4 = 2^2$$

$$\text{lnr of } 6^{33} \text{ modulo } 107: \quad 15 = 3 \cdot 5$$

$$\text{lnr of } 6^{34} \text{ modulo } 107: \quad 90 = 2 \cdot 3^2 \cdot 5$$

By taking the logarithm base 6 modulo 107 of both sides, and using the properties of discrete logarithms (from proposition 43), we get the following system of congruences:

$$24 \equiv \log 2 + \log 3 + \log 7 \pmod{106}$$

$$6 \equiv 2 \cdot \log 2 \pmod{106}$$

$$33 \equiv \log 3 + \log 5 \pmod{106}$$

$$34 \equiv \log 2 + 2 \cdot \log 3 + \log 5 \pmod{106}$$

To solve this system, we need to reduce the following matrix to row echelon form using an analogue of Gauss–Jordan elimination for matrices representing congruences.

$$\begin{vmatrix} 1 & 1 & 0 & 1 & \vdots & 24 \\ 1 & 0 & 0 & 0 & \vdots & 6 \\ 0 & 1 & 1 & 0 & \vdots & 33 \\ 1 & 2 & 1 & 0 & \vdots & 34 \end{vmatrix}$$

When this is done, we achieve this reduced matrix. (Verify.)

$$\begin{vmatrix} 1 & 0 & 0 & 0 & \vdots & 3 \\ 0 & 1 & 0 & 0 & \vdots & 104 \\ 0 & 0 & 1 & 0 & \vdots & 35 \\ 0 & 0 & 0 & 1 & \vdots & 23 \end{vmatrix}$$

Thus, we have

$$\log_6 2 = 3$$

$$\log_6 3 = 104$$

$$\log_6 5 = 35$$

$$\log_6 7 = 23$$

Now, we try to evaluate $\log_{6,107} 57$ (the purpose of all this work, remember?). First, we pick a random integer $k = 38$, and try to write $b \cdot g^k$ as a product of members of S. It turns out that we can:

$$\text{lnr of } 57 \cdot 6^{38} \text{ modulo } 107 = 35 = 5 \cdot 7.$$

Taking the logarithm base 6 of both sides, and by using the properties of discrete logarithms, we get

$$\log 57 + 38 \equiv \log 5 + \log 7$$

$$\equiv 35 + 23$$

$$\equiv 58 \pmod{106}.$$

Thus, we obtain our final result,

$$\log_{6,107} 57 = 58 - 38 = 20. \quad \text{(Verify!)}$$

Some parts of this algorithm are not clear; for instance, how many primes t should be in the set S? The answer is not clear, since it depends on the abilities of the computing device. If t is too large, the corresponding system of congruences may take up too much memory, and take too long to solve. On the other hand, if t is too small, it will be harder to find elements which can be written as a product of members of S; the search for these elements could take too long. This type of time–memory tradeoff always depends on the hardware being used; thus, we leave this part of the algorithm unspecified.

Another part of the algorithm that is unclear is when it directs one to "attempt to write the element as a product of members from S." If we are using the first t primes, we can do this by simply taking the prime factorization of the element (say E), and checking if each factor of E is in the set S. However, if E is a large prime, or is composite but is difficult to factor because it has large prime factors, the time to do this could be prohibitive. Thus, we should probably submit E to a primality test; if it turns out to be a probable prime, we should reject E and choose another random integer. Otherwise, we can try to factor E, but enforce some time limit to do this.

Many of these decisions for the index–calculus algorithm are heavily dependent on the hardware, and the software, such as the implementation of large integer arithmetic. Thus, the decisions on how to implement the index–calculus algorithm are often made based on experimentation.

EXERCISES

1. Prove part (b) of proposition 37.

2. Write a logPohligHellman() method in the BigIntegerMath class to compute discrete logs using the Pohlig–Hellman algorithm.

3. Prove part (c) of proposition 43.

4. The BigInteger class provides a modPow() method to perform modular exponentiation, but you should consider how to write such a method. Write an efficient method to perform modular exponentiation, say a modPow(BigInteger base, BigInteger exponent, BigInteger modulus) method. Put it in the BigintegerMath class. For help, refer to the following:

Implementing Modular Exponentiation. Notice that many cryptosystems require us to raise integers to large powers modulo n. It is easy to write an algorithm that does a poor job of this. Consider the relatively easy problem of raising 2 to the 340th power modulo 341; that is, compute the lnr x of

$$2^{340} \equiv x \pmod{341}.$$

Do we compute 2^{340}, then compute the least nonnegative residue? Of course not; if the numbers involved were only moderately larger, the storage space of computers would be quickly maxed out trying to contain such a large number.

Our second alternative may be to write a loop which executes 339 times, begins with a value of the base 2, then multiplying the product times 2 each time and taking the lnr modulo 341 on each iteration. This is better, but only moderately larger exponents could make this far too slow. For example, an exponent larger than a trillion would cause the loop to execute more than a trillion times, and even supercomputers would take a while to crank through such a loop.

A much better alternative is to do repeated squarings and multiplications, taking the lnr after each operation. To see this, we rewrite 2^{340} as

$$2^{340}$$
$$= 2^{170 \cdot 2}$$
$$= (2^{170})^2$$
$$= ((2^{85})^2)^2$$
$$= (((2^{42 \cdot 2 \cdot 1})^2)^2)^2$$
$$= (((2(2^{42})^2)^2)^2)^2$$
$$= (((2(2^{21 \cdot 2})^2)^2)^2)^2$$
$$= (((2((2^{21})^2)^2)^2)^2)^2$$
$$= (((2((2^{10 \cdot 2 \cdot 1})^2)^2)^2)^2)^2$$
$$= (((2((2(2^{10})^2)^2)^2)^2)^2)^2$$
$$= (((2((2(2^{5 \cdot 2})^2)^2)^2)^2)^2)^2$$
$$= (((2((2((2^5)^2)^2)^2)^2)^2)^2)^2$$
$$= (((2((2((2^{2 \cdot 2 \cdot 1})^2)^2)^2)^2)^2)^2)^2$$
$$= (((2((2((2(2^2)^2)^2)^2)^2)^2)^2)^2)^2.$$

Computing 2^{340} modulo 341 then becomes a matter of calculating

$$(((2((2((2(2^2)^2)^2)^2)^2)^2)^2)^2$$
$$\equiv (((2((2((2(4)^2)^2)^2)^2)^2)^2)^2$$
$$\equiv (((2((2((32)^2)^2)^2)^2)^2)^2$$

$$\equiv (((2((2(1)^2)^2)^2)^2)^2$$

$$\equiv (((2(2^2)^2)^2)^2)^2$$

$$\equiv (((2(4)^2)^2)^2)^2$$

$$\equiv ((32^2)^2)^2$$

$$\equiv (1^2)^2$$

$$\equiv 1 \ (\text{mod } 341).$$

Writing these computations out is far uglier than actually doing them. You will notice that calculating 2^{340} modulo 341 this way only requires 9 squarings, and only 3 multiplications by the base 2. This is a dramatic improvement over 339 multiplications, and this improvement becomes even more obvious as we use much larger exponents.

To do this, it may help to look at the binary representation of 340; that is,

$$340 = 101010100_{(\text{base } 2)}$$

When calculating the lnr x of

$$2^{340} \equiv x \ (\text{mod } 341)$$

You may see an efficient way to determine when to square, and when to multiply by the base.

5. Write the following constructor for the Int class.

```
public Int(int bitlength, int certainty, Random r);
```

It should generate probable primes of the desired bitlength. They should be prime with probability exceeding $1 - 0.25^{\text{certainty}}$.

CHAPTER 14

Exponential Ciphers

In the last chapter, we discussed how to solve congruences of the form

$$a^x \equiv b \pmod{p}$$

for x, where a and b are known, and p is prime. Cryptosystems based on exponential congruences can be quite difficult to crack. We will consider such ciphers now.

14.1 DIFFIE–HELLMAN KEY EXCHANGE

The first public key scheme was invented by Diffie and Hellman. Though it could not be used to send messages, it could establish secret keys for use in secret key cryptosystems. An eavesdropper "tapping the line" would be unable to determine what the generated key was.

The steps to Diffie–Hellman (DFH) are as follows:

1. Two users agree on using a large prime p, and g, a generator modulo p. At current levels of computing power, p should be at least 1024 bits in length. It doesn't matter if a third party hears this exchange and knows these numbers g and p.

2. Next, user 1 chooses a private number, say x. User 2 chooses his own secret number, say y.

3. User 1 then calculates $g^x \pmod{p}$ and sends this quantity to User 2. User 2 similarly computes $g^y \pmod{p}$ and sends this to User 1.

4. User 1 then takes the value received from User 2 and raises it to his x power, and User 2 likewise computes the value received from User 1 to his y power. Thus, they both compute $K \equiv (g^x)^y \equiv g^{xy} \equiv (g^y)^x \pmod{p}$. This value K can then be used as a key in subsequent secret key sessions.

14.2 WEAKNESSES OF DIFFIE–HELLMAN

Why is this secure? Note that even if a third party is listening, and hears all of the following transmissions, he will know the value of g, p, g^x, and g^y. Is this enough to compute the K value? No! In order to compute K, the eavesdropper must do either of two things:

- Raise g^x to the y power (mod p), which he cannot do because he does not know y, or

- Raise g^y to the x power (mod p), which he cannot do because he does not know x.

Note that though the eavesdropper does not know x or y, he does know g^x and g^y. How easy is it to obtain x, for example, if you know what g^x is? Nearly impossible! This is, of course, the discrete logarithm problem, and it means solving a congruence of the form

$$z \equiv g^x \ (\text{mod } p)$$

for x. We know this problem is intractable when the modulus p is large, and when g is a generator modulo p. Thus, anyone using DFH with confidence in the difficulty of the discrete logarithm problem can generate as many keys as desired and use them with other cryptosystems.

Later we will see a Diffie–Hellman Key Exchange. To do this, we will need to cover some of the Java networking classes, so I've saved this topic for the upcoming chapter, Establishing Keys and Message Exchange.

14.3 THE POHLIG–HELLMAN EXPONENTIATION CIPHER

This cipher is based on Fermat's Little Theorem (FLT), and is called the Pohlig–Hellman exponentiation cipher. Let p be a large safe prime, and let e be some integer relatively prime to $p - 1$. At current levels of computing power, p should be at least 1024 bits in length. Our plaintext message P is a nonnegative integer less than p. The enciphering transformation is

$$C \equiv P^e \ (\text{mod } p), 0 \le P < p, 0 \le C < p.$$

To decrypt, we must first find an inverse of e modulo $p - 1$, call it d. We know this inverse exists because e is relatively prime to $p - 1$; thus, d must satisfy the congruence

$$ed \equiv 1 \ (\text{mod } p - 1).$$

This congruence has a unique solution for d modulo $p - 1$ and is easily solved using the extended Euclidean algorithm. Once d is calculated, one may decrypt in the following way:

$$P \equiv C^d \ (\text{mod } p).$$

Why does this work? Why does raising the ciphertext to the d power recover the plaintext? If we recall Fermat's Little Theorem, it is easy to show why:

$$C^d$$

$$\equiv (P^e)^d$$

$$\equiv P^{ed}$$

$\equiv P^{k(p-1)+1}$ (Since $ed \equiv 1 \pmod{p-1}$, $ed = k(p-1)+1$ for some integer k.)

$\equiv (P^{p-1})^k P$

$\equiv 1^k P$ (Here is where FLT comes in.)

$\equiv P \pmod{p}$.

Note that the conditions in the hypothesis of Fermat's Little Theorem are satisfied; that is, p is prime and does not divide P, a nonnegative integer less than p.

14.4   WEAKNESSES OF THE POHLIG–HELLMAN CIPHER

Suppose we are using Pohlig–Hellman and manage to get our hands on the plaintext P associated with some ciphertext C. Finding the encryption key e then means solving the congruence

$$C \equiv P^e \pmod{p}$$

for e. This is an exponential congruence, and as we know, these are quite difficult to solve. Thus, when using this cipher, even if we obtain some plaintext knowing that it corresponds to certain ciphertext, it still does not help us in cracking the cipher. Hence, the Pohlig–Hellman cipher is resistant even to a known plaintext attack. It is very important that a cipher not be vulnerable to such an attack, since it is considered too great a security risk. This exponentiation cipher is quite resistant to cryptanalysis, provided the proper precautions are taken. We list some of the potential weaknesses of this cipher.

Inadequate Block Size   The block size (and thus the prime modulus p) must be chosen large enough; say greater than 500 decimal digits for the prime p.

Weak Primes   The quantity $p - 1$ should have at least one large prime factor, otherwise p could be vulnerable to certain discrete log finding algorithms.

Low Order Messages modulo p   Since we encrypt with Pohlig–Hellman using the transformation

$$C \equiv P^e \pmod{p},$$

the plaintext message may not be a generator modulo p, and in fact may have low order. This makes the discrete logarithm problem easier to solve. Some method must be employed to ensure the message is of high order modulo p; perhaps by judicious use of salt. Note finally that Pohlig–Hellman is a secret key cipher. Divulging the encryption key e to anyone is the same as handing them the decryption key d, since finding it merely means solving the congruence $ed \equiv 1 \pmod{p-1}$ for d, which is very easily done.

Memoryless Cipher   Pohlig–Hellman is a static cipher. That is, it always maps a particular plaintext block to the same ciphertext block. We discussed CBC earlier to cope with this problem, but here we will cover a different solution. It has some advantages over CBC, but can only be used for a secret key cipher.

14.5 CIPHER FEEDBACK MODE (CFB)

Like CBC, CFB uses an initialization vector (IV) to start the encryption and decryption. What may seem strange is that only the encryption transformation is used for both encryption and decryption; the decryption key is never needed. (This makes CFB unsuitable for public key ciphers, of course.)

Suppose the cipher maps m-bit blocks to n-bit blocks, where $m \leq n$. Let $E_k(x)$ denote the encipherment of x using the secret encryption key k. The IV is an m-bit quantity that need not be secret. Let r be a positive integer not exceeding n, and divide the plaintext message into r-bit blocks, $x_1, x_2, \ldots, x_w$. We proceed as follows:

1. Let $I_1 = IV$

2. For i from 1 through w do:

    a) Let $U_i = E_k(I_i)$.

    b) Let t_i be the r least significant bits of U_i. (Suppose the least significant bits are to the right.)

    c) Let $c_i = x_i \oplus t_i$.

    d) Shift I_i toward the left r bit positions, and append c_i; assign this value to I_{i+1}.

The ciphertext is the set of r-bit blocks $c_1, c_2, \ldots, c_w$. Figure 14.1 is a diagram of the CFB mode of operation.

To decrypt, we go through nearly the same process, with only the ciphertext blocks and plaintext blocks exchanging roles in step 2.(c).

FIGURE 14.1

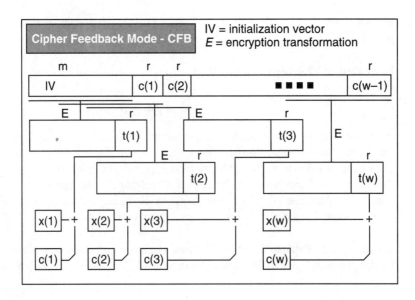

1. Let $I_1 = \text{IV}$

2. For i from 1 through w do:

   a) Let $U_i = E_k(I_i)$.

   b) Let t_i be the r least significant bits of U_i. (Suppose the least significant bits are to the right.)

   c) Let $x_i = c_i \oplus t_i$.

   d) Shift I_i toward the left r bit positions, and append c_i; assign this value to I_{i+1}.

This cipher mode has a great benefit; using it we can process message blocks which are smaller than the cipher block length. This is necessary for some applications, in which a single byte (or even a bit) must be processed as soon as it enters the stream. (Many networked applications work this way; telnet, for example.)

CFB has an advantage over CBC, in that errors do not propagate very far down the stream. With CBC, each ciphertext block is produced based on the previous ciphertext block, and a single bit inversion in one of these blocks changes all of the blocks following it. This is not likely to happen during the encryption phase, but is quite possible on the receiving end of the message, after it has passed possibly thousands of miles over a noisy channel. One incorrect bit in any block destroys all the blocks following.

A bit error using CFB propagates only a small distance. If you see how each ciphertext block is used, you will see why. In the ith step of the algorithm, a ciphertext block c_i is appended to a left-shifted I_i, then continues to be shifted left until it is eventually shifted out of the m-bit register. If the bit error is in block c_i, for example, then it will only affect those blocks processed while c_i remains in the register.

EXAMPLE. We will use CFB with Pohlig–Hellman, using a small prime. In reality, a safe prime at least a thousand bits in length should be used. The quantities will be expressed in binary. We will process 3 bits of the message at a time. Suppose the prime modulus is

$$p = 1101011111111,$$

the encryption exponent is

$$e = 111111110000,$$

the initialization vector is

$$\text{iv} = 10110011,$$

and the message (divided into 3-bit blocks) is

$$x_1 = 101, x_2 = 110, x_3 = 011.$$

We begin by setting $I_1 = $ to the initialization vector:

$$I_1 = \text{iv} = 10110011.$$

We then compute

$$u_1 \equiv I_1{}^e \equiv 0101101100011 \pmod{p},$$

and t_1 is the three rightmost bits:

$$t_1 = 011.$$

This is $\oplus$-ed with the first plaintext block to yield the first ciphertext block.

$$c_1 = t_1 \oplus 101 = 011 \oplus 101 = 110$$

We now form the next value I_2 by shifting I_1 to the left three bits, and appending c_1. The three most significant bits of I_1 are lost.

$$I_2 = 10011110.$$

From here on out, the process goes exactly the same way:

$$U_2 \equiv I_2^e \equiv 111101111 \pmod{p}$$

$$t_2 = 111$$

$$c_2 = t_2 \oplus 110 = 001$$

$$I_3 = 11110111$$

$$U_3 \equiv I_3^e \equiv 1011100100 \pmod{p}$$

$$t_3 = 100$$

$$c_3 = t_3 \oplus 011 = 111$$

The final ciphertext message (in 3-bit blocks) is:

$$c_1 = 110, c_2 = 001, c_3 = 111$$

Java Algorithm   Using the BigInteger class in Java, it is easy to write code to perform Pohlig–Hellman exponentiation encryption/decryption. Here, we add a couple of methods, pohligHellmanEncipher() and pohligHellmanDecipher(), to our Ciphers class. It calls the same pad(), block(), unPad() and unBlock() methods we defined earlier, but it does not use salt, or CFB. You will be asked to do CFB in the exercises.

```java
import java.math.*;
public class Ciphers {
    public static byte[] pohligHellmanEncipher(byte[] msg,BigInteger e,BigInteger p)
{
        //Compute the plaintext block size
        int blockSize=(p.bitLength()-1)/8;
        //Check the enciphering exponent
        if (!(p.subtract(BigIntegerMath.ONE).gcd(e).equals(BigIntegerMath.ONE)))
            throw new IllegalArgumentException
                ("Enciphering key is not relatively prime to (modulus minus one).");
        byte ba[][]=block(pad(msg,blockSize),blockSize);
        //Begin the enciphering
```

```
        for (int i=0;i<ba.length;i++) ba[i]=getBytes(new
            BigInteger(1,ba[i]).modPow(e,p));
        //Return to a 1D array.
        //The ciphertext block size is one byte greater than plaintext block size.
        return unBlock(ba,blockSize+1);
    }
    public static byte[] pohligHellmanDecipher(byte[] msg,BigInteger d,BigInteger p)
{
        //Compute the ciphertext block size
        int blockSize=(p.bitLength()-1)/8+1;
        //Check the deciphering exponent
        if (!(p.subtract(BigIntegerMath.ONE).gcd(d).equals(BigIntegerMath.ONE)))
            throw new IllegalArgumentException
                ("Deciphering key is not relatively prime to (modulus minus one).");
        byte[][] ba=block(msg,blockSize);
        //Begin the deciphering
        for (int i=0;i<ba.length;i++) ba[i]=getBytes(new
            BigInteger(1,ba[i]).modPow(d,p));
        //Go from blocks to a 1D array, and remove padding; return this
        return unPad(unBlock(ba,blockSize-1),blockSize-1);
    }
//...Other methods
}
```

An applet (called TestPohligHellmanCipherApplet) to view the behavior of this cipher can be run from the book's website. The applet generates a safe prime to use as the modulus. The applet actually uses a salted version of Pohlig–Hellman. You will see that if you encipher the same plaintext multiple times, you will receive a different ciphertext each time. The methods to encipher/decipher this way are in the Ciphers class.

```
public static byte[] pohligHellmanEncipherWSalt
(byte[] msg,BigInteger e,BigInteger p,SecureRandom sr) {
    //Compute the plaintext block size
    int blockSize=(p.bitLength()-1)/8;
    if (blockSize<5) throw new IllegalArgumentException
        ("Block size must be >= 5 bytes");
    //Check the enciphering exponent
    if (!(p.subtract(BigIntegerMath.ONE).gcd(e).equals(BigIntegerMath.ONE)))
        throw new IllegalArgumentException
        ("Enciphering key is not relatively prime to (modulus minus one).");
    byte[][] ba=block(pad(msg,blockSize-4),blockSize-4);
    //Begin the enciphering
    for (int i=0;i<ba.length;i++) {
        ba[i]=addSalt(ba[i],sr);
        ba[i]=getBytes(new BigInteger(1,ba[i]).modPow(e,p));
    }
```

```
   //Return to a 1D array.  The ciphertext block size is one byte greater than
   //plaintext block size.
   return unBlock(ba,blockSize+1);
}


public static byte[] pohligHellmanDecipherWSalt(byte[] msg,BigInteger d,BigInteger
p) {
   //Compute the ciphertext block size
   int blockSize=(p.bitLength()-1)/8+1;
   //Check the deciphering exponent
   if (!(p.subtract(BigIntegerMath.ONE).gcd(d).equals(BigIntegerMath.ONE)))
      throw new IllegalArgumentException
      ("Deciphering key is not relatively prime to (modulus minus one).");
   byte[][] ba=block(msg,blockSize);
   //Begin the deciphering
   for (int i=0;i<ba.length;i++) {
      ba[i]=getBytes(new BigInteger(1,ba[i]).modPow(d,p));
      ba[i]=removeSalt(ba[i]);
   }
   //Go from blocks to a 1D array, and remove padding; return this
   return unPad(unBlock(ba,blockSize-5),blockSize-5);
}
```

You can see that these methods call a couple of helper methods, addSalt() and removeSalt(), also in the Ciphers class.

```
//Method to add salt to blocks
private static byte[] addSalt(byte[] b,SecureRandom random) {
   byte[] answer=new byte[b.length+4];
   byte[] salt=new byte[4];
   random.nextBytes(salt);
   //Put salt in front
   System.arraycopy(salt,0,answer,0,4);
   //Copy the message over
   System.arraycopy(b,0,answer,4,b.length);
   return answer;
}


//Method to remove salt
private static byte[] removeSalt(byte[] b) {
   byte[] answer=new byte[b.length-4];
   //Copy the message over
   System.arraycopy(b,4,answer,0,answer.length);
   return answer;
}
```

FIGURE 14.2

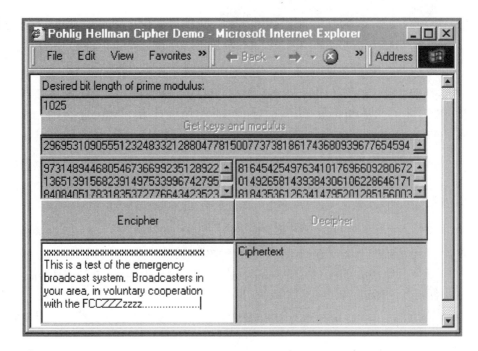

Figure 14.2 is a screen shot of TestPohligHellmanCipherApplet. Give it a try and see how it works.

14.6 THE ELGAMAL CIPHER

Since DFH, there has been an explosion of public key algorithms. The proposed national standard, backed by the National Security Agency (NSA), is called ElGamal. Though it is a very interesting algorithm, it is possible that NSA has already broken it, which could explain their enthusiasm for it. ElGamal is similar to Diffie–Hellman key exchange and Pohlig–Hellman in that breaking it requires solving the discrete logarithm problem. This is opposed to RSA (which we will soon discuss), which depends on the intractability of factoring integers with large prime factors.

This is how ElGamal works: First, the recipient of a message must choose a large random safe prime p, and a generator g modulo p. At current levels of computing power, p should be at least 1024 bits in length. Then he selects a random integer a such that $1 < a < p - 1$, and computes the least nonnegative residue r of g^a modulo p. That is,

$$r \equiv g^a \pmod{p} \qquad (0 \leq r < p).$$

He makes public the values p, g, and r. The private key is a.

Now, for someone to send a message to this individual, she must do the following: Suppose P is the plaintext message, considered as an integer, with $0 \leq P < p$. The sender then selects a random integer k such that $1 \leq k \leq p - 2$ (it is very important that the sender choose a different random value for each message); then she computes the two values

$$c \equiv g^k \pmod{p} \qquad\qquad (0 \leq c < p)$$

$$d \equiv Pr^k \equiv P(g^a)^k \pmod{p} \quad (0 \leq d < p).$$

The ciphertext to send is the pair of values c and d; that is,

$$C = (c, d).$$

The intended recipient decrypts C by using the private key a to first compute the lnr z of an inverse of c^a modulo p; that is,

$$z \equiv (c^a)' \pmod{p} \qquad (0 \leq z < p).$$

He then recovers the plaintext P by computing

$$P \equiv zd \pmod{p} \qquad (0 \leq P < p).$$

Why does this last computation recover the plaintext? If one references how each quantity was created, it becomes obvious:

$$zd \equiv (c^a)' \cdot P \cdot r^k \equiv ((g^k)^a)' \cdot P \cdot (g^a)^k \equiv (g^{ak})' \cdot g^{ak} \cdot P \equiv P \pmod{p}.$$

EXAMPLE.   We will now demonstrate ElGamal using very small numbers. The intended recipient first chooses a prime $p = 2357$, and $g = 2$, a generator modulo 2357. She then chooses a random integer $a = 2001$ which will serve as the private key. She then computes

$$r = 2034 \equiv 2^{2001} \pmod{2357}.$$

She makes public the values of p, g, and r.
Suppose now someone wishes to send the message (regarded as an integer)

$$P = 1622$$

to the aforementioned recipient. She must first generate a random integer $k = 835$ then compute the two values

$$c = 731 \equiv 2^{835} \pmod{2357}$$

$$d = 1326 \equiv 1622 \cdot 2034^{835} \pmod{2357}$$

She then sends these 2 values; the ciphertext is

$$C = (731, 1326)$$

To decrypt, the recipient must first find an inverse of c^a modulo p; that is,

$$z = 794 \equiv 1980' \equiv (731^{2001})' \pmod{2357}.$$

She then retrieves the plaintext by computing the lnr of zd modulo p.

$$P = 1622 \equiv 794 \cdot 1326 \pmod{2357}.$$

Note that ElGamal basically doubles the size of the message. For this reason, cryptographers often ignore the national standard in favor of other cryptosystems.

System-Wide Parameters   Note that there is no particular reason why everyone in a system could not use the same values for the prime p and the generator g with ElGamal. Each individual would only then need to choose a private value for a. This has been suggested, and has received limited use in practice.

14.7   WEAKNESSES OF ELGAMAL

ElGamal can be broken provided proper precautions are not taken. We describe the most important weakness here.

Equal Encryption Exponent Attack   It is very important that when enciphering using the transformations

$$c \equiv g^k \pmod{p} \qquad (0 \le c < p)$$

$$d \equiv Pr^k \equiv P(g^a)^k \pmod{p} \quad (0 \le d < p).$$

that the sender choose a different random value of k for each plaintext message. If the message must be separated into blocks, a different value of k must be used on each block. If not, plaintext can be easily derived by an adversary. To see this, suppose the same value for k was used to encipher the plaintext messages P and P^*. Their corresponding ciphertext pairs are (c, d), and (c^*, d^*). Note then that we have

$$d \cdot (d^*)' \equiv P(g^a)^k \cdot (P^*(g^a)^k)' \pmod{p},$$

where d' and $(d^*)'$ are inverses of d and d^* modulo p, respectively. Thus

$$P^* \cdot d \cdot (d^*)' \equiv P \pmod{p}.$$

Thus, if either message, P or P^*, were known to an adversary, they could easily derive the other message. Thus, this is a known plaintext attack coupled with carelessness on the part of the sender. If the sender always used the same value for k, an adversary would need only one plaintext message to retrieve any others.

EXAMPLE.   Here we see this type of attack, which you will be asked to program in Java. We begin by finding a safe prime:

$p = 3213876088517980551083924184682325205044405987565585670609523$

It turns out that $g = 2$ is a generator for this prime. The sender's private ElGamal key will be:

$a = 1897456254164942343917965235766273117568497123443633417036846$

We compute the sender's public key value r as the lnr of g^a modulo p:

$r = 2063540830854289477395627063716322702415230040026373835561574$

To execute this attack we have two plaintext messages; suppose the first is unknown to the adversary:

$$P = 302498753092857093287593028759302857093275903475240963 46$$

The second plaintext message, however, is known to the adversary:

$$P^* = 9238652389765892365982365826589265892569823659826892659823$$

We will choose a random k for encryption, but we will make the mistake of using the same k for both messages:

$$k = 2388424515437026664851549783676880762378680269832085250306583$$

We now compute the ciphertext values for both messages, and send them. The adversary now has both ciphertext messages.

$$c \equiv g^k \pmod p \equiv$$
$$16428880205113883998514374765220985326482329818251802 1833998$$

$$d \equiv P \cdot r^k \pmod p \equiv$$

$$242369927295936507129991969696534780912801909834187753 7393147$$

$$c^* = c \equiv g^k \pmod p \equiv$$

$$16428880205113883998514374765220985326482329818251802 1833998$$

$$d^* \equiv P^* \cdot r^k \pmod p \equiv$$
$$1394500791523696367305442526712905312818729871045966459248084$$

With this information, the adversary computes inverse of d^* modulo p; this is easily done:

$$(d^*)' = 1711642693000210140982699304286061941393356166206543 62864166$$

The adversary can now obtain the first plaintext message without decrypting, by computing the lnr of $P^* \cdot d \cdot (d^*)'$ modulo p:

$$302498753092857093287593028759302857093275903475240963 46.$$

This should convince you that you should never use the same value for k to encrypt multiple messages.

14.8   THE RSA CIPHER

Rivest, Shamir, and Adleman created the RSA cipher (hence the acronym RSA). They were among the first to patent their work in public key cryptography, and they even claimed their patent included all forms of public key cryptography! Regardless, their patent has now expired.

RSA works like this:

1. The receiver of a message generates two large strong primes, p and q, forms their product, say $n = pq$, and makes public the value of n. At current levels of computing power,

n should be at least 1024 bits in length. Everyone knows n, but not its two factors, p or q.

2. The receiver then chooses an integer $e < n$, such that $(e,(p - 1)(q - 1)) = 1$. The value for e is made public.

3. The receiver also computes a decryption key, d, which is an inverse of e modulo $(p - 1)(q - 1)$. This inverse exists since e was chosen relatively prime to $(p - 1)$ $(q - 1)$. That is, d must satisfy the congruence

$$ed \equiv 1 \ (\text{mod} \ (p - 1)(q - 1)).$$

The sender of the message can send a message $P < n$ by computing with the enciphering transformation

$$C \equiv P^e \ (\text{mod} \ n) \qquad\qquad\qquad 0 \le C < n.$$

5. The receiver gets the ciphertext message C, and can retrieve the plaintext by computing $P \equiv C^d \ (\text{mod} \ n)$.

This cipher looks remarkably similar to the Pohlig–Hellman exponentiation cipher. Decryption worked in that case because of Fermat's Little Theorem. FLT will also help us prove that decryption works here. Note that since

$$ed \equiv 1 \ (\text{mod} \ (p - 1)(q - 1))$$

there is an integer k such that $ed = 1 + k(p - 1)(q - 1)$. Now, suppose the plaintext message P is relatively prime to p; that is, $(P, p) = 1$. Then, by FLT,

$$P^{p-1} \equiv 1 \ (\text{mod} \ p).$$

Thus, we also have the following:

$$P^{ed} \equiv P^{1+k(p-1)(q-1)} \equiv P(P^{(p-1)})^{k(q-1)} \equiv P \cdot 1^{k(q+1)} \equiv P \ (\text{mod} \ p).$$

On the other hand, even if P is not relatively prime to p, we still have

$$P^{ed} \equiv P \ (\text{mod} \ p),$$

since both sides are congruent to 0 modulo m. Similarly, we can also show that in all cases,

$$P^{ed} \equiv P \ (\text{mod} \ q).$$

Now, since p and q are certainly relatively prime, by proposition 26 we have

$$P^{ed} \equiv P \ (\text{mod} \ n).$$

Now, simply note that

$$C^d \equiv (P^e)^d \equiv P^{ed} \equiv P \ (\text{mod} \ n)$$

and we have our proof that decryption always works, whether or not the plaintext message P is relatively prime to the modulus n.

EXAMPLE.   We will demonstrate RSA using small numbers. To establish a public and private key, an individual first selects two primes, say $p = 563$ and $q = 2357$. So, $n = 563 \cdot 2357 = 1326991$. Finally, he selects an integer $e = 3$ relatively prime to $(p - 1)(q - 1) = 1324072$, and computes the inverse of e modulo $(p - 1)(q - 1)$ by solving

$$3d \equiv 1 \bmod (1324072)$$

for d. This yields

$$d \equiv 882715 \pmod{1324072}.$$

The values for n and e are made public; d, p, and q remain private.

Suppose someone wants to send the message (regarded as an integer)

$$P = 1107300$$

to the aforementioned individual. They must simply calculate and send the ciphertext

$$C = 875102 \equiv 1107300^3 \pmod{1326991}.$$

To decrypt, the recipient uses the decryption key to derive the plaintext thus:

$$P = 1107300 \equiv 875102^{882715} \pmod{1326991}.$$

14.9   WEAKNESSES OF RSA

RSA can be compromised given certain conditions. We will examine these issues here.

Small Encryption Exponent   It has been suggested that a small encryption exponent in RSA be used since it speeds up encryption. For example, all users could use $e = 3$ as their public encryption key. This doesn't help recover their decryption exponents, since this still seems to involve factoring each of their moduli (each still chooses a different modulus). However, a small common value for e allows one to compute the eth root (with the aid of the Chinese Remainder Theorem) when the same message is sent to multiple entities. Recall that a similar problem occurs with the Rabin cipher.

Suppose $e = 3$ for some individual, and they send the same message m (enciphered) to three different entities, having respective moduli n_1, n_2, and n_3. The ciphertext sent to each entity will be denoted c_1, c_2, and c_3. An eavesdropper intercepting these messages merely has to find the simultaneous solution x to the system

$$x \equiv c_1 \pmod{n_1}$$

$$x \equiv c_2 \pmod{n_2}$$

$$x \equiv c_3 \pmod{n_3}.$$

Since $m^3 < n_1 n_2 n_3$, (and these moduli are almost certainly pairwise relatively prime) the lnr of the x obtained using CRT is in fact, m^3. Thus, to recover m, one needs only compute the ordinary cube root of x. The eavesdropper needs no knowledge of the private decryption keys.

EXAMPLE. Here we see this type of attack. You will be asked to program this in Java. We will use $e = 3$, a small RSA encryption exponent. The private primes $p1$ and $q1$ for the first recipient will be

$p1 = $ 179769313486231590772930519078902473361797697894230657273430081157732675805500963132708477322407536021120113879871393357658789768814416622492847430639474124377767893424865485276302219601246094119453082952085005768838150682342462881473913110540827237163350510684586298239947245938479716304835356329624224137859

$q1 = $ 359538626972463181545861038157804946723595395788461314546860162315465351611001926265416954644815072042240227759742786715317579537628833244985694861278948248755535786849730970552604439202492188238906165904170011537676301364684925762947826221081654474326701021369172596479894491876959432609670712659248448276687

and so the public modulus of the first recipient is

$n1 = $ 646340121426220146014297533773399039208882053394309680642606908550493102777357817863944028230458269273774359218437960389882391183009818421901763047728965662412617547346019921835003955007793042135921152767681351365535844372852395123236761886769523409411632917040726100857751517830821316172151047982478607716803918058340827477683169176315227971638380003141234015213715286981934574126958310812212353843734392842382104560615275941849712736764525520559801471208444488841303619868703237828364738114662819239227238184943188232325983560711367060575557374757848121466511362604986541276943834825366579731809108470421496863793133.

The private primes $p2$ and $q2$ of the second recipient will be

$p2 = $ 287630901577970545236688830526243957378876316630769051637488129852372281288801541012333563715852057633792182207794229372254063630103066595988555889023158599004428629479784776442083551361993750591124932723336009230141041091747940610358260976865323579461360817095338077183915593501567546087736570127398758619564

$q2 = $ 287630901577970545236688830526243957378876316630769051637488129852372281288801541012333563715852057633792182207794229372254063630103066595988555889023158599004428629479784776442083551361993750591124932723336009230141041091747940610358260976865323579461360817095338077183915593501567546087736570127398758619899

and so the public modulus of the second recipient is

$n2 = $ 827315355425561786898300843229950770187369028344716391222536842944631171555018006865848356134986584670431179799600589299049460714252567580034256701093076047888150460602905499948805062409975093933979075542632129

478858807972510657577430552150649899640468901338121294090979219428234512
847003533414175726178704338701976613396997023846923989429400915267675371
224072946225492282228797405663320182508126374511091622289958902650991068
621751297833605381900481249551537274059332054881942134979356683844461315
857197697481081258955632608022896552417746308879672265471807920624327017
057749253168131337219010124364276404953144761357.

The values for the third recipient follow:

$p3$ = 354111029957378467196233665181683335942980501967557747587069433392443
66354248746209746766217298983045140174450682725781109897153957417542916
040491337203319097489754734608074368268882013823897755753670014930080870
848303015557260084193760775969411802919046594091514825570101726091141999
723275760769674074440206l

$q3$ = 537250577580301119169902718622943611515464373762117373724433164996
83971883057143513630903120528766504955760962910142965550004592007536183
4704417904769891758186341525914238321657828217670692153125327204540654867
795987726325808014350172260902692229856033303728223284940139917347963269
33040505799501161620255577

$n3$ = 190246355372156893903225782350292600167477369758759824713970150155
833032560573732156154986990101160748711956621018724350255640687762304205
144517420437252812678611421725439723210501596142807702910144484328413464
009410879198942831308327834478772050471428586982951345191112660759887497
098234128606203524070530199477782074583416481614110088865594576679523571
008070891377916006088569389740523909478410532054423032367945632587585577
649911547160430568562503586541625305374277808808231279409769887944404948
587431526155196203679667198209757555886992928257029955739785822695049305
578021206595674009896187315568772022945351419l.

Here is the plaintext message, which will be enciphered using the public information of all three recipients, and sent to each of them.

P = 327562836508236509237590237590823750923875098275908237590827359082\
75908723095873209875093285790328750932875093248750983275098327509832759\
08237509837095730928750932875092385872365897236589236593027509432759034\
5732658972659823569823659823568926589236509578093672398568923659823659\
365982365982365982569825698235698265398236598269852732095689236589237932
865982365982365987263986598236589726895698236598236598723658972

The three ciphertext messages follow (remember that all three recipients are using the same encryption exponent $e = 3$):

$c1$ = 29852288355285620833884276741963562062821478738279455589916857970780\
77854306787783992568624318014109425772341743388920108913938591038814111
839772619456653274001839218157096089847009660629844237128793654287567350

24040110693379683123838271272606550342096994503193458750596050020203927101020420506490601544316102184565378675263602526079912255429933308526293775468161694805357459666494818093633847140459951939335094731175024933660256637305408508565446696846743517313867784277126910778607676468310472515908580339924768983948071002423189955295524086656450041608246132538291285639811279975799247355177851762197212093956297320

$c2 = 16286983518735228505840113496918055700047960329750616066339974975250894466786593649586940796439731971714973648579964628952756390697386846725808247246350123364251824728684405000577233656908306660838469990709494371183440981716872319937648396756921247290698985908758743411248226003010386914137647769501871476851826732558313018035079597905992082481553177956845505791440702248084940208130754599931889430653577464075295729219681632788900620750598115948837855900651606672958729969095386594621689577676203663696374637520566486504552000041248343493856740588118792122227244169316401463892991226040987253568658204443662929478165630$

$c3 = 12567783837800213521200299914797114622076420797206177684473093808580938325308332512752655068693755790871997590027458508437110805679513183420442283465242611891567416821943641070051981230872763796105042888016717025300494644541461194457425228032425313318614186520722586565382438019917243091905720890203872957452684366165431133548225626913824877304107770894899866371960770489484155556132768782853292020545589228629366651712164492852409158186141379757758419440311040383774470301077963093119315090023781825727351989076473102076691623614368347638568431352532118619990795887055439812204212124790288640996535404057617561041475.$

The adversary now simply needs to apply the Chinese Remainder Theorem to find a unique solution for P^3 modulo $n1 \cdot n2 \cdot n3$. In this case, the value obtained for P^3 is:

$P^3 = 35146644579287030560978762514660233813201904405872997059321157686969057377829284941234246676938106391540980571794946783416042520644800859304488733999135105591808406273916612785137477738245321317364295788681805335465969730516794476072244986887791034416435574279329447358441021200655134501526472612037973822456380922536060527302564690617164640272412886689926648463239266014724261719075482210633000087822697701339375033682153613414246952996334229702577090503403981847586883612308946772156712485558762524437182168413264536794758538672881823263582829463147033139812269360214321815513448852638693832272626096817507319671132054594443971378460131228623684279087419200303612750672879004633969288353455772445271994079248616463120920524224029603941002829411794654577026980400314923836141921334511242566502623353840339717981385895280926677274480737559384205544192161514315139833402636047689372269449103806561532691281049854874944500806019396722033121279338682650414049675178754354860014765098679096909819551305579820

04847131609795611687578444766431359782982807664706432139830408029286104018112198187458403535738453126194087007359013225950707584860854262289713296583020549314264992505723858709585501542812091026748685649206916026789970058857114079794206712144194648.

Since the adversary knows that P^3 must be less than $n1 \cdot n2 \cdot n3$, she simply needs to take a normal cube root to retrieve the plaintext.

$P = (P^3)^{1/3}$= 32756283650823650923750923750923750923875098275908237590827359082375908237590872309587320987509328579032875093287509324875098327509832750983275908237509837095730928750932875092385872365897236589236593027509432759034285732658972659823569823659823568926589236509578093672398568923659823659823659823659825698256982356982653982365982698527320956892365892379328659823659823659872639865982365897268956982365982365987236589723658972.

Note that nowhere during this attack does the adversary need to know any of the private info of any of the recipients. Of course, this attack can be circumvented by salting messages. Another way of getting around this attack is NOT to use a small encryption exponent with RSA.

Common Modulus Attack   It has also been suggested for RSA that all entities in a system could use the same modulus n. Each user would choose their own distinct enciphering exponent e and its corresponding deciphering exponent d. However, a common value for n is far worse than everyone using the same value for e, as it allows anyone knowing a single pair (e^*, d^*) of exponents to determine the private keys of everyone using the same modulus. You should consider how this is done.

Java Algorithm   Following are two methods in the Ciphers class to do encryption and decryption using RSA. Neither salt nor CBC is used. Of course, these methods use the helper methods in the Ciphers class to block, unblock, pad and unpad.

```java
public static byte[] RSAEncipher(byte[] msg,BigInteger e,BigInteger n) {
   //Compute the plaintext block size
   int blockSize=(n.bitLength()-1)/8;
   byte[][] ba=block(pad(msg,blockSize),blockSize);
   //Begin the enciphering
   for (int i=0;i<ba.length;i++) ba[i]=getBytes(new
      BigInteger(1,ba[i]).modPow(e,n));
   //Return to a 1D array.  The ciphertext block size is one byte greater than
plaintext block size.
   return unBlock(ba,blockSize+1);
}

public static byte[] RSADecipher(byte[] msg,BigInteger d,BigInteger n) {
   //Compute the ciphertext block size
```

```
   int blockSize=(n.bitLength()-1)/8+1;
   byte[][] ba=block(msg,blockSize);
   //Begin the deciphering
   for (int i=0;i<ba.length;i++) ba[i]=getBytes(new
      BigInteger(1,ba[i]).modPow(d,n));
   //Go from blocks to a 1D array, and remove padding; return this
   return unPad(unBlock(ba,blockSize-1),blockSize-1);
}
```

The methods to encipher/decipher with salt are also in the Ciphers class.

```
public static byte[] RSAEncipherWSalt
(byte[] msg,BigInteger e,BigInteger n,SecureRandom sr) {
   //Compute the plaintext block size
   int blockSize=(n.bitLength()-1)/8;
   if (blockSize<5) throw new IllegalArgumentException
      ("Block size must be >= 5 bytes");
   byte[][] ba=block(pad(msg,blockSize-4),blockSize-4);
   //Begin the enciphering
   for (int i=0;i<ba.length;i++) {
      ba[i]=addSalt(ba[i],sr);
      ba[i]=getBytes(new BigInteger(1,ba[i]).modPow(e,n));
   }
   //Return to a 1D array.  The ciphertext block size is one byte greater than
   //plaintext block size.
   return unBlock(ba,blockSize+1);
}

public static byte[] RSADecipherWSalt(byte[] msg,BigInteger d,BigInteger n) {
   //Compute the ciphertext block size
   int blockSize=(n.bitLength()-1)/8+1;
   byte[][] ba=block(msg,blockSize);
   //Begin the deciphering
   for (int i=0;i<ba.length;i++) {
      ba[i]=getBytes(new BigInteger(1,ba[i]).modPow(d,n));
      ba[i]=removeSalt(ba[i]);
   }
   //Go from blocks to a 1D array, and remove padding; return this
   return unPad(unBlock(ba,blockSize-5),blockSize-5);
}
```

TestRSACipherApplet is on the book's website to test the RSA methods. The applet actually uses a salted version of RSA. You will see that if you encipher the same plaintext multiple times, you will receive a different ciphertext each time. (See Figure 14.3.)

FIGURE 14.3

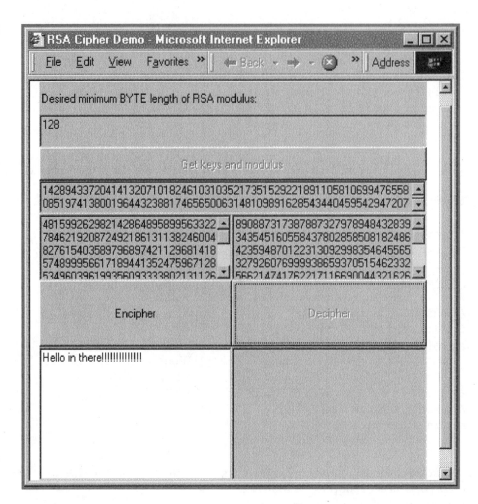

EXERCISES

1. Write a pohligHellmanEncipherWCFB() and pohligHellmanDecipherWCFB() method in the Ciphers class to use CFB.

2. Write the elGamalEncipher() and elGamalDecipher() methods in the Ciphers class.

3. Write the RSAEncipherWCBC() and RSADecipherWCBC() methods in the Ciphers class to use CBC.

4. Write a Java program to retrieve ElGamal messages using the equal enciphering exponent attack.

5. Write a Java program to retrieve RSA messages when all entities use the same small encryption exponent.

6. It has been proposed that each entity using RSA use a common modulus (but distinct encryption and decryption exponents). Why is it crucial that each entity choose its own modulus?

CHAPTER 15

Establishing Keys and Message Exchange

15.1 ESTABLISHING KEYS

Since its appearance, public key cryptography has been used to establish secret keys over an unsecure connection. Thus, communicants with no secret key to share can establish one by using a public key protocol, and some public keys generated "on the fly."

To demonstrate this key exchange I have written a couple of classes. However, in order to see how they work we must cover some of the methods of the Java networking classes. To get two computers to talk to each other, we will use two classes from the java.net package: Socket and ServerSocket. A socket represents an abstraction of a connection between computers. The way data is transferred between machines is quite complicated, and a socket insulates the programmer from this. Thus, socket I/O in most languages is similar to keyboard I/O, or file I/O. In Java, this is certainly the case.

To set up a socket between machines, one machine starts out by listening for a connection on a designated port (the server) and one starts out by talking to the server (the client).

In Java, we set up a server by doing something like this:

```
ServerSocket ss = new ServerSocket(54321);

Socket connectionServerSide = ss.accept();
```

This server will listen on port 54321 for a request from a client. When it receives such a request, the accept() method from the ServerSocket class will create (and return) a socket between the server and the client.

There are 65535 logical ports that a server can use; however, some are set aside for use with standard protocols. A list of some of these standardized ports follows. (See Table 15.1.) Do not use them unless you are writing a server for that purpose.

Most standard protocols are on the low end of the range of 1 thru 65535. If you use a port greater than 10000, say, you will probably be fine. Another potential problem with running a server is that you may not have permission to bind to (listen on) a port. You may need to see your system administrator to obtain permission to do this.

Setting up the client side of a socket is simple. You simply request a connection to a server running on a specified port.

TABLE 15.1

Protocol	Port
echo	7
discard	9
daytime	13
ftp-data	20
ftp	21
telnet	23
smtp	25
time	37
whois	43
finger	79
http	80
pop3	110
nntp	119
RMI registry	1099

```
Socket connectionClientSide =
    new Socket("WupAssGameMachine",54321);
```

The server's name can be any of the following:

1. Its name on a network (if the client is also part of that network),

2. Its domain name on the Internet (if it has one), or

3. Its IP (Internet Protocol) address (this is a number in dotted quad format, like 127.0.0.1). Any computer connected to the Internet will have an IP address.

If anything goes wrong in setting up, the ServerSocket and socket constructors can throw various exceptions, as listed in Table 15.2.

TABLE 15.2

ServerSocket()	Socket()
IOException	IOException
BindException	UnknownHostException

How these exceptions are handled is up to the application. Once the socket exists between client and server, both client and server can prepare for input and output by using the getInputStream() and getOutputStream() methods from the Socket class. Each returns an InputStream object, and an OutputStream object, respectively. We usually pass these objects into constructors, which transform the streams into objects that can be more easily read from or written to; for example, if the server needs to send text data to the client, the programmer may do something like this:

```
PrintStream toClient =
    new PrintStream(connectionServerSide.getOutputStream());
```

To send text data, we can use any of the methods from the PrintStream class:

```
toClient.println("Howdy, client!");
```

The client can set up output in the same way. To receive text data, the client can set up a BufferedReader object, like this:

```
BufferedReader fromServer = new BufferedReader(
    new InputStreamReader(connectionClientSide.getInputStream());
```

To receive the text data, we have now at our disposal any of the methods from the BufferedReader class:

```
String greetings = fromServer.readLine();
```

One should close a socket prior to exiting a program, or at any time during the program when we wish to break the connection. Either the client or the server can close the socket, using the close() method from the socket class, as the server does here:

```
connectionServerSide.close();
```

In Java, attempting to close a Socket which has already been closed does nothing. ServerSockets should also be closed (once the Socket has been closed, of course):

```
ss.close();
```

15.2   DIFFIE–HELLMAN KEY EXCHANGE APPLICATION

You now know everything you need to know to set up a line of communication between computers using Java. Hence, I will now show you a couple of programs called DiffieHellmanListener (the server) and DiffieHellmanInitiator (the client), which set up a connection with each other and establish a secret key over an unsecure line. Here is the code for the server side.

```
import java.security.*;
import java.math.*;
import java.net.*;
import java.io.*;
public class DiffieHellmanListener {
    public static void main(String[] args) throws IOException {
```

```
//Start by listening on port 11111
ServerSocket ss=new ServerSocket(11111);
//Wait for a connection
Socket socket=ss.accept();
//Open input and output streams on the socket
BufferedReader in=new BufferedReader(new
    InputStreamReader(socket.getInputStream()));
PrintStream out=new PrintStream(socket.getOutputStream());

//Capture p,g,gtox values from client
BigInteger p=new BigInteger(in.readLine());
BigInteger g=new BigInteger(in.readLine());
BigInteger gtox=new BigInteger(in.readLine());

//Produce your own secret exponent
SecureRandom sr=new SecureRandom();
BigInteger y=new BigInteger(p.bitLength()-1,sr);

//Raise g to this power
BigInteger gtoy=g.modPow(y,p);

//Send this to client
out.println(gtoy);

//Raise gtox to y power-this is the secret key
BigInteger key=gtox.modPow(y,p);
System.out.println
    ("The secret key with "+socket.getInetAddress().toString()+" is:\n"+key);
int c=System.in.read();
    }
}
```

The client side of this connection is equally simple:

```
import java.security.*;
import java.math.*;
import java.net.*;
import java.io.*;
public class DiffieHellmanInitiator {
    static BufferedReader k=new BufferedReader(new InputStreamReader(System.in));
    public static void main(String[] args) throws IOException {
        //Make a safe prime and generator
        SecureRandom sr=new SecureRandom();
        PrimeGenerator pg=new PrimeGenerator(1025,10,sr);
        BigInteger[] pandg=pg.getSafePrimeAndGenerator();
        //Make your secret exponent
        BigInteger x=new BigInteger(pandg[0].bitLength()-1,sr);
```

```
//Raise g to this power
BigInteger gtox=pandg[1].modPow(x,pandg[0]);

//Open a connection with a server waiting for info
System.out.println("Enter host name or IP address of server:");
String host=k.readLine();
//Server should be listening on port 11111
Socket socket=new Socket(host,11111);
//Open input and output streams on the socket
BufferedReader in=new BufferedReader(new
    InputStreamReader(socket.getInputStream()));
PrintStream out=new PrintStream(socket.getOutputStream());

//Send the values p,g,gtox to server
out.println(pandg[0]);
out.println(pandg[1]);
out.println(gtox);

//Get the gtoy value from server
BigInteger gtoy=new BigInteger(in.readLine());

//Raise gtoy to x power-this is the secret key
BigInteger key=gtoy.modPow(x,pandg[0]);
System.out.println("The secret key is:\n"+key);
k.readLine();
    }
}
```

Here is a sample run of the server (which was started first) and the client (started second on a different machine).

Server:

```
The secret key with **********/********** is:
121141996366069247972668406101715272882810606295028494880493816079792
128909711913425221065203246229296289019227474910482061933998953299929
747753068016087465910738004515719368489010404514526849086194982928867
966610646711588437785046440184200142675145862622605625817760288575244
650960340277864713806977500153330
```

Client:

```
Enter host name or IP address of server:
**********
The secret key is:
121141996366069247972668406101715272882810606295028494880493816079792
```

212890971191342522106520324622929628901922747491048206193399895329992974775306801608746591073800451571936848901040451452684908619498292886796661064671158843778504644018420014267514586262260562581776028857524465096034027786471380697750015333301

Here, for reasons of anonymity, I have replaced the computers' names and/or IP addresses with asterisks.

15.3   MESSAGE EXCHANGE

Certainly, the most common use of cryptography has been to exchange messages. A natural question to ask is, "which cryptographic method is best?" This is a loaded question, because the answer is, "It depends." Most algorithms are superior in some ways, but inferior in others. We can make a table of the ciphers we have covered, as shown in Table 15.3, listing the advantages, disadvantages, and weaknesses of each. (I consider a weakness different than a mere disadvantage.) Some of the weaknesses can be described as potential weaknesses, since they can be corrected.

15.4   CIPHER CHAT APPLICATION

I have written a chat program to pass enciphered messages back and forth between a machine running as a client, and another running as a server. The two chatters do not need to share a secret key, since the client and the server each generate a public key/private key pair, then send the public key to the other. It doesn't matter if anyone "listening in" captures either of these public keys. After the client and the server know the other's public key, either can send encrypted messages.

I should note that the messages in this application are not text, but arrays of bytes. Of course, this is because the messages are enciphered. Thus, the PrintStream and Buffered-Reader classes are not appropriate for doing IO. We must use something appropriate for reading/writing raw bytes, like DataInputStream, and DataOutputStream.

To create these, we would do something like this:

```
DataInputStream in=new
        DataInputStream(connection.getInputStream());
```

and

```
DataOutputStream out=new
        DataOutputStream(connection.getOutputStream());
```

To write an array of bytes to the stream, we could use one of the write() methods from DataOutputStream, like this.

```
byte[] msg = new byte[100];

...

out.write(msg);
```

TABLE 15.3

Algorithm	Advantages	Disadvantages	Weaknesses
Rabin	Quick encryption—only a modular scanning is required. Can sign messages.	Relatively slow decryption—correct root must be found. Must be padded with redundant bits for deciphering.	Must use strong primes. Static cipher—salt or CBC required. If salt not used, vulnerable to chosen ciphertext attack, adaptive chosen ciphertext attack, and square root attack.
Blum-Goldwasser	Quick encryption. Stream cipher—can work with small quantities. Randomization is part of the encryption process.		Vulnerable to chosen ciphertext attack.
Pohlig-Hellman		Secret key cipher—distribution of keys difficult.	Must use safe primes. Message may be of low order modulo p. Static cipher—salt or CFB required.
El Gamal	Not a static cipher—randomization is part of the encryption process. Can sign messages.	Ciphertext is at least twice as long as the plaintext.	Must use safe primes. Must use a different random value k for each block.
RSA	Quick encryption if a small enciphering exponent is used. Can sign messages.	Decryption relatively slow due to modular exponentiation to large powers. Encryption may also be slow if a small encryption exponent is not used.	Must use strong primes. Message may be of low order modulo n. Static cipher—salt or CFB required. If small encryption exponent is used without salt, vulnerable to a root attack. Vulnerable to common modulus attack if multiple entities choose to use the same modulus.

To read bytes from the input stream into a byte array, we could use one of the read() methods from DataInputStream:

```
byte[] buffer = new byte[100];
...
int numBytes = in.read(buffer);
```

After execution of the last statement here, the array buffer will be filled up with as many bytes that were read, and this read() method returns how many bytes were read. You should make the input buffer at least as long as the number of bytes you expect to receive, or not all the bytes will be read in. This should be adequate for you to understand the byte IO in the chat program that follows.

I'll start with a screen shot of the CipherChat Server, because looking at the GUI helps to explain the components we will see later in the code. (See Figure 15.1.) It has a button to disconnect from the client (it starts out disabled), a field to type messages in, and an output area which displays incoming messages, plus information on the connection.

Here is the code for CipherChatServer, which can be found on the book's website. I will explain the code as I present it.

```java
import java.io.*;
import java.net.*;
import java.awt.*;
import java.awt.event.*;
import java.math.*;
import java.security.*;
public class CipherChatServer extends Frame implements ActionListener {
```

The following are all the objects the server will need. They are:

1. The graphical components for the chat window.

2. The objects used for input and output.

3. The networking objects required to establish a connection.

FIGURE 15.1

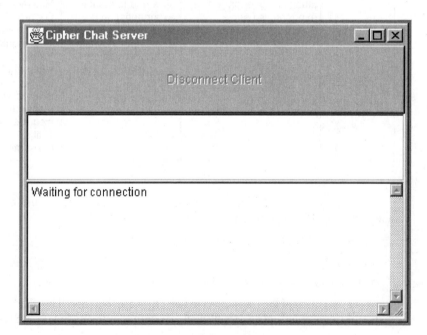

4. The crypto objects to store the server's public and private keys, and to store the public key of the client. Two variables store the length of the ciphertext, and the length of the plaintext.

```
private Button disconnectButton=new Button("Disconnect Client");
private TextField enterField=new TextField();
private TextArea displayArea=new TextArea();
private Panel top=new Panel();
private Panel bottom=new Panel();

private DataOutputStream output;
private DataInputStream input;
private String message="";

private static ServerSocket server;
private Socket connection;

private BigInteger p,q,modulus,decipherExp,recipModulus;
private SecureRandom sr=new SecureRandom();
private int ciphertextBlockSize;
private int plaintextBlockSize;
```

The constructor does the typical thing for a GUI; it lays out all the components on the frame, and displays it. However, this constructor also produces the public and private keys of the server when it calls the makeKeys() method, which we will see later.

```
public CipherChatServer() {
    //Lay components on frame and display it
    super("Cipher Chat Server");
    //Establish keys for RSA cipher
    makeKeys();
    setLayout(new GridLayout(2,1));
    top.setLayout(new GridLayout(2,1));
    bottom.setLayout(new GridLayout(1,1));
    add(top);
    add(bottom);
    disconnectButton.setEnabled(false);
    disconnectButton.addActionListener(this);
    top.add(disconnectButton);
    enterField.setEnabled(false);
    enterField.addActionListener(this);
    top.add(enterField,BorderLayout.NORTH);
    bottom.add(displayArea);
    setSize(400,300);
    show();
}
```

The makeKeys() method is called early by the constructor to set up the sender's public and private keys. Since we use RSA with salt, each communicant can use the enciphering exponent *e* = 3. Of course, each has its own modulus, and deciphering key, which are created here. Strong primes are used.

```
private void makeKeys() {
    PrimeGenerator pg=new PrimeGenerator(513,10,sr);
    do {
        p=pg.getStrongPrime();
    } while(p.subtract(BigIntegerMath.ONE).mod(BigIntegerMath.THREE).equals
            (BigIntegerMath.ZERO));
    do {
        q=pg.getStrongPrime();
    } while(q.subtract(BigIntegerMath.ONE).mod(BigIntegerMath.THREE).equals
            (BigIntegerMath.ZERO));
    modulus=p.multiply(q);
    //Use 3 as enciphering exponent - OK since we are using salt
    decipherExp=BigIntegerMath.THREE.modInverse
        (p.subtract(BigIntegerMath.ONE).multiply(q.subtract(BigIntegerMath.ONE)));
    ciphertextBlockSize=(modulus.bitLength()-1)/8+1;
    plaintextBlockSize=ciphertextBlockSize-6;
}
```

Note that the plaintext block size is computed as 6 bytes less than the ciphertext block size. This is because we need to take off 1 byte to get the plaintext under the modulus (all plaintext blocks must be smaller than the modulus), 4 bytes for the salt, and 1 byte for a pad byte (remember that the decipher method always removes padding).

Once the keys exist, they can be sent to the other communicant. This task is handled here by the exchangeKeys() method. It will be called from a point in the program soon after a socket has been set up between the two parties.

```
private void exchangeKeys() {
    try {
        byte[] buffer=new byte[ciphertextBlockSize];
        input.read(buffer);
        recipModulus=new BigInteger(1,buffer);
        output.write(modulus.toByteArray());
    } catch (IOException ioe) {
        System.err.println("Error establishing keys");
    }
}
```

Two components on this window can generate an ActionEvent object:

1. The user hit the enter key while in the message entry field. This means a message is to be sent. The text is captured from the field, enciphered using the recipient's public key, and sent down the output stream.

2. The user clicked on the disconnect button. This sends a final one byte message of ZERO (enciphered) to the recipient. This special message signifies that this is the last transmission for the connection.

These cases are handled here in the actionPerformed() method.

```
public void actionPerformed(ActionEvent e) {
   Object source=e.getSource();
   //User pressed enter in message entry field-send it
   if (source==enterField) {
      //Get the message
      message=e.getActionCommand();
      try {
         //Encipher the message
         if (message.length()>plaintextBlockSize)
            message=message.substring(0,plaintextBlockSize);
         byte[] ciphertext=Ciphers.RSAEncipherWSalt
            (message.getBytes(),BigIntegerMath.THREE,recipModulus,sr);
         //Send to the client
         output.write(ciphertext);
         output.flush();
         //Display same message in output area
         displayArea.append("\n"+message);
         enterField.setText("");
      } catch ( IOException ioe ) {
         displayArea.append("\nError writing message");
      }
   //Server wishes disconnect from the client
   } else if (source==disconnectButton) {
         try {
            byte[] lastMsg=new byte[1];
            lastMsg[0]=0;
            output.write(Ciphers.RSAEncipherWSalt
               (lastMsg,BigIntegerMath.THREE,recipModulus,sr));
            output.flush();
            closeAll();
         } catch (IOException ioe) {
            displayArea.append("\nError in disconnecting");
         }
   }
}
```

Note that before a message is encrypted and sent, it may be truncated so that it does not exceed the plaintext block size.

The go() method is where the server does most of its work. It continually loops (until someone closes the application) listening for incoming connections. When the accept()

method returns a Socket object, a connection exists. The server then opens up its IO streams, and exchanges its public key (just the modulus—both parties will use 3 as their enciphering exponent) with the client. It then enables the disconnect button on the frame, and makes the message entry field editable. Finally, it enters into a loop, listening for messages from its input stream. If the disconnect message 0 is sent from the client, or if there is no more input to be read, the server disconnects by calling the closeAll() method, which you will soon see. The server then loops back up to the top, and waits for another connection.

```java
public void go() {
    try {
        while (true) {
            displayArea.setText("Waiting for connection");
            //accept() halts execution until a connection is made from a client
            connection = server.accept();

            displayArea.append("\nConnection received from:"
                            +connection.getInetAddress().getHostName());

            //Set up the IO streams
            output = new DataOutputStream(connection.getOutputStream());
            output.flush();
            input = new DataInputStream(connection.getInputStream() );

            //Exchange public keys with the client-send yours, get theirs
            exchangeKeys();

            //Send connection message to client
            message = connection.getLocalAddress()
                .getLocalHost()+":Connection successful";
            byte[] ciphertext=Ciphers.RSAEncipherWSalt
                (message.getBytes(),BigIntegerMath.THREE,recipModulus,sr);
            //Send to the client
            output.write(ciphertext);
            output.flush();

            //Enable disconnect button
            disconnectButton.setEnabled(true);
            //Messages may now be entered
            enterField.setEnabled(true);

            try {
                //Read as long as there is input
                byte[] buffer=new byte[ciphertextBlockSize];
                boolean disconnectMsgSent=false;
                while (!disconnectMsgSent&&input.read(buffer)!=-1) {
```

```
                 //Decipher the bytes read in
                 byte[]
                    plaintext=Ciphers.RSADecipherWSalt(buffer,decipherExp,modulus);
                 if (plaintext.length==1&&plaintext[0]==0) {
                    disconnectMsgSent=true;
                    closeAll();
                 } else {
                    //convert to a string and display
                    message = new String(plaintext);
                    displayArea.append("\n"+message);
                 }
              }
           //Socket was closed from client side
           } catch (SocketException se) {
              //close connection and IO streams, change some components
              closeAll();
           }
           closeAll();
        }
     } catch (Exception exc) {
        exc.printStackTrace();
     }
}
```

Here is the closeAll() method. It puts a "Connection closing" string in the display area, then shuts down its IO streams, then the socket. It turns off the message entry field, and disables the disconnect button.

```
//Close socket and IO streams, change appearance/functionality of some components
private void closeAll() throws IOException {
   displayArea.append("\nConnection closing");
   output.close();
   input.close();
   connection.close();
   //Disable message entry
   enterField.setEnabled(false);
   //We are not connected-turn off the disconnect button
   disconnectButton.setEnabled(false);
}
```

Of course, here is the main() method of CipherChatServer, which simply sets up the GUI, binds to a port for listening, then calls the go() method.

```
public static void main(String[] args) throws IOException {
   CipherChatServer ccs=new CipherChatServer();
   ccs.addWindowListener(
      new WindowAdapter() {
```

```
        public void windowClosing(WindowEvent e) {
            System.exit(0);
        }
      }
  );
  server = new ServerSocket(55555);
  ccs.go();
  server.close();
 }

}
```

The client side of the chat program is pretty much the same, except it must initiate the connection with the server. Either the client or the server can break the connection, but the client must reinitiate, if desired. Figure 15.2 shows a screen shot of the client.

It contains an area to type in the name of the server to connect to, and a button to connect. This button changes appearance once a connection exists; the label changes to "Disconnect from server above." The client also contains a field to type messages in, and an output area for incoming messages, and connection information.

```
import java.io.*;
import java.net.*;
```

FIGURE 15.2

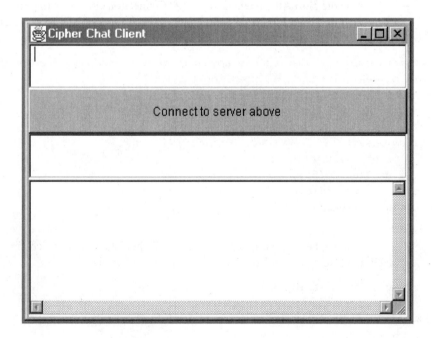

```
import java.awt.*;
import java.awt.event.*;
import java.math.*;
import java.security.*;
public class CipherChatClient extends Frame implements ActionListener {
```

The following are all the objects the client will need. They are:

1. The graphical components for the chat window.

2. The objects used for input and output.

3. The networking objects required to establish a connection.

4. The crypto objects to store the client's public and private keys, and to store the public key of the server. Two variables record the length of the ciphertext, and the length of the plaintext.

5. A Thread object. Since the client's go() method (which just reads the input stream) cannot be called from the main method (since a connection may not yet exist), but is called from the actionPerformed() method, it does not exist in a separate thread from the frame. Thus, the read() method will block execution and won't allow interactivity with the frame, unless it runs in a separate thread. (Note that the chat server does not have this problem.)

```
private TextField serverField=new TextField();
private Button connectButton=new Button("Connect to server above");
private TextField enterField=new TextField();
private TextArea displayArea = new TextArea();
private Panel top=new Panel();
private Panel bottom=new Panel();

private DataOutputStream output;
private DataInputStream input;

private String message="";
private String chatServer;

private Socket connection=null;
private InetAddress clientName;
private InetAddress serverName;

private BigInteger p,q,modulus,decipherExp,recipModulus;
private SecureRandom sr=new SecureRandom();
private int ciphertextBlockSize;
private int plaintextBlockSize;

private static Thread listener=null;
```

The constructor does the typical thing for a GUI; it lays out all the components on the frame, and displays it. However, this constructor also produces the public and private keys of the client when it calls the makeKeys() method, which we will see later.

```
public CipherChatClient() {
    super("Cipher Chat Client");
    //Establish keys for RSA cipher
    makeKeys();
    //Lay out the components and display the frame
    setLayout(new GridLayout(2,1));
    top.setLayout(new GridLayout(3,1));
    add(top);
    bottom.setLayout(new GridLayout(1,1));
    add(bottom);
    connectButton.addActionListener(this);
    enterField.setEnabled(false);
    enterField.addActionListener(this);
    top.add(serverField);
    top.add(connectButton);
    top.add(enterField);
    bottom.add(displayArea);
    setSize(400,300);
    show();
}
```

The client does a lot of work in its actionPerformed() method. The ActionEvents generated here may mean more than one thing. The events are:

1. The user hit enter in the message entry field, and wants to send the message. We send this message down the output stream the way we did for the server.

2. The user pressed the connect/disconnect button. This can mean one of two things:

    a) We are currently connected, and the client wishes to disconnect. To disconnect, we must first send the terminate message 0 (enciphered) to the server. Then we call the closeAll() method, which closes the streams and sockets, and changes the appearance/functionality of components on the GUI.

    b) We are currently disconnected, and the client wishes to connect. To connect (or reconnect) the client must attempt to establish a socket with the specified server, open its IO streams, exchange public keys with the server, and enable the message entry field. It then calls the go() method, which listens for input in a separate thread.

All of these cases are handled here.

```
public void actionPerformed(ActionEvent e) {
    Object source=e.getSource();
    //Client pressed enter in the message entry field-send it
    if (source==enterField) {
```

```
      //Get the message
      message=e.getActionCommand();
      try {
         //Encipher the message
         if (message.length()>plaintextBlockSize)
             message=message.substring(0,plaintextBlockSize);
         byte[] ciphertext=Ciphers.RSAEncipherWSalt
             (message.getBytes(),BigIntegerMath.THREE,recipModulus,sr);
         //Send to the server
         output.write(ciphertext);
         output.flush();
         //Display same message in client output area
         displayArea.append("\n"+message);
         enterField.setText("");
      } catch (IOException ioe) {
         displayArea.append("\nError writing message");
      }
   } else if (source==connectButton) {
      if (connection!=null) { //Already connected-button press now means disconnect
         try {
            //Send final message of 0
            byte[] lastMsg=new byte[1];
            lastMsg[0]=0;
            output.write(Ciphers.RSAEncipherWSalt
                (lastMsg,BigIntegerMath.THREE,recipModulus,sr));
            output.flush();
            //close connection and IO streams, change some components
            closeAll();
         } catch (IOException ioe) {
            displayArea.append("\nError closing connection");
         }
      } else {//Not connected-connect
         //Get name of server to connect to
         chatServer=serverField.getText();
         displayArea.setText("Attempting connection to "+chatServer);
         try {
            //Set up the socket
            connection = new Socket(chatServer,55555);

            displayArea.append
                ("\nConnected to: "+connection.getInetAddress().getHostName());

            //Set up the IO streams
            output = new DataOutputStream(connection.getOutputStream());
            output.flush();
```

```
        input = new DataInputStream(connection.getInputStream());

        //Exchange public keys with the server-send yours, get theirs
        exchangeKeys();

        //Change appearance/functionality of some components
        serverField.setEditable(false);
        connectButton.setLabel("Disconnect from server above");
        enterField.setEnabled(true);
        //Set up a thread to listen for the connection
        listener = new Thread(
          new Runnable() {
            public void run() {
              go();
            }
          }
        );
        listener.start();
      } catch (IOException ioe) {
        displayArea.append("\nError connecting to "+chatServer);
      }
    }
  }
}
```

The makeKeys() method here is the same as the one in CipherChatServer.

```
private void makeKeys() {
   PrimeGenerator pg=new PrimeGenerator(513,10,sr);
   do {
      p=pg.getStrongPrime();
   } while(p.subtract(BigIntegerMath.ONE).mod(BigIntegerMath.THREE).equals
         (BigIntegerMath.ZERO));
   do {
      q=pg.getStrongPrime();
   } while(q.subtract(BigIntegerMath.ONE).mod(BigIntegerMath.THREE).equals
         (BigIntegerMath.ZERO));
   modulus=p.multiply(q);
   //Use 3 as enciphering exponent - OK since we are using salt
   decipherExp=BigIntegerMath.THREE.modInverse(p.subtract(BigIntegerMath.ONE)
     .multiply(q.subtract(BigIntegerMath.ONE)));
   ciphertextBlockSize=(modulus.bitLength()-1)/8+1;
   plaintextBlockSize=ciphertextBlockSize-6;
}
```

The exchangeKeys() method here is the same as the one in CipherChatServer, except the client sends its key first, then waits for the public key of the server.

```
private void exchangeKeys() {
   try {
      output.write(modulus.toByteArray());
      byte[] buffer=new byte[ciphertextBlockSize];
      input.read(buffer);
      recipModulus=new BigInteger(1,buffer);
   } catch (IOException ioe) {
      System.err.println("Error establishing keys");
   }
}
```

The go() method is where the client enters into a loop, listening for messages from its input stream. It then proceeds to read input; if the disconnect message 0 is sent from the server, or if there is no more input to be read, the client disconnects by calling its closeAll() method, which you will soon see. This method will be called whenever the client clicks on "Connect to server above."

```
private void go() {
   try {
      //Read as long as there is input
      byte[] buffer=new byte[ciphertextBlockSize];
      boolean disconnectMsgSent=false;
      while (!disconnectMsgSent&&input.read(buffer)!=-1) {
         //Decipher the bytes read in
         byte[] plaintext=Ciphers.RSADecipherWSalt(buffer,decipherExp,modulus);
         if (plaintext.length==1&&plaintext[0]==0) {
            disconnectMsgSent=true;
            closeAll();
         } else {
            //convert to a string and display
            message = new String(plaintext);
            displayArea.append("\n"+message);
         }
      }
   } catch (IOException ioe) {
      //Server disconnected-we can reconnect if we wish
   }
}
```

The closeAll() method for the client is similar to the one for the server. It closes its IO streams, then the socket. It ensures to set the socket to null, since this is how the client tests for a connection. The client then changes its button to say "Connect to server above" again, and shuts off the message entry field.

```
//Close socket and IO streams, change appearance/functionality of some components
private void closeAll() throws IOException {
   displayArea.append("\nConnection closing");
   output.close();
```

```
        input.close();
        connection.close();
        //We are no longer connected
        connection=null;
        //Change components
        serverField.setEditable(true);
        connectButton.setLabel("Connect to server above");
        enterField.setEnabled(false);
    }
```

Here is the main() method of CipherChatClient, which simply sets up the GUI.

```
public static void main( String args[] ) throws IOException {
    final CipherChatClient ccc = new CipherChatClient();
    ccc.addWindowListener(
        new WindowAdapter() {
            public void windowClosing(WindowEvent e) {
                System.exit(0);
            }
        }
    );
}

}
```

Note that this chat program makes no attempt to authenticate its users. That is, you don't know if the person on the other end of the socket is actually whom he or she claims to be (without, perhaps, asking a few personal questions). To provide authentication, the keys would not be generated for each connection, but would already be on file with a Trusted Third Party, or TTP (see the chapter on cryptographic applications for discussion of a TTP). Each communicant can check the received public keys against this database. It would be virtually impossible for a chatter to pretend to be someone else without knowledge of his or her decryption keys. (They certainly would have a hell of a time trying to carry on an intelligent conversation with you without being able to decrypt your messages!)

EXERCISE

Realistically, a chat program should function both as a multithreaded server, and a multithreaded client. This would allow you to start your chat program and initiate connections with multiple chatters, while at the same time listening for connections from other chatters wishing to connect with you. Write an enciphered chat program with this capability, and use a cipher other than RSA.

CHAPTER 16

Cryptographic Applications

The classical use of cryptography was to use it to pass secret messages between enti-ties. More recently, cryptography has shown its usefulness in many other ways. We will investigate some of these topics in this chapter.

16.1 SHADOWS

The Chinese Remainder Theorem has many important applications in cryptography. One of these applications is the protection of vital information from both disclosure (whether inten-tional or not), and from loss. Suppose there is a secret that must be protected from exposure. This might be done by giving separate individuals (who may not even know each other) a piece of the information. To retrieve it, everyone supplies his or her piece and the secret is recovered. However, if one of these persons dies, or if his piece of the information has become somehow inaccessible, we must be able to protect the secret from being lost. That is, we should require that any subset of these individuals (of a predetermined minimum size) be able to reconstruct the secret. CRT provides us with a way to do this.

Let the secret be represented by N, a large integer. From this N we will construct a sequence of integers $s_1, s_2, \ldots, s_r$, called "shadows," and give them to r different individ-uals. We generate the shadows thus: Choose a prime p greater than N, and a sequence of pair-wise relatively prime integers not divisible by p, say $m_1, m_2, \ldots, m_r$ such that $m_1 < m_2 < \ldots < m_r$, and such that

$$m_1 m_2 \ldots m_{r'} > p m_r m_{r-1} \ldots m_{r-r'+2}.$$

This last inequality says that if we take the smallest r' integers, their product must be greater than p times the largest $r' - 1$ integers. This implies that if $M = m_1 m_2 \ldots m_{r'}$, then M/p is greater than the product of any subset of $r' - 1$ integers from $\{m_1, m_2, \ldots, m_r\}$. Now, choose a random integer $u < M/p - 1$, and let

$$N' = N + up,$$

so that $0 \leq N' < M$. This is so since

$$0 \leq N' = N + up < p + up = (u + 1)p < (M/p)p = M.$$

Now, this is how to produce the shadows, $s_1, s_2, \ldots, s_r$; let s_j be the least nonnegative residue of N' (mod m_j); that is,

$$s_j \equiv N' \;(\text{mod } m_j) \qquad 0 \leq k_j < m_j, \text{ and } i = 1, 2, \ldots, r.$$

In order to recover the secret N from the shadows, we will need at least r' of them, so say we have some subset of the shadows $s_{j_1}, s_{j_2}, \ldots, s_{j_{r'}}\}$. Using CRT, we can find the least nonnegative residue of N' modulo M_j where $M_j = m_{j_1} m_{j_2} \ldots m_{j_{r'}}$. Now, note that $M \leq M_j$ (since $M = m_1 m_2 \ldots m_{r'}$ is the product of the r' smallest integers), and thus, since

$$0 \leq N' < M \leq M_j,$$

the least nonnegative residue obtained by using CRT is in fact N', the very integer we seek. We then recover the secret N by computing

$$N = N' - up.$$

However, if we have fewer than r' shadows to work with, we cannot determine N', and hence cannot retrieve the secret N. To see this, suppose we only have $r' - 1$ shadows s_{i_1}, $s_{i_2}, \ldots, s_{i_{r'}-1}$. CRT allows us to determine the lnr (say z) of N' modulo M_i where $M_i = m_{i_1}$, $m_{i_2}, \ldots, m_{i_{r'}-1}$, and so we know that

$$N' = z + yM_i \text{ where } y = 0, 1, \ldots, M/M_i.$$

Now, we know (by our choice of p and the moduli) that M/p is greater than any product of $r' - 1$ of the moduli, so since

$$M/p > M_i$$

we have

$$M/M_i > p.$$

This tells us that as y traverses the integers smaller than M/M_i, y takes on every value modulo p, and so also does N', since $N' = z + yM_i$ and since M_i is relatively prime to p. (Recall that all of the moduli are chosen so that they are not divisible by p.) Thus, we cannot pin N' (and hence N) down to any value, because N' could be in any of the residue classes modulo p.

EXAMPLE.   Suppose we want to hide the secret number $N = 10$ from prying eyes. (Of course, we are choosing an example with ridiculously small values so that you can readily observe how this works.) We choose a prime greater than the secret, say $p = 11$. Now, suppose we want to have $r = 5$ shadows, and we wish to be able to recover the secret N from at least $r' = 3$ of the shadows. We choose the moduli as

$$m_1 = 17$$

$$m_2 = 19$$

$$m_3 = 23$$
$$m_4 = 24$$
$$m_5 = 25.$$

Note that none of the moduli are divisible by 11, and that the product of the 3 smallest moduli is greater than the prime $p = 11$ times the two largest moduli:

$$M = 17 \cdot 19 \cdot 23 = 7429 > 6600 = 11 \cdot 24 \cdot 25.$$

Now, we choose a random integer u smaller than $M = 7429/11 \cong 675.36$, say $u = 439$, and then we compute

$$N' = N + up = 10 + 439 \cdot 11 = 4839.$$

The shadows are the least nonnegative residues of N' modulo each modulus m_i. Thus,

$$s_1 \equiv 11 \pmod{17}$$
$$s_2 \equiv 13 \pmod{19}$$
$$s_3 \equiv 9 \pmod{23}$$
$$s_4 \equiv 15 \pmod{24}$$
$$s_5 \equiv 14 \pmod{25}.$$

Now, suppose we wish to reconstruct the secret N from any 3 of the shadows, say $s_2 = 13$, $s_3 = 9$, and $s_5 = 14$. First we find N' using the Chinese Remainder Theorem, as follows:

$$N' = 13 \cdot 575 \cdot 575' + 9 \cdot 475 \cdot 475' + 14 \cdot 437 \cdot 437'$$
$$= 13 \cdot 575 \cdot 4 + 9 \cdot 475 \cdot 20 + 14 \cdot 437 \cdot 23$$
$$= 256114$$
$$\equiv 4839 \pmod{10925} \ (10925 = 19 \cdot 23 \cdot 25)$$

Once we have N', we recover the secret N by taking

$$N = N' - up$$
$$= 4839 - 439 \cdot 11$$
$$= 10.$$

It doesn't matter which 3 shadows we use to reconstruct N; any 3 will do, as you may like to verify. However, if we try to pull the secret N out of only 2 shadows, we should fail. Suppose we try to reconstruct N from $s_1 = 11$, and $s_4 = 15$. We use CRT to form the quantity

$$N' = 11 \cdot 24 \cdot 24' + 15 \cdot 17 \cdot 17'$$
$$= 11 \cdot 24 \cdot 5 + 15 \cdot 17 \cdot 17$$
$$= 5655$$
$$\equiv 351 \pmod{408}.$$

TABLE 16.1

1st Shadow	1st Modulus	2nd Shadow	2nd Modulus	Value for N'
11	17	13	19	317 (mod 323)
11	17	9	23	147 (mod 391)
11	17	15	24	351 (mod 408)
11	17	14	25	164 (mod 425)
13	19	9	23	32 (mod 437)
13	19	15	24	279 (mod 456)
13	19	14	25	89 (mod 475)
9	23	15	24	423 (mod 552)
9	23	14	25	239 (mod 575)
15	24	14	25	39 (mod 600)

This is, of course, an incorrect value for N'. We will see that if we try any other pair of shadows, a similarly hopeless situation results. Consult Table 16.1, which shows all the combinations of shadow pairs, and the corresponding values for N'.

None of the values obtained here for N' are correct. Because of the requirements in our choice of the moduli and the prime p, two shadows simply do not provide us with enough information to reconstruct N' (and thus N).

Java Algorithm   We can write programs to demonstrate shadow making and key reconstruction. To do this, we will define two classes:

The ShadowBuilder Class   This will define a constructor that will accept a master key, and the number of shadows to generate. It generates the shadows and their respective moduli, plus the values of u, and the prime p as described above. Methods are provided to retrieve all these values. This class exhibits some differences from the scheme described above. First, it sets the minimum number of shadows required for reconstruction at just over half the total number of shadows; for example, if the total number of shadows generated is 7, 4 of them will be required to recover the master key, and if 8 shadows are produced, 5 will be required for reconstruction. Second, the class produces a sequence of prime numbers for the moduli; these will certainly fulfill the requirement to be pairwise relatively prime.

The KeyRebuilder Class   This class is for recovering the master key. It will define a constructor that accepts some shadows and their respective moduli, plus the values of u and p. It assumes that enough shadows are being used, and that the moduli are pairwise relatively prime. It reconstructs the master key from the shadows using the Chinese Remainder Theorem, and provides a method to return the master key as a BigInteger.

The ShadowBuilder class definition follows:

```java
import java.math.*;
import java.security.*;
public class ShadowBuilder {

    //The shadows
    BigInteger[] shadow;

    //The moduli
    //The i-th modulus is for the i-th shadow
    BigInteger[] modulus;

    //Two other values needed to reconstruct the master key
    BigInteger randomMultiplier;
    BigInteger reconstructingPrime;

    //This constructor accepts the master key, the number of shadows to
    //generate, and the tolerance to set for the primes.  These will be
    //used for the moduli, rather than a set of pairwise relatively prime
    //integers.  The minimum number of shadows required to reconstruct
    //is set at r/2+1.
    public ShadowBuilder(BigInteger K, int r, int primeTolerance) {
        int s=r/2+1;
        int KeySize=K.bitLength();
        //Generate a probable prime reconstructingPrime larger than K
        SecureRandom sr=new SecureRandom();
        reconstructingPrime=new BigInteger(KeySize+1,primeTolerance,sr);
        //Generate r primes for the moduli
        modulus=new BigInteger[r];
        for (int index=0;index<r;index++) {
            modulus[index]=new BigInteger(KeySize+2,primeTolerance,sr);
        }
        //Choose a random multiplier less than the product of any s of the primes.
        //This will be so if the bitlength is less than (s-1)*(KeySize-1).
        randomMultiplier=new BigInteger(s*(KeySize-1)-KeySize-1,sr);
        //Compute K0=K+randomMultiplier*reconstructingPrime
        BigInteger K0=K.add(randomMultiplier.multiply(reconstructingPrime));
        //Generate the r shadows
        shadow=new BigInteger[r];
        for (int index=0;index<r;index++) {
            shadow[index]=K0.mod(modulus[index]);
        }
    }

    //Methods to return the values the constructor generated.
```

```
public BigInteger[] getShadows() {
   return shadow;
}
public BigInteger[] getModuli() {
   return modulus;
}
public BigInteger getRandomMultiplier() {
   return randomMultiplier;
}
public BigInteger getReconstructingPrime() {
   return reconstructingPrime;
}


}
```

Here is the KeyRebuilder class definition:

```
import java.math.*;
public class KeyRebuilder {

BigInteger masterKey;

   //This constructor reconstructs the master key from a sequence of shadows
   //and moduli.  It is assumed that enough shadows are being used to do this.
   //It is further assumed that the moduli are pairwise relatively prime
   public KeyRebuilder(BigInteger[] shadow, BigInteger[] modulus,
        BigInteger randomMultiplier, BigInteger reconstructingPrime) {
      //Produce a parallel array for each Mi, product of all mj where i!=j for CRT
      BigInteger[] M;
      M=new BigInteger[modulus.length];
      //BigM is the product of all the moduli
      BigInteger BigM=new BigInteger("1");
      for (int index=0;index<modulus.length;index++) {
             //Multiply BigM by modulus[index]
             BigM=BigM.multiply(modulus[index]);
             //Start forming each M[index]
             M[index]=new BigInteger("1");
             for (int index2=0;index2<modulus.length;index2++) {
                   //If index=index2, do not multiply M[index] by m[index2]
                   if(index!=index2) {
                      M[index]=M[index].multiply(modulus[index2]);
                   }
             }
      }
      BigInteger K0=new BigInteger("0");
      //Produce K0 using the Chinese Remainder Theorem with the shadows
```

```
for (int index=0;index<modulus.length;index++) {
        BigInteger MInv=M[index].modInverse(modulus[index]);
        K0=K0.add(shadow[index].multiply(M[index].multiply(MInv))).mod(BigM);
    }
    //The master key is K0 - tp where t is multiplier, p is reconstructing prime
    masterKey=K0.subtract(randomMultiplier.multiply(reconstructingPrime));
}


//Method to return the master key
public BigInteger getMasterKey() {
    return masterKey;
}


}
```

Figure 16.1(a)–(d) shows an applet (called TestShadowApplet) to test the ShadowBuilder and KeyRebuilder classes.

FIGURE 16.1

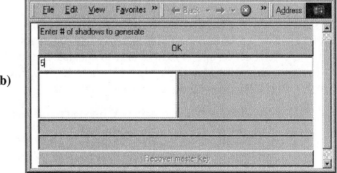

(a)

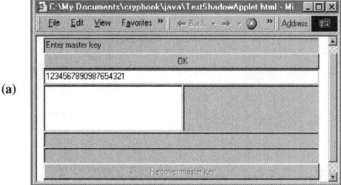

(b)

FIGURE 16.1

(c)

(d)

16.2 DATABASE ENCRYPTION

The Chinese Remainder Theorem can also play a role in enciphering databases. It can be done so that a particular user only has access to their data. A database is a collection of records $R_1, R_2, \ldots, R_n$. We can regard each record as an integer, for they are basically stored this way.

We first choose a sequence $p_1, p_2, \ldots, p_n$ of distinct primes with $p_i > R_i$ for $i = 1, 2, \ldots, n$. As the enciphered database we will use an integer C that is congruent to R_i modulo p_i $\forall$ i. Such an integer exists and is computable by the CRT. Let $M = p_1 p_2 \ldots p_n$ and let $M_i = M/p_i$ for each i. Now, let $w_i = M_i M'_i$ where M'_i is an inverse of M_i modulo p_i.

We compute the enciphered database as

$$C \equiv \Sigma \, w_i R_i \pmod{M} \qquad 0 \le C < M, \, i = 1, 2, \ldots, n.$$

We call $w_1, w_2, \ldots, w_n$ the write subkeys of the database cipher, for these will be required to write to the database; that is, they are required to construct C. The moduli, however, p_1,

$p_2, \ldots, p_n$ are all that is needed to read a record from the database; thus, we call them the read subkeys. Note that C, by construction, is congruent R_i modulo p_i for any i; that is,

$$C \equiv R_i \ (\text{mod } p_i) \qquad\qquad i = 1, 2, \ldots, n.$$

Each individual i gets the pair of values w_i, and p_i; this gives them read/write access to only their data.

EXAMPLE.   Suppose the records in our database are

$$R_1 = 234$$
$$R_2 = 201$$
$$R_3 = 147.$$

We choose 3 primes, each greater than their associated record; say

$$p_1 = 499$$
$$p_2 = 503$$
$$p_3 = 563.$$

To encipher the database, we must find an integer C that simultaneously solves

$$C \equiv 234 \ (\text{mod } 499)$$
$$C \equiv 201 \ (\text{mod } 503)$$
$$C \equiv 147 \ (\text{mod } 563).$$

Thus, we compute

$$M = 141311311$$
$$M_1 = 141311311/499 = 283189$$
$$M_2 = 141311311/503 = 280937$$
$$M_3 = 141311311/563 = 250997.$$

and we find inverses of each M_i modulo p_i.

$$M_1' = 283189' \equiv 384 \ (\text{mod } 499)$$
$$M_2' = 280937' \equiv 350 \ (\text{mod } 503)$$
$$M_3' = 250997' \equiv 301 \ (\text{mod } 563)$$

Thus, the write subkeys are

$$w_1 = 283189 \cdot 384 = 108744576$$
$$w_2 = 280937 \cdot 350 = 98327950$$
$$w_3 = 250997 \cdot 301 = 75550097.$$

TABLE 16.2

i	C	is congruent to	R_i	modulo	p_i
1	74111215		234		499
2	74111215		201		503
3	74111215		147		563

Using the write subkeys, we encipher the records by forming the sum

$$C \equiv w_1 R_1 + w_2 R_2 + w_3 R_3$$

$$\equiv 108744576 \cdot 234 + 98327950 \cdot 201 + 75550097 \cdot 147$$

$$\equiv 56316012993$$

$$\equiv 74111215 \ (\mathrm{mod}\ 141311311).$$

To retrieve a particular record R_i from the database, we simply compute the least non-negative residue of C modulo p_i. Table 16.2 shows all the retrieved records.

Editing a Record   Note that modifying some record R_i to some new value R_i' with this scheme is particularly easy, for it does not involve recomputing the entire sum

$$C \equiv \Sigma\, w_i R_i \ (\mathrm{mod}\ M) \qquad\qquad 0 \le C < M,\ i = 1, 2, \ldots, n.$$

All we have to do is compute the difference between the new value and the old value:

$$D = R_i' - R_i,$$

then add this to the sum to get a new enciphered value for the database.

$$C' \equiv C + w_i D \ (\mathrm{mod}\ M).$$

This works because

$$C' \equiv C + w_i D$$

$$\equiv w_1 R_1 + w_2 R_2 + \ldots + w_i R_i + \ldots + w_n R_n + w_i D$$

$$\equiv w_1 R_1 + w_2 R_2 + \ldots + w_i R_i + \ldots + w_n R_n + w_i(R_i' - R_i)$$

$$\equiv w_1 R_1 + w_2 R_2 + \ldots + w_i R_i - w_i R_i + \ldots + w_n R_n + w_i R_i'$$

$$\equiv w_1 R_1 + w_2 R_2 + \ldots + w_i R_i' + \ldots + w_n R_n \ (\mathrm{mod}\ M).$$

EXAMPLE.   Suppose in our previous example that individual 2 wishes to change

$$R_2 = 201$$

to the new value

$$R_2' = 103.$$

TABLE 16.3

i	C	is congruent to	R_i	modulo	p_i
1	47141263		234		499
2	47141263		103		503
3	47141263		147		563

We compute the difference

$$D = 103 - 201 = -98$$

and form the modified sum

$$C' \equiv 74111215 + 98327950 \cdot (-98) \equiv -9562027885 \equiv 47141263 \ (\text{mod } 141311311).$$

To verify that this works see Table 16.3, in which we have once again recovered the 3 records.

16.3 LARGE INTEGER ARITHMETIC

CRT provides us with a particularly novel way to do arithmetic with very large nonnegative integers. We usually represent numbers using a single radix, like

$$4231 = 4 \cdot 10^3 + 2 \cdot 10^2 + 3 \cdot 10^1 + 1 \cdot 10^0$$

or

$$100011_{\text{base 2}} = 1 \cdot 2^5 + 0 \cdot 2^4 + 0 \cdot 2^3 + 0 \cdot 2^2 + 1 \cdot 2^1 + 1 \cdot 2^0.$$

The Chinese Remainder Theorem tells us that the representation of an integer x such that

$$x \equiv a_1 \ (\text{mod } m_1)$$

$$x \equiv a_2 \ (\text{mod } m_2)$$

$$\vdots$$

$$x \equiv a_n \ (\text{mod } m_n),$$

where the moduli are pairwise relatively prime, is unique modulo $M = m_1 m_2 \ldots m_n$. Thus, we can either represent x in its "composed" representation, or in its "decomposed" representation. Using multiple moduli to represent an integer in this way is called a mixed radix system, or a residue number system.

EXAMPLE.   Take the integer 73, and note that

$$73 \equiv 9 \pmod{64}$$

$$73 \equiv 19 \pmod{27}$$

$$73 \equiv 23 \pmod{25}$$

$$73 \equiv 24 \pmod{49}.$$

We can thus represent the integer 73 as the vector

$$(9, 19, 23, 24)$$

where the moduli are here understood to be 64, 27, 25, and 49. There is no other positive integer less than $M = 64 \cdot 27 \cdot 25 \cdot 49 = 2116800$ that is represented by this vector. In fact, every integer between 0 and 2116799 has a unique such representation.

This motivates us to consider perhaps representing integers in this way; we can do arithmetic with such integers by instead doing the arithmetic with their smaller residues.

EXAMPLE.   We take now the integer 1907833, and note that

$$1907833 \equiv 57 \pmod{64}$$

$$1907833 \equiv 13 \pmod{27}$$

$$1907833 \equiv 8 \pmod{25}$$

$$1907833 \equiv 18 \pmod{49}.$$

Using this representation, and the representation of 73 given earlier, we can then compute $1907833 - 73$ by computing

$$57 - 9 \equiv 48 \pmod{64}$$

$$13 - 19 = -6 \equiv 21 \pmod{27}$$

$$8 - 23 = -15 \equiv 10 \pmod{25}$$

$$18 - 24 = -6 \equiv 43 \pmod{49}$$

This gives the vector

$$(1, 4, 9, 40)$$

which is, in fact, the decomposed representation of $1907760 = 1907833 - 73$. Taking the lnr of 1907760 modulo, each of the moduli easily checks this. We can multiply, add, and subtract (as long as the result of the subtraction is nonnegative) with numbers as large as $M - 1 = 2116799$ using this mixed radix representation. This works because of propositions 20 and 21.

But why should we do this? There are two good reasons:

1. We can reduce arithmetic with very large integers to arithmetic with much smaller integers. If we choose the moduli carefully, we can arrange it so that none of the integers exceeds the word size of our computer. Thus, we can work quickly with a language's primitive integer type. Integer need to be converted to and from their "large" representation only for input and output purposes.

2. The arithmetic operations with the decomposed representation are completely independent of each other, so they can be done in parallel, significantly reducing operation time on multiprocessor machines. This is not true with arithmetic using normal radix representation.

The IntCRT Class   This class represents nonnegative integers as a series of residues modulo a series of moduli, where the moduli are all unique primes. It adds/multiplies two IntCRT objects together by adding/multiplying their residues together. The moduli are all primes not exceeding the largest value for a Java int, and hence the residues do not exceed the maximum int value either. This allows us to implement the moduli and residues as dual arrays of primitive type long (we use long since a multiplication of two residues may exceed the maximum int value). Here is an outline of the IntCRT class, with descriptions interspersed with the code.

```
import java.util.*;
import java.math.*;
public class IntCRT {
```

IntCRT objects will consist of

1. The moduli, which are stored in a static array of type long. Once they are set up, they are used by all subsequently declared IntCRT objects. Since they use the same moduli, they must all specify the same maximum modulus bit length (the bit length of the product of all the moduli) to be added or multiplied together.

2. The residues, which are the corresponding residues for each modulus.

3. A variable to record the maximum modulus bit length.

```
//IntCRT objects are based on a series of ints modulo a series of long primes
//The primes are stored here in this static array-all IntCRT objects will share
this array
static long[] moduli=null;

//A parallel array of residues for each IntCRT object holds its mixed radix
representation
long[] residues=null;

//The maximum size of the modulus - computations must not exceed this modulus
int maxModulusBitLength=0;
```

There is a single public constructor, which reads in a string of digits, and parses it as a BigInteger, say *n*. If this is the first IntCRT object created, we must set up the moduli. We begin with the largest odd primitive int value, and test it for primality. If it succeeds, we add it to the moduli, and if not, we subtract two from this number and continue in the same way until we have a product of moduli whose bit length exceeds the maximum modulus bit length specified in the constructor. We then produce the residues by taking the BigInteger *n* modulo each modulus. We convert each residue to a primitive long. Do not be concerned that we use the BigInteger class here (it seems like cheating). We only use it for input/output purposes. The addition/multiplication of IntCRT objects (the bulk of processing time for crypto purposes) will be done entirely with the primitive type residues.

```java
//This constructor produces the residues from the string of decimal digits
//Also produces the prime moduli
public IntCRT(String digitString, int maxModulusBitLength) {

    //If modulus<=64 bits, we might as well be using ints
    if (maxModulusBitLength<65) throw new IllegalArgumentException
        ("The maximum modulus bit length must be at least 65 bits");
    this.maxModulusBitLength=maxModulusBitLength;

    //If the prime moduli are not yet set up, set them up
    if (moduli==null) setupModuli();

    //The residues are long, but each will be no larger than an int
    //This is because multiplication of residues may exceed the size of an int,
    //requiring a long to store
    residues=new long[moduli.length];

    //Get the string and make it into a BigInteger; BigInteger only used for IO
    //conversions,
    //not for calculations
    BigInteger n=new BigInteger(digitString);
    if (n.compareTo(BigIntegerMath.ZERO)<0) throw new IllegalArgumentException
        ("IntCRT objects must be nonnegative.");
    if (n.bitLength()>=maxModulusBitLength) throw new IllegalArgumentException
        ("IntCRT objects must be less than maximum modulus bit length = "
+maxModulusBitLength+".");
    //Make each residue
    for (int i=0;i<residues.length;i++)
residues[i]=n.mod(BigInteger.valueOf(moduli[i])).longValue();
}

//Private constructor to make IntCRT object by passing in residues
private IntCRT(long[] residues) {
    this.residues=residues;
}
```

```
//Set up the prime moduli
private void setupModuli() {
    //Don't know how long array should be-start with a Vector
    Vector vector=new Vector();
    BigInteger two=BigInteger.valueOf(2);
    //Start with the largest possible int-this is an odd number
    BigInteger test=BigInteger.valueOf(Integer.MAX_VALUE);
    //bigBubba will be the product of all the primes
    BigInteger bigBubba=BigInteger.valueOf(1);
    //When this product is big enough (has long enough bit length) we have enough
    //primes
    while (bigBubba.bitLength()<maxModulusBitLength) {
        //If test is prime, add it to the vector, and multiply bigBubba by it
        if (test.isProbablePrime(10)) {
            vector.addElement(test);
            bigBubba=bigBubba.multiply(test);
        }
        //Subtract two from the test number-test is always odd
        test=test.subtract(two);
    }
    //We know the size of our array of primes-create the array
    moduli=new long[vector.size()];
    //Copy the prime moduli into the array
    for (int i=0;i<vector.size();i++)
        moduli[i]=((BigInteger)vector.elementAt(i)).longValue();
}
```

The addition and multiplication methods follow. Note that the work is done entirely with primitive types. The code is not written to do these operations in parallel; however, this would be a great exercise for you.

```
public IntCRT add(IntCRT other) {
    //IntCRT objects must be using the same moduli
    if (maxModulusBitLength!=other.maxModulusBitLength) throw new
IllegalArgumentException
("IntCRT objects must have same maximum modulus bit length to be added together");
    long[] answer=new long[residues.length];
    //Add i-th residue of this to i-th residue of other, take residue mod i-th
    //moduli
    for (int i=0;i<residues.length;i++)
        answer[i]=(residues[i]+other.residues[i])%moduli[i];
    return new IntCRT(answer);
}

public IntCRT multiply(IntCRT other) {
    //IntCRT objects must be using the same moduli
```

```
    if (maxModulusBitLength!=other.maxModulusBitLength) throw new
IllegalArgumentException
("IntCRT objects must have same modulus bit length to be multiplied together");
    long[] answer=new long[residues.length];
    //Multiply i-th residue of this by i-th residue of other, may produce a long
    //Take residue mod i-th moduli
    for (int i=0;i<residues.length;i++)
        answer[i]=(residues[i]*other.residues[i])%moduli[i];
    return new IntCRT(answer);
}
```

The toString() method takes the residues and moduli, and "recomposes" the BigInteger using the solveCRT() method from the BigIntegerMath class. We then convert it to a string by calling the toString() method from the BigInteger class.

```
public String toString() {
    //Make an array of BigIntegers for each modulus
    BigInteger[] m=new BigInteger[moduli.length];
    //We reconstruct a BigInteger from the residues by using the Chinese Remainder
    //Theorem
    for (int i=0;i<moduli.length;i++) m[i]=BigInteger.valueOf(moduli[i]);
    //Make an array of BigIntegers for each residue
    BigInteger[] r=new BigInteger[residues.length];
    for (int i=0;i<residues.length;i++) r[i]=BigInteger.valueOf(residues[i]);
    //Reconstruct the BigInteger and return it as a string
    BigInteger whopper=BigIntegerMath.solveCRT(r,m)[0];
    return whopper.toString();
}
```

```
}//End of IntCRT class
```

Figures 16.2, 16.3, and 16.4 are shots of TestIntCRTApplet.

FIGURE 16.2

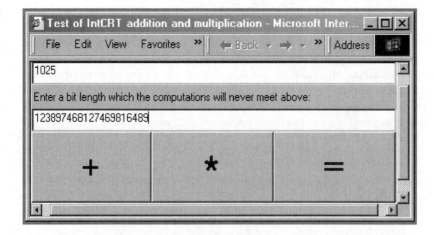

FIGURE 16.3

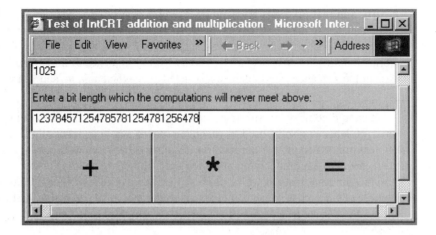

FIGURE 16.4

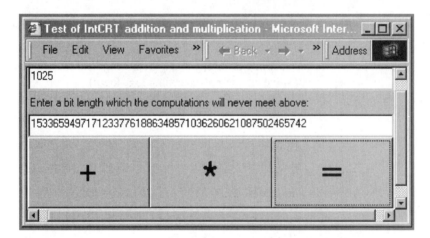

16.4 RANDOM NUMBER GENERATION

Many cryptosystems depend on the ability to generate random numbers, where random means in the sense that the values could not be easily predicted by an adversary. Perhaps surprisingly, this is difficult to do in practice. Without special hardware, a computer cannot truly generate random numbers; they can merely produce what we call pseudorandom numbers based on some deterministic mathematical algorithm, and an initial number called a seed. If either the seed or the transformation is not chosen carefully enough, an adversary can predict, to a high degree of accuracy, the pseudorandom numbers produced.

EXAMPLE. Conventional random number generators are insufficient for protecting the secrecy of the numbers they generate. An example is a linear congruential generator, which produces a sequence $x_1, x_2, \ldots$ of pseudorandom numbers given by the affine transformation

$$x_n \equiv ax_{n-1} + b \pmod{m} \qquad n \geq 1, 0 \leq x_n < m.$$

The values a, b, and m are parameters which define the generator; x_0 is the seed which generates the sequence. If any of these values are compromised, or can be guessed, this generator cannot produce unpredictable numbers. It turns out that with this particular transformation, this is rather easy to do; given a partial sequence of these random numbers, the rest of the sequence can often be constructed even when a, b, m, and x_0 are unknown.

It should come as no surprise that many of the same transformations that we use to encrypt data can also be used to generate random numbers. After all, the purposes of disguising messages and the purposes of disguising the previous numbers and the seed in a sequence of pseudorandom numbers are very similar. A random number generator able to produce integers that cannot be predicted by an adversary are suitable for cryptography; these are called cryptographically secure pseudorandom bit generators (CSPRBG). Descriptions of two such generators follow; the first resembles Rabin, while the second resembles RSA.

Blum–Blum–Shub Pseudorandom Bit Generator   To generate pseudorandom numbers or bitstreams:

1. Choose two secret strong primes, p and q, both congruent to 3 modulo 4. Form $n = pq$. Choose j as a positive integer not exceeding $\log_2(\log_2 n)$

2. Select a random integer seed s such that

   - $2 \le s < n$

   - s and n are relatively prime.

   Compute x_0 = the lnr of s^2 modulo n.

3. Repeat for as long as desired:

   - Compute x_i = the lnr of $x_{i-1}{}^2$ modulo n.

   - Let z_i be the j least significant bits of x_i.

4. The output sequence is $z_1, z_2, z_3, \ldots$.

EXAMPLE.   For this example we will use small primes; in reality, we must use large, strong primes. Suppose we choose $p = 11351$, $q = 11987$. So $n = 136064437$. We compute j as 4, the largest integer not exceeding $\log_2(\log_2(n)) = 4.75594$, and we will select as our seed $s = 80331757$. We wish to generate a stream of 2 blocks, each of bit length 4; we compute the values

$$x_0 \equiv s^2 \equiv 80331757^2 \equiv 131273718 \pmod{136064437}$$

$$x_1 \equiv x_0{}^2 \equiv 131273718^2 \equiv 47497112 \pmod{136064437}$$

$$z_1 \equiv 47497112 \equiv 8 \equiv 1000_{\text{base 2}} \pmod{2^4} \text{ (the 4 least significant bits of } x_1)$$

$$x_2 \equiv x_1^2 \equiv 47497112^2 \equiv 69993144 \pmod{136064437}$$

$$z_2 \equiv 69993144 \equiv 8 \equiv 1000_{\text{base } 2} \pmod{2^4} \text{ (the 4 least significant bits of } x_2)$$

The final "random" bitstream produced is

$$10001000.$$

Admittedly, it isn't much to look at. We need to generate a much larger stream, and will do so in the next example.

EXAMPLE.   Here we produce a much longer stream of 100 blocks, each of bit length 4. We will use exactly the same parameters $p = 11351$, $q = 11987$, $n = pq = 136064437$, $j = 4$, and the seed $s = 80331757$.

```
1000 1000 0101 1111 1110 0101 1101 0001 0000 0000 0000 1000 1100 1101
0001 0101 0110 1010 1110 0110 0110 0000 1011 0011 1000 1010 1100 1010
0000 1101 1110 0100 0111 1111 1010 0000 1011 1001 1110 1001 1100 0100
0011 1000 0101 1000 0010 1001 0100 0101 1111 0001 0110 1100 0101 0000
0110 1011 1001 0001 0000 0101 0011 1100 0111 0011 0101 0111 0000 1000
0010 1111 1111 1100 0110 0001 0011 1110 0111 0001 1111 0010 1111 1100
1011 0011 1111 1111 1110 1010 1000 1001 0111 0111 0010 0100 1001 0010
1100
```

You may wish to check these values, or write a program to check them. (I recommend the latter.)

The CSPRBG Class   I have designed a class which implements the Blum–Blum–Shub algorithm for generating random bitstreams. For convenience, the modulus $n = pq$ will be fixed at 1025–1026 bits. Using this bit length for n, we should choose no more than 10 of the least significant bits after each squaring. For convenience again, we will choose the 8 least significant bits, allowing us to easily place them in a byte array using the method fillBytes(). We can also retrieve a single byte using the getRandomByte() method. The code for the CSPRBG class follows.

```java
import java.math.*;
import java.security.*;
public class CSPRBG {
   BigInteger p,q,n,seed;
   public CSPRBG(byte[] seed) {
      this.seed=new BigInteger(seed);
      if (this.seed.bitLength()<515) throw new
         IllegalArgumentException("Seed too small");
      SecureRandom sr=new SecureRandom(seed);
      //Use a secureRandom object to get the strong primes
      PrimeGenerator pg=new PrimeGenerator(513,16,sr);
      do {p=pg.getStrongPrime();}
```

```
        while (!p.mod(BigIntegerMath.FOUR).equals(BigIntegerMath.THREE));
        do {q=pg.getStrongPrime();}
        while (!q.mod(BigIntegerMath.FOUR).equals(BigIntegerMath.THREE));
        n=p.multiply(q);
    }
    //Fills an array of bytes with random data
    public void fillBytes(byte[] array) {
        for (int i=0;i<array.length;i++) {
            //Seed is continually squared
            seed=seed.multiply(seed).mod(n);
            //Least significant byte of residue is the i-th random byte
            byte b=seed.byteValue();
            array[i]=b;
        }
    }
    //Returns a single byte of pseudorandom data
    public byte getRandomByte() {
            seed=seed.multiply(seed).mod(n);
            return seed.byteValue();
    }
}
```

Figures 16.5, 16.6, and 16.7 are screen shots of the test applet (TestCSPRBGApplet). You first enter a seed as a large integer, then press the button repeatedly to get random bytes, which are displayed as decimal integers in the range -128 thru 127.

Micali-Schnorr Pseudorandom Bit Generator To generate pseudorandom numbers or bitstreams:

1. Choose two secret strong primes, p and q, and form $n = pq$.

Let N equal the bit length of n.

FIGURE 16.5

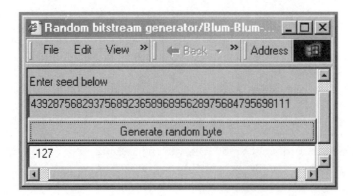

FIGURE 16.6

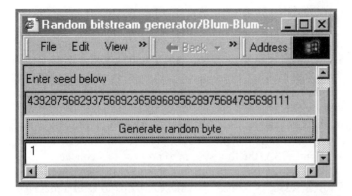

FIGURE 16.7

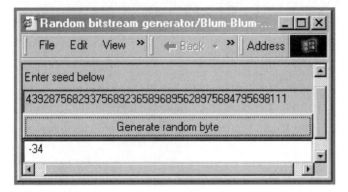

Choose an exponent e such that

- $1 < e < (p - 1)(q - 1)$
- e is relatively prime to $(p - 1)(q - 1)$
- $80e \leq N$.

Let k be the largest integer not exceeding $N(1 - 2/e)$.

Let $r = N - k$.

2. Select a random seed x_0 of bitlength r.

3. For $i = 1$, to Z do:

- Compute y_i = the lnr of x_{i-1}^e modulo n.
- Let x_i be the r most significant bits of y_i.
- Let z_i be the r least significant bits of y_i.

4. The output sequence is $z_1, z_2, z_3, \ldots, z_Z$.

The numbers z_i may not be large enough for an application's purposes; in this case, one concatenates as many of the numbers together as necessary to form a sufficiently large integer.

16.5 SIGNING MESSAGES

Signing messages is a concept which arose with public key cryptography. When you receive a message encrypted with your public key, how do you know the message is from whom claims to have sent it? After all, your encryption keys are public, and so anyone can encrypt messages to you. Signing is a way for the sender to modify the message in a way that could only be done by her.

Each public key scheme usually defines a method to perform signing. Sometimes the signing closely resembles the enciphering mechanism, but often it does not. We will first cover signing with RSA, the first system to propose this concept.

Signing with RSA   Suppose individual A wants to send a message P to individual B using RSA in such a way so that B knows the message could only have come from individual A. Suppose A uses the RSA modulus $n = pq$, and the exponents e and d, while individual B uses $n^* = p^*q^*$, and the exponents e^* and d^*. Of course, neither party knows the other's private key. Individual A does the following:

1. Individual A computes

$$C_1 \equiv P^d \ (\mathrm{mod} \ n)$$

using her decryption exponent. (No one else can do this if A is protecting her private key.)

2. If $C_1 \geq n^*$, it is necessary for A to separate C_1 into blocks before applying the transformation

$$C \equiv C_1^{e^*} \ (\mathrm{mod} \ n^*)$$

and form the final ciphertext to send to B.

To decrypt the message sent by A, B does the following:

1. B decrypts the message C by applying

$$C_1 \equiv C^{d^*} \ (\mathrm{mod} \ n^*)$$

to regain C_1.

2. B then computes

$$P \equiv C_1^{e} \ (\mathrm{mod} \ n)$$

using A's public information to recover the plaintext.

Actually, it isn't necessary for A to encrypt the message a second time using B's public information if she isn't concerned with who reads the message. B could simply decrypt with A's public key to retrieve the plaintext. However, anyone else could do the same thing. If privacy (in addition to integrity) is an issue (and it usually is), both transformations are involved.

Is this all there is to it? No. Establishing one's identity couldn't possibly be this easy. For example, is it possible someone could publish his or her public key values using someone else's identity? If this is not regulated in some way, the answer is yes. Most public key schemes in use provide a mechanism by which individuals must establish their identity with an entity called a "Trusted Third Party" or TTP, when publishing their keys. If necessary, these TTPs can establish that the individual using a certain set of keys is actually the person he or she claims to be. The TTP does not need to know anyone's private keys to do this.

EXAMPLE.   For simplicity's sake, we will use small parameters, and so that blocking will not be an issue, we will arrange it so that $n < n^*$.

Suppose individual A (the sender) chooses $p = 7$ and $q = 19$, so that $n = 133$. Individual A chooses $e = 5$ as the encryption exponent, and computes $d = e' = 5' \equiv 65 \pmod{108}$.

Individual B (the recipient) chooses $p^* = 11$ and $q^* = 23$, so that $n^* = 253$. Individual B chooses $e = 9$ as the encryption exponent, and computes $d = e' = 9' \equiv 49 \pmod{253}$.

A wishes to send the message $P = 93$ to B with a signature. Individual A first computes

$$C_1 \equiv 93^{65} \equiv 4 \pmod{133}$$

No one else can do this because A's decryption exponent is private. Individual A then encrypts using B's public encryption exponent and modulus:

$$C \equiv 4^9 \equiv 36 \pmod{253}.$$

This is the final ciphertext, which is sent to B. $C1$ is first recovered by decrypting with B's private decryption exponent:

$$36^{49} \equiv 4 \equiv C_1 \pmod{253}.$$

No one can do this except B, and so privacy is assured. Finally, B uses A's public exponent and modulus to recover the plaintext P:

$$4^5 \equiv 93 \equiv P \pmod{133}.$$

Java Algorithm   Writing the methods to sign with RSA in this way are easy since most of the work has already been done. The methods to do this (from the Ciphers class) follow.

```
public static byte[] RSAEncipherSigned(
byte[] msg,
BigInteger dSender,
BigInteger nSender,
BigInteger eRecip,
BigInteger nRecip,
SecureRandom sr) {

    return RSAEncipherWSalt
        (RSAEncipherWSalt(msg,dSender,nSender,sr),eRecip,nRecip,sr);
}


public static byte[] RSADecipherSigned(
byte[] msg,
BigInteger dRecip,
BigInteger nRecip,
```

```
BigInteger eSender,
BigInteger nSender) {

    return RSADecipherWSalt(RSADecipherWSalt(msg,dRecip,nRecip),eSender,nSender);
}
```

Of course, the variables *eSender*, *dSender*, and *nSender* refer to the message sender's key information, while *eRecip*, *dRecip*, and *nRecip* refers to the recipient's keys. Note that neither the sender nor the recipient needs to know the other's private info for message exchange. Also, note that enciphering is an application of *RSAEncipher() twice*, first using the sender's private exponent, then using the recipient's public exponent. It is done this way so that padding and blocking issues will be handled correctly. Because of the symmetric nature of the RSA enciphering and deciphering transformations, this works. Likewise, deciphering involves applying *RSADecipher() twice* with different exponents. You will find that writing methods to sign using other algorithms won't be quite so easy.

Following is the output of a simple console program TestRSACipherSigned. The code can be found on the book's website:

```
Plaintext message:

Little Willy Willy won't GO HOME!!!!!!!!!!!!!!!!!!!!!!!!!!!!!!!!!!!!!

Sender's keys:

n=477823173909498405997193614062827870319711697063408892059106005116510909
1324842762783453285232353074783464254995516764280738329563279965438228948
9280441812866482827362912397521119899724567407854726573606946785783804821
1490867893827447459512197749446350191839654657188532964841056340856133204
8607351598198101709

e=833129746446438599032679468347081594856478586251792124851156162222872371
9387882814550117641490108129879776898385160468375233192812901537663393120
6775135511580272006739510422068301894064631602466966489594485010052428466
8889081939342459055418763799023158612672616635656825520516281014459754981
0696099572097327

d=468483891642423302250714496666046374112247137991151120406092727014998268
5021302587703288508227050307879046123080765550452834966641081393777954381
8758048336718320130340924290800346871151831153200675204844684724839023305
8288674199969230216110595131611445634490421710900628837913761448368073145
108476860945640143

Recipient's keys:

n=400300648901310455561641439066399772102781394265593840916989629340257812
8705290677954932329334228417935240465475883900295598468088922991924243392
77730359089626351125443267309018481637322550902644045356241675200020795l
```

9356433725290818322063237477659539960679619018282576265414797224176810239
4461794720293192639

e=1073897546771631301622641198261606337509693528009697337882014837390100003774703137721988755652034217634736416790256976187329068002009493889017144337965064160547094535922354431198904536464821168309068889027430457499760109104727012011311098964646341231797382360474439424184703023571994984526858491783340807165

d=341204278197491655422588736306802438438852069123933952917047305752354168499010091359026204518569891972265492221968149078409284214574471096638649650892539138073989681927493778329092286576144239515174415777136569306123999162911588324300355102269082575368258631783857744577803847668997336044509358887363459579267

Doubly enciphered signed message:

```
Ü¡… ??-au¡?(dRc(µß¶š«Ùáà6R.K>;▯,>▯ÿÍŠE-ÌC9B▯¿cd_øT»%ìß?{▯ŒW9'Q
     n½?Á?‡ü¿/CH30ôÜ
▯Áµ?)ÙjÁ™<R-1@øA
£µ▯ù¯-{èüÜ\±by|©▯-R,ÙèYpL0â?Sú▯▯Òᵒ▯Æôs22!H³^Õᵒ°KP▯· Ë)´▯ã¬-¼
ëkû▯Õ▯ŸÛf¨--P▯ú  pR▯MY9@/+   áœ1«%Q·¶v²y▯E=ùu-‚Zcê™7ß-
Ñqp·?±▯_?W½íúŸæœ▯▯p  MÓíË▯xᵃ=z}©xÀG▯âñᵒB▯▯"Ýá Ý▯Àè
▯†™1
```
Doubly deciphered signed message:
Little Willy Willy won't GO HOME!!

Signing with Rabin   Rabin signatures are simple to produce. Suppose individual A wants to send a message P to individual B using Rabin in such a way so that B knows the message could only have come from A. Suppose A uses the Rabin modulus $n = pq$, while B uses $n^* = p^* q^*$. (The primes involved now are all congruent to 3 modulo 4, as required by Rabin.) Of course, neither party knows the other's private key. A does the following:

1. A computes a square root of P modulo n (if P has such a square root); that is, she computes a value, say C_1, such that

$$C_1^2 \equiv P \ (\mathrm{mod} \ n).$$

This transformation can produce up to four roots; it doesn't matter which root she chooses. (No one else can do this if A is protecting her primes p and q, as computing a square root modulo n without its prime factorization is an intractable problem.)

Note that a particular message may not have a square root modulo n. The sender must salt the message (or salt each block) in such a way that the salted result has a square root modulo n. This isn't difficult, because the odds of some random integer having a square root modulo n is quite likely. The amount of salt to use for this purpose is agreed on beforehand.

2. If $C_1 \geq n^*$, it is necessary for A to separate C_1 into blocks, and add redundancy before applying the transformation

$$C \equiv C_1^2 \ (\text{mod } n^*)$$

and form the final ciphertext to send to B.

To decrypt the message sent by A, B does the following:

1. B decrypts the message C by sending it through his decryption machine to regain C_1. That is, it computes the square roots of C modulo n^*. If redundancy was added at the proper point, his decryption machine can determine the correct root congruent to C_1 out of the four possible roots calculated.

2. B then computes

$$P \equiv C_1^2 \ (\text{mod } n)$$

using A's public modulus to recover the plaintext.

Once again, the enciphering and deciphering transformations are used not only to ensure that the message was from the sender, but also to ensure that no one other than the intended recipient can decipher it.

EXAMPLE. For simplicity's sake, we will use small parameters. Suppose individual A (the sender) chooses $p = 10259$, and $q = 10739$, so that $n = 110171401$. Individual B (the recipient) chooses $p^* = 10691$, and $q^* = 11351$, so that $n^* = 121353541$. Note that all primes are congruent to 3 modulo 4. (There is a table in the appendices listing all primes less than 12000, plus their lnr's modulo 4.)

A wishes to send the message $P = 1696082$ to B with a signature. This message may not have a square root modulo n. A first checks this, and discovers that it does not; so by adding salt (just a single digit will do here), she eventually obtains a value that has a square root; namely,

$$P' = 16960824$$

A then computes the square roots of 16960824 modulo 110171401. B does this by computing

$$x \equiv \pm P^{(p-1)/4} q q_{p'} \pm P^{(q-1)/4} p p_{q'} \ (\text{mod } n)$$

where $q_{p'}$ is an inverse of q modulo p, and $p_{q'}$ is an inverse of p modulo q. The values desired are

$$p_{q'} = 1320$$

$$q_{p'} = 8998$$

This yields the four roots

$$x \equiv 50253700 \ (\text{mod } 110171401)$$

$$x \equiv 40866715 \ (\text{mod } 110171401)$$

$$x \equiv 59917701 \pmod{110171401}$$

$$x \equiv 69304686 \pmod{110171401}.$$

No one else can do this since only A knows the values of p and q. A selects one of these roots (it doesn't matter which), say $x = 59917701$. To compute the final ciphertext, it is necessary that A reblock the text and add redundancy so that B's decryption machine can select the correct root out of the four possible roots generated by the decryption transformation. Thus, the message is split into

$$x_1 = 59915991$$

$$x_2 = 77017701$$

A then encrypts using B's public modulus:

$$C_1 \equiv 59915991^2 \equiv 20072206 \pmod{121353541}.$$

$$C_2 \equiv 77017701^2 \equiv 11711668 \pmod{121353541}.$$

This is the final ciphertext, which is sent to B. To recover the plaintext, B must first solve for the square roots of C_1 and C_2 modulo 121353541:

$$x \equiv \pm C^{(p+1)/4} q^* q^*_{p^{*\prime}} \pm C^{(q+1)/4} p^* p^*_{q^{*\prime}} \pmod{n^*}$$

where $q^*_{p^{*\prime}}$ is an inverse of q^* modulo p^*, and $p^*_{q^{*\prime}}$ is an inverse of p^* modulo q^*. The values desired are

$$p^*_{q^{*\prime}} = 2253$$

$$q^*_{p^{*\prime}} = 8569$$

This yields the four roots for C_1:

$$x \equiv 36623739 \pmod{121353541}$$

$$x \equiv 61437550 \pmod{121353541}$$

$$x \equiv 84729802 \pmod{121353541}$$

$$\rightarrow x \equiv 59915991 \pmod{121353541}.$$

Since the last root is the one possessing redundancy, it is chosen as the correct root. The redundancy is discarded to yield $x_1 = 5991$. It is highly unlikely that another root will possess this redundancy (especially if we use large redundant blocks).

The four roots for C_2 are:

$$x \equiv 28117593 \pmod{121353541}$$

$$x \equiv 44335840 \pmod{121353541}$$

$$x \equiv 93235948 \pmod{121353541}$$

$$\rightarrow x \equiv 77017701 \pmod{121353541}$$

It so happens that the last root is again the correct one. The redundancy is discarded to give $x_2 = 7701$. Since no one can do this except B, privacy is assured. Finally, B reforms the message $x = 59917701$ and uses A's public modulus to recover the plaintext P' (with salt):

$$59917701^2 \equiv 16960824 \equiv P' \pmod{133}.$$

The salt is removed, and the plaintext is regained:

$$P = 1696082.$$

16.6   MESSAGE DIGESTS

A message digest is basically a fixed-size compressed version of an arbitrary length message. This compression is done by way of something called a digest function, which is really a special type of hash function.

You have probably heard the term hash function before, for we use them when we construct hash tables. A hash table is a way of storing data so that it can be retrieved very quickly. The hash function maps a data item to an index in a table; a "good" hash function is one that very rarely maps two different data items to the same index. This property is known as collision resistance.

EXAMPLES.   Suppose we represent the data as large integers, and suppose the hash function is defined as

$$h(x) = \text{lnr of } x \text{ modulo } 2^{64}.$$

Thus, the hash value is merely the trailing 64 bits of the binary representation of x. If the data items are evenly distributed, this may be a suitable mapping for a hash table.

For example, if $x = 2009009954064294883069219470104030543000$, then

$$h(x) = 12493796564522152668$$

$$\equiv 2009009954064294883069219470104030543000 \pmod{2^{64}}$$

or

$$h(x) = 1010110101100010111000011100011111001100010101101011001011011100_{\text{base 2}}.$$

However, since data are rarely evenly distributed, we might choose a hash function such as this one:

$$g(x) = \text{lnr of } x \text{ modulo } p$$

where p is a large prime. Since any message x not divisible by p will be relatively prime to p, an overabundance of messages having the same trailing digits will tend to be spread out among the range of hash values.

Most of these "classical" hash functions are not suitable for cryptography, however. For reasons which will become apparent, a hash function, say h, used to produce message digests must also satisfy the following properties:

> **Definition**
>
> A hash function h is a digest function if it satisfies all of the following properties:
>
> 1. Given a hash value $h(m)$, it must be extremely difficult to determine m.
> 2. Given a message m, it must be extremely difficult to find another message m' such that $h(m) = h(m')$.
> 3. It must be extremely difficult to find any two messages, say m and m', for which $h(m) = h(m')$.

Property 2 looks very much like property 3, but they are quite different. The former says that if we start with a given message, we can't find another that maps to the same hash value. The latter does not specify that we start with a particular message; it only requires that we cannot find any two messages that map to the same digest.

A hash function that satisfies these three properties will be called a digest function. Sometimes we will also refer to the function as a digest, but we also use the word digest to refer to the output of a digest function; the intended meaning should be clear from the context.

If we take the hash functions from the previous examples, it is easy to see that they could not be digest functions, since they fail some of the required properties. For example, any two messages with the same trailing 64 bits will map to the same hash value using function h. The function g likewise fails to have property 2.

Digest functions are very much like good ciphers, in that the values they produce must look random to the point that an adversary cannot tell what the originating data was. There are three important differences between digest functions and ciphers, however; they are:

1. A cipher is intended to be reversible, given a certain secret key. Digests are specifically intended not to be reversible, no matter what information one has.
2. A digest function compresses the data, whereas a cipher generally does not. In fact, a cipher usually expands the data.
3. Digest functions use no keys; the scrambling effect that they produce comes about by the nature of the mathematical transformation itself. Such a digest is referred to as a Modification Detection Code (MDC); the name signifies the basic purpose. However, other digests use keys; such a digest is called a Message Authentication Code (MAC).

Now we will cover a specific digest function; namely, the Modular Arithmetic Secure Hash, Algorithm 2 (MASH–2).

MASH–2 The following produces an n bit digest of a message x of bitlength b such that $0 \leq b < 2^{n/2}$.

1. Choose two primes such that their product, M, is m bits in length.
2. The integer n is chosen as the largest multiple of 16 not exceeding m; n is the bitlength of the digest.
3. $H_0 = 0$ is an initialization vector; we will define another n bit constant A, such that

$$A = 11110000 \ldots 0000_{\text{base } 2}.$$

4. Pad the message x with zeros, if necessary, to make the bitlength of x a perfect multiple of $n/2$. Divide x up into t blocks, each of bitlength $n/2$ (t may be 1). Add another $n/2$ bit block, which is the ($n/2$) bit representation of b. We represent this as:

$$x = x_1, x_2, \ldots, x_t, x_{t+1}.$$

Note that each of the blocks is a multiple of 8.

5. For each i from 1 through t, divide x_i into 4-bit blocks; insert the bits 1111 before each 4-bit block. This produces an n-bit block, say y_i, from each x_i. Then divide x_{t+1} into 4-bit blocks, but this time, insert the bits 1010 before each 4-bit block. This yields the expanded message

$$y = y_1, y_2, \ldots, y_t, y_{t+1}.$$

6. Now, to compute the digest. For i from 1 through $t + 1$ do the following:

- Compute $F_i = $ lnr of $((H_{i-1} \oplus y_i) \text{ OR A})^{257}$ modulo M (where OR means bitwise inclusive–or, and $\oplus$ represents bitwise exclusive–or).
- Let G_i be the n rightmost bits of F_i.
- Compute $H_i = G_i \oplus H_{i-1}$.

7. The digest is H_{t+1}.

EXAMPLE. We will again use very small numbers. Let the message be $x = 45 = 101101$ (binary), and so the bitlength b of x is $b = 6 = 110$ (binary). Let $p = 6911$ and $q = 6947$; thus, $M = 48010717 = 10110111001001010111011101$ (binary). The bitlength m of M is 26, so we choose $n = 16$. The IV (initialization vector) H_0 is 0, and the constant A is 1111000000000000 (binary). We pad the message with zeros so that it is a multiple of 16/2 = 8; that is,

$$x = 10110100.$$

Now we divide this up into 8 bit blocks; in this case, there is only one such block ($t = 1$). We append another block, which is the 8-bit representation of b, or 00000110. So, we have

$$x_1 = 10110100$$

$$x_2 = 00000110.$$

We divide the message up by splitting each block x_i (where $i \le t$) into 4-bit blocks, and inserting 1111 before each such 4-bit block. For x_1 this yields

$$y_1 = 1111101111110100.$$

The last block is split in the same way, but 1010 is inserted before each block. Hence, for x_2 we have

$$y_2 = 1010000010100110.$$

Now, to produce the digest:

$F_1 \equiv ((H_0 \oplus y_1) \text{ OR A})^{257} \equiv ((0000000000000000 \oplus 1111101111110100) \text{ OR}$
$1111000000000000)^{100000001} \equiv (1111101111110100 \text{ OR } 1111000000000000)^{100000001} \equiv$
$1111101111110100^{100000001} \equiv 1010110110100101100101011 \pmod{}$
$1011011100100101011011011101).$

G_1 is taken to be the 16 rightmost bits of F_1; so

$$G_1 = 1010010100101011.$$

We take H_1 by computing

$$H_1 = G_1 \oplus H_0 = 1010010100101011.$$

We compute H_2 in the same way:

$F_2 \equiv ((H_1 \oplus y_2) \text{ OR A})^{257} \equiv ((1010010100101011 \oplus 1010000010100110) \text{ OR}$
$1111000000000000)^{100000001} \equiv (0000010110001101 \text{ OR } 1111000000000000)^{100000001} \equiv$
$1111010110001101^{100000001} \equiv 1000100010110010000000101011 \pmod{}$
$10110111001001010111011101).$

$G_2 = 1100100000010111$

$H_2 = G_2 \oplus H_1 = 1100100000010111 \oplus 1010010100101011 = 0110110100111100.$

The final digest value is 0110110100111100.

Of course, this was a lot to go through for such a tiny message; in fact, in this case, the digest is larger than the message! Of course, we could have used a message up to $2^8 - 1 = 255$ bits in length for this example.

The MASH2 Class I have designed a class to generate digests of messages using the MASH–2 algorithm. The digestOf() method accepts a message as a byte array, and returns the digest as a byte array.

```java
import java.math.*;
import java.security.*;
public class MASH2 {

    //Define some handy values
    static BigInteger two=BigInteger.valueOf(2);
    static BigInteger ten=BigInteger.valueOf(10);//=binary 1010
    static BigInteger fifteen=BigInteger.valueOf(15);//=binary 1111
    static BigInteger sixteen=BigInteger.valueOf(16);
    static BigInteger exp=BigInteger.valueOf(257);

    BigInteger modulus;

    public MASH2(BigInteger modulus) {
        this.modulus=modulus;
    }
```

```java
public byte[] digestOf(byte[] msg) {
    //Convert message to BigInteger-easier to work with
    //Ensure the BigInteger is positive using BigInteger(int signum,byte[] b)
    //constructor
    BigInteger msgInt=new BigInteger(1,msg);

    //b is bitlength of msg
    BigInteger b=BigInteger.valueOf(msgInt.bitLength());

    //n is largest multiple of 16 not exceeding bitlength of modulus
    int n=modulus.bitLength()/16*16;

    //Check that msg is not too large for use with MASH2
    if (b.compareTo(two.pow(n/2))>0) throw new IllegalArgumentException
        ("Message is too large");

    //Pad msg with enough zeros to make it a multiple of n/2
    int amountToShift=msgInt.bitLength()%(n/2)==0?0:(n/2)-
        msgInt.bitLength()%(n/2);
    msgInt=msgInt.shiftLeft(amountToShift);

    //Define variable for 2 raised to n power
    BigInteger twon=two.pow(n);

    //Define initialization vector H
    BigInteger H=BigInteger.valueOf(0);
    //Define n bit binary numeric constant A=11110000...0000
    BigInteger A=BigInteger.valueOf(15).multiply(two.pow(n-4));

    //Process the first t blocks
    int t=msgInt.bitLength()/(n/2);
    BigInteger prevH;
    for (int i=0;i<t;i++) {
        prevH=H;
        H=BigInteger.valueOf(0);
        //Process the 4 bit nybbles-there are n/8 of them
        BigInteger rem;
        for (int j=n/2-4;j>=0;j-=4) {
            //Each byte begins with 1111B
            H=H.shiftLeft(4).or(fifteen);
            //Shift msg to right and keep last 4 bits
            rem=msgInt.shiftRight(j+n/2*(t-1-i)).mod(sixteen);
            //Append this remainder to H
            H=H.shiftLeft(4).or(rem);
        }
```

```
      //Compute the new digest value for H
      H=prevH.xor(H).or(A).modPow(exp,modulus).mod(twon).xor(prevH);
   }
   //Process the t+1 block
   prevH=H;
   H=BigInteger.valueOf(0);
   //Process the 4 bit nybbles
   BigInteger rem;
   for (int j=n/2-4;j>=0;j-=4) {
      //Each byte in last block begins with 1010B
      H=H.shiftLeft(4).or(ten);
      //Shift b to right and keep last 4 bits
      rem=b.shiftRight(j).mod(sixteen);
      //Append this remainder to H
      H=H.shiftLeft(4).or(rem);
   }
   //Compute the final digest value as a BigInteger
   H=prevH.xor(H).or(A).modPow(exp,modulus).mod(twon).xor(prevH);
   //Convert to a byte array and return-call helper method getBytes().
   return getBytes(H);
}


//Converting BigInteger to a byte array may force an extra byte for a sign bit.
//We remove this byte if it is produced
private static byte[] getBytes(BigInteger big) {
   byte[] bigBytes=big.toByteArray();
   if (big.bitLength()%8!=0) return bigBytes;
   else {
      byte[] smallerBytes=new byte[big.bitLength()/8];
      System.arraycopy(bigBytes,1,smallerBytes,0,smallerBytes.length);
      return smallerBytes;
   }
}

}
```

 TestMASH2Applet is an applet on the book's website you can use to view the behavior of MASH-2. A modulus about 1024 bits in length is generated. You enter a message, then press a button to see its digest. The digest is displayed as a base 10 integer. (See Figure 16.8.)

One of the drawbacks of MASH-2 is that the digest it produces can be rather large. To be secure, the size of the modulus should be at least 1024 bits, which implies that the digest will likewise be 1024 bits, or 128 bytes long. For most applications, digests should be around 128 *bits* long.

FIGURE 16.8

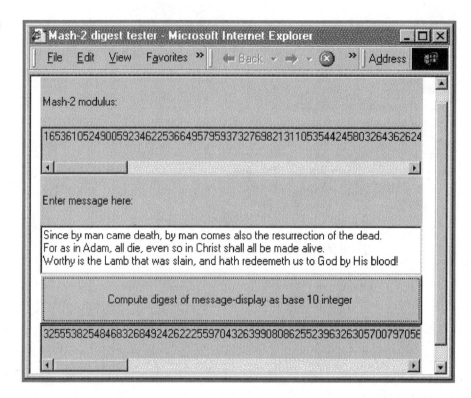

Uses of Message Digests   Digests are most commonly used for two purposes:

1. Ensuring data integrity. This refers to methods that the recipient of data can use to determine whether or not this data has been modified. It is sometimes possible for an adversary, even without knowledge of keys, to modify a message in such a way so that it appears valid to the recipient.

2. Providing authentication of the origin of data. This means that the recipient can ascertain whether or not a message is from the entity that claims to have sent it. Signing messages in the manner described earlier can do this.

When you think about it, each of these two objectives is necessary for the other. To argue this, consider a message of which origin you cannot be sure; then knowing whether or not it has been modified is not useful information. On the other hand, if you cannot be sure whether or not a message has been modified, then knowing its true origin does not help. Thus, a digest must always be used to provide assurances of both the integrity and the authentic origin of data.

Here are some examples of how a digest can be used to do this.

Transmission of a Digest by Secure Means   The sender of a message computes a digest for the plaintext message. The message is sent (probably encrypted, but perhaps not if privacy is not a concern) via an insecure channel, whereas the digest is sent by way of a secure channel. Here, a secure channel may mean:

- An electronic means of data communication known to be safe.
- The telephone, where voice recognition provides the authentication.
- Transporting the data by trusted physical means.

When this is done, the recipient of a message can compute the digest for it, then compare this to the digest received. If they match, the recipient accepts the message as authentic and unmodified (since the digest was sent via secure means.)

Due to the logistical problems involved, this type of assurance is rarely used. The mere problem of not being able to guarantee a "secure" channel is the reason cryptography evolved in the first place. However, this example is given to make you realize the importance of never sending a digest along the same lines of communication as a message. An adversary can capture both the message and the digest. He can then construct a new message, compute a digest for it, and then send them to you. This is easily done even if a public key encryption scheme is being used. (Think about it; everyone knows your public key, and everyone knows the digest function.)

Signing the Digest   One of the problems with signing messages in the manner described earlier is that basically, the sender does double encryption, and double decryption is done by the recipient. This may be too costly in terms of computer resources, especially if messages are being transmitted in real time (like an audio or video signal).

One solution is for the sender, say A, to produce a digest from the plaintext. A then singly encrypts the message using the public key of the recipient, say B. A then doubly encrypts only the digest, first using the private key of A, then B's public key. The message and the digest are then sent. It doesn't matter now if the digest is sent with the message. B decrypts the message, then decrypts the digest first using B's private key, then A's public key. B then calculates a digest of the decrypted message. If it matches the decrypted digest, B accepts the message. See Figure 16.9.

Why does this work? Could an adversary capture the message and the digest, and produce a new message and digest? Since the digest was first encrypted using A's private key, an adversary has no way to duplicate this. The best she can do is "guess" a digest value for her modified message, in the hopes that it will match the digest computed by B from her bogus message. If the digest size is large enough, say 128 bits, this is extremely unlikely; in this case, the probability of all 128 bits matching is $1/2^{128}$, or less than 2.939×10^{-39}.

Encrypting Digest with Message   The situation of sending a digest along the same line of communication as the message is not necessarily unique to public key cryptosystems. Data authentication is also important for secret key cryptosystems. Even with secret key ciphers, it is sometimes possible for an adversary to modify a message so that it appears meaningful to the recipient. This is actually quite easy if the message possesses little structure; for example, a series of widely ranging numbers in binary format. The adversary does not need to know the secret key to do this. (If they knew the secret key, you would be up the creek anyway!)

FIGURE 16.9

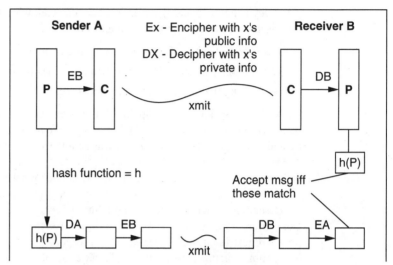

We deal with this very simply: we compute a digest for the plaintext message, then append it to the message. This larger message is then encrypted, and sent. The decryptor checks that the tail end of the decrypted message is the digest of the data that precedes it. Without knowledge of the secret key, it is highly unlikely that an adversary can construct a message that decrypts to a message having this special structure; that is, with the tail of the message being a perfect digest of the rest of the data. (See Figure 16.10.)

Note here that we cannot attach a digest to a message in this way if we are using a public key system, and encrypting using only the recipient's public information. It should be obvious why this is so.

16.7 SIGNING WITH ELGAMAL

The ElGamal signature scheme was specifically intended to work with digests. Suppose a sender, say A, is using the public key (p, g, y), and the private key a, where p is a large, safe

FIGURE 16.10

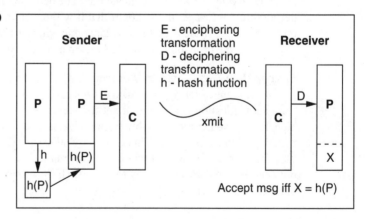

prime, g is a generator modulo p, and y is the lnr of g^a modulo p. Suppose d is a public message digest function. To generate a signed digest of a message P, A must do the following:

1. Select a random integer k between 1 and $p - 2$ (inclusive), such that k is relatively prime to $p - 1$.
2. Calculate r, the lnr of g^k modulo p.
3. Find k', an inverse of k modulo $p - 1$. (This inverse exists due to our choice of k.)
4. Calculate s, the lnr of $k'(d(P) - ar)$ modulo $(p - 1)$. (Only A can do this step, as only A knows the private key a.)
5. The signature is the pair of integers, r and s.

To verify that this signature is valid, the recipient B must do this:

1. Verify that r is between 1 and $p - 1$; if not, reject the signature.
2. Using A's public information, calculate v, the lnr of $y^r r^s$ modulo p.
3. Calculate $d(P)$, the digest of the message P.
4. Compute w, the lnr of $g^{d(P)}$ modulo p.
5. If $v = w$, accept the signature as valid; otherwise, reject it.

Why does this work? Well, because

$$s \equiv k'(d(P) - ar) \pmod{p - 1},$$

we have

$$ks \equiv k\,k'(d(P) - ar)$$
$$\equiv d(P) - ar \pmod{p - 1}.$$

Thus, by subtracting ar from both sides, we have

$$d(P) \equiv ar + ks \pmod{p - 1}.$$

Because of the properties of discrete logarithms, this then yields

$$g^{d(P)} \equiv g^{ar + ks} \pmod{p}.$$

But note that by construction of v and w, and because of the previous congruence, we must have

$$w \equiv g^{d(P)} \equiv g^{ar + ks} \equiv (g^a)^r r^s \equiv y^r r^s \equiv v \pmod{p}.$$

Thus, the signature is valid iff $v = w$.

EXAMPLE.   For this example, we will use a simple hash function, but unsuitable for cryptographic purposes. For simplicity's sake, we will not use salt, or CBC. Suppose A is using the public prime

$p = 768416655531999472553972503490662169854881508111468141690052585033772353811145704262633807570477286149198100781782215658227986987692047241181534570445703122494213057666371119117944205153516492397844122051887566688$

7574706804224094930150661111156295398663728459674020860553762128961778707620918767139240759217479797.

This choice of p is a safe prime; we know the factorization of $p - 1$, which has at least one large prime factor; in this case, $p - 1 = 2zt$, where

$$z = 362,$$

and

$t = 10613489717292810394391885407329587981421015305407018531630560566764811516728531826831958668100515002060747248367157674837403135189116674601954897381846728211246036708099048606601439297700504038644255829445960865866815893376000131118992625844138529556165370800654724945516246034477594900028893324777956849747 9.$

A chooses a generator modulo p,

$$g = 2.$$

A chooses a private value for a:

$a = 45366932286305017454823998962543872234171279575807307127836833791199106589647221361411404680513932826550438110018938792808421883674318765239855541004504826749690514434467452187115574562871476458097782440492959459114595918998192357354718847375845084259186299700677238352348768625876330302043529365424071172153676.$

A computes the public value of y, the lnr of g^a modulo p:

$y = 72405527325288150957658884104015272584081190726722616665216885768981792648756490795465192629719933522111280634525813759194585725104834320113080568963585169373833696783851877954777289700977387406787351042208644765952479766680050092506982307058232778318910085313419726295369615642136040676327159300158548622476503.$

The plaintext message which A must sign is

$P = 47495233644665988426542797641862170747046710526789245391156504620320517515571648723939384358595186200968673256615798341680398991554123874397908150043241195926795222914754565141859355539104925268550584190056601904838582629751247671428189205507655795265722620866029099708789775077073512480224582285200694189809167.$

We will assume P has already been encrypted using public information of the recipient B, and sent to B. A creates a signature for this message by doing the following:
A selects a random integer k such that $0 \leq k \leq p - 2$ and $(k, p - 1) = 1$; say

$k = 82856917389970632286253786630664077566635236475196324460901196566466248841746038786260869442047228630531155629906195900348240923300503772304032557920752115786554083917562470624809498551255955210906062137226118215 9$

07367426672859790890178550005235715982194744315060307555486157771312984
57166748765201121009594717.

A then calculates r, the lnr of g^k modulo p:

r = 75498068930901596713465212228968107301133708588093175478835443495046
58689452027727440730628293467447779556271545462398144979866730979135966
18187706415730448305962740003790259873593478841192742794988274985183707
33508857687070847979356504748344434443482341750430309156841679728553674
4959938944736337026588945192
25.

The value for r is the first part of the signature. Now, A must find an inverse of k modulo $p - 1$; this is easily done using the extended Euclidean algorithm:

k' = 41476618378700412297173224500420810670339064876850101272695099201480
40909661356549509986713778218842987157548817549818549010185909875969239
23474297418780395649640823967899438653445882201671706143611508708336501
16512052394573930927553494824898854134339214385016217721200185633500260
41130221516326398843115285674
9.

A must compute a digest of the plaintext message. A uses the public hash function

$$d(x) \equiv x \pmod{q} \qquad 0 \le d(x) < q$$

where the prime q is:

$q = 10931809682175872911$

$= 1001011110110101100101101111110010011010010001001100111110001111_{\text{base 2}}.$

(Note that the binary representation of q is 64 bits; it will produce a 64-bit digest.) A calculates $d(P)$:

$$d(P) \equiv 7763193083250062093 \pmod{q}.$$

Now, A calculates the final part of the signature:

$s \equiv k'(d(P) - ar) \equiv$
50412964547291244886607923945931220915528315989181820611618158433628477
40608777801280275748083146568549013171666554370962283165579964915036974
13041178568111884781202739723644461510362506102063431227543591653744230
58923266118434727390510960743059856469094244323861240121853603519934530
1596399005935356773095888
49 $(\bmod\ p - 1)$.

The values of r and s are sent to B. To verify that this signature is valid, B must first check that r is between 1 and $p - 1$. This checks, so B continues in this way:

B then calculates the two values v and w. B can compute w because the hash function is public:

$v \equiv y^r r^s \equiv$
43890836505049217211214115926691601468943012262276785040999060333913856
52789956216926890449589142338693394589084888160249340683798561005143061
51

64119498985245557763472039670206557538701771143948315395042004039616450967280727260953220234211129435233938791614241443043366921696427914064194709191846832151545994886 (mod p)

and

$$w \equiv g^{d(P)} \equiv$$
4389083650504921721121411592669160146894301226227678504099906033391385652789956216926890449589142338693394589084888160249340683798561005143061516411949898524555776347203967020655753870177114394831539504200403961645096728072726095322023421112943523393879161424144304336692169642791406419470
9191846832151545994886.

B takes note of the fact that v and w are equal, and accepts the signature.

Storing Passwords or Passphrases as Digests A system administrator has a peculiar problem. She must store the passwords or passphrases of all her users, so that she can compare these entries to the entered passwords when a user attempts a login. However, she must be able to protect these passwords, so unauthorized users cannot obtain them. Ideally, it would be best if the system administrator herself could not obtain the passwords.

Cryptographically secure digest functions provide a solution. A user's password is not stored, but rather, a digest of the password is stored. When a user attempts a login, a digest of the password is taken, then compared against this user's entry in a table. If an adversary somehow obtains the hashed password list, it does him little good if the digest function is a good one; that is, it will be nearly impossible for him to obtain any particular password from its digest. Even the system administrator does not know any particular password; only the user who created it knows (assuming he or she didn't forget it). Various operating systems grant access based on such an idea; Figure 16.11 illustrates this process:

16.8 ATTACKS ON DIGEST FUNCTIONS

There are various approaches to defeating a digest function. To defeat a digest function, one must be able to produce a bogus message, say P', which hashes to the same value as

Figure 16.11

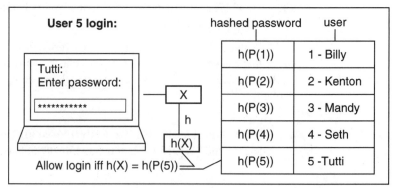

the message P. In addition to other parties, both the verifier (receiver), and the signer (sender) of a message may wish to have this ability. Why?

If a third party is able to produce a bogus message P', such that $h(P) = h(P')$, he may be able to convince the signer to sign P', then later claim this signature is for P. The meanings of P and P' may be totally different. For example, suppose you want your secretary to draft a message P that orders your company bank to transfer funds to more conservative stocks. Instead, by careful construction, he drafts a fraudulent message P' which orders the bank to transfer 1.3 million company dollars to his Swiss bank account! By virtue of this careful construction, it so happens that $h(P)$ and $h(P')$ are equal. The bank receives the bogus message, accepts it as authentic, and the next day your secretary is nowhere to be found. The verifier (an employee of the bank, in this case) may also want to be able to do this (if he also leans toward dishonest activity).

The signer can also do this. Suppose you are a high-ranking official of your government, and you want to send a message P' ordering the death of millions of innocent civilians. By careful construction, you are able to produce a message P that instead conveys great love and affection for the masses. It so happens that $h(P) = h(P')$. You send the message P' to your generals, who accept it as genuine, and then carry out your orders. Later, when NATO is trying you for crimes against humanity, you whip out the message P, claiming that it was the message you really sent. You claim that some adversary confiscated the message P and sent P' in its place. The act of denying that you sent a signed message is known as repudiation. A good digest function enforces nonrepudiation; that is, it makes it far too difficult for a signer to find a bogus message to use in place of the real one.

Now do you see why a digest function must have the three required properties? If you recall, they are:

1. Given a hash value $h(m)$, it must be extremely difficult to determine m.

2. Given a message m, it must be extremely difficult to find another message m' such that $h(m) = h(m')$.

3. It must be extremely difficult to find any two messages, say m and m', for which $h(m) = h(m')$.

The Birthday Attack   The following illustrates a method to defeat a digest function, known as the birthday attack. It is based on the following well-known principle: If you select (with replacement) from a set of m objects, with high probability, you can expect to draw some element twice within $\sqrt{m}$ selections.

The way we normally hear this is from the birthday problem: If you select randomly from the population, the odds are high that you will encounter 2 people with the same birthday within about $19 \cong \sqrt{365}$ selections.

In the birthday attack, we assume the individual with bad intent can make modifications to both the real message (P), and the bogus message (P'). Suppose the digest function produces an n-bit hash. Thus, there are 2^n possible hashes (2 choices for each bit.) Note before we begin that $\sqrt{(2^n)} = 2^{n/2}$. This is what to do:

1. Generate a table of $t = 2^{n/2}$ minor modifications to the message P (add a space, delete a semicolon, use a similar word, etc., etc. . . .). Label these modified messages $P_1, P_2, \ldots, P_t$.

2. For i from 1 through t, generate the hash $h(P_i)$, and store it with the message P_i.

3. Generate a minor modification of the bogus message P', say P^*. Search the table for a message P_k such that $h(P_k) = h(P^*)$ for some k. (The search of the table can be done in constant time if a hash table is used.)

4. If the search is successful, stop. The current P^* is the fraudulent message, to send in place of P_k. If the search is not successful, return to step 3.

Depending on n (the hash size), the birthday attack can have enormous storage requirements. If $n = 64$, the table will contain $2^{32} \cong 4$ billion elements. If each modified message and its hash takes, say, one thousand bytes each, then we are talking storage space of about 4 terabytes. Though this seems large, it is feasible, or soon will be. Thus, digest functions which produce 128 bit (or larger) hashes are preferable.

Note that it may be possible for the "bad guy" to modify only the bogus message. This considerably increases the amount of selections one should make before expectations of finding a match are high. As an example, suppose your birthday is July 15. How many people should you randomly sample from the population so that the odds are greater than 50 percent that you will find someone with your birthday?

There are many other attacks on digest functions. Unfortunately, due to space considerations, we cannot cover them here. An excellent reference for this topic (and many other topics in cryptography) is *The Handbook of Applied Cryptography*, by Menezes, van Oorschot, and Vanstone, published by CRC.

16.9   ZERO KNOWLEDGE IDENTIFICATION

Sometimes all that is desired in an exchange between two parties is that one be assured of the identity of the other. (This is common among military protocols.) There are various ways to do this, but one of the most interesting ways is to use "Zero Knowledge Identification." This refers to convincing someone that you are who you claim to be by convincing them that you know certain information that only you could know, but without revealing that information to anyone, including the entity you are trying to convince! In these types of exchanges, the entity trying to prove their identity is called the respondent, and the entity trying to establish the identity of the respondent is called the challenger.

For example, suppose individual A is known to be using a public modulus n, where n is the product of two large strong primes both congruent to 3 modulo 4, say p and q. A can convince another individual, say B, that he knows these primes, without revealing them to B. If A can do this, B is assured that A is really who he claims to be. A and B proceed in this way:

1. Let A (the respondent) choose n as the product of two strong primes, p and q. A also chooses some integer s such that s has a square root modulo n. The integers s and n are public, and registered with a Trusted Third Party (TTP). A computes t, the lnr of a square root of s modulo n; that is, he computes t such that

$$t^2 \equiv s \pmod{n} \qquad 0 \le t < n.$$

The value of t is kept private. Note that only A should be able to calculate t, as only he knows the prime factors of n.

2. A chooses a random positive integer r less than n, and sends to B (the challenger) two values:

$$z_1 = \text{lnr of } r^2 \text{ modulo } n, \text{ and}$$

$$z_2 = \text{lnr of } sz_{1'} \text{ modulo } n,$$

where $z_{1'}$ is an inverse of z_1 modulo n.

3. B checks that $z_1 z_2 \equiv s$ modulo n. He then randomly chooses either $c = 0$ or $c = 1$ and sends c to A.

4. A will respond in one of two ways:

- If $c = 0$, A sends the message r to B.
- If $c = 1$, A sends the lnr of tr' modulo n, where r' is an inverse of r modulo n.

5. B now computes the lnr of m^2 modulo n, and does one of two things:

- If $c = 0$, he checks that $r^2 \equiv z_1 \pmod{m}$.
- If $c = 1$, he checks that $(tr')^2 = t^2 r'^2 \equiv sz_1 \equiv z_2 \pmod{n}$.

After this process, B knows that A can compute t, a square root of s modulo n, but he cannot compute t himself, and t is never revealed to him. These are the only values that B knows (modulo n): $z_1 \equiv r^2$, $z_2 \equiv s(r^2)' \equiv sr'^2$, s, and exactly one of r or tr'. Note that B can never be given both r and tr', for this allows him to calculate t. This process can be repeated as often as necessary with different random values for r until B is convinced that A knows t. However, it is absolutely vital that A choose a different value for r every time. Why?

EXAMPLE.   Suppose A is using the public modulus

$n =$
274767815982245548988790206801956651309342982830065216921948667831130363
270253391613297772360579492679629996501029139838682116550051160900059917
252079335683044082645443287136361829237904549448424168235143278727967298
537931735369900497614908459888542386548176723918689759709749816846741951
438624571462267660236650416857894422109721140233441189969425961870588371
894903496708435357401553646260714625504652954935134556139340783655294871
737383374223242600468713011439066059016281996201542058384927054227873607
471972731775123706246506154077712330891353812432890865488929521246586593
805509406956432735591716835142616776177720051153

which is the product of two large, strong (and private) primes congruent to 3 modulo 4; namely,

$p =$
200766270232954088077041575959108612757411238838003505144742064111712514
438539012193632244782163192814569872158475903654023762579506771732582156

26739711285945794099392942183793253143931816436660620039075177872926503795085555604962599651899765121244080690200474454983224437339641808775896661805199361161973267635391

$q =$

136859550991023357674233837751193444637145211672745580838508211454534324823686210424604005719046718052981484190707562992713417956940416543355152315219159854859002395777579635185385039269578229009584384066590554210488182334714799737615710384650453125076807810092764555005612188062536100529729582192738972213180427.

A is using the following public identifier:

$s =$

655888759462533346896099455125955297863619815052059946417712093279459636342631365262945091607400550526643865410801510951287478034133829455860917289602594107432247734813074447586090300953100896097041105461066228022450166033881770704236319990387444689492432645953381065640248889649060248175467020832162871151166044236329570436283893628145176691891823037121955814938541733991912989896275607617952520860767797954234828253534756762094155814794971779899171546943797691420279291340595160862830887928416259974179143970911859299229488556748722670747759415492038884902807323535046135389513570970637001674827508837421741060864541027797.

This value for s has a square root modulo n; let's say,

$t =$

165939251694010184592593767485127540635808807933739119951718497170488592148972055777285530210620518273692388315164078449283411444102820207961683880417477924017600541987600931639085385971444581959989319417992193306141335450460118404029149636306714968895603334454397709463970275583243016901423853053941948601770260591458870529845193261034683705291970236037633310907364071581496095213148290413871725043392307378067658837187041433121406416290503339428815946362864700618273596792458170735372510429224074039038301648162396953994412378543760633875395589555679973650286550990104663372816929390018566375288205090035695870984674369844.

This value for t is kept private. To convince B that he can indeed compute t, without revealing t, A first chooses a random integer less than n, say

$r =$

173651607556993658543074931792348037298652767890536649836378803212048174119600416703769869733860342049288372423745801528669105373390624108185926747940578397289745643201766424420162191119041288192344657982273471518628215332496677780952733934200916926981810730240920232847296029476965497809662739704519945187970453408466395941396051840775986075125108182246279299702785594609410635181141522115473272018306542018693995053351421839424696911117540694875175647980201822766135826987878547070039026905448088441503482709036662431574895978524539775437034803554754381419475994272847508134837308772864371800567653105828673708366963334060.

A computes z_1, the lnr of r^2 modulo n, then sends this to B.

$z_1 =$
63690737291663041763995066002816628171949205542921736422045748959303786616533345937931577287578777337037541907245190619182026856650879956802273173727653237932730236799540949166036640396067096006368790208263953521451704572089983481089922202109679272366316833510515738367728341281090988890017949190862656857701787085332407191771344848452681843460609190812839743239539173185250158849003287069362341076698100394134863541161919354903211440548148854461283108399370076457835460381060108060892102815095326918418621906140804028643052737070898387615059953558402717556755855784801790608315799225620380440437470494606638185674708753382.

A then computes an inverse of z_1 modulo n; this is easily done using the extended Euclidean algorithm:

$z_{1'} =$
24686172151689476425285741157786711310645494035006286634731332325375000630921044179357982377162544583401649557996354268258181277736237542509570131890429076716439748993874961156458008996169101420288661718418746509628163149961479592922502072125659460329728515775688208547283773829348479566694430550274597461011879047993856792856929479213820332943350151945975640416410899815016899604425867054633862988960432431433337967835481291126293458406150873293686420839273011870893591808700733222664860467108213167975050959549757844949562068463476731051310304494771648902657814806383987207842481116358933225458494226492425817166857486241.

A needs this value to compute z_2, the lnr of $sz_{1'}$ modulo n. A sends z_2 to B:

$z_2 =$
12747551368556672544689085272061309536032718760398865194123141585315757833145659715320949400473621097769957891699946603245667759512751963415999052154083795705653834510602567377352418578663500405203386328924994294867935184018822939774485842157483331734800366091767355035374482205516573611123451290411688927269940694884275511560908678812201013167698353117595208115364428275176203894832414383245435425552409594836430325290312727856645586787665484241168762391821058930035142514569910831114779624225402915977657087219661928479181676359706037896699964314397374669653325227844772298279026787779574072094948369447747820013063852307388.

B receives the two values z_1 and z_2, then checks that the lnr of their product is equal to s. If you care to do the calculations, you will see this is true.

$z_1 z_2 =$
24686172151689476425285741157786711310645494035006286634731332325375000630921044179357982377162544583401649557996354268258181277736237542509570131890429076716439748993874961156458008996169101420288661718418746509628163149961479592922502072125659460329728515775688208547283773829348479566694430550274597461011879047993856792856929479213820332943350151945975640

16410899815016899604425867054633862988960432431433337967835481291126293458406150873293686420839273011870893591808700733222664860467108213167975050959549757844949562068463476731051310304494771648902657814806383987207842481163589332254584942264924258171668574862418

$\times$

127475513685566725446890852720613095360327187603988651941231415853157578331456597153209494004736210977699578916999466032456677595127519634159990521540837957056538345106025673773524185786635004052033863289249942948679351840188229397744858421574833317348003660917673550353744822055165736111234512904116889272699406948842755115609086788122010131676983531175952081153644282751762038948324143832454354255524095948364303252903127278566455867876654842411687623918210589300351425145699108311147796242254029159776570872196619284791816763597060378966996431439737466965332522784477229827902678779574072094948369447747820013063852307384

$\equiv$

655888759462533346896099455125955297863619815052059946417712093279459636342631365262945091607400505266438654108015109512874780341338294558609172896025941074322477348130744475860903009531008960970411054610662280224501660338817707042363199903874446894924326459533810656402488896490602481754670208321628711511660442363295704362838936281451766918918230371219558149385417339919129898962756076179525208607677979542348282535347567620941558147949717798991715469439796914202792913405951608628308879284162599741791439709118592992294885567487226707477594154920388849028073235350461353895135709706370016748275088374217410608645410279741

$\equiv s \pmod{n}$.

B then decides randomly whether to send a 0 or 1 back to A; suppose he sends the value 1. Based on this, A returns the least nonnegative residue modulo n to tr' where r' is an inverse of r modulo n. First, A computes r':

$r' =$
764099968690517121353391255537826929750924022145231920293817937632484200823244999903844151729958088746605736494045667481382068184503010229657204324741870974090123392049287708272219558696413394357793284604912718755591336387596862510056826243493640606882949339406701718749418165555632969778993258001186079998310245516683439718610351326287706100768787955581515819601632478429513623086926648395375078113392282117379085848769481062034764830179215068677951322660617601740480059922020216720433340230781653771458887609228294973191663746577397725012728968435241942794317479187819506033859036560577789529935727667635975177196008829264

The value which A sends to B is therefore

$tr' \equiv$
806863988054169024920301405295203174706259473118276369760225652423019997525913534708697658713793930280015474876469073032943300741644028317049787631296437500635771334741355725945454918382262962438730708821951004673206

3221982677027682219574644478156596648034259201625794258589871363371520439578030398462472559658341543739620385505494303453498511871847453150845811888827290782855452209158581847907874837698037750312261364313174865624583504184820486171774455102057367509927587851672018642910324549466616562816802079928403326841790704444055995636115902228001656164492260407559173911635634931359062322458271768089779844860822413 (mod n).

Finally, B squares this, and since he sent a 1, he checks that the lnr of $(tr')^2$ is z_2. If you do the computation, you will see that this is so:

$(tr')^2 \equiv$
12747551368556672544689085272061309536032718760398865194123141585315757833145659715320949400473621097769957891699946603245667759512751963415999052154083795705653834510602567377352418578663500405203386328924994294867935184018822939774485842157483331734800366091767355035374482205516573611123451290411688927269940694884275511560908678812201013167698353117595208115364428275176203894832414383245435425552409594836430325290312727856645586787665484241168762391821058930035142514569910831114779624225402915977657087219661928479181676359706037896699964314397374669653325227844772298279026787795740720949483694477478200130638523073 8

$\equiv z_2$ (mod n).

Java Algorithm   I have written a couple of Java programs to do this kind of exchange. Here the respondent acts as a client, sending a request for approval from the challenger, which acts as a server. The respondent connects to the challenger, sends the values for n and s, then generates r, z_1, and z_2. It sends z_1 and z_2 to the challenger, then waits for the challenge, a 0 or a 1. It responds to the challenge, then waits for a response from the challenger, either "Y" meaning approved, or "N" meaning not yet approved. If the respondent is not yet approved, it generates new values for r, z_1, and z_2, and begins again. Here is the Respondent class.

```java
import java.math.*;
import java.net.*;
import java.io.*;
import java.security.*;
public class Respondent {
    static BufferedReader k=new BufferedReader(new InputStreamReader(System.in));

  public static void main(String[] args) throws IOException {

      //Define some handy values
      BigInteger zero=BigInteger.valueOf(0);
      BigInteger one=BigInteger.valueOf(1);
      BigInteger two=BigInteger.valueOf(2);
      BigInteger three=BigInteger.valueOf(3);
      BigInteger four=BigInteger.valueOf(4);
```

```
//Generate two strong primes congruent to 3 mod 4
SecureRandom sr=new SecureRandom();
PrimeGenerator pg=new PrimeGenerator(513,10,sr);
BigInteger p=null,q=null;
do {
   p=pg.getStrongPrime();
} while (!p.mod(four).equals(three));
do {
   q=pg.getStrongPrime();
} while (!q.mod(four).equals(three));

//Form the modulus as the product of these primes
BigInteger modulus=p.multiply(q);
//Choose a random value t and square it modulo the modulus to form s
BigInteger t=new BigInteger(modulus.bitLength()-1,sr);
//s is your identifying number
BigInteger s=t.modPow(two,modulus);
//The values of s and the modulus should be made publicly available
//with a Trusted Third Party (TTP)

System.out.println("Enter host name or IP address of challenger:");
String host=k.readLine();
Socket socket=new Socket(host,12345);
PrintStream out=new PrintStream(socket.getOutputStream());
BufferedReader in=new BufferedReader(new
   InputStreamReader(socket.getInputStream()));
//Send the values for the modulus, and s, to the challenger-we do not send t
//of course
out.println(modulus.toString());
out.println(s.toString());

String approved="N";
//The challenges begin
do {
   System.out.println("You have yet to be approved.");

   //Generate the random value r
   BigInteger r=new BigInteger(modulus.bitLength()-1,sr);
   //Compute z1 and z2
   BigInteger z1=r.modPow(two,modulus);
   BigInteger z2=s.multiply(z1.modInverse(modulus)).mod(modulus);
   //Send z1 and z2 to the challenger
   out.println(z1.toString());
   out.println(z2.toString());
```

```
    //Challenger will send back a 0 or a 1
    int challenge=Integer.parseInt(in.readLine());
    //If a 0 was sent, return r to the challenger
    if (challenge==0) out.println(r.toString());
    //Otherwise, send tr' modulo the modulus to the challenger
    else
        out.println(t.multiply(r.modInverse(modulus)).mod(modulus).toString());

    //Challenger will now either send "Y" (approved) or "N" (not approved)
    approved=in.readLine().toUpperCase();
} while (!approved.equals("Y"));

    //If we get here, we succeeded
    System.out.println("Your claim of identity has been accepted.");
    k.readLine();
    }
}
```

The Challenger class is a server which loops forever simply listening for connections on port 12345. (I didn't choose this port for any particular reason.) It establishes a socket with a respondent using the accept() method. So that the challenger can deal with multiple respondents at once, it is threaded. It will produce a new Challenger object (a subclass of Thread) for each new connection. If any response from a respondent does not check, the challenger closes the connection immediately.

```
import java.math.*;
import java.net.*;
import java.io.*;
import java.security.*;
public class Challenger extends Thread {
    static BufferedReader k=new BufferedReader(new InputStreamReader(System.in));

    //socket is the connection between challenger and respondent
    Socket socket=null;
    //trials is the number of challenges the respondent must satisfy
    static int trials=0;
    static SecureRandom r=null;

    //The constructor only sets the socket field
    public Challenger(Socket s) {
        socket=s;
    }

    public static void main(String[] args) throws IOException {
```

```
System.out.println
    ("Enter the number of challenges to issue per respondent:");
trials=Integer.parseInt(k.readLine());
r=new SecureRandom();
//Bind the challenger to port 12345
ServerSocket ss=new ServerSocket(12345);

//Loop forever
while (true) {
    //Create a new thread for every incoming connection
    //this allows challenger to handle multiple respondents
    Challenger c=new Challenger(ss.accept());
    c.start();
    }
}


public void run() {
    try {
        System.out.println("Request received from "
            +socket.getInetAddress().toString());
        //Create the IO streams
        PrintStream out=new PrintStream(socket.getOutputStream());
        BufferedReader in=new BufferedReader
            (new InputStreamReader(socket.getInputStream()));

        //Read in modulus and s key values
        //These should be checked against a database with a TTP
        BigInteger modulus=new BigInteger(in.readLine());
        BigInteger s=new BigInteger(in.readLine());
        BigInteger[] z=new BigInteger[2];

        //Begin challenging the respondent
        for (int i=0;i<trials;i++) {
            //Read in z1 and z2; here labeled z0 and z1 for convenience
            z[0]=new BigInteger(in.readLine());
            z[1]=new BigInteger(in.readLine());
            //Check that their product = s
            if (!z[0].multiply(z[1]).mod(modulus).equals(s)) {
                System.out.println("Product not congruent to s-closing connection");
                break;
            }

            //Issue the challenge-a random 0 or 1
            int challenge=Math.abs(r.nextInt())%2;
            out.println(challenge);

            //Get the response
            BigInteger response=new BigInteger(in.readLine());
```

```
      //Check the response, based on the value of challenge
      if (!response.modPow(BigIntegerMath.TWO,modulus).equals(z[challenge]))
      {
         System.out.println("Response does not check-closing connection");
         break;
      }

      if (i<trials-1) out.println("N");
      else {
         out.println("Y");
         System.out.println("Respondent approved.");
      }
   }

   //Close the connection with this respondent
   socket.close();
} catch (IOException ioe) {
   System.out.println(ioe.toString());
}
  }
}
}
```

Here is a test run of Respondent and Challenger running on two different computers.

Respondent:

```
Enter host name or IP address of challenger:
**********
You have yet to be approved.
You have yet to be approved.
You have yet to be approved.
You have yet to be approved.
You have yet to be approved.
Your claim of identity has been accepted.
```

Challenger:

```
Enter the number of challenges to issue per respondent:
5
Request received from **********/**********
Respondent approved.
```

Note that I have crossed out the names/IP addresses of the machines running these pro-grams.

I should mention that the Respondent and Challenger programs fail to do something important. First, the respondent would not generate new values of n and s for each exchange. These values should already exist and be published with a TTP. Secondly, the challenger should check received values for n and s against values in a database maintained by the TTP. This way, the respondent can be verified as having a certain set of keys, and that an impersonator would have a very tough time "pretending" to be that person without knowledge of their private information. (In this case, this means being able to compute a square root of s modulo n without knowing the prime factors of n.)

EXERCISES

1. Here, a set of shadows and their corresponding moduli are given, plus values for the reconstructing prime p and the random multiplier u. Use all the shadows given to reconstruct the master key, which will be immediately recognizable.

Shadows	Moduli
1835256971	2142418429
298859542	1247760289
611228613	2061443389
1052969410	1817116199
1343567939	1614361069
1045659651	1250119291
1399180591	1478137559
1725515793	2084068787

   The random multiplier is: 724799153237188128058363304731475

   The reconstructing prime is: 764018977

2. Modify the ShadowBuilder constructor so that the user can specify the minimum number of shadows required for construction (as opposed to just over half, as I have written it), and to compute the values for u and p accordingly.

3. Design a Java class to produce random bitstreams according to the Micali–Schnorr method.

4. Write a RabinEncipherSigned() and RabinDecipherSigned() method for the Ciphers class to perform encryption and decryption of signed messages.

5. Write methods in the Ciphers class to send and receive signed messages with ElGamal.

6. When two parties, B (the challenger) and A (the respondent) are using zero knowledge identification as described in the text, A must be sure never to repeat a random value for r. Why?

7. Consider how you could modify the IntCRT class to handle negative integers, subtraction, and division, then do this modification.

8. Modify the CSPRBG class (or write your own) to generate random bitstreams using the Micali–Schnorr method.

APPENDIX I

List of Propositions

Proposition 1. If x, y, and z are integers with $x|y$ and $y|z$, then $x|z$.

Proposition 2. If c, x, y, m, and n are integers such that $c|x$ and $c|y$, then $c|(mx + ny)$.

Proposition 3. (The Division Algorithm.) If y and b are integers such that $b > 0$, then $\exists$ unique integers q and r such that $0 \le r < b$ and $y = bq + r$. This q is called the quotient, r the remainder, b the divisor, and y the dividend.

Proposition 4. Every positive integer greater than 1 has a prime divisor.

Proposition 5. There are infinitely many primes.

Proposition 6. If n is composite, then n has a prime factor not exceeding the square root of n.

Proposition 7. Let x, y, and z be integers with $(x, y) = d$. Then

a. $(x/d, y/d) = 1$

b. $(x + cy, y) = (x, y)$.

Proposition 8. The gcd of integers x and y, not both zero, is the least positive integer that is a linear combination of x and y.

Proposition 9. $(a_1, a_2, a_3, \ldots, a_n) = ((a_1, a_2), a_3, \ldots, a_n)$.

Proposition 10. If c and d are integers and $c = dq + r$ where q and r are integers, then $(c, d) = (d, r)$.

Proposition 11. (The Euclidean Algorithm.)   Let $r_0 = c$ and $r_1 = b$ be integers such that $c \geq b > 0$. If the division algorithm is successively applied to obtain $r_j = r_{j+1}q_{j+1} + r_{j+2}$ with $0 < r_{j+2} < r_{j+1}$ for $j = 0, 1, 2, \ldots, n - 2$ and $r_{n+1} = 0$, then $(c, b) = r_n$.

Proposition 12.   Let x and y be positive integers. Then

$$(x, y) = s_n x + t_n y$$

where the s_n and t_n are defined recursively as

$$s_j = s_{j-2} - q_{j-1}s_{j-1} \text{ for } j = 2, \ldots, n$$

$$s_0 = 1$$

$$s_1 = 0$$

$$t_j = t_{j-2} - q_{j-1}t_{j-1} \text{ for } j = 2, \ldots, n$$

$$t_0 = 0$$

$$t_1 = 1$$

and the q_j and r_i are as in the Euclidean algorithm.

Proposition 13.   If a, b, and c are positive integers with a and b relatively prime, and such that $a|bc$, then $a|c$.

Proposition 14.   Suppose $a_1, a_2, \ldots, a_n$ are positive integers, and p is a prime which divides $a_1 a_2 \ldots a_n$. Then there is an integer i such that $1 \leq i \leq n$ and $p|a_i$.

Proposition 15. (The Fundamental Theorem of Arithmetic.)   Every positive integer n greater than 1 can be written in the form $n = p_1 p_2 \ldots p_n$ where each p_i is prime, $i = 1, 2, \ldots, n$. Furthermore, this representation is unique.

Proposition 16.   Let a and b be integers with $d = (a, b)$. If $d|c$, the integer solutions x and y of the equation $ax + by = c$ are $x = x_0 + bn/d$, $y = y_0 - an/d$, where $x = x_0$, $y = y_0$ is a particular solution. If $d \nmid c$, the equation has no integer solutions.

Proposition 17.   Integers a and b are congruent modulo m iff $\exists$ an integer k such that $a = b + km$.

Proposition 18.   Let a, b and c be integers, and let m be a positive integer. Then

a. $a \equiv a \pmod{m}$

b. $a \equiv b \pmod{m}$ implies $b \equiv a \pmod{m}$

c. $a \equiv b \pmod{m}$ and $b \equiv c \pmod{m}$ implies $a \equiv c \pmod{m}$.

Proposition 19.   Let a, b, and c be integers, and let m be a positive integer. Suppose $a \equiv b \pmod{m}$. Then

a. $a + c \equiv b + c \pmod{m}$

b. $a - c \equiv b - c \pmod{m}$

c. $ac \equiv bc \pmod{m}$.

Proposition 20. Let a, b, and c be integers, and let m be a positive integer. Suppose $a \equiv b \pmod{m}$, and $c \equiv d \pmod{m}$. Then

a. $a + c \equiv b + d \pmod{m}$

b. $a - c \equiv b - d \pmod{m}$

c. $ac \equiv bd \pmod{m}$.

Proposition 21. Let a, b, and c be integers, and m a positive integer. Let $d = (c, m)$, and suppose $ac \equiv bc \pmod{m}$. Then $a \equiv b \pmod{m/d}$.

Proposition 22. Suppose $ax \equiv b \pmod{m}$, where a, b, and m are all positive integers. Let $d = (a, m)$. If $d \nmid b$, the congruence has no solution for x. If $d | b$, then there are exactly d incongruent solutions modulo m, given by $x = x_0 + tm/d$, where x_0 is a particular solution to the linear diophantine equation $ax + my = b$, and $t = 0, 1, \ldots, d - 1$.

Proposition 23. When matrices are used to represent a system of linear congruences, the three elementary row operations for matrices do not affect the solution(s) of the corresponding system of congruences modulo n.

Proposition 24. Suppose two $n \times k$ matrices A and B are such that $A \equiv B \pmod{m}$. Then $AC \equiv BC \pmod{m}$ for any $k \times p$ matrix C, and $DA \equiv DB \pmod{m}$ for any $q \times n$ matrix D.

Proposition 25. Suppose integers $a_1, a_2, \ldots, a_n$ are pairwise relatively prime. Then $(a_1 a_2 \ldots a_n) | c$ if and only if $a_1 | c, a_2 | c, \ldots, a_n | c$.

Proposition 26. Let $a \equiv b \pmod{m_1}$, $a \equiv b \pmod{m_2}$, $\ldots, a \equiv b \pmod{m_n}$ where a_1, $a_2, \ldots, a_n$ are pairwise relatively prime. Then we have $a \equiv b \pmod{m_1 m_2 \ldots m_n}$.

Proposition 27. (The Chinese Remainder Theorem.) Suppose $m_1, m_2, \ldots, m_n$ are pairwise relatively prime. Then the system of congruences

$$x \equiv a_1 \pmod{m_1}$$

$$x \equiv a_3 \pmod{m_3}$$

$$\ldots$$

$$x \equiv a_n \pmod{m_n}$$

has a unique solution modulo $M = m_1 m_2 \ldots m_n$, namely,

$$x \equiv a_1 M_1 y_1 + a_2 M_2 y_2 + \ldots + a_n M_n y_n \pmod{M}$$

where $M_i = M/m_i$ and y_i is an inverse of M_i modulo m_i $\forall\ i = 1, 2, \ldots, n$.

Proposition 28. If p is an odd prime and $p \neq a$, then the congruence $x^2 \equiv a$ (mod p) has either no solutions or exactly two incongruent solutions modulo p.

Proposition 29. (Fermat's Little Theorem.) Let p be prime and b an integer such that $p \nmid b$. Then $b^{p-1} \equiv 1$ (mod p).

Proposition 30. Let p be a prime congruent to 3 modulo 4, and a an integer such that $p \nmid a$. Then if the congruence $x^2 \equiv a$ (mod p) has solutions, they are $x \equiv a^{(p+1)/4}$ (mod p), and $x \equiv -a^{(p+1)/4}$ (mod p).

Proposition 31. Let $n = pq$ where p and q are primes congruent to 3 modulo 4, and let a be an integer such that $0 < a < n$. Suppose the equation $x^2 \equiv a$ (mod n) has a solution. Then all the solutions are given by

$$x \equiv \pm(zqq_{p'} \pm wpp_{q'})\ (\text{mod } n)$$

where $z = a^{(p+1)/4}$, $w = a^{(q+1)/4}$, $q_{p'}$ is an inverse of q modulo p, and $p_{q'}$ is an inverse of p modulo q.

Proposition 32. Let $n = pq$, where p and q are primes congruent to 3 modulo n. Suppose a is an integer relatively prime to n, and that the congruence

$$ax^2 + bx + c \equiv 0\ (\text{mod } n)$$

has a solution. Then all the solutions are given by

$$x \equiv (\pm(a'((2'b)^2 a' - c))^{(p+1)/4} - 2'a'b)qq_{p'} + (\pm(a'((2'b)^2 a' - c))^{(q+1)/4} - 2'a'b)pp_{q'}$$
$$(\text{mod } n).$$

Proposition 33. There are infinitely many primes of the form $4k + 3$.

Proposition 34. Let p be prime, and suppose $x^2 \equiv 1$ (mod p). Then $x \equiv 1$ (mod p) or $x \equiv -1$ (mod p).

Proposition 35. If n is prime and b is a positive integer such that $n \nmid b$, then n passes Miller's test for the base b.

Proposition 36. Suppose n is an odd, composite positive integer. Then n fails Miller's test for at least 75 percent of the test bases b where $1 \leq b \leq n - 1$.

Proposition 37. If p is prime and b an integer such that $p \nmid b$, then

a. the positive integer x is a solution to $b^x \equiv 1$ (mod p) iff $|b|_p$ divides x.
b. $|b|_p$ divides $p - 1$.

Proposition 38. Suppose p is prime and b an integer such that $p \nmid b$. Then, if i and j are nonnegative integers, $b^i \equiv b^j$ (mod p) iff $i \equiv j$ (mod $|b|_p$).

Proposition 39.   If g is a generator modulo p, then the sequence of integers $g, g^2, \ldots,$ g^{p-1} is a permutation of $1, 2, \ldots, p-1$.

Proposition 40.   If $|b|_p = t$ and u is a positive integer, then $|b^u|_p = t/(t, u)$.

Proposition 41.   Let r be the number of positive integers not exceeding $p-1$ that are relatively prime to $p-1$. Then, if the prime p has a generator, it has r of them.

Proposition 42.   Every prime has a generator.

Proposition 43.   Let p be prime, and let g be a generator modulo p. Suppose a and b are positive integers not divisible by p. Then we have all of the following:

a. $\log 1 \equiv 0 \pmod{p-1}$
b. $\log(ab) \equiv \log a + \log b \pmod{p-1}$
c. $\log(a^k) \equiv k \cdot \log a \pmod{p-1}$

where all logarithms are taken to the base g modulo p.

APPENDIX **II**

Information Theory

Information theory is closely related to cryptography. Cryptanalysts use results obtained by information theorists to help them crack ciphers, and cryptographers use similar results when crafting cryptosystems and choosing keys. Information theory provides tools that allow us to measure the amount of information in a message. Cryptographers attempt to keep this information to a minimum, while cryptographers exploit this tiny amount of information to help them determine a probable plaintext for a given ciphertext.

AII.1 ENTROPY OF A MESSAGE

If we define the amount of information in a message as the minimum number of bits (including fractions of a bit!) needed to encode all possible meanings of the message, we can obtain a measure of that information. For example, suppose we are looking at the following bit stream message

101001101000101010100000101010001000101010011010100001001000101010100100

which we know indicates a month of the year. Regardless of the actual length of the message, we could say that the message contains only about 3 or 4 bits of information, since it only takes that many bits to code up all possible months. (See Table A2.1.)

We define the entropy $E(M)$ of a message M as

$$E(M) = \log_2 n$$

where n is the number of possible meanings of M, where each meaning is equally likely. Thus the entropy of a message M' signifying the month is

$$E(M') = \log_2 12 \cong 3.58496250072115618145373894394778.$$

TABLE A2.1

Month	Code
January	0000
February	0001
March	0010
April	0011
May	0100
June	0101
July	0110
August	0111
September	1000
October	1001
November	1010
December	1011

Questions

What is the entropy of a message that signifies

1. A day of the week?

2. A day in the month of May?

3. A time of day in hours, minutes, and seconds?

What entropy means to a cryptanalyst is that the analyst needs only to learn at most only 4 bits of a message representing a month to discern the month. For example, consider the 12 messages in Table A2.2, which represent all of the months in a year:

In this case, examining only the first 2 bits and the last 2 bits of one of these messages will tell you the month. We say that the number of bits required to determine the meaning of a message is the uncertainty of a message. In general, entropy and uncertainty are equal. Obviously, for the cryptanalyst, the lower the entropy, the better.

AII.2   RATE OF A LANGUAGE

What is the entropy of any English message? This is what the analyst really wants to know. If we are using only upper case letters (there are 26 such letters), then certainly the entropy is no more than

Month	Message
January	0001010010000010100111001010101010000001010100100010110100000000000
February	0000110010001010100001001010010010101010100000101010010110010000000001
March	0101101010000010101001001000011010010000000000000000000000000000000010
April	0100001010100000101001001001001010011000000000000000000000000000000011
May	0001101010000010101100100000000000000000000000000000000000000000000000
June	0001010010101010100111001000101000000000000000000000000000000000000001
July	0101010010101010100110001011001000000000000000000000000000000000000010
August	0100001010101010100011101010101010100110101010000000000000000000000011
September	10100110100010101010000010101000100010101001101010000100100010101010100100
October	100111100100111101010110010001010100110101000010010001010101001000000001
November	100111100100111101010110010001010100110101000010010001010101001000000010
December	1000100010001010100001101000101010011010100001001000101010100100000000011

TABLE A2.2

$$R = \log_2 26 \cong 4.7004397181410921603968126542567.$$

This upper bound R of the entropy is called the absolute rate of a language. For English, the value above says that each letter contains about 5 bits of information. In truth, the actual amount of information in each letter is much lower than this.

To find a better estimate of the entropy of a language, we may want to compute the entropy for messages of size $1, 2, \ldots, N$, and use some averaging technique to obtain an estimate.

$$r_N = [E(M_1)/1 + E(M_2)/2 + \ldots + E(M_N)/N]/N$$

Here M_i represents messages of length i. If we use large values of N, and if we assume the entropy converges to some value as N approaches infinity, we can get a good estimate of the entropy of a language.

$$r = \lim r_N \text{ (as } N \to \infty).$$

We call this value r the rate of a language. Many studies have been done to compute r for English, and the best estimates obtained so far are around

$$r = 1.3.$$

This means each letter in an English message contains only slightly more than a single bit of information. If we express the redundancy of a language as its absolute rate minus its rate, i.e.,

$$D = R - r$$

then clearly English is a very redundant language, for we have in this case

$$D = R - r \cong 4.7 - 1.3 = 3.4.$$

This means that on the average, English messages are only about 28 percent real information, and 72 percent wasted space. Such a low value is beneficial to a cryptanalyst, since, conceivably, it means the analyst only has to determine around a single bit for each letter in a message to determine the message. If we encode characters in bytes (as we usually do), the analyst would only need to determine 1 out of every 8 bits to successfully recover a plaintext message. (Of course, finding these bits, and making them hard to find is the continuing battle between cryptanalyst and cryptographer!)

If we want to measure the entropy of a cipher, we can simply measure the entropy of its key space K. If each key in a key space K is equally likely for a 64-bit cipher, then, since there are 2^{64} possible keys to use, the entropy of the cipher is

$$E(K) = \log_2 2^{64} = 64$$

Of course, for a cryptographer, the higher the entropy of a cipher, the better.

AII.3 CRYPTOGRAPHIC TECHNIQUES

In general, a cryptographer wants to decrease the redundancy in messages (likewise, increase the entropy), since as we have seen, the more redundant a language is, the easier messages are to cryptanalyze. This is done using techniques that can be separated into categories: confusion, and diffusion.

AII.4 CONFUSION

This technique is intended to make statistical analysis more difficult by replacing plaintext items with ciphertext items possessing less redundancy (hence, greater entropy).

This is commonly done through simple substitution. For example, the Caesar cipher substitutes letters with other letters, though, as we have seen, the substituted letters contain as much redundancy as the plaintext letters, so do little to protect the information. Other substitution methods replace entire blocks of characters with other blocks. If, on the average, half of the bits of a substituted block change with every bit change in a plaintext block, and if one is unable to predict which bits will change, we have ciphertext that appears to have greater entropy than the plaintext.

In practice, however, the conditions required for a successful substitution are often not met; that is, sometimes the analyst is able to predict how many bits of ciphertext will change for some bit change in the plaintext, and can even know which ciphertext bits will change. They can do this with careful study of the ciphertext, and of the mathematical transformation used.

AII.5 DIFFUSION

Diffusion spreads the redundancy in the plaintext throughout the ciphertext. That is, it makes the crucial bits that the cryptanalyst seeks harder to find. Most often, transposition is used to accomplish this. Early transposition ciphers, which mapped characters to characters, obviously did not diffuse the redundancy of messages well, since the same characters were simply rearranged. A statistical analysis of the ciphertext yielded much the same frequency distribution as normal text, and rearranging the letters was often quite simple. When transposition was eventually used with fractionation (i.e., moving single bits, or parts of the plaintext different than the size of a character), it was much more effective.

AII.6 COMPRESSION

There is a good technique for generally decreasing the redundancy in a message: compress it. A compressed message contains the same amount of information as the original in less space. That is, compressed messages contain less redundancy. For this reason, cryptographers often compress messages before enciphering them. This also has the added benefit of yielding a shorter message that can be stored and transmitted using less resources.

There are many excellent compression techniques. Often, the compression method is linked to the type of data it is intended to compress. For example, a compression algorithm intended to compress text would be different from one intended to compress a bit map image. Good compression algorithms exploit the particular redundant characteristics of the data they are supposed to compress.

EXAMPLE. Here is a simple example of compressing text consisting of only upper case English letters. The typical encoding of characters is 1 byte each; however, we know that we can reduce this to 5 bits per character, because we can code up each character as shown in Table A2.3.

The last character in the table will be a special marker character we may pad our bytes with when compressing. We will remove it should we decompress the message. Given the length of these characters, we should be able to fit 3 characters into 2 bytes. We can do this in the simplest way; suppose we want to compress the message "DOG."

We skip the first bit of the first byte, and place the character bits after that, as shown in Table A2.4.

If we have a message that is not a multiple of 3 bytes, we use the pad character for the last 1 or 2 characters. Random salt can be placed in the unused bit.

Java Algorithm Here is a Java program that compresses text according to this scheme:

```java
import java.math.*;
public class CharCompressDemo {
    static int posA='A';
    public static void main(String[] args) {
        String incoming=args[0].toUpperCase();

        if (incoming.length()%3==1) incoming+="{[";
```

TABLE A2.3

Character	Code
A	00000
B	00001
C	00010
D	00011
E	00100
F	00101
G	00110
H	00111
I	01000
J	01001
K	01010
L	01011
M	01100
N	01101
O	01110
P	01111
Q	10000
R	10001
S	10010
T	10011
U	10100
V	10101
W	10110
X	10111
Y	11000
Z	11001
<pad character>	11010

TABLE A2.4

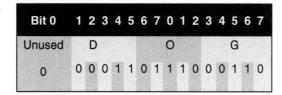

Bit 0	1 2 3 4 5 6 7 0 1 2 3 4 5 6 7
Unused	D O G
0	0 0 0 1 1 0 1 1 1 0 0 0 1 1 0

```java
    else if (incoming.length()%3==2) incoming+="[";

    byte[] original=incoming.getBytes();

    BigInteger origNum=new BigInteger(1,original);
    System.out.println("Original string in binary:\n"+origNum.toString(2));

    byte[] compressed=new byte[2*incoming.length()/3];

    compress(original,compressed);

    BigInteger compNum=new BigInteger(1,compressed);
    System.out.println("Compressed string in binary:\n"+compNum.toString(2));

}

public static void compress(byte[] o,byte[] c) {
    for (int i=0,j=0;i<o.length-2;i+=3,j+=2) {
        int c1=o[i]-posA;
        int c2=o[i+1]-posA;
        int c3=o[i+2]-posA;

        int res1=0,res2=0;

        //Do the first compressed byte
        //Put 1st value shifted 2 bits up
        res1=res1|(c1<<2);
        //Put first 2 bits of 2nd value in lo position
        res1=res1|(c2>>>3);

        //Do the second compressed byte
        //Put last 3 bits of 2nd value in high position-mask out first 5 bits
        res2=res2|((c2&7)<<5);
        //Put 3rd value in lo position
        res2=res2|c3;
```

```
        c[j]=(byte)res1;
        c[j+1]=(byte)res2;


      }

    }

  }
```

Here is a sample run of the program. Check its results for correctness (bear in mind that the program does not display the leading zeros).

```
C:\ java>java CharCompressDemo LOULOUSKIPTOMYLOUSKIPTOMY
LOUMYDARLIN

Original string in binary:

1001100010011110101010101001100010011110101010101010011010010
1101001001010100000101010001001111010011010101100101001100010
0111101010101010100110100101101001001010100000101010001001111
0100110101011001010011000100111101010101010011010101100101000
10001000001010100100100110001001001001110

Compressed string in binary:

1011011101010000101101110101000100100101001000001111100110111
0001100110000101100111010100100100010100100001111010011011100
1100011000010110111001010001100110000000110000010001001011010
0001101
```

You may want to write a program that decompresses messages of this type; consider how you might do this. The topic of compression is as interesting as anything in cryptography, and I encourage you to study it.

Recommended Reading

Kaufman, Charlie, Radia Perlman and Mike Speciner. *Network Security—Private Communication in a Public World*. Upper Saddle River: Prentice Hall, 1995.

Knudsen, Johnathan. *Java Cryptography*. Sebastopol: O'Reilly, 1998.

Koblitz, Neal. *A Course in Number Theory and Cryptography*, 2d ed. New York: Springer-Verlag, 1994.

Menezes, Alfred, Paul van Oorschot and Scott Vanstone. *Handbook of Applied Cryptography*. CRC Press, 1997.

Rosen, Kenneth. *Elementary Number Theory and Its Applications*. Boston: Addison-Wesley, 1993.

Rosing, Michael. *Implementing Elliptic Curve Cryptography*. Greenwich: Manning, 1999.

Smith, Richard. *Internet Cryptography*. Boston: Addison-Wesley, 1997.

Stallings, William. *Cryptography and Network Security*, 2d ed. Upper Saddle River: Prentice Hall, 1999.

Stephenson, Neal. *Cryptonomicon*. New York: Perennial, 2000.

Trappe, Wade and Lawrence Washington. *Introduction to Cryptography with Coding Theory*. Upper Saddle River: Prentice Hall, 2002.

Wayner, Peter. *Disappearing Cryptography*. Chestnut Hill: AP Professional, 1996

Index